Trading Option Volatility

A Breakthrough in Option Valuation, Yielding
Practical Insights into Strategy Design, Simulation,
Optimization, Risk Management, and Profits

BRIAN JOHNSON

DISCLAIMER

COVER IMAGE

The fractal image on the cover is a graphical metaphor for the seemingly stable patterns of price behavior that can suddenly and unexpectedly devolve into chaos, resulting in discrete price and volatility changes as new equilibrium conditions are negotiated by market participants. The chaotic pattern illustrates the unique challenges of trading and forecasting option volatility and the potential edge that can be derived from applying a volatility framework that is both theoretically correct and consistent with the actual market-implied term structure of volatility.

TABLE OF CONTENTS

INTRODUCTION

Brian Johnson, an investment professional with over 30 years of experience, a former university derivatives professor, and an author of four pioneering books on options, introduces his latest book: *Trading Option Volatility*.

This new in-depth book represents a breakthrough in option valuation, which has profound implications for option strategy design, option and volatility trading, and even for calculating accurate and reliable option risk metrics (Greeks). Drawing on his extensive background in option-valuation and on decades of experience in investment management and trading, Brian Johnson has developed a practical new analytical framework that generates theoretically correct and internally consistent, current and future option prices, volatility index futures prices, and risk metrics (Greeks) - across all term structures of volatilities and all term structures of interest rates. All of the required documentation, formulas, and examples are included to allow the dedicated reader to implement this new framework in practice.

This new framework eliminates the invalid and unrealistic constant volatility and constant interest rate assumptions of the Black-Scholes-Merton (BSM) and conventional binomial option models (BOM), correcting the sizable errors that result from these assumptions. Both the BOM and BSM use *different* interest rate and volatility assumptions to describe the *same* time period when evaluating different options. This means that current and future option values calculated by the BOM and BSM are *incorrect* and *inconsistent*, as are the Greek (risk metrics) values – which rely on these invalid assumptions!

Created especially for readers who have some familiarity with options, this practical guide begins with an accessible primer on all aspects of volatility, followed by a two-chapter primer on the binomial options model, followed by a primer on the Black-Scholes-Merton model.

Building on that foundation, Chapter 5 provides a comprehensive explanation and detailed examples of the new option valuation and volatility aggregation framework cited above. Chapters 6 and 8, plus the accompanying comprehensive Supplement, execute and document a logical, step-by-step validation plan for all elements of this framework.

The remaining chapters provide a wealth of new and practical insights for the volatility trader. You will find it fascinating that the simple, objective trade management strategies of Gamma-Scalping and Portfolio Insurance can be used to solve for the theoretical values and profits of any option or option strategy. Even more important, the *Gamma-Scalping strategy can extract the realized value from an option over time, completely offsetting the loss from time decay – in the appropriate realized volatility environment.* Evaluating the notorious Portfolio Insurance strategy even provides insights into managing Option Income Strategies. Finally, a number of practical and detailed volatility trade examples are examined in actual market environments.

Formulas are included to facilitate the understanding of important concepts, and to provide further research opportunities for inquisitive traders. The book also includes hundreds of graphs and tables to illustrate how the framework and tools can be used in practice.

A user-friendly Excel spreadsheet is also included with *Trading Option Volatility*. The spreadsheet uses actual market data to solve for forward volatilities, which are applied to identify and quantify volatility pricing anomalies in equity index options and volatility index futures contracts. The resulting forward volatilities are also used to calculate structurally-consistent True Vega metrics for ATM options, VIX futures, and their corresponding calendar spreads. All of the spreadsheet functions are automated through the use of push-button macros, making spreadsheet operation as simple as possible.

1) VOLATILITY PRIMER

Volatility is arguably the single most important (and most inadequately understood) option concept. The term volatility is used in a number of different ways when discussing options; I will explain several different types of volatility in this chapter and explore how they are used in practice. One or two of these volatility concepts may be new to you.

Volatility at its most basic level is used to describe the distribution of rates of return. In an option context, it is the distribution of rates of return of the underlying security - not of the option itself. The underlying security is what the option contract gives the option buyer the right to buy or sell: stock, index, futures, etc. The higher the volatility, the wider the distribution of returns. The lower the volatility, the narrower the distribution of returns. Volatility can be used to describe the past distribution of returns (derived from historical price changes), the expected future distribution of returns, or the actual realized distribution of returns over the holding period of the option strategy. Finally, the return calculations used in the volatility calculations can utilize all of the periodic prices of the underlying security or just the terminal (beginning and ending) prices. We will explore each of these volatility concepts in this chapter.

Why is volatility so important? Because volatility is synonymous with the price of the option. If you know the market's estimate of expected future volatility (implied volatility), you also know the price of the option (for a given option model) – and vice versa. We will explore the most widely used option models in the next three chapters; two chapters will be devoted to the Binomial Option Model (BOM) and one chapter will be dedicated to the Black-Scholes-Merton (BSM) model.

Both models require the same input values to calculate an option value: the price of the underlying security (S), the strike price of the option (K), the time until option expiration in years (t), the annual continuously-compounded risk-free interest rate (r), the dividend yield (q), and the annualized volatility (σ). The simultaneous yield of the U.S. T-bill with a comparable maturity is typically used as a proxy for the risk-free interest rate. As a result, when valuing an option, we know the real-time values of S, K, t, and r with certainty. For short-dated options, we arguably have a very precise estimate for q as well. The only value we do *not* know with virtual certainty is the future annualized volatility (σ) or future distribution of returns of the underlying security.

However, if we know the current option price, we could use the BOM or BSM to calculate the future annualized volatility *implied* by that market price. This is called *implied* volatility for obvious reasons and represents the market's consensus estimate of the expected future volatility of the returns of the underlying security. If we have our own forecast of expected future annualized volatility, we could use the BOM or BSM to calculate our own estimate of the value of the option. We could then compare our estimate of the option value to the current option price to identify anomalies and prospective profit opportunities.

This is why volatility is so critical. It is the only option model input that is not known with certainty. As a result, volatility determines the price of the option today, the fair value of the option today, and the price and fair value of the option in the future. Note: the price and fair value of options will differ when the market's estimate of volatility diverges from the future realized volatility – more on that later.

Unfortunately, there are a number of well-known deficiencies in the BOM and BSM models, many of which I will review in the next three chapters. For now, it is important to recognize that the BOM and BSM both assume that volatility and interest rates will be constant over the life of every option. These assumption are violated in practice for interest rates and for volatility. In fact, they are wildly inaccurate, especially for volatility. These fallacious assumptions have very unfortunate consequences: both the BOM and BSM use *different* interest rate and volatility assumptions to describe the *same* time period when evaluating different options. This means that current and future option values calculated by the BOM and BSM are *incorrect* and *inconsistent*, as are the Greek (risk metrics) values – which rely on these invalid assumptions!

Until now, there has never been an objective framework that eliminated the invalid constant interest rate and constant volatility assumptions, allowing us to solve for and use the complete term structure of interest rates and term structure of volatilities to calculate accurate and theoretically consistent: current option values, expected future option values, current Greeks, and expected future Greeks. I call this framework the Johnson Aggregation Framework (JAF), which will be explained in detail in Chapter 5.

However, before I can introduce the JAF and explore its practical implications, we need to examine several measures of volatility and explore how volatility affects option values (this chapter), plus review the BOM and

BSM in more detail (subsequent three chapters). Portions of the following crucial material on volatility also appeared in my previous books; however, I have made a number of important revisions and additions to the material in this chapter.

Asymmetrical Payoff Functions

The key to understanding option valuation (and the role of volatility) is the asymmetrical payoff function. Let's begin with a simple analogy: the flip of a fair coin. If the flip turns up heads, I would immediately pay you $10. If the flip turns up tails, I would pay you $0. Would you want to play? Of course, as many times possible – until my money runs out. The payoffs are asymmetric – in your favor.

Would I want to play? Never. I also recognize that the payoffs are asymmetric in your favor. More interesting: could I be incentivized to play? We assumed the coin flip is fair, so the probability of heads is 50% and the probability of tails is 50%. Your probability-weighted or expected payoff would be $5 [(50% x $10) + (50% x $0)]. My probability-weighted expected payoff would be the opposite of yours: negative $5 [(50% x -$10) + (50% x $0)].

If you paid me $6 to play one round of the game, I would definitely play. My expected *profit* (not payoff) per round would now equal $1 (a receipt of $6 to play the game, *plus* the same expected payoff of *negative* $5). Assuming perfect knowledge (and risk-neutrality), you would be willing to pay me a maximum of $5 and I would be willing to accept a minimum of $5. The resulting market-clearing, no-arbitrage price would be $5 per flip.

The next interesting question is what happens to our equilibrium price if we double the payoffs to $20 and $0, from $10 and $0. The probability-weighted expected payoffs would also double to positive $10 for you and negative $10 for me. You would *now* be willing to pay a maximum of $10 per flip and I would require a minimum of $10 per flip, setting a new market-clearing, equilibrium price of $10 per flip – twice the initial price.

In this analogy, you represent the buyer of an option and I represent the seller of the option. The payoffs of the coin flip symbolize the payoffs of the call or put option at expiration. The magnitude or spread of the payoffs represent volatility. The higher the volatility, the higher the payoffs – and vice versa. The price paid per flip represents the price of an option. Therefore, as volatility increases, the magnitude of the payoffs increases. This is a direct cause and effect relationship. As the expected level of volatility increases, the values of both call and put options also increase. The reason is asymmetry. Increasing volatility magnifies the value of asymmetry. Decreasing volatility diminishes the value of asymmetry.

Let me now summarize the payoff and profit and loss functions for European call and put options (no dividends) in a convenient table (Figure 1.1) for future reference. The Max function calculates the maximum of the two values in the brackets that are separated by a comma. In the case of the long call option, the payoff would equal $Max (S_E - K, 0)$, which would ensure the payoff to the option buyer would always be greater than or equal to zero. Similarly, the payoff to the seller (short call) would always be less than or equal to zero. The only difference between the payoff and profit or loss formulas is subtracting the initial price paid by the option buyer (long) and adding the initial price received by the option seller (short).

Figure 1.1 Option Payoff Matrix

Instrument	$ Payoff	$ Profit or Loss
Long Call	$Max (S_E - K, 0)$	$Max (S_E - K, 0) - C_0$
Short Call	$- Max (S_E - K, 0)$	$- Max (S_E - K, 0) + C_0$
Long Put	$Max (K - S_E, 0)$	$Max (K - S_E, 0) - P_0$
Short Put	$- Max (K - S_E, 0)$	$- Max (K - S_E, 0) + P_0$

S_E: Stock price at Expiration
K: Strike Price
C_0: Call price today (time 0)
P_0: Put price today (time 0)

In the preceding analogy, I assumed that the payoffs occurred instantaneously, but payoffs could occur in the future – as they do with options. In that case, the value of the option would equal the *present value* of the probability-weighted future payoffs. In other words, first calculate the future payoffs and the risk-neutral probabilities of each payoff; then discount the probability-weighted expected future payoff back to the present at the risk-free interest rate. Assuming positive interest rates, the value today will be worth less than the expected or probability-weighted future payoffs.

The important conclusion from this exercise is that *the current value of almost any type of derivative instrument equals the present value of its future probability-weighted payoffs*. The Binomial Option Model (BOM) and the Black-Scholes-Merton (BSM) model are elegant means of calculating the present value of the probability weighted future payoffs for discrete and continuous distributions, respectively. Now let's explore volatility further.

Volatility Assumptions & Conventions

Volatility is a measure of price dispersion and is typically expressed as a one standard deviation (SD) *annualized* percentage price change in the underlying security based on a log-normal return distribution. Figure 1.2 depicts the normal and log-normal price distributions of a $100 non-dividend paying stock, one year into the future. The assumed risk-free interest rate was 0.25% and the annual standard deviation was 25%. The future stock price is shown on the independent x-axis and the probability is shown on the dependent y-axis. The percentages were calculated in increments of $1 and Microsoft Excel connected the probabilities using a smooth curve. The normal distribution is represented by the dashed purple line and the log-normal distribution is depicted by the solid blue line.

First, note that the normal distribution is symmetric and is centered (approximately) at the current stock price of $100. The symmetry of a normal price distribution leads to a very significant problem when valuing options: negative prices for the underlying security. In practice, there is no upper bound on stock prices (provided there are investors who are willing to pay more for the stock), but stock prices cannot drop below zero. As a result, it is not practical to use normal price distributions when pricing options.

The Black-Scholes-Merton (BSM) model assumes that the non-instantaneous returns of the underlying security are distributed log-normally, which means that the natural log of the ending prices divided by the beginning price (ending price/beginning price) are distributed normally. This also means the BSM assumes that the *continuously compounded* returns of the underlying security are *normally* distributed.

Returns of the underlying security that are *not* continuously compounded (and the underlying security prices themselves) are assumed to be log-normally distributed, and continuously compounded returns of the underlying security are normally distributed. This is internally consistent, but tends to confuse many derivative students who focus only on the continuously compounded normally distributed returns, but fail to recognize the resulting log-normal distribution of prices and non-instantaneous returns.

Prices derived from a log-normal distribution cannot drop below zero, but are not limited in how much they can increase.

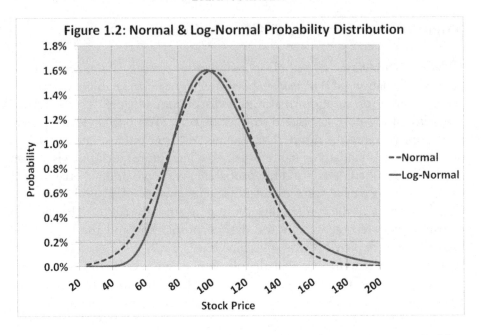

Figure 1.2: Normal & Log-Normal Probability Distribution

The above return distributions were calculated for a one-year holding period. However, there are obviously many different options, all with varying amounts of time remaining until expiration. As a result, the industry convention is to express volatility in annual terms, regardless of the time remaining until expiration for a given option.

This yields two important benefits. First, the annualized volatility estimate can be used directly in the BOM and BSM models. Even more important, the resulting annualized volatilities are directly comparable across all variables: time, underlying security, strike price, time to expiration, option type, etc. This further elevates the importance of volatility relative to other option metrics.

Annualized Volatility and Expected Price Changes

Just because volatility is expressed in annual terms does not mean that it cannot be used to calculate expected price changes for other periods. When price changes are assumed to be independent (as is the case in the BOM and BSM models), the dispersion of prices or volatility is a function of the square root of time. The following formula can be used to calculate the expected future price of an underlying security under the simplifying assumptions of a 0% risk-free rate and a 0% dividend yield:

$$S_T = S_0 \times EXP(N * \sigma * (TD/252)^{0.5})$$

S_T = Stock Price T years into the future
S_0 = Stock Price today (Zero years into the future)
EXP represents the Excel function e raised to a power,
e = 2.718281828 (base of natural logarithm)
N = Number of standard deviations (can be positive or negative)
σ = Annualized volatility, typically expressed as a percentage
TD = Number of trade days in the holding period
252 = Approximate number of trading days in calendar year

You will note that the number of trade days (TD) was used in the above formula, instead of the number of calendar days. All of the formulas in this book use trade days, as does the accompanying spreadsheet. The improved precision of trade days is important in all volatility-related calculations, especially for near-term options.

Now let's use the above formula to forecast a hypothetical negative one standard deviation price change for a $100 stock, 42 trading days in the future, assuming an annual volatility of 25%.

$$S_T = S_0 \times EXP(N * \sigma * (TD/252)^{0.5})$$
$$S_T = 100 \times EXP(-1 * 0.25 * (42/252)^{0.5})$$
$$S_T = 100 \times EXP(-1 * 0.25 * (0.408248))$$
$$S_T = 100 \times EXP(-0.102062) = 90.29$$

The resulting price of $90.29 represents a 9.71% decline (not continuously compounded) from the initial stock price of $100. If we repeat this calculation for a range of time periods (measured in trade days), we can construct the graph in Figure 1.3, which depicts the positive and negative one standard deviation percentage price changes as a function of the number of trading days. The initial price of the non-dividend paying stock was $100; the assumed risk-free interest rate was 0.00% and the annual standard deviation was 25%.

The number of trading days is shown on the independent x-axis and the percentage price change is shown on the dependent y-axis. The negative one SD percentage price changes are represented by the dashed red line and the positive one SD percentage price changes are depicted by the solid green line. The red circle on the dashed red line represents the percentage price change for the hypothetical negative one SD move over 42 trade days (approximately two months). Note: in practice, price changes are not limited to moves of one-standard deviation. Similar graphs could be constructed for price changes resulting from moves of any number of standard deviations.

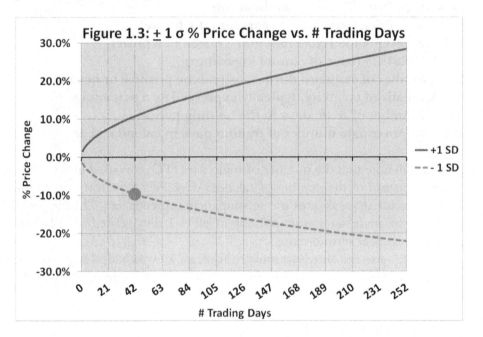

The ability to forecast expected price changes for a given level of annualized volatility is a critical element of option trading. It should be one of the main tools in your option trading toolbox. I use this formula on a daily basis. We will apply this formula more systematically when we explore the Binomial Option Model (BOM) in the next two chapters.

Realized Terminal Volatility (RTV)

While forecasting expected price changes for a given level of annualized volatility is extremely important, when designing option strategies, it can also be useful to forecast the expected *non-annualized* percentage price change of the underlying security over a range of future holding periods. I call this metric Realized Terminal Volatility (RTV), which represents the expected continuously compounded percentage price change of the underlying security from the analysis date to the end of the specified period in the future. These return forecasts are not annualized and are not directional. In other words, a 21-trade day RTV forecast of 4% would imply an expected price change of *plus or minus* 4% (continuously compounded) from now until the close, 21 trading days in the future.

Realized Extreme Volatility (REV)

I also use a related volatility forecast when implementing option strategies: Realized Extreme Volatility (REV). Realized Extreme Volatility is a forecast of the *maximum* percentage price change of the underlying security *at any time during the specified period* in the future. As was the case with the Realized Terminal Volatility, the Realized Extreme Volatility forecasts are not annualized and are not directional. If the Realized Terminal Volatility forecast was plus or minus 4% (continuously compounded) for the next 21 days, the Realized Extreme Volatility forecast might be plus or minus 5.6% (also continuously compounded). By definition, the REV forecast will always be greater than or equal to the RTV. The RTV and REV are extremely useful when designing option strategies, especially for selecting strike prices and planning adjustment levels. I will use these forecasts in specific examples in later chapters, but wanted to introduce them now, because they are both volatility metrics. The specific volatility forecasting tool I use for all volatility forecasts is the AI Volatility Edge (AIVE) Platform, which is explained in the Resources chapter at the end of this book.

Multiple Volatilities

Until now, I have ignored the fact that the term "volatility" is used to describe several different concepts, all of which are relevant to this book. The remainder of this chapter will explain three vital types of volatility measures: Implied Volatility (IV), Historical Volatility (HV), and Realized Volatility (RV).

Implied Volatility (IV)

I already touched on Implied Volatility earlier in this chapter, but it is also important to include it here – in the context of the other core volatility concepts. Implied Volatility is a measure of expected or forward-looking volatility. Specifically, it is the market's consensus estimate of future volatility. It is expressed in annualized percentage terms.

Since we know the values of the other variables that are required to calculate the value of an option (S, K, t, r, *and* q) and we also can observe the market price of the option (C_0 or P_0), we can use an option valuation formula, such as the BOM or BSM, to solve for the *implied volatility (IV)* using an iterative process. .

Do you see why this is called implied volatility? Implied volatility is the expected level of volatility *implied by* or embedded in the price of the option. In other words, IV represents the market's estimate of the future level of volatility of the underlying security, as determined by the price of the option.

If we know the option price, we can solve for the corresponding implied volatility. Similarly, if we know the expected level of volatility, we can solve for the price of the option. The relationship between the price of an option and the expected level of volatility of the underlying security is completely deterministic, but it does require an option valuation model, which relies on a given set of assumptions. However, as explained earlier, the most important assumptions regarding volatility and interest rates are violated in practice.

In Chapter 5, I will explain how to model the expected price dispersion accurately and consistently for options with different expiration dates using the Johnson Aggregation Framework. Chapter 5 will formally document the mathematical relationship between discrete estimates of future volatility and interest rates and explain how these values can be aggregated for use in option valuation, scenario analysis, and optimization.

Historical Volatility (HV)

The second volatility concept that we will need is historical volatility, which is a measure of past or backward-looking volatility. Practitioners use past levels of price volatility as a means of forecasting future levels of price volatility, which are then used to forecast option prices. To be useful as an estimate of implied volatility, historical volatility must be expressed in the same units as implied volatility. In other words, historical volatility must represent an annualized volatility of the historical continuously compounded periodic returns of the underlying security.

Realized volatility is similar to historical volatility, except that realized volatility is forward-looking. I will explain realized volatility in the next section, but I wanted to mention now that the same steps are required to calculate both historical and realized volatility.

To calculate the annualized historical (or realized) volatility of a return series, annualize the root mean squared continuously compounded daily returns of the underlying security.

To calculate the annualized historical (or realized) volatility:
1. Calculate the ratio of the daily closing prices (closing price/previous closing price).
2. Calculate the natural log of the daily price ratios (from step 1).
3. Square the continuously compounded or log returns (from step 2).
4. Calculate the average of the squared log returns (from step 3).
5. Calculate the square root of the average of the squared log returns (from step 4).
6. Annualize the root mean squared (RMS) log returns (from step 5).

While I did use the term standard deviation before, you should note that we *did not* and *should not* use the formula for standard deviation to calculate historical (or realized) volatility. Standard deviation measures the deviation *around the mean or average value of a data series*, while the root mean squared return measures the deviation *around zero*.

The expected daily return for all assets is *approximately* zero under BOM and BSM assumptions, which is consistent with the historical root mean squared (RMS) calculation. The standard deviation calculation implicitly assumes that the *expected* daily return equals the *average* daily return, which is grossly inaccurate for real-world historical data. Using standard deviation to measure historical or realized volatility can significantly understate volatility, especially for small data sets. Using systematically biased (understated) volatility estimates would result in potentially catastrophic trading losses.

If you are a purist, you could subtract the actual expected daily return from the continuously compounded daily return before squaring the result. However, in recent interest rate environments, this expected daily return value would be less than 0.01%, which is why I am comfortable advocating the RMS calculation. Do not under any circumstances use the standard deviation around the average daily return to estimate historical or realized volatility – even though it is recommended in several derivative textbooks!

The hypothetical example in Figure 1.4 illustrates the potential magnitude of the problem of using standard deviation as a measure of historical volatility. The twelve daily returns are listed in the first column, all of which equal 2.02%. The natural logs of one plus the daily returns (which equal the continuously compounded daily returns) are provided in the next column, followed by the squared log returns in column three.

Each of the *continuously compounded* daily returns equals 2.00%, which means that the mean or arithmetic average of the log returns also equals 2.00%. Therefore, the daily deviations from the average must all equal zero, as does the standard deviation (SD) around the mean. Using the standard

13

deviation formula, we would have calculated a historical volatility of 0.00% for a security that was moving in price by 2.02% per day!

Daily Return	Log Return	Log Return Squared	Dev from Mean Squared
2.02%	2.00%	0.04%	0.0017%
2.02%	2.00%	0.04%	0.0017%
2.02%	2.00%	0.04%	0.0017%
2.02%	2.00%	0.04%	0.0017%
2.02%	2.00%	0.04%	0.0017%
2.02%	2.00%	0.04%	0.0017%
2.02%	2.00%	0.04%	0.0017%
2.02%	2.00%	0.04%	0.0017%
2.02%	2.00%	0.04%	0.0017%
2.02%	2.00%	0.04%	0.0017%
2.02%	2.00%	0.04%	0.0017%
2.02%	2.00%	0.04%	0.0017%
	Period	RMS	SD
	Daily	2.00%	0.00%
	Annual	31.75%	0.00%

Figure 1.4: Historical Volatility

Unlike the standard deviation formula, the root mean squared (RMS) formula provides an accurate and representative historical volatility measure and is not affected by the historical average level of volatility. The daily RMS for the hypothetical example was 2.00% (steps 1-6). You will recall that volatility is a function of the square root of time. We can use this fact to calculate an annualized historical volatility from the daily historical volatility.

If we assume there are 252 trade days per calendar year, we multiply the daily volatility value of 2% by the square root of 252 to arrive at the annualized historical volatility (see formula below).

Annual Volatility = Periodic Volatility * ((252/TD) ^ 0.5)
NTD = Number of trade days in the return period (1 for daily)

Annual Volatility = Periodic Volatility * ((252/NTD) ^ 0.5)
Annual Volatility = 2.00% * ((252/1) ^ 0.5) = 31.75%

If we determined that the resulting historical volatility of 31.75% was a fair and unbiased estimate of future volatility, we could use the value of 31.75% as a forecast of the future level of annualized volatility in the BOM or BSM to estimate the value of an option on the underlying security. There are many other sophisticated techniques available for further refining our volatility forecasting as well, but the historical standard deviation around a historical average return should not be used as an input to these models in practice. RMS is preferred.

Realized Volatility (RV)

Realized Volatility (RV) is the annualized volatility of the periodic (typically daily) continuously compounded returns of the underlying security actually realized (earned) over one or more future holding period(s). The holding period could equal the full time to expiration of the option of interest, or it could be a shorter period. In fact, a complete term structure of realized volatilities could be calculated.

To calculate realized volatility, *we use the exact same RMS calculation that I presented in the previous section.* The only difference is that we use the actual daily returns of the underlying security realized in the future, instead of the historical daily returns earned in the past.

I recognize that we do not know the actual future daily returns of the underlying security in advance. Fortunately, we can still use the realized volatility RMS calculation on a historical dataset to help us develop a model to forecast realized volatility. After the fact, we can also use Realized Volatility to help us explain the performance of an option strategy over the specific holding period.

Realized volatility is probably the most important core volatility concept, but it is rarely mentioned in the option trading community. The term may even be new to you. Why is realized volatility so important? While Implied Volatility (IV) represents the *market price* of an option, Realized Volatility (RV) represents the *value* of the option – what the option is actually worth.

Let's walk through a simple, hypothetical IV and RV example. Using the market price of an option in conjunction with an options valuation model (such as the BOM or BSM), we can calculate the implied volatility of the option, which represents the market's estimate of future price volatility. We can also calculate historical volatility, which can be used by itself, or preferably in a volatility model, to estimate future realized volatility. Why would we need two estimates of future volatility? Because the market's estimate of future volatility is frequently wrong, and these errors can be significant.

If we could come up with a more accurate estimate of realized volatility than the market's implied volatility estimate, then we could design option strategies to exploit these anomalies and use our unique insight and earn excess returns.

We will look at specific strategy examples later, but for now, let's assume that the market's annualized implied volatility estimate was only 15%, but the annualized historical volatility was 20%, which our volatility model determined was likely to persist in the future.

In this hypothetical example, it would appear that the market's implied volatility estimate is too low. Since volatility is synonymous with price, option prices would also be too low. In other words, if we believe our annualized future volatility estimate of 20% is more accurate than the market's implied volatility estimate of 15%, then options must be cheap or undervalued and should be purchased.

How could we profit from such a trade? Let's ignore directional price changes and focus on volatility. If we purchased undervalued options at the market's implied volatility of only 15%, and the market's implied volatility estimate of 15% converged to our future realized volatility estimate of 20%, then the prices of our options would increase and we would earn an excess return. In other words, implied volatility would increase; the increase in implied volatility would act simultaneously through positive Vega to boost both option prices and the value of our long option positions. After the implied volatility converged to our realized volatility estimate, we would sell our position and capitalize on our excess returns.

What if the market's implied volatility estimate (15% annualized) never changed, but our expected future level of realized volatility over the life of the option (20% annualized) proved to be correct? What would this mean and how would it affect the performance of our strategy? It would mean that we were ultimately correct and the *realized volatility* experienced over the life of the option was equal to our future realized volatility forecast of 20%, which was based (to some degree) on *historical volatility*.

In this scenario, we would have expected to earn an excess return (on average) because the *realized volatility* experienced over the life of the option was greater than the market's *implied volatility*, despite the fact that the market's estimate of implied volatility did not change. Why would we have expected to earn an excess return on average? Because option payoff functions are asymmetric and the undervalued options we purchased would have benefited from a higher than expected level of volatility.

However, simply buying an undervalued call or put option and holding it until it expires would not have guaranteed an excess return. Why? Because we would have still been exposed to the directional bias in a simple long call or put option. Even if we knew the future annualized realized volatility would be 20% (RMS of the daily continuously compounded returns) with absolute certainty in advance, we would only experience one of the infinite number of possible price paths over the life of the option. In many of those 20% realized volatility paths, our simple long call or put option would expire worthless. *On average*, we would expect to earn excess returns, but not in every case. By holding the long directional call or put option to expiration without adjustments of any kind, *realized terminal volatility* (based on only the starting and ending prices) would be the more relevant than realized volatility (based on all of the daily returns), but realized terminal volatility would not be sufficient either - due to the unhedged directional exposure.

Are there alternative strategies that could exploit anomalies between implied and realized volatility more effectively? Fortunately, there are. I will examine several of these trading strategies in Chapters 11 and 12. In addition, the same chapters will explore the theoretical and practical applications of this fascinating subject in great detail, including the implications for gamma scalping, delta hedging, portfolio insurance, and a broad selection of option income strategies.

In summary, implied volatility represents the *market price* of an option, realized volatility represents the *actual value* of an option, and historical volatility can be used to help forecast implied volatility and realized volatility. RMS is the preferred metric for calculating historical and realized volatility. Material divergences between implied and realized volatility can be exploited, but more sophisticated trading strategies are required.

2) BINOMIAL: HEDGE FRAMEWORK PRIMER

Every undergraduate or graduate derivatives student studied option models in exhaustive detail, but many non-professionals have never even been introduced to the topic. There are even a number of investment professionals who never had this opportunity. A basic understanding of option models (including their assumptions and limitations) is invaluable for option traders and is a prerequisite for understanding and evaluating the Johnson Aggregation Framework (JAF) that I will explain and demonstrate in the coming chapters.

From a practical perspective, learning more about option models will help option traders gain new insights into option valuation, scenario analysis, and risk management. I will attempt to highlight a number of those insights. For the former derivative student, this option model primer will reinforce some ideas and may provide a new perspective on several concepts.

Option models use mathematical formulas and I recognize that all traders do not share the same level of proficiency with, or affinity for, mathematics. As a result, I will present the required formulas and numerical examples for those who are interested. For those who are not mathematically inclined, I would suggest skimming (or potentially even skipping) the formulas, and focusing on my explanations of the formulas - which provide intuition into the cause-and-effect relationships that are embedded in the models. The next two chapters will be devoted to the Binomial Option Model (BOM). Chapter 2 will focus on the Binomial Hedge Framework and Chapter 3 will explain how to use Binomial Backward Induction to value options. Chapter 4 will investigate the Black-Scholes-Merton (BSM) Options Model.

To remain consistent with the Black-Scholes-Merton model assumptions, I will assume that options are European – may only be exercised at expiration and not before. For ease of explanation, all examples will assume that dividends are zero, although this assumption is not required. All of the models discussed in this book can be used to accurately value European options by reducing the value of the underlying stock (or index) price by the present (or discounted) value of all of the dividends to be received during the life of the option. All present value calculations require the use of the appropriate risk-free interest rate – more on that later.

For our purposes, we will assume *long-term (not instantaneous)* stock returns and the resulting future stock prices are log-normally distributed, which is consistent with the BSM assumptions. This also implies that *instantaneous* or *continuously compounded* stock returns are *normally* distributed, but practitioners should focus on the non-instantaneous log-normal distribution of stock returns and prices. To make the formulas more intuitive, I will typically assume each option applies to one share of stock, rather than the typical 100 shares per option contract.

Binomial Model Introduction

The Binomial Options Model (BOM) is the single most powerful and flexible option valuation model currently in use. The BOM can be used to value virtually every type of option or derivative security. The most notable exception to this is path-dependent options, which require a Monte Carlo simulation or similar sampling approach. However, a binomial (or multinomial) process is still the foundation for the Monte Carlo simulation.

Conceptually, the BOM is very simple. It is called a Binomial model because there are *two* possible future states or outcomes in each period, the *UP* state and the *DOWN* state. Options are *derivative* securities, which means that option values are *derived* from or determined by an underlying security or index. The underlying security is typically assumed to be a stock in most textbook examples, so I will follow that convention here.

The first step in the binomial valuation process is to determine the two possible stock prices one period in the future. These prices are a function of the stock price today, the length of time between today and the future state price, and the expected volatility or dispersion of the returns of the underlying stock price.

Let's begin with a simple one-period binomial option example, with the initial stock price (S_0) equal to 100, the strike price (K) also equal to 100, the time to expiration (t) equal to one-year (1.0), the annualized standard deviation of the continuously compounded expected stock returns (σ) equal to 20%, and the annual risk-free rate of interest (r) equal to 4% (continuously compounded). Note: e represents the base of a natural logarithm – approximately 2.7182818.

There are many different binomial models, all of which are very similar and yield consistent results at the limit. In Chapters 2 and 3, I will use the binomial framework and several of the formulas presented in the textbook I used to teach derivatives at the University of North Carolina's Kenan-Flagler Business School: *Fundamentals of Futures and Options Markets* by John C. Hull. However, I use a slightly different notation. All calculations in the examples below are rounded, but the formulas provide exact results.

We can use the following formula to solve for the future value of the stock in the UP state (S_U) and the future value of the stock in the DOWN state (S_D).

$$S_U = S_0 * e^{\sigma \sqrt{t}} = 100 * e^{0.20\,(1.0)} = 100 * 1.22140 = 122.140$$
$$S_D = S_0 * e^{-\sigma \sqrt{t}} = 100 * e^{-0.20\,(1.0)} = 100 * 0.81873 = 81.873$$

The next step is to calculate the payoffs for the call and put options in the UP state and in the DOWN state. Note that we are calculating the payoffs, not the profits or losses. We do not know the value of the option yet; that is what we are trying to determine. We use the future payoff amounts to calculate the value of the options.

Call Option Payoff = Max (S_E – K, 0)
S_E = Stock price at Expiration
C_U = Value of Call Option in UP state
C_D = Value of Call Option in DOWN state

C_U = Max (122.140– 100.00, 0) = 22.140
C_D = Max (81.873 - 100.00, 0) = 0.000

If the stock price increased to 122.140, then the call option would be in the money at expiration and the holder of the option could buy the stock at 100.00 and resell it for 122.140 for a payoff of 22.140. Conversely, if the stock price dropped to 81.873, the holder of the call option would choose NOT to exercise (why buy the stock for 100 when it is trading at 81.873) and the option would expire worthless.

The calculations for the put option are similar, but reversed:

Put Option Payoff = Max (K - S_E, 0)
P_U = Value of Put Option in UP state
P_D = Value of Put Option in DOWN state

P_U = Max (100.00 – 122.140, 0) = 0.000
P_D = Max (100.00 – 81.873, 0) = 18.127

If the stock price decreased to 81.873, then the put option would be in the money at expiration and the holder of the option could purchase the stock at the market price of 81.873 and exercise the option to sell the stock at 100 for a payoff of 18.127. Conversely, if the stock price increased to 122.140, the holder of the put option would choose NOT to exercise (why sell the stock for 100 when it is trading at 122.140) and the option would expire worthless.

Binomial Hedge Framework – Call Option

Now that we know the future state payoffs of the stock, call option, and put option, we can use the binomial hedge framework to calculate the theoretical value of the call option and the put option in our example above ($S_0 = 100$, $K = 100$, $\sigma = 20\%$, $r = 4\%$). If we can construct a perfect hedge that results in the same position value in both the UP and the DOWN states, then the position would be riskless and must earn the risk-free rate of return. We can use this insight to construct the hedges and calculate the values of the call and put option.

The first step is to find the fractional number of shares of stock, that when combined with a one-share short position in calls or puts, would result in a riskless or hedged position. We will refer to the fractional number of shares of stock per one-share short position in the option as Delta (Δ). To solve for Delta, we set the future value of the hedged position in the UP state equal to the future value of the hedged position in the DOWN state and use algebra to solve for the value of Delta (Δ).

$\Delta S_U - C_U = \Delta S_D - C_D$
$\Delta(122.140) - 22.143 = \Delta(81.873) - 0$
$\Delta(40.27) = 22.140$
$\Delta = 22.140 / 40.27 = 0.54983$ Shares of Stock

I initially used the formula above because it is more intuitive to set the future value of the hedged position in the UP state equal to the future value of the hedged position in the DOWN state. This formula reinforces the idea of a riskless hedged position with the same position payoffs in both the UP and DOWN state that must earn a return equal to the risk-free interest rate.

However, it is more efficient to use the formula below and solve for Delta directly. The other advantage of the formula below is that it expresses Delta as the change in the value of the call option per one-unit change in the value of the underlying stock. In other words, it quantifies the price sensitivity of the call option with respect to a change in the price of the underlying stock. If you are an option trader, this is the same Delta metric that you use every day to construct your option strategies. By changing the terms used in the numerator and denominator, this formula can be used to calculate a wide range of sensitivities or risk metrics.

$$\Delta = (C_U - C_D) / (S_U - S_D)$$

To construct a perfect riskless hedge (same payoffs in UP and DOWN state), we would buy 0.549863 shares of stock per one-share short position in the call option.

We can use this information to solve for the value of the call option. The LHS of the equation below $(\Delta S_0 - C_0)$ equals the value of the hedged position today. The quantity $(\Delta S_D - C_D)$ on the RHS of the equation below represents the value of the hedged position in the DOWN state (which must also equal the value in the UP state) one period in the future. Since this represents the *future value* of the hedged position, to equate this value to the hedged value today, we have to discount this future value back to the present by multiplying by e^{-rt}.

$$\Delta S_0 - C_0 = (\Delta S_D - C_D)e^{-rt}$$

By rearranging terms, we can isolate the value of the call option on the LHS of the equation.

$$C_0 = \Delta S_0 + (- (\Delta S_D - C_D)e^{-rt})$$

$C_0 = \Delta S_0 + (- (\Delta S_D - C_D) e^{-rt})$
$C_0 = (0.54983)100.00 + -[(0.54983)81.873 - 0] (e^{-.04})$
$C_0 = (.54983)100.00 - 43.251$
$C_0 = \mathbf{11.732}$

The RHS of the equation above represents the *replicating portfolio* for the call option. The one-period binomial replicating portfolio will always include delta shares of stock and some amount "invested" at the risk-free interest rate until the end of the binomial period.

Note that the RHS includes a positive sign, followed immediately by a negative sign. This allows us to consistently follow the convention where a negative sign represents borrowing (or a short position) and a positive sign represents investing (or a long position). In the case of the call option, the amount invested at the risk-free interest rate will be negative, which indicates borrowing is required. How much is borrowed? The present value of the future value of the hedged portfolio value (which is the same in the UP and DOWN state).

We have already done this calculation above. We simply need to recognize that the second term in the equation represents the amount invested at the risk-free interest rate.

$C_0 = \Delta S_0 + (- (\Delta S_D - C_D)e^{-rt})$
$C_0 = (0.54983)100.00 + - [(0.54983)81.873 - 0] (e^{-.04})$
$C_0 = (0.54983)100.00 - 43.251$

In this case, the amount invested at the risk-free interest rate equals negative 43.251, which means that the replicating portfolio for the call option requires the purchase of 0.54983 shares of stock, which is financed by *borrowing (due to the negative parameter value)* 43.251 at the risk-free interest rate (4%) for one period. This replicating portfolio will produce the exact same one-period payoffs as the call option in the UP state and in the DOWN state.

Binomial Hedge Framework – Put Option

We can use the same binomial hedge framework to calculate the theoretical value of the put option in our example above ($S_0 = 100$, $K = 100$, $\sigma = 20\%$, $r = 4\%$).

As was the case for the call option, the first step is to find Delta (Δ): the fractional number of shares of stock that, when combined with a one-share short position in a put option, would result in a riskless or hedged position. To solve for the Delta of the put option, we set the future value of the hedged position in the UP state equal to the future value of the hedged position in the DOWN state and use algebra to solve for the value of Delta (Δ).

$\Delta S_U - P_U = \Delta S_D - P_D$
$\Delta(122.140) - 0 = \Delta(81.873) - 18.13$
$\Delta(40.27) = -18.13$
$\Delta = -18.13 / 40.27 = -0.45017$ Shares of Stock

As I demonstrated with the call option, we can also use the price sensitivity formula below to solve for the Delta of the put option directly.

$\Delta = (P_U - P_D) / (S_U - S_D) = -0.45017$

To construct a perfect riskless hedge (same payoffs in UP and DOWN state), we would *sell* 0.45017 shares of stock per one-share short position in the put option. Note: we would need to *sell* stock due to the negative Delta of the put option.

We can use the value of Delta to solve for the value of the put option. The LHS of the equation below $(\Delta S_0 - P_0)$ equals the value of the hedged position today. The quantity $(\Delta S_U - P_U)$ on the RHS of the equation below represents the value of the hedged position in the UP state (which must also equal the value in the DOWN state) one period in the future. Note: I typically use the DOWN state for call options and the UP state for put options, since the option payoffs are typically zero – which makes the math a little easier. Since this represents the *future value* of the hedged position, to equate this value to the hedged value today, we have to discount this future value back to the present by multiplying by e^{-rt}.

$$\Delta S_0 - P_0 = (\Delta S_U - P_U)e^{-rt}$$

By rearranging terms, we can isolate the value of the put option on the LHS of the equation.

$$P_0 = \Delta S_0 + (- (\Delta S_U - P_U)e^{-rt})$$

$P_0 = \Delta S_0 + (- (\Delta S_U - P_U)\ e^{-rt})$
$P_0 = (- 0.45017)100.00 + -[(- 0.45017)122.14 - 0]\ (e^{-.04})$
$P_0 = (- 0.45017)100.00 + 52.828$
$P_0 = \mathbf{7.811}$

The RHS of the equation above represents the *replicating portfolio* for the put option. The one-period binomial replicating portfolio will always include Delta shares of stock and some amount "invested" at the risk-free interest rate until the end of the binomial period.

In the case of the put option, the amount invested at the risk-free interest rate will be positive, which indicates investing (not borrowing) is required. How much is invested? The present value of the future value of the hedged portfolio value (which is the same in the UP and DOWN state).

We have already done this calculation above. We simply need to recognize that the second term in the equation represents the amount invested at the risk-free interest rate.

$P_0 = \Delta S_0 + (- (\Delta S_U - P_U)e^{-rt})$
$P_0 = (- 0.45017)100.00 + - [(-0.45017)122.14 - 0] (e^{-.04})$
$P_0 = (- 0.45017)100.00 + 52.828$

In this case, the amount invested at the risk-free interest rate equals 52.828, which means that the replicating portfolio for the put option requires the *sale* of 0.45017 shares of stock, with 52.828 invested at the continuously-compounded risk-free interest rate of 4% for one period. This replicating portfolio will produce the exact same one-period payoffs as the put option in the UP state and in the DOWN state.

Practical Observations

Options behave like leveraged instruments and involve a substantial amount of risk. As a result, it probably seems strange to discount future cash flows at the risk-free interest rate. This implies that option investors only require an expected return equal to the risk-free interest rate. The key observation is that we have constructed hedged portfolios with the same riskless payoffs, which must earn a rate of return equal to the return earned by investing at the risk-free interest rate. If that was not the case, riskless arbitrage would be possible.

It may also seem odd that I did not mention probabilities when discussing the UP and DOWN states. In fact, we were able to calculate the theoretical values of the call and put options without knowing anything about the probabilities of the payoffs. Again, the key is the hedged portfolio concept. We have constructed a hedged portfolio that earns the same rate of return in the UP state and in the DOWN state. As a result, we are indifferent to which state actually occurs one period into the future.

This is an example of the *risk neutral* framework that is widely used to value many types of derivative instruments. The alternative would be to use a risk-averse valuation framework, where investors would require higher returns for taking on more risk (systematic risk in the case of the Capital Asset Pricing Model – CAPM). I will discuss CAPM in more detail in Chapter 3. For now, systematic risk represents the sensitivity of the value of an asset to changes in the overall market. The greater the change in the value of an asset in response to a change in the overall market, the greater the systematic risk of the asset. Beta is the primary metric used to quantify the systematic risk of individual assets and portfolios. I will explain Beta in more detail below, including how to use the binomial framework to calculate the Beta of call and put options.

The risk-averse framework is more appealing intuitively than the risk-neutral framework, but would be much more complex to apply in practice. The reason is that the systematic risk or Beta of every option changes continuously, which means that the required rate of return would also change continuously. We obviously want to calculate accurate and realistic option values, so which framework should we use? Fortunately, the risk-neutral valuation framework and the risk-averse valuation framework generate the exact same option values! After over 30 years of working with option models, I still find this result remarkable. I will demonstrate this result in Chapter 3. For now, this means we can use the much easier risk-neutral valuation framework without reservations. However, we will need to be careful to recognize some intermediate calculations will only apply to the risk-neutral framework and may not be generalized to the risk-averse environment.

As I explained above, we did not need to use probabilities to apply the binomial hedge framework, but there are actually implicit risk-neutral UP and DOWN state probabilities embedded in the hedge framework calculations. We will calculate these implicit probabilities directly in the next chapter when we use the more common binomial lattice to calculate the values of call and put options.

When first exposed to the binomial hedge framework, many derivative students and traders tend to confuse the riskless hedged portfolio and the replicating portfolio. Let me revisit this concept briefly before we continue. The riskless hedge portfolio was constructed with a one share short position in the option (put or call) combined with Delta shares of stock. This hedged portfolio generated the exact same payoff in the UP and DOWN states.

The hedged portfolio using the call option required the sale of one call option (on one share of stock) and the simultaneous *purchase* of 0.54983 shares of stock. The *initial* value of the hedged call portfolio was $\Delta S_0 - C_0$ $(0.54983(100) - 11.732 = 43.251)$. The *ending* value of the hedged call portfolio in the DOWN state (which was the same as the UP state) equaled $\Delta S_D - C_D$ $(0.54983(81.873) - 0.0 = 45.02)$. Buying the hedged call portfolio was equivalent to investing 43.251 for the one year period and earning a continuously compounded rate of return of 4% $[\ln(45.02/43.251)]$, exactly equal to the risk-free interest rate available at the beginning of the period.

The hedged portfolio using the put option required the sale of one put option (on one share of stock) and the simultaneous *sale* of 0.45017 shares of stock. The *initial* value of the hedged put portfolio was $\Delta S_0 - P_0$ (-$0.45017(100) - 7.811 = -52.828$). The *ending* value of the hedged put portfolio in the UP state (which was the same as the DOWN state) equaled $\Delta S_U - P_U$

(-0.45017 (122.14) – 0) = - 54.984. Buying the hedged put portfolio was equivalent to *borrowing* 52.828 for the one year period and *paying* a continuously compounded rate of return of 4% [ln(54.984/52.828)], exactly equal to the risk-free interest rate available at the beginning of the period.

Note: the hedged call portfolio required *selling* stock and the hedged put portfolio required *buying* stock. Both hedged portfolios required selling a call or put option on one share of stock. The resulting hedged portfolio was equivalent to either *investing* or *borrowing* for one period at the risk-free interest rate. The initial value of the hedged call portfolio was *positive* (an asset earning the risk-free rate of interest) and the initial value of the hedged put portfolio was *negative* (a liability paying the risk-free rate of interest). Note: the hedged portfolio would only be hedged for one period. In the binomial framework, Delta changes every period, resulting in a different hedged portfolio from period to period.

Replicating portfolios are different from *hedged* portfolios. Hedged portfolios combine positions in stocks and options and are riskless. Hedged portfolios are equivalent to either investing or borrowing at the risk-free interest rate. Replicating portfolios combine borrowing or lending with long or short positions in stock to exactly replicate the payoffs of a call or put option for one period. They are not riskless; they replicate risky investments in call or put options.

In our earlier example, the *replicating* portfolio for the call option required the *purchase* of 0.54983 shares of stock, which is financed by *borrowing (due to the negative parameter value)* 43.251 at the risk-free interest rate (4%) for one period. The *replicating* portfolio for the put option requires the *sale* of 0.45017 shares of stock, with 52.828 *invested* at the continuously-compounded risk-free interest rate of 4% for one period. Note that stock purchases are required for the call replicating portfolio and stock sales are required for the put replicating portfolio, which is logical given that calls are bullish and puts are bearish. The respective *borrowing* and *lending* components of the call and put replicating portfolios directly follow from the required *purchase* and *sale* of stock in the call and put replicating portfolios.

Finally, I wanted to introduce the Put-Call Parity formula, which is fundamental to understanding the theoretical and practical relationship between call options, put options, the underlying stock, and the riskless asset (borrowing or lending). Per our usual convention, positive values represent purchases or long positions and negative values represent sales or short positions. When applied to the risk-free asset, positive values represent investing at the risk-free rate of interest and negative values represent borrowing at the risk-free rate of interest. To remain consistent with the original Black-Scholes-Merton (BSM) formula, I am still assuming no dividends, but there is a comparable Put-Call Parity formula that includes dividends.

We can use algebra to rearrange the Put-Call Parity formula in many different forms. In fact, we can express the value of any one of the instruments in terms of the other three instruments. This means that we can exactly replicate a European call option or put option using the other three instruments. Similarly, we could also exactly replicate a stock or riskless borrowing or lending with the other three instruments – under the normal BSM and BOM assumptions. In my derivative classes, I typically started with the following form of the Put-Call Parity formula.

$$C - P = S - Ke^{-rt}$$

This formula indicates that a long call option and a short put option (with the same strike prices and expiration dates) has the exact same value and payoffs as a long stock position with K dollars borrowed at the risk-free rate of interest for t years. This implies that a long call plus a short put is equivalent to a leveraged stock position. Every option trader should be aware of this formula and the underlying relationship between the above assets.

We can use the Put-Call Parity formula to confirm the values of the call and put options that we calculated earlier with the binomial hedge framework.

$$C - P = S - Ke^{-rt}$$
$$11.732 - 7.811 = 100 - 100e^{-0.04(1.0)}$$
$$3.921 = 100 - 96.079$$
$$3.921 = 3.921 \text{ Confirmed}$$

I will not review the alternative forms of the Put-Call Parity formula below in detail, but I wanted to include them for your reference. They document how each of the respective assets can be replicated exactly using the other three assets.

$$C = \ S - Ke^{-rt} + P$$
$$P = -S + Ke^{-rt} + C$$
$$S = Ke^{-rt} + C - P$$
$$Ke^{-rt} = S - C + P$$

Binomial Option Beta

As I mentioned above, there is an important measure of systematic risk that can be derived from the binomial state prices: the Beta of the option. Beta is covered extensively in most undergraduate and graduate level finance classes. Beta is a widely-used measure of systematic (undiversifiable) risk and represents the percentage change in the value of an asset in response to a 1% change in the value of the broad-market index. If the Beta of an asset is stable over time, it can be calculated by regressing the periodic returns of the asset against the periodic returns of the index. Beta is useful on the asset level, but is an even more valuable risk metric for portfolios.

Finally, Beta is a critical component of the Capital Asset Pricing Model (CAPM), which states that the required or expected return of an asset equals the risk-free rate of return, plus Beta times the market risk premium (MRP). The market risk premium equals the expected return of the market in excess of the risk-free rate of interest $(R_m - R_f)$.

$$R_i = R_f + \beta * (R_m - R_f)$$

Unfortunately, we cannot use a regression to calculate the Beta of a call or put option. Why? Because the option Betas are not stable. They are highly sensitive to changes in the value of the underlying security and to the passage of time. However, we can use the state prices in the binomial to derive the Betas of the call and put options using the formula below. For this example, I will assume the Beta of the underlying stock equals 1.0 (which is usually relatively stable and *could* typically be calculated with a linear regression).

$$\beta_C = \beta_S * \Delta_C (S_0 / C_0) = 1.0 * 0.54983 (100/ 11.732) = \textbf{4.687}$$
β_C = Beta of call option
β_S = Beta of Stock

What does this formula mean and why does it work? Since the Beta of the stock is assumed to be 1.0, CAPM suggests that the value of the stock would increase by 1% for every 1% increase in the market index. The 1% increase in the stock price would act on a base of $100 (the current price of the stock), resulting in a one dollar increase in the price of the stock, from $100 to $101.

In order to calculate the Beta of the option, there are two adjustments required: one for the Delta of the option and a second for the relative price difference between the price of the stock and the price of the option.

The 1% increase in the stock price would result in a one dollar increase in the price of the stock, but the price of the option will not change on a dollar-for-dollar basis with the price of the stock. Using a linear estimate, it will only change by Delta. As a result, we also need to multiply the expected price change of one dollar in this example by Delta to calculate the price change of the option.

In the earlier call option example, the option price will only increase by 0.55 for every dollar increase in the price of the stock, which will reduce the Beta of the option relative to the stock. However, the 0.55 change in the price of the option will act on a much smaller initial option price of the call option (11.732), versus the much larger price of the stock (100). Therefore, to find the percentage price change in the option for a 1% change in the broad market, we also have to multiply by (S_0 / C_0), which correctly adjusts the Beta of the stock by the relative price ratio of the option versus the stock (which could be interpreted as a leverage ratio). Since the price of the stock will exceed the value of the option, this multiplier will increase the magnitude of the Beta of the option, relative to the Beta of the stock.

$$\beta_C = \beta_S * \Delta_C (S_0 / C_0) = 1.0 * 0.54983 (100/ 11.732) = \mathbf{4.687}$$

The resulting Beta of the call option is 4.687, which represents a 4.687% change in the value of the call option for a 1% increase in the value of the broad-market index (S&P 500 for example). However, as with Delta, the Beta of every option will change as a function of time and as a function of the price of the underlying stock across all nodes of the binomial tree. It will not be stable. As was the case with Delta, it is only applicable at a specific point in time.

It is also possible to calculate the Beta of a portfolio; in fact, Beta is the most widely used risk measure in portfolio management. The Beta of a portfolio equals the market-value weighted Beta of every position in the portfolio. As a result, it should be possible to calculate the Beta of the call replicating portfolio. And that Beta should equal the Beta we derived above. Let's work through the Beta calculation using the formula below. We will use BC_{RP} to denote the Beta of the call replicating portfolio, "I" to denote the amount invested at the risk-free interest rate, and β_I to denote the beta of the risk-free investment. I have previously defined all of the other terms.

To calculate the Beta of the call replicating portfolio, we multiply the market value of each position (stock or risk-free investment) by its respective Beta, add the results together, then divide by the combined market value of the replicating portfolio.

$\mathbf{BC_{RP} = [(\beta_S * S * \Delta_C) + (\beta_I * I)] / [(S * \Delta_C) + I]}$
$BC_{RP} = [(1.0 * 100.0 * 0.54983) + (\beta_I * -43.251)] / [(100.00 * 0.54983) + -43.251]$
$BC_{RP} = [(54.983) + (0 * -43.251)] / [(54.983) -43.251]$
$BC_{RP} = 54.983/ 11.732 = \mathbf{4.687}$

BC_{RP} = Beta of Call Replicating Portfolio
I = Amount invested at the risk-free interest rate
B_I = Beta of Risk-free Investment = zero by definition

The Beta of the call replicating portfolio exactly matches the Beta of the call option we calculated directly. In addition, the value of the replicating portfolio in the denominator above exactly equals the value of the call option we calculated using the binomial hedge framework.

I will not provide the detailed explanation of the put option Beta calculations here, but the same formulas are used. Here are the resulting Beta calculations for a one-year put option with a strike price of 100. The formulas use the values from the earlier put option example that were derived using the binomial hedge framework. The replicating portfolio Beta derivation is also shown. As expected, both formulas generate the same values for the Beta of the put option.

$\beta_P = \beta_S * \Delta_P (S_0 / P_0) = 1.0 * (- 0.45017) (100/ 7.811) = \mathbf{- 5.763}$

$\mathbf{BP_{RP} = [(\beta_S * S * \Delta_P) + (\beta_I * I)] / [(S * \Delta_C) + I]}$
$BP_{RP} = [(1.0 * 100.0 * -0.45017) + (\beta_I * 52.828)] / [(100.00 * 0.54983) + -43.251]$
$BP_{RP} = [(-45.017) + (0 * 52.828)] / [(-45.017) + 52.828]$
$BP_{RP} = -45.017 / 7.811 = \mathbf{- 5.763}$

BP_{RP} = Beta of Put Replicating Portfolio
I = Amount invested at the risk-free interest rate
B_I = Beta of Risk-free Investment = zero by definition

Practical Observations

Before proceeding, let's take another step back from the mathematical formulas to explore the implications of the Beta calculations and gain some further insights into what they mean. First, note the magnitude of the Betas of the call and put options relative to the Beta of the stock. The Beta of the call option is 4.687 versus an assumed Beta of 1.0 for the stock. In other words, the Beta of the call option is over four times as large as the Beta of the stock, which means it has over four times the systematic risk of the stock (on a percentage basis).

$$\beta_C = \beta_S * \Delta_C (S_0 / C_0) = 1.0 * 0.54983 (100/ 11.732) = \mathbf{4.687}$$

This is due almost entirely to the implicit leverage of controlling a 100-dollar stock with an investment of only 11.73 dollars. Granted, the call option value only changes by 0.55 for a one-dollar move in the price of the stock, but the implied leverage of the call option results in a much higher Beta.

Similarly, the Beta of the put option in the earlier example is more than five times the Beta of the stock (- 5.763 versus 1.0), but the Beta of the put option is negative. In fact, given that the Delta of a put option will always be less than or equal to zero and the price of a put option will always be greater than or equal to zero, the Beta of a put option will *always* be less than or equal to zero. This explains why put options are so desirable for hedging equity portfolios. Given that Delta and put option prices are both widely available on all broker platforms, it is easy to calculate option Betas in real time for portfolio hedging purposes.

Before I leave the topic of Beta, I want to emphasize the importance of calculating the Betas of all of your trading vehicles, including individual stocks, bonds, ETFs, and even futures contracts. This will help you understand how each of your investments contributes to your overall level of systematic risk. As I explained before, *if the Beta of an asset is stable over time*, it could be calculated by regressing the periodic returns of the asset against the periodic returns of the index. For example, daily returns over a one-year period could be used in the regression. Not surprising, the slope term in the regression equals Beta.

However, I break down the Beta calculation when evaluating my trading instruments. The slope term in the regression (Beta) also equals the correlation between the asset and the index multiplied by the ratio of the standard deviation of the asset returns divided by the standard deviation of the market returns. For illustration purposes, let's assume the returns of an asset had a correlation of 0.50 with the returns of the market. Let's also assume that the annualized standard deviation of the asset's returns was 20.0% and the standard deviation of the market's returns was 15%. The resulting Beta calculation is shown below.

$\beta_A = \rho_{AM} (\sigma_A / \sigma_M) = 0.50(0.20 / 0.15) = 0.50(1.333) = 0.667$
β_A = Beta of the asset
ρ_{AM} = Correlation between the returns of the asset and the index
σ_A = Standard deviation of the asset returns (RMS would be better)
σ_M= Standard deviation of the market returns (RMS would be better)

Breaking down Beta into its two components, correlation and the relative volatility of the asset versus the index, provides much more insight into the sources of systematic risk and the effectiveness of the hedge. In the example above, the Beta is only 0.667, which is less than the market Beta of 1.0. This implies a lower level of systematic risk. However, the relative volatility of the asset returns is much higher than the index (0.20 / 0.15 = 1.333). The reason for the lower asset Beta is due entirely to the relatively low correlation of 0.50. In practice, I would also look at longer time periods to better understand the long-term correlation and relative volatility between the asset and index returns. This would ensure these values are stable before using the resulting Beta for hedging purposes.

Put/Call Parity Revisited

The importance of the Put/Call Parity relationship for European options cannot be overstated. I demonstrated earlier that the put and call values we calculated using the binomial hedge framework satisfied the Put/Call Parity formula

$$(C - P = S - Ke^{-rt}).$$

If the Put/Call Parity formula holds for the market value of each instrument, then it must also hold for risk measures, such as Beta and Delta. We have already calculated the values of Delta for the call and put options. The Delta of the stock equals one by definition and the Delta of the risk-free investment equals zero (it does not change in response to a change in the value of the underlying stock). The Delta calculations below demonstrate that Put/Call Parity holds for Delta as well.

$\Delta_C - \Delta_P = \Delta_S - \Delta_{Ke\text{-}rt}$
$0.54983 - (-0.45017) = 1.0 - 0.0$
1.0 = 1.0 Confirmed

We can also verify that the Put/Call Parity formula holds for our Beta calculations as well. We have already calculated the values of Beta for the call and put options. We assumed that the Beta of the stock equals zero in our example. The Beta of the risk-free investment equals zero (it does not change in response to a change in the value of the market). The Beta calculations below demonstrate that Put/Call Parity also holds for Beta.

$$(C\beta_C - P\beta_P)/(C - P) = (S\beta_S - Ke^{-rt}\beta_{Ke-rt})/(S_S - Ke^{-rt})$$
$$(11.732(4.687) - 7.811(-5.763)/(11.732 - 7.811) =$$
$$= (100.00(1.0) - 100.00(e^{0.04(1)})(0.0))(100.00 - 100.00(e^{0.04(1)})$$
25.503 = 25.503 Confirmed

Why is the Beta so large? Because the left and right-side of the equations both represent highly-leveraged investments in stock. This is easier to see on the right-side of the equation where we borrow $96.08 to buy a stock valued at $100. We have the systematic risk of a $100 investment in stock on a net investment of only $3.92. Leverage increases Beta.

Summary

This completes our review of the binomial hedge framework. We used the hedge framework to find option payoffs, call and put hedge portfolios, and call and put replicating portfolios. We solved for call and put option Deltas and Betas and used a combination of these values to solve for the theoretical values of call and put options. In doing so, we also discovered that these option values are not dependent on the probabilities of the future UP and DOWN states, uncovering the risk-neutral environment that is used throughout the industry to value many types of derivative instruments. Finally, I demonstrated that the Put/Call Parity relationship holds for market values and risk measures (including Delta and Beta) of European options.

The hedge framework is important and is very instructive, but it is much more efficient to calculate the implied probabilities of the up and down state directly and use those probabilities with backward induction (working backwards through the binomial tree or lattice) to solve for the value of the option today. This is particularly true for binomial trees in practice, where the number of nodes is large. The next chapter will explain how to use backward induction to calculate option values using the entire binomial lattice and will compare and contrast the results from risk-neutral and risk-averse (CAPM) environments.

3) BINOMIAL: BACKWARD INDUCTION PRIMER

As a general rule (with very few exceptions), *the value of a derivatives instrument equals the present value of the probability-weighted future cash flows.* While backward induction sounds complicated, the process we will use for each interval is quite simple:

1. Determine the future cash flows, payoffs, or values in each future state
2. Determine the probability of each future state occurring
3. Calculate the expected or probability-weighted future value
4. Discount the expected value back to the beginning of the interval

Note: if this was an American option, there would be one additional step in this process. We would compare the above probability-weighted present value of the future up and down states to the *payoff* of exercising the option at the beginning of the interval. With an American option, this comparison would be made at the beginning of every node of the tree. This illustrates the power of the Binomial Option Model (BOM). It is not possible to calculate the value of American options using the Black-Scholes-Merton (BSM) model.

To demonstrate the above four-step process for European options, I will begin with a simple one-period, risk-neutral binomial lattice and will work through a detailed example of all the resulting lattice calculations for the call option. I will continue with a single-period CAPM (risk-averse) example, a multi-period risk-neutral example, and a multi-period CAPM binomial example. For multi-period examples, we begin at the far right-side of the tree or lattice (at the expiration of the option) and work backwards through the tree until we reach time zero, or today.

Due to space limitations, I will severely limit the number of nodes in the multi-period examples. We use many more intervals in the binomial lattice when valuing options in practice. The Binomial Option Model (BOM) values converge to the Black-Scholes-Merton (BSM) values as the number of intervals in the binomial tree approaches infinity and the length of each interval approaches zero. I will demonstrate this convergence in later chapters.

Backward Induction: One-Period / Risk-Neutral

For the one-period risk-neutral example, let's continue using the same values we used in the one-period binomial hedge framework example from Chapter 2: initial stock price (S_0) equal to 100, strike price (K) also equal to 100, time to expiration (t) equal to one-year (1.0), annualized standard deviation of the continuously compounded expected stock returns (σ) equal to 20%, and the annual risk-free rate of interest (r) equal to 4% (continuously compounded). You will recall that "e" represents the base of a natural logarithm – approximately 2.7182818. Using the same scenario values will make it easy to validate our results. The valuation results should be identical to those we calculated in Chapter 2.

We calculated the one-period, future UP and DOWN state values for the stock, call, and put options in Chapter 2. I duplicated these calculations from Chapter 2 below. This gives us the future payoffs or values that we require in step one of our process:

1. Determine the future cash flows, payoffs, or values in each future state

$S_U = S_0 * e^{\sigma\sqrt{t}} = 100 * e^{0.20 \, (1.0)} = 100 * 1.22140 = 122.140$
$S_D = S_0 * e^{-\sigma\sqrt{t}} = 100 * e^{-0.20 \, (1.0)} = 100 * 0.81873 = 81.873$

Call Option Payoff = Max (S_E – K, 0)
$C_U = \text{Max} (122.140 - 100.00, 0) = 22.140$
$C_D = \text{Max} (81.873 - 100.00, 0) = 0.000$

Put Option Payoff = Max (K - S_E, 0)
$P_U = \text{Max} (100.00 - 122.140, 0) = 0.000$
$P_D = \text{Max} (100.00 - 81.873, 0) = 18.127$

That brings us to Step 2: Determine the probability of each future state occurring. In a risk-neutral environment, the probability of the UP state (Pr_U) and the probability of the DOWN state (Pr_D) are functions of the return of the underlying stock in the UP state and the DOWN state, and the return earned on a riskless investment over the interval. Below are the values we will need for the probability formula, followed by the probability formulas for the UP and DOWN states.

$U = e^{\sigma\sqrt{t}} = S_U/S_0 = 1.22140$
$D = e^{-\sigma\sqrt{t}} = S_D/S_0 = 0.81873$
$R = e^{rt} = 1.04081$
t = Length of interval in years (1.0)

$Pr_U = (R - D) / (U - D)$
$Pr_U = (1.04081 - 0.81873) / (1.22140 - 0.81873) = 55.152\%$

$Pr_D = (U - R) / (U - D)$ or $1 - Pr_U$
$Pr_D = (1.22140 - 1.04081) / (1.22140 - 0.81873) = 44.848\%$

$Pr_D = 1 - Pr_U$
$Pr_D = 1 - 55.152\% = 44.848\%$

The probability formulas can also be written directly as functions of r, t, and sigma, instead of R, U, and D. The results are obviously the same.

$Pr_U = (e^{rt} - e^{-\sigma\sqrt{t}}) / (e^{\sigma\sqrt{t}} - e^{-\sigma\sqrt{t}}) = 55.152\%$
$Pr_D = (e^{\sigma\sqrt{t}} - e^{rt}) / (e^{\sigma\sqrt{t}} - e^{-\sigma\sqrt{t}}) = 44.848\%$

Due to the unrealistic limitations in the Binomial Options Model (and in the Black-Scholes-Merton model), interest rates and volatility are both assumed to be constant over the life of every option. As a result, the above values of sigma, r, U, D, and R are the same in every interval (in multi-period cases), which only requires us to calculate these values one time for the entire binomial lattice.

It may not be obvious from Hull's risk-neutral probability formulas above, but the implied probabilities of the UP and DOWN states force the *expected* return of the underlying stock to equal the effective (not continuously compounded) risk-free return over the period. In finance, the term *expected* return does not signify the most likely return. Instead, *expected* means probability-weighted. Now that we have the probabilities of the UP and DOWN state for the risk-neutral environment, we can move on to Step 3: Calculate the probability-weighted future value. We can calculate the expected future value at the end of period one for the underlying stock (ES_1), the call option (EC_1), and the put option (EP_1) by applying the risk-neutral probabilities to the UP and DOWN state payoffs at the end of the period.

$ES_1 = (Pr_U * S_U) + (Pr_D * S_D)$
$ES_1 = (55.152\% * 122.140) + (44.848\% * 81.873) = 104.081$

$EC_1 = (Pr_U * C_U) + (Pr_D * C_D)$
$EC_1 = (55.152\% * 22.140) + (44.848\% * 0.000) = 12.211$

$EP_1 = (Pr_U * P_U) + (Pr_D * P_D)$
$EP_1 = (55.152\% * 0.000) + (44.848\% * 18.127) = 8.130$

There is only one remaining step in the process, Step 4: Discount the expected value back to the beginning of the interval. In a risk-neutral environment, we discount the expected future value of each instrument back to the beginning of the interval. Since we are using a one-period example, the beginning of the interval will coincide with today. The resulting discounted values will equal the current or present value of each instrument.

$S_0 = (ES_1) e^{-rt}$
$S_0 = (104.084) e^{-0.04(1.0)} = 100.000$

$C_0 = (EC_1) e^{-rt}$
$C_0 = (12.211) e^{-0.04(1.0)} = 11.732$

$P_0 = (EP_1) e^{-rt}$
$P_0 = (8.130) e^{-0.04(1.0)} = 7.811$

Note, the values of each instrument calculated with the backward induction process exactly equal the values we calculated in Chapter 2 using the binomial hedge framework. This will always be the case. Furthermore, we can now demonstrate that the expected (probability-weighted) returns of each instrument will equal the return earned on a risk-free investment over the period. The intermediate values below are rounded for presentation purposes, but the final results reflect the full precision of all intermediate calculations.

Expected Returns: One-Period / Risk-Neutral

Rate of return = (Ending Value / Beginning Value) – 1.0

UP State Returns:
Stock = (122.140 / 100.000) – 1.0 = 22.14%
Call = (22.140 / 11.732) – 1.0 = 88.72%
Put = (0.000 / 7.811) – 1.0 = -100.00%

DOWN State Returns:
Stock = (81.873 / 100.000) − 1.0 = -18.13%
Call = (0.00 / 11.732) − 1.0 = -100.00%
Put = (18.127 / 7.811) − 1.0 = 132.07%

Probability-Weighted Return = $Pr_U Ru + Pr_D Rd$
Should equal the effective risk-free rate = e^{rt} - 1

Probability-Weighted (Expected) Risk-Neutral Returns:
Stock = 0.55152 (22.14%) + 0.44848 (-18.13%) = 4.081%
Call = 0.55152 (88.72%) + 0.44848 (-100.00%) = 4.081%
Put = 0.55152 (-100.00%) + 0.44848 (132.07%) = 4.081%

In each case, we have demonstrated that the expected return for each security equals the effective risk-free rate earned over the one-year period ($e^{rt} − 1 = e^{0.04} − 1 = 1.0481 − 1 = 4.081\%$).

Binomial Call Lattice: One-Period / Risk-Neutral

That completes our one-period backward induction example. All of the input values, intermediate calculations, and derived metrics for the call option are shown below in the complete one-period binomial lattice (Figure 3.1). The table at the top-left of the diagram lists all of the input values, as well as the intermediate calculations that we have already reviewed (U, D, Pr_U, Pr_D). In addition, the continuously compounded risk-free return and the effective annual risk-free return are also shown. Finally, the MRP represents the annual market risk premium for the Capital Asset Pricing Model (CAPM). The continuously compounded MRP and the effective annual MRP are both shown. Since this is a risk-neutral example, the MRP equals zero.

For each node in the binomial lattice, the corresponding table includes the following values (in order): the value of the stock, the amount of borrowing or lending required in the replicating portfolio, the value of the European option, the Delta of the European option, the Beta of the European option, the expected return of the stock, the expected return of the option, and the probability of that node occurring. We calculated several of these values in the previous chapter (borrowing or lending required in replicating portfolio, Delta, and Beta) and I will not review the calculations here. However, note that these results are identical to the values we calculated in Chapter 2.

Figure 3.1 Risk-Neutral

		European Call Option		
S_0	100.000			
Rf (C)	4.000%			
Rf EAR	4.081%			
MRP (C)	0.000%			
MRP EAR	0.000%			
Strike	100.000			
Time	1.000	Cum R_s	4.081%	
Up	1.2214	Cum R_O	4.081%	
Down	0.8187		1	1
Pru	55.152%	Stock	122.140	
Prd	44.848%	-B/+L	N/A	
		Eur Call	22.140	
0	0	Δ_{OPT}	N/A	
Stock	100.000	β_{OPT}	N/A	
-B/+L	-43.25	ROR_s	N/A	
Eur Call	11.732	ROR_{Opt}	N/A	
Δ_{OPT}	0.550	Prob	55.15%	
β_{OPT}	4.687			
ROR_s	4.081%	Stock	81.873	
ROR_{Opt}	4.081%	-B/+L	N/A	
Prob	100.00%	Eur Call	0.000	
		Δ_{OPT}	N/A	
		β_{OPT}	N/A	
		ROR_s	N/A	
		ROR_{Opt}	N/A	
		Prob	44.85%	

Finally, at the top of each column (period), the cumulative probability-weighted returns of the underlying stock and option are both provided. These cumulative return values are not continuously compounded. I will use these binomial trees throughout the remainder of this chapter to compare and contrast calls versus puts, risk-neutral versus risk-averse (CAPM) environments, and single versus multi-period examples.

Binomial Put Lattice: One-Period / Risk-Neutral

The one-period, risk-neutral binomial lattices for both the call option and the put option are shown side-by-side in Figure 3.2 below. I will not provide the put calculations here, but the formulas for the put option and the backward induction process for the put option are identical to those we used in the call option example.

Figure 3.2 Risk Neutral

European Call Option

S_0	100.000		
Rf (C)	4.000%		
Rf EAR	4.081%		
MRP (C)	5.000%		
MRP EAR	5.336%		
Strike	100.000		
Time	1.000	Cum R_s	9.417%
Up	1.2214	Cum R_O	29.091%
Down	0.8187	1	1
Pru	68.404%	Stock	122.140
Prd	31.596%	-B/+L	N/A
		Eur Call	22.140
0	0	Δ_{OPT}	N/A
Stock	100.000	β_{OPT}	N/A
-B/+L	-43.25	ROR_s	N/A
Eur Call	11.732	ROR_{Opt}	N/A
Δ_{OPT}	0.550	Prob	68.40%
β_{OPT}	4.687		
ROR_s	9.417%	Stock	81.873
ROR_{Opt}	29.091%	-B/+L	N/A
Prob	100.00%	Eur Call	0.000
		Δ_{OPT}	N/A
		β_{OPT}	N/A
		ROR_s	N/A
		ROR_{Opt}	N/A
		Prob	31.60%

European Put Option

S_0	100.000		
Rf (C)	4.000%		
Rf EAR	4.081%		
MRP (C)	5.000%		
MRP EAR	5.336%		
Strike	100.000		
Time	1.000	Cum R_s	9.417%
Up	1.2214	Cum R_O	-26.674%
Down	0.8187	1	1
Pru	68.404%	Stock	122.140
Prd	31.596%	-B/+L	N/A
		EUR Put	0.000
0	0	Δ_{OPT}	N/A
Stock	100.000	β_{OPT}	N/A
-B/+L	52.83	ROR_s	N/A
EUR Put	7.811	ROR_{Opt}	N/A
Δ_{OPT}	-0.450	Prob	68.40%
β_{OPT}	-5.763		
ROR_s	9.417%	Stock	81.873
ROR_{Opt}	-26.674%	-B/+L	N/A
Prob	100.00%	EUR Put	18.127
		Δ_{OPT}	N/A
		β_{OPT}	N/A
		ROR_s	N/A
		ROR_{Opt}	N/A
		Prob	31.60%

What observations can we make from comparing the one-period, risk-neutral lattices for the call and put options? First, there are many similarities. As would be expected, the input variable and intermediate calculations describing the environment (risk-free rate, UP and DOWN state multipliers, UP and DOWN state probabilities, stock prices at each node, etc.) and the option characteristics (strike price and time to expiration) are the same for call and put options. This ensures the call and put option values are consistent, which we already verified with the Put/Call Parity formula introduced in Chapter 2.

In this risk-neutral environment, the rates of return for the stock, call option, and put option are also identical at every node. I provided the return formulas and calculated the rates of return for each instrument earlier in this chapter, and the periodic returns are also shown in the lattice.

So, which lattice values are different for the put and call option? Obviously, the value of the call option will not equal the value of the put option, nor should it. However, Put/Call Parity will be valid at every node of the tree for the European put and call options, not just at the initial node (time zero). The Delta of the call and put options at every node will also be very different (and have the opposite sign), but they are related as well. The

41

Delta of a put option at every node will equal the Delta of the call option, minus 1.0. As demonstrated in Chapter 2, the Put/Call Parity relationship applies to the risk measures (including Delta and Beta) as well as to the values of the financial instruments.

We calculated the call and put option Betas and risk-free replicating portfolio investments in Chapter 2. As expected, both sets of values are different for the call and put options and they both have different signs. In Chapter 2, I also demonstrated that the Betas and replicating portfolios are through the Put/Call Parity formula. Each of these Put/Call Parity relationships can be verified at each node of the binomial lattices, but I will not repeat those calculations here.

Binomial Call Lattice: One-Period / Risk-Averse (CAPM)

The one-period, risk-neutral and risk-averse (CAPM) binomial lattices for the call option are shown side-by-side in Figure 3.3 below.

Figure 3.3 Risk Neutral & Risk Averse

Risk Neutral — European Call Option:

S_0	100.000			
Rf (C)	4.000%			
Rf EAR	4.081%			
MRP (C)	0.000%			
MRP EAR	0.000%			
Strike	100.000			
Time	1.000	Cum R_s	4.081%	
Up	1.2214	Cum R_O	4.081%	
Down	0.8187	1	1	
Pru	55.152%	Stock	122.140	
Prd	44.848%	-B/+L	N/A	
		Eur Call	22.140	
0	0	Δ_{OPT}	N/A	
Stock	100.000	β_{OPT}	N/A	
-B/+L	-43.25	ROR_s	N/A	
Eur Call	11.732	ROR_{Opt}	N/A	
Δ_{OPT}	0.550	Prob	55.15%	
β_{OPT}	4.687			
ROR_s	4.081%	Stock	81.873	
ROR_{Opt}	4.081%	-B/+L	N/A	
Prob	100.00%	Eur Call	0.000	
		Δ_{OPT}	N/A	
		β_{OPT}	N/A	
		ROR_s	N/A	
		ROR_{Opt}	N/A	
		Prob	44.85%	

Risk Averse — European Call Option:

S_0	100.000			
Rf (C)	4.000%			
Rf EAR	4.081%			
MRP (C)	5.000%			
MRP EAR	5.336%			
Strike	100.000			
Time	1.000	Cum R_s	9.417%	
Up	1.2214	Cum R_O	29.091%	
Down	0.8187	1	1	
Pru	68.404%	Stock	122.140	
Prd	31.596%	-B/+L	N/A	
		Eur Call	22.140	
0	0	Δ_{OPT}	N/A	
Stock	100.000	β_{OPT}	N/A	
-B/+L	-43.25	ROR_s	N/A	
Eur Call	11.732	ROR_{Opt}	N/A	
Δ_{OPT}	0.550	Prob	68.40%	
β_{OPT}	4.687			
ROR_s	9.417%	Stock	81.873	
ROR_{Opt}	29.091%	-B/+L	N/A	
Prob	100.00%	Eur Call	0.000	
		Δ_{OPT}	N/A	
		β_{OPT}	N/A	
		ROR_s	N/A	
		ROR_{Opt}	N/A	
		Prob	31.60%	

A comparison of the binomial lattices for the call option in the risk-neutral and risk-averse environments yields some interesting insights. To ensure an apples-to-apples comparison, the option characteristics (strike price and time to expiration) are the same for the call options in both environments.

There are similarities in the environmental variables, but also some important differences. First, the initial stock price is the same (100), as is the continuously compounded risk-free interest rate (4.00%). Perhaps surprising, the UP (1.2214) and DOWN (0.8187) state multipliers are also the same in both environments, as are the underlying stock prices in the UP (122.14) and DOWN (81.873) state. Even more surprising for many, the call and put option prices, Deltas, and Betas are the same for comparable nodes in both environments.

As you will recall from the binomial hedge framework in Chapter 2, we determined that the option prices are not dependent on probabilities. Given that, it follows that the option prices must be the same in the risk-neutral and risk-averse environments. If the prices for both environments are the same at every node, then the risk metrics (Beta and Delta) must also be the same.

So, what is different and why? In the risk-averse (CAPM) environment, investors demand a higher rate of return for exposure to systematic risk. CAPM states that the required or expected return of an asset equals the risk-free rate of return, plus Beta times the market risk premium (MRP). The market risk premium equals the expected return of the market in excess of the risk-free rate of interest $(R_m - R_f)$. In other words, the Market Risk Premium (MRP) represents the additional return required for each additional unit of systematic risk – as measured by Beta.

$$R_i = R_f + \beta * (R_m - R_f)$$
$$R_i = R_f + \beta * (MRP)$$

In the risk-averse (CAPM) lattice above, the continuously compounded MRP is 5.00% and the effective annual MRP is 5.336% or $(e^{0.05} - 1)$. In the risk-free environment, the MRP is 0.00% by definition. The resulting expected or required returns for the underlying stock (with an assumed Beta of 1.0) could be derived using the CAPMs. Note effective annual rates of return are used in the formula for the risk-free interest rate and for the MRP.

Risk-Neutral $R_S = R_f + \beta * (MRP)$
Risk-Neutral R_S = 4.081% + 1.0 * (0.000%) = **4.081%**

Risk-Averse $R_S = R_f + \beta * (MRP)$
Risk-Averse $R_S = 4.081\% + 1.0 * (5.336\%) = \mathbf{9.417\%}$

The CAPM results exactly match the binomial lattice returns of the underlying stock in both the risk-neutral and risk-averse environments. If the underlying stock prices are the same in both environments at each corresponding node, then the probabilities must be different – and they are.

Earlier in this chapter, we calculated the implied probabilities for the risk-neutral environment, which ensured the probability-weighted return of the underlying stock exactly equaled the effective return earned by the risk-free investment. The formulas we used to calculate the risk-neutral probability of the UP state are shown again below.

$Pr_U = (R - D) / (U - D)$
$Pr_U = (e^{rt} - e^{-\sigma\sqrt{t}}) / (e^{\sigma\sqrt{t}} - e^{-\sigma\sqrt{t}})$

The simplified risk-averse probability formula for a one-year, one-period example is shown below.

$Pr_U = (RR - D) / (U - D)$
$RR = e^{(r + MRP)t} = e^{(0.04 + 0.05)1.0} = \mathbf{1.09417}$
$Pr_U = (e^{(r + MRP)t} - e^{-\sigma\sqrt{t}}) / (e^{\sigma\sqrt{t}} - e^{-\sigma\sqrt{t}})$

$Pr_U = (1.09417 - 0.81873) / (1.22140 - 0.81873) = \mathbf{68.404\%}$
$Pr_D = 1 - Pr_U = \mathbf{31.596\%}$

The resulting UP and DOWN state probabilities for the risk-averse environment are 68.404% and 31.596% respectively, which match the probabilities (rounded) shown in the risk-averse binomial lattice (Figure 3.3 above). We can use the probability-weighted return formula below to calculate the expected rate of returns for the stock and the call option in the risk-averse environment, which are consistent with the returns in the risk-averse lattice.

Probability-Weighted Return = $Pr_U R_u + Pr_D R_d$

Probability-Weighted (Expected) Risk-Averse Returns:
Stock: $R_S = 0.68404 (22.14\%) + 0.31596 (-18.13\%) = 9.417\%$
Call: $R_C = 0.68404 (88.72\%) + 0.31596 (-100.00\%) = 29.091\%$

Given the high Beta of the call option (4.687), it should be no surprise that the required or expected return of the call option is much higher than the underlying stock. What still amazes me is that CAPM explains the required return on the call option exactly.

$$R_C = R_f + \beta * (MRP)$$
$$R_C = 4.081\% + 4.687 * (5.336\%) = 29.091\%$$

We can use our choice of risk-free interest rates and market risk premiums and create a risk-averse binomial lattice to evaluate any European call or put option. The resulting risk-averse lattice will have the same state prices for the underlying stock and for the option at every node. The resulting risk-averse Deltas and Betas will be identical to those we calculated using the binomial hedge framework and using the risk-free lattice.

The risk-averse implied probabilities are derived from the risk-free interest rate and the market risk premium. The resulting returns for stocks and options will be different than those in the risk-free environment, but will be exactly explained by CAPM.

Binomial Put Lattice: One-Period / Risk-Averse (CAPM)

The one-period, risk-neutral and risk-averse (CAPM) binomial lattices for the put option are shown side-by-side in Figure 3.4 below. The option characteristics (strike price and time to expiration) for the put option are still identical to the option characteristics for the call option. In addition, the risk-neutral and risk-averse environments for the put option are exactly the same as the corresponding environments we just reviewed in detail for the call option (Figure 3.3 above). This includes the state prices for the underlying stock at each node, the implied probabilities for both environments, and the risk-free rate and MRP.

As was the case with the call option, the values of the put option must be the same in both environments at each node. The resulting Deltas and Betas must also be the same for both environments. As demonstrated below, the implied risk-averse probabilities will be different, which results in different required or expected rates of return.

Figure 3.4 Risk Neutral & Risk Averse

European Put Option (left panel)

S_0	100.000	**European Put Option**		
Rf (C)	4.000%			
Rf EAR	4.081%			
MRP (C)	0.000%			
MRP EAR	0.000%			
Strike	100.000			
Time	1.000	Cum R_S	4.081%	
Up	1.2214	Cum R_O	4.081%	
Down	0.8187	1	1	
Pru	55.152%	Stock	122.140	
Prd	44.848%	-B/+L	N/A	
		EUR Put	0.000	
0	0	Δ_{OPT}	N/A	
Stock	100.000	β_{OPT}	N/A	
-B/+L	52.83	ROR_S	N/A	
EUR Put	7.811	ROR_{Opt}	N/A	
Δ_{OPT}	-0.450	Prob	55.15%	
β_{OPT}	-5.763			
ROR_S	4.081%	Stock	81.873	
ROR_{Opt}	4.081%	-B/+L	N/A	
Prob	100.00%	EUR Put	18.127	
		Δ_{OPT}	N/A	
		β_{OPT}	N/A	
		ROR_S	N/A	
		ROR_{Opt}	N/A	
		Prob	44.85%	

European Put Option (right panel)

S_0	100.000	**European Put Option**		
Rf (C)	4.000%			
Rf EAR	4.081%			
MRP (C)	5.000%			
MRP EAR	5.336%			
Strike	100.000			
Time	1.000	Cum R_S	9.417%	
Up	1.2214	Cum R_O	-26.674%	
Down	0.8187	1	1	
Pru	68.404%	Stock	122.140	
Prd	31.596%	-B/+L	N/A	
		EUR Put	0.000	
0	0	Δ_{OPT}	N/A	
Stock	100.000	β_{OPT}	N/A	
-B/+L	52.83	ROR_S	N/A	
EUR Put	7.811	ROR_{Opt}	N/A	
Δ_{OPT}	-0.450	Prob	68.40%	
β_{OPT}	-5.763			
ROR_S	9.417%	Stock	81.873	
ROR_{Opt}	-26.674%	-B/+L	N/A	
Prob	100.00%	EUR Put	18.127	
		Δ_{OPT}	N/A	
		β_{OPT}	N/A	
		ROR_S	N/A	
		ROR_{Opt}	N/A	
		Prob	31.60%	

The probability-weighted return of the put option in the risk-neutral environment equals the effective return earned by investing at the risk-free interest rate (4.081%). The probability-weighted return for the put option in the risk-averse environment is quite different – a remarkable negative 26.674%! How could the expected or required rate of return of a put option be negative 26.674%?

The answer is the benefit of reducing systematic risk (hedging) in a risk-averse (CAPM) environment. As you will recall, the Beta of the put option was extremely negative (-5.763). By applying CAPM, we can calculate the expected rate of return (adjusted for intermediate rounding errors).

$$R_P = R_f + \beta * (MRP)$$
$$R_P = 4.081\% + -5.763 * (5.336\%) = -26.674\%$$

We can use the probability-weighted return formula below to verify the expected rate of return for the put option in the risk-averse environment, which is consistent with the return in the risk-averse lattice.

Probability-Weighted Return = $Pr_U Ru + Pr_D Rd$

Probability-Weighted (Expected) Risk-Averse Return:
Put: $R_P = 0.68404$ (-100.00%) $+ 0.31596$ (132.07%) $= -26.674\%$

Binomial Call Lattice: Three-Period / Risk-Neutral

Now that we have fully explored the simple one-year, one-period binomial examples for the call and put option in the risk-neutral and risk-averse environments, let's move on to the multi-period binomial. Due to space limitations, I will limit the number of periods or intervals used in these examples to three. To ensure the returns and input values are somewhat intuitive, I will still use one-year intervals. The resulting lattice will now value *three-year options, NOT one-year options*. As a result, the new three-year option values should NOT be compared to the earlier one-year, one-period examples. The three-year, three-period, risk-neutral binomial lattice for the call option is shown in Figure 3.5 below.

Before looking for insights in the multi-period binomial lattice, I need to elaborate on the backward induction process for a multi-period tree. So far, we have only used a lattice with a single period or interval. To calculate the value of an option today, we followed the four-step process I introduced at the beginning of this chapter for a single interval.

1. Determine the future cash flows, payoffs, or values in each future state
2. Determine the probability of each future state occurring
3. Calculate the expected or probability-weighted future value
4. Discount the expected value back to the beginning of the interval

In a multi-period lattice, the four-step backward induction process is the same, but we have to repeat the process for every node, working backwards through the tree. This requires us to start at the far right-side of the tree (at option expiration) and work backwards until we reach the first node of the tree (time zero or today). Once we complete the process, we will know the value of the option at every node throughout the tree, and be able to derive the intermediate ancillary values (replicating risk-free investment) and risk metrics (Delta and Beta) at every node as well.

I will use the following notation to refer to a specific node in the multi-period tree. The first value in the subscript will represent the period number, starting at zero for today, and ending at three for the end of the third period (three years into the future). The second value in the subscript will represent the node number, beginning with one at the top node of each column in the lattice. For example, the call price at the first node at the end of the third period would be $C_{3,1}$ (82.212) in Figure 3.5 below.

Now that we have the requisite notation, we can use backward induction to solve for the value of the call option at every node of the lattice. The values of the call option at the far-right side of the lattice are simply the intrinsic values of the call option at option expiration or Max (S – K, 0). Therefore, we will begin the backward induction calculations for the nodes in period two and work backward to period zero (today). I will not repeat the calculations of the ancillary values and risk metrics for each node.

$$Cn,m = [(Pr_U * C_{n+1,m}) + (Pr_D * C_{n+1,m+1})]e^{-rt}$$
$$C_{2,1} = [(0.55152 * 82.212) + (0.44848 * 22.140)]e^{-0.04(1)} = 53.104$$
$$C_{2,2} = [(0.55152 * 22.140) + (0.44848 * 0.000)]e^{-0.04(1)} = 11.732$$
$$C_{2,3} = [(0.55152 * 0.000) + (0.44848 * 0.000)]e^{-0.04(1)} = 0.000$$

$$C_{1,1} = [(0.55152 * 53.104) + (0.44848 * 11.732)]e^{-0.04(1)} = 33.194$$
$$C_{1,2} = [(0.55152 * 11.732) + (0.44848 * 0.000)]e^{-0.04(1)} = 6.217$$

$$C_{0,1} = [(0.55152 * 33.194) + (0.44848 * 6.217)]e^{-0.04(1)} = 20.268$$

With respect to the three-year, three-period lattice, the risk-free rate and volatility are the same values that we used in the one-year example, and are the same in each period. The resulting UP (1.2214) and DOWN (0.8187) state multipliers are also the same as our one-year example and are the same in all three periods. The same is true for the expected risk-neutral returns of stocks and options. Options and stocks still earn the risk-free return in every period - in the risk-neutral environment.

So, what is different? Obviously, the value of a three-year call option (20.368) is greater than the value of a one-year call option (11.732). The initial Delta and Beta values of the three-year call option will also be different from the comparable values of the one-year call option, but the formulas used to derive these values are identical to the formulas we used earlier.

The most interesting observation from the three-period call example is that Delta and Beta are not constant. As the price of the stock moves up, Delta increases accordingly, becoming progressively more responsive to changes in the underlying stock price. The resulting call replicating portfolio also changes as Delta increases, requiring larger positions in the underlying stock, which requires additional borrowing.

Figure 3.5 Risk Neutral

	Cum R_s	12.750%
	Cum R_O	12.750%

European Call Option

S_0	100.000
Rf (C)	4.000%
Rf EAR	4.081%
MRP (C)	0.000%
MRP EAR	0.000%
Strike	100.000
Time	3.000
Up	1.2214
Down	0.8187
Pru	55.152%
Prd	44.848%

Node 0

0	0
Stock	100.000
-B/+L	-46.73
Eur Call	20.268
Δ_{OPT}	0.670
β_{OPT}	3.306
ROR_S	4.081%
ROR_{Opt}	4.081%
Prob	100.00%

Node 1

Cum R_S	4.081%
Cum R_O	4.081%
1	**1**
Stock	122.140
-B/+L	-69.55
Eur Call	33.194
Δ_{OPT}	0.841
β_{OPT}	3.095
ROR_S	4.081%
ROR_{Opt}	4.081%
Prob	55.15%

Stock	81.873
-B/+L	-22.92
Eur Call	6.217
Δ_{OPT}	0.356
β_{OPT}	4.687
ROR_S	4.081%
ROR_{Opt}	4.081%
Prob	44.85%

Node 2

Cum R_s	8.329%
Cum R_O	8.329%
2	**2**
Stock	149.182
-B/+L	-96.08
Eur Call	53.104
Δ_{OPT}	1.000
β_{OPT}	2.809
ROR_S	4.081%
ROR_{Opt}	4.081%
Prob	30.42%

Stock	100.000
-B/+L	-43.25
Eur Call	11.732
Δ_{OPT}	0.550
β_{OPT}	4.687
ROR_S	4.081%
ROR_{Opt}	4.081%
Prob	49.47%

Stock	67.032
-B/+L	0.00
Eur Call	0.000
Δ_{OPT}	0.000
β_{OPT}	0.000
ROR_S	4.081%
ROR_{Opt}	0.000%
Prob	20.11%

Node 3

3	**3**
Stock	182.212
-B/+L	N/A
Eur Call	82.212
Δ_{OPT}	N/A
β_{OPT}	N/A
ROR_S	N/A
ROR_{Opt}	N/A
Prob	16.78%

Stock	122.140
-B/+L	N/A
Eur Call	22.140
Δ_{OPT}	N/A
β_{OPT}	N/A
ROR_S	N/A
ROR_{Opt}	N/A
Prob	40.92%

Stock	81.873
-B/+L	N/A
Eur Call	0.000
Δ_{OPT}	N/A
β_{OPT}	N/A
ROR_S	N/A
ROR_{Opt}	N/A
Prob	33.28%

Stock	54.881
-B/+L	N/A
Eur Call	0.000
Δ_{OPT}	N/A
β_{OPT}	N/A
ROR_S	N/A
ROR_{Opt}	N/A
Prob	9.02%

The Beta of the call option also changes from node to node. As the price of the underlying stock increases, Delta increases, but the implicit amount of leverage decreases. The net effect of these two relationships determines how Beta changes from node to node for the call option. The changes in Delta and Beta are critical to understand for all option traders. The binomial lattice is an excellent tool for understanding how and why these changes occur.

Binomial Call Lattice: Three-Period / Risk-Averse (CAPM)

The three-period, risk-averse binomial lattice for the call option is shown in Figure 3.6 below. All of the option characteristics (except the time to expiration) and environmental values are identical to those used in our earlier CAPM example. Note that the UP and DOWN state multipliers and implied risk-averse probabilities are identical to the earlier one-period CAPM example.

As we should now expect, the state prices for the underlying stock and the call option are the same (at each node) as those in the three-year, three-period risk-neutral call example (Figure 3.5 above). The Deltas, Betas, and replicating portfolio investments are also the same in both environments at every node in the lattice. As we observed in the one-period risk-neutral/CAPM comparison, the MRP, implied probabilities, and probability-weighted returns are different in both environments.

We can demonstrate that CAPM holds at every node in the binomial lattice.

$R_S = R_f + \beta * (MRP)$
$R_S = 4.081\% + 1.0 * (5.336\%) = 9.417\%$

$R_C = R_f + \beta * (MRP)$
$R_{C0} = 4.081\% + 3.306 * (5.336\%) = 21.721\%$
$R_{C1,1} = 4.081\% + 3.095 * (5.336\%) = 20.598\%$
$R_{C1,2} = 4.081\% + 4.687 * (5.336\%) = 29.091\%$
$R_{C2,1} = 4.081\% + 2.809 * (5.336\%) = 19.072\%$
$R_{C2,2} = 4.081\% + 4.687 * (5.336\%) = 29.091\%$
$R_{C2,3} = $ N/A or Undefined (Value of the call option equals zero at node 2,3)

The CAPM returns (adjusted for intermediate rounding effects) exactly match the probability-weighted returns in the binomial lattice (Figure 3.6 below). The expected return of the stock is constant at every node, due to the fact that the risk-free rate, implied probabilities, Delta, and Beta of the stock are constant over time and at each node. The expected return of the call option changes at every node in response to changes in Delta and Beta. Per CAPM, investors require higher returns for taking on incremental levels of systematic risk. As Beta increases, the required return also increases, and vice versa.

Figure 3.6 Risk Averse — European Call Option

Parameters:

S0	100.000
Rf (C)	4.000%
Rf EAR	4.081%
MRP (C)	5.000%
MRP EAR	5.336%
Strike	100.000
Time	3.000
Up	1.2214
Down	0.8187
Pru	68.404%
Prd	31.596%

Node 0 (0)

Stock	100.000
-B/+L	-46.73
Eur Call	20.268
ΔOPT	0.670
βOPT	3.306
RORs	9.417%
RORopt	21.721%
Prob	100.00%

Period 1

Cum Rs 9.417% · Cum Ro 21.721%

	Node 1 (1)	Node
Stock	122.140	81.873
-B/+L	-69.55	-22.92
Eur Call	33.194	6.217
ΔOPT	0.841	0.356
βOPT	3.095	4.687
RORs	9.417%	9.417%
RORopt	20.598%	29.091%
Prob	68.40%	31.60%

Period 2

Cum Rs 19.722% · Cum Ro 47.616%

	Node 2 (2)		
Stock	149.182	100.000	67.032
-B/+L	-96.08	-43.25	0.00
Eur Call	53.104	11.732	0.000
ΔOPT	1.000	0.550	0.000
βOPT	2.809	4.687	0.000
RORs	9.417%	9.417%	9.417%
RORopt	19.072%	29.091%	0.000%
Prob	46.79%	43.23%	9.98%

Period 3

Cum Rs 30.996% · Cum Ro 78.276%

	Node 3 (3)			
Stock	182.212	122.140	81.873	54.881
-B/+L	N/A	N/A	N/A	N/A
Eur Call	82.212	22.140	0.000	0.000
ΔOPT	N/A	N/A	N/A	N/A
βOPT	N/A	N/A	N/A	N/A
RORs	N/A	N/A	N/A	N/A
RORopt	N/A	N/A	N/A	N/A
Prob	32.01%	44.35%	20.49%	3.15%

Binomial Put Lattice: Three-Period / Risk-Neutral

The three-period, risk-neutral binomial lattice for the put option is shown in Figure 3.7 below. The resulting lattice will now value *three-year put options, NOT one-year put options*. As a result, the new three-year option values should NOT be compared to the earlier one-year, one-period examples. The three-year, three-period, risk-neutral binomial lattice for the put option is shown in Figure 3.7 below.

The risk-free rate and volatility are the same values that we used in the one-year example and are the same in each period. The resulting UP (1.2214) and DOWN (0.8187) state multipliers are also the same as our one-year example and are the same in all three periods. The same is true for the expected risk-neutral returns of stocks and options. Put options and stocks still earn the risk-free return in every period - in the risk-neutral environment.

Figure 3.7 Risk Neutral — European Put Option

	Cum Rs	12.750%
	Cum Ro	12.750%

Input parameters:

S_0	100.000
Rf (C)	4.000%
Rf EAR	4.081%
MRP (C)	0.000%
MRP EAR	0.000%
Strike	100.000
Time	3.000
Up	1.2214
Down	0.8187
Pru	55.152%
Prd	44.848%

Period 0 (Cum Rs 4.081%, Cum Ro 4.081% at period 1):

0	0
Stock	100.000
-B/+L	41.96
EUR Put	8.960
Δ_{OPT}	-0.330
β_{OPT}	-3.683
ROR_S	4.081%
ROR_{Opt}	4.081%
Prob	100.00%

Period 1:

1	1
Stock	122.140
-B/+L	22.76
EUR Put	3.366
Δ_{OPT}	-0.159
β_{OPT}	-5.763
ROR_S	4.081%
ROR_{Opt}	4.081%
Prob	55.15%

Stock	81.873
-B/+L	69.39
EUR Put	16.655
Δ_{OPT}	-0.644
β_{OPT}	-3.166
ROR_S	4.081%
ROR_{Opt}	4.081%
Prob	44.85%

Period 2 (Cum Rs 8.329%, Cum Ro 8.329%):

2	2
Stock	149.182
-B/+L	0.00
EUR Put	0.000
Δ_{OPT}	0.000
β_{OPT}	0.000
ROR_S	4.081%
ROR_{Opt}	0.000%
Prob	30.42%

Stock	100.000
-B/+L	52.83
EUR Put	7.811
Δ_{OPT}	-0.450
β_{OPT}	-5.763
ROR_S	4.081%
ROR_{Opt}	4.081%
Prob	49.47%

Stock	67.032
-B/+L	96.08
EUR Put	29.047
Δ_{OPT}	-1.000
β_{OPT}	-2.308
ROR_S	4.081%
ROR_{Opt}	4.081%
Prob	20.11%

Period 3 (Cum Rs 12.750%, Cum Ro 12.750%):

3	3
Stock	182.212
-B/+L	N/A
EUR Put	0.000
Δ_{OPT}	N/A
β_{OPT}	N/A
ROR_S	N/A
ROR_{Opt}	N/A
Prob	16.78%

Stock	122.140
-B/+L	N/A
EUR Put	0.000
Δ_{OPT}	N/A
β_{OPT}	N/A
ROR_S	N/A
ROR_{Opt}	N/A
Prob	40.92%

Stock	81.873
-B/+L	N/A
EUR Put	18.127
Δ_{OPT}	N/A
β_{OPT}	N/A
ROR_S	N/A
ROR_{Opt}	N/A
Prob	33.28%

Stock	54.881
-B/+L	N/A
EUR Put	45.119
Δ_{OPT}	N/A
β_{OPT}	N/A
ROR_S	N/A
ROR_{Opt}	N/A
Prob	9.02%

As we saw in the three-year call example above, the value of a three-year put option (8.960) is greater than the value of a one-year put option (7.811). The initial Delta and Beta values of the three-year put option are also different from the comparable values of the one-year put option.

In addition, the Delta and Beta are not constant. As the price of the stock moves down, Delta decreases accordingly (becomes more negative), becoming progressively more responsive (in a negative direction) to changes in the underlying stock price. The resulting put replicating portfolio also changes as Delta decreases (becomes more negative), requiring larger short positions in the underlying stock, which generates additional funds to be invested at the risk-free interest rate.

The Beta of the put option also changes from node to node. As the price of the underlying stock decreases, Delta becomes more negative, but the implicit amount of leverage decreases as the put option increases in value. The net effect of these two relationships determines how Beta changes from node to node for the put option.

Binomial Put Lattice: Three-Period / Risk-Averse (CAPM)

The three-period, risk-averse binomial lattice for the put option is shown in Figure 3.8 below.

All of the option characteristics (except the time to expiration) and environmental values are identical to those used in our earlier CAPM example. Note that the UP and DOWN state multipliers and implied risk-averse probabilities are identical to the earlier one-period CAPM example.

The state prices for the underlying stock and the put option are the same (at each node) as those in the three-year, three-period risk-neutral put example (Figure 3.7 above). The Deltas, Betas, and replicating portfolio investments are also the same in both environments at every node in the lattice. As we observed in the one-period risk-neutral/CAPM comparison, the MRP, implied probabilities, and probability-weighted returns are different in both environments.

We can demonstrate that CAPM holds at every node in the binomial lattice for the put option.

$R_P = R_f + \beta * (MRP)$
$R_{P0} = 4.081\% + -3.683 * (5.336\%) = -15.575\%$
$R_{P1,1} = 4.081\% + -5.763 * (5.336\%) = -26.674\%$
$R_{P1,2} = 4.081\% + -3.166 * (5.336\%) = -12.816\%$
$R_{P2,1} = N/A$ or Undefined (Value of the put option equals zero at node 2,1)
$R_{P2,2} = 4.081\% + -5.763 * (5.336\%) = -26.674\%$
$R_{P2,3} = 4.081\% + -2.308 * (5.336\%) = -8.234\%$

Figure 3.8 Risk Averse — European Put Option

S_0	100.000
Rf (C)	4.000%
Rf EAR	4.081%
MRP (C)	5.000%
MRP EAR	5.336%
Strike	100.000
Time	3.000
Up	1.2214
Down	0.8187
Pru	68.404%
Prd	31.596%

Node 0

0	0
Stock	100.000
-B/+L	41.96
EUR Put	8.960
Δ_{OPT}	-0.330
β_{OPT}	-3.683
ROR_S	9.417%
ROR_{Opt}	-15.575%
Prob	100.00%

Node 1 — Cum R_S 9.417%, Cum R_O -15.575%

1	1		1	1
Stock	122.140		Stock	81.873
-B/+L	22.76		-B/+L	69.39
EUR Put	3.366		EUR Put	16.655
Δ_{OPT}	-0.159		Δ_{OPT}	-0.644
β_{OPT}	-5.763		β_{OPT}	-3.166
ROR_S	9.417%		ROR_S	9.417%
ROR_{Opt}	-26.674%		ROR_{Opt}	-12.816%
Prob	68.40%		Prob	31.60%

Node 2 — Cum R_S 19.722%, Cum R_O -29.955%

2	2
Stock	149.182
-B/+L	0.00
EUR Put	0.000
Δ_{OPT}	0.000
β_{OPT}	0.000
ROR_S	9.417%
ROR_{Opt}	0.000%
Prob	46.79%

2	2
Stock	100.000
-B/+L	52.83
EUR Put	7.811
Δ_{OPT}	-0.450
β_{OPT}	-5.763
ROR_S	9.417%
ROR_{Opt}	-26.674%
Prob	43.23%

2	2
Stock	67.032
-B/+L	96.08
EUR Put	29.047
Δ_{OPT}	-1.000
β_{OPT}	-2.308
ROR_S	9.417%
ROR_{Opt}	-8.234%
Prob	9.98%

Node 3 — Cum R_S 30.996%, Cum R_O -42.671%

3	3
Stock	182.212
-B/+L	N/A
EUR Put	0.000
Δ_{OPT}	N/A
β_{OPT}	N/A
ROR_S	N/A
ROR_{Opt}	N/A
Prob	32.01%

3	3
Stock	122.140
-B/+L	N/A
EUR Put	0.000
Δ_{OPT}	N/A
β_{OPT}	N/A
ROR_S	N/A
ROR_{Opt}	N/A
Prob	44.35%

3	3
Stock	81.873
-B/+L	N/A
EUR Put	18.127
Δ_{OPT}	N/A
β_{OPT}	N/A
ROR_S	N/A
ROR_{Opt}	N/A
Prob	20.49%

3	3
Stock	54.881
-B/+L	N/A
EUR Put	45.119
Δ_{OPT}	N/A
β_{OPT}	N/A
ROR_S	N/A
ROR_{Opt}	N/A
Prob	3.15%

The above CAPM returns (adjusted for intermediate rounding effects) exactly match the probability-weighted returns in the risk-averse binomial lattice (Figure 3.8 above). The expected returns of the put option change at every node in response to changes in Delta and Beta. Per CAPM, investors are willing to accept increasingly negative returns for progressive reductions in systematic risk. As Beta becomes more negative, the required return also decreases (becomes more negative). Conversely, as the Beta of the put option becomes less negative (reducing the effectiveness of the market hedge), hedgers require higher (less negative) returns on the put investment.

Invalid and Inconsistent BOM Assumptions

The Binomial Option Model is more flexible, but more computationally intensive than the Black-Scholes-Merton (BSM) model. It is a discrete model that generates option values that converge to those of the BSM model as the number of intervals increases and the length of each interval decreases.

Given the large number of intervals required to reduce the magnitude of valuation errors (induced by the discrete valuation framework) to an acceptable level, the nodes of the binomial lattice must recombine. In other words, an UP move followed by a DOWN move, must result in the same underlying stock price as a DOWN move followed by an UP move. This recombination was demonstrated in all of the lattice exhibits in this chapter.

The result is that the number of terminal nodes only increases by one node for each additional interval. For a recombining binomial lattice, 250 intervals would result in 251 terminal prices and 1000 intervals would result in 1001 terminal prices. This is a manageable problem for today's computers, even when evaluating the entire option chain or matrix.

The only way to force the nodes in a binomial to recombine is to use constant length intervals, AND a *constant volatility assumption in each period or interval*. Unfortunately, this is wildly inaccurate. Options with different expiration dates have different implied volatilities, often dramatically different. As a result, each option across the entire term structure of volatilities would require its own unique binomial matrix, with its own unique constant volatility assumption. The resulting volatility assumptions would be inconsistent for every option. This results in invalid and inconsistent current option values, future option values, and risk metrics (Greeks). This is a serious deficiency in the BOM and represents a major problem for all option traders.

The standard BOM also assumes that interest rates are constant across all option expirations as well. While this is not as serious as the constant volatility assumption, it is also incorrect and inconsistent.

If the nodes in the lattice were not forced to recombine, we could use the entire term structure of volatilities and interest rates to generate a non-recombining binomial lattice. Unfortunately, the number of terminal nodes would double with each additional interval. The resulting number of terminal nodes would equal 2^N, where N equals the number of binomial intervals.

For a non-recombining binomial lattice, 250 intervals would result in 1.80925E+75 terminal prices, and 1000 intervals would result in 1.0715E+301 terminal prices. Due to the enormous number of terminal prices, I was forced to use scientific notation to express the results. For 250 intervals, 1.80925E+75 equals 1.80925 multiplied by 10 to the 75th power (75 zeros). For 1000 intervals, 1.0715E+301 equals 1.0715 multiplied by 10 to the 301th power (301 zeros)!

Even for a relatively modest number of intervals (250 or 1000), it would not be practical or even possible to calculate the resulting number of terminal prices in a non-recombining binomial lattice – even for a single option. The BOM cannot accommodate realistic and consistent interest rate and volatility assumptions and its results are inconsistent and invalid.

The Johnson Aggregation Framework (JAF) will be introduced in Chapter 5. The JAF will correct these serious deficiencies by eliminating the invalid constant interest rate and constant volatility assumptions, allowing us to solve for and use the complete term structure of interest rates and term structure of volatilities to calculate accurate and theoretically consistent current option values, expected future option values, and Greeks. Before we can proceed with the JAF, we need to complete the foundation with a review of the Black-Scholes-Merton (BSM) option model.

4) BSM OPTION MODEL PRIMER

The Black-Scholes-Merton (BSM) option pricing model is one of the most important contributions to the field of finance, as is the Binomial Options Model (BOM). While there are invalid assumptions and practical limitations in both models, that in no way diminishes the significance of these models.

The BSM model provided the first consistent, objective algorithm for approximating the value of European, non-dividend paying options. Unlike the BOM (which was developed later), the BSM was continuous. It did not require discrete periods or repeated and computationally intensive backward induction calculations to solve for the value of an option. Instead, the BSM model can be expressed as a single formula that can be solved instantly by today's computers. This made options much more accessible to individual and institutional investors.

Perhaps most important, the BSM formula is continuously differentiable. In other words, through the use of calculus (not presented here), it is possible to calculate the sensitivity of the BSM option value to instantaneous, independent changes in each of the respective input variables. This led to sophisticated risk metrics for options and option strategies and provided the foundation for risk management. The BSM model was revolutionary and its impact on the world of finance, options, and derivatives cannot be overstated.

Unfortunately, the BSM formula itself is somewhat dense and is not very intuitive, especially for the typical first-year derivatives student or retail trader. Unlike the BOM, it is not possible in the BSM model to open up the hood (lattice) and evaluate how and why all of the intermediate option values, ancillary values, and risk metrics change over time and in response to changes in the value of the underlying stock.

That is why I always introduced the Binomial Option Model (BOM) before the Black-Scholes-Merton (BSM) model in my Undergraduate and Graduate-level derivatives classes, and why I chose to do so here as well. Our understanding of the BOM model will help us understand each element of the BSM formula and how those elements relate to similar elements in the binomial model.

BSM Call Option Formula

In this section, I will present the BSM formula for European call options. In the following section, I will use the BSM formula to calculate the specific call option value, ancillary values, and risk metrics for the same three-year, risk-neutral call option that we evaluated with the binomial backward induction process in Chapter 3. The general form of the BSM formula is shown below in Figure 4.1 and all ancillary results in the following section should be interpreted as risk-neutral, not risk-averse.

$$C = SN(d_1) - Ke^{-rt}N(d_2)$$

$$d_1 = \frac{\ln\left(\frac{S}{K}\right) + \left(r + \frac{\sigma^2}{2}\right)t}{\sigma\sqrt{t}}$$

$$d_2 = d_1 - \sigma\sqrt{t}$$

Figure 4.1

In addition to the input variables from the last chapter, the BSM formula includes two intermediate values (d_1 and d_2) as well as the corresponding functions $N(d_1)$ and $N(d_2)$. The function $N(d_1)$ and $N(d_2)$ represent the normal Cumulative Density Functions (CDF) of the values d_1 and d_2. The normal Cumulative Density Function equals the area under the standard normal curve from negative infinity up to the value specified in the function (d_1 or d_2 in this case).

The values of "d" can be interpreted as the number of standard deviations above the mean (positive values of d) or below the mean (negative values of d) of a standard normal distribution. The graphs below in Figure 4.2 should help clarify how to interpret the normal CDF function.

As you can observe in the graphs below, normal CDF values range from zero to one (or 100%). The graphical example below illustrates the normal CDF for a d-value of 1.0 (one standard deviation above the mean). The resulting normal CDF for a d-value of +1.0 is 84.13%. The normal CDF is easy to calculate using Microsoft Excel: NORMDIST(1, 0, 1, *TRUE*) = 84.13%.

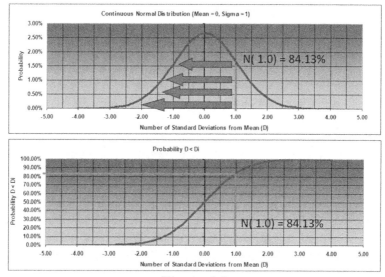

Figure 4.2

There are related functions, N-prime of d_1 and d_2 ($N'(d_1)$ and $N'(d_2)$), that are used in the calculation of the Greeks. The N-prime function is not used in the BSM formula, but it is derived from the BSM formula. To be complete, I will also include a brief definition of the N-prime function and an example here.

The functions $N'(d_1)$ and $N'(d_2)$ represent the normal Probability Mass Function (PMF) of the values d_1 and d_2. The normal Probability Mass Function (PMF) represents the area under the standard normal curve from $(d - 0.5)$ to $(d + 0.5)$. In other words, the PMF represents the area under the standard normal curve for the one-unit range, centered on the user-specified d-value.

As was the case for the CDF, the values of "d" can be interpreted as the number of standard deviations above the mean (positive values of d) or below the mean (negative values of d) of a standard normal distribution. The graphs below in Figure 4.3 should help clarify how to interpret the normal PMF function.

As you can observe in the graphs below, normal PMF values range from zero to a maximum theoretical value of positive one (or 100%). The graphical example below illustrates the normal PMF for a d-value of 1.0. The resulting normal PMF for a d-value of +1.0 is 24.20%. The normal PMF is easy to calculate using Microsoft Excel: NORMDIST(1, 0, 1, *FALSE*) = 24.20%. Note the FALSE parameter in the PMF function. The formula for $N'(x)$ is also shown in the bottom graph in Figure 4.3.

For readers with an aptitude for mathematics, a great deal of insight is available from studying the BSM formula and the formulas for the Greeks, but that is beyond the scope of this book.

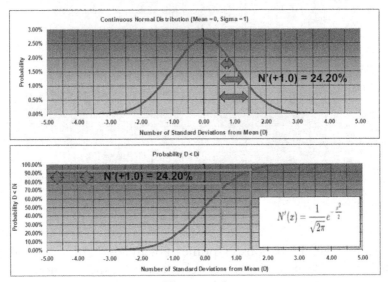

Figure 4.3

Now that we have reviewed all of the inputs and intermediate functions used in the BSM formula, let's use the BSM to calculate the value of the three-year call option, its ancillary values and risk metrics, and then compare the results to the values we found using the Binomial lattice in Chapter 3.

BSM: Three-Year, Risk-Neutral ATM Call Option

As a refresher, here are the input values that we used for the three-year call option, risk-neutral example (Figure 3.5) in the last chapter: initial stock price (S_0) equal to 100, strike price (K) also equal to 100, time to expiration (t) equal to three-years (3.0), annualized standard deviation of the continuously compounded expected stock returns (σ) equal to 20%, annual risk-free rate of interest (r) equal to 4% (continuously compounded), and the Market Risk Premium (MRP) equal to 0% (risk neutral).

In Figure 4.4 below, I have entered each of the input values into the BSM formula for the European call option from earlier in this chapter (Figure 4.1) and provided every step in the calculation of the value of the call option. The intermediate values shown in Figure 4.4 are rounded, but the full-precision of these values were used in the actual BSM call option calculation.

The first step in applying the BSM formula for the call option is to calculate d_1(0.5196) and d_2(0.1732). The resulting normal CDF values for d_1 and d_2, N(0.5196) and N(0.1732), equal 0.6983 and 0.5688 respectively.

$$C = 100.0N(0.5196) - 100.0e^{-0.04(3.0)}N(0.1732)$$
$$C = 100.0(0.6983) - 100.0(0.8869)(0.5688)$$
$$C = 100.0(0.6983) - 50.444$$
$$C = 19.389$$

$$d_1 = \frac{\ln\left(\frac{100.0}{100.0}\right) + \left(0.04 + \frac{0.20^2}{2}\right)3.0}{0.20\sqrt{3.0}} = 0.5196$$

$$d_2 = 0.520 - 0.20\sqrt{3.0} = 0.1732$$

Figure 4.4

The resulting BSM value of the three-year call option is 19.389. This compares to a binomial value of the three-year call option in Chapter 3 of 20.268. To facilitate the comparisons of the BSM and BOM values, I have included the three-year, three-period, risk-neutral binomial lattice from Chapter 3 below (Figure 3.5).

The BOM value of the call option is overstated by 0.879 or approximately 4.5%. I artificially limited the binomial lattice in Chapter 3 to three periods/intervals due to space limitations, but this is a perfect example of why a large number of intervals is required when using the BOM to value options – to approximate a more realistic continuous distribution.

We can also use the BSM to calculate the risk metrics (Delta and Beta) and the replicating portfolio for the three-year call option. Unlike the binomial example, all of these values are continuous, not discrete. As a result, these values will also change continuously in response to changes in all of the BSM input values.

Unlike the BOM, the BSM calculation of Delta is simple. In fact, we have already done the calculation. The Delta of the call option equals $N(d_1)$ in the BSM formula. If you refer to Figure 4.4, d_1 equals 0.5196 and N(0.5196) equals 0.6983. This compares to a Delta of 0.670 for the BOM, which is relatively close.

Figure 3.5 Risk Neutral

European Call Option — binomial tree

Cum R_S	12.750%
Cum R_O	12.750%

Input parameters:

S_0	100.000
Rf (C)	4.000%
Rf EAR	4.081%
MRP (C)	0.000%
MRP EAR	0.000%
Strike	100.000
Time	3.000
Up	1.2214
Down	0.8187
Pru	55.152%
Prd	44.848%

Node 0:

0	0
Stock	100.000
-B/+L	-46.73
Eur Call	20.268
Δ_{OPT}	0.670
β_{OPT}	3.306
ROR_S	4.081%
ROR_Opt	4.081%
Prob	100.00%

Node 1:

Cum R_S	4.081%
Cum R_O	4.081%

1	1
Stock	122.140
-B/+L	-69.55
Eur Call	33.194
Δ_{OPT}	0.841
β_{OPT}	3.095
ROR_S	4.081%
ROR_Opt	4.081%
Prob	55.15%

Stock	81.873
-B/+L	-22.92
Eur Call	6.217
Δ_{OPT}	0.356
β_{OPT}	4.687
ROR_S	4.081%
ROR_Opt	4.081%
Prob	44.85%

Node 2:

Cum R_S	8.329%
Cum R_O	8.329%

2	2
Stock	149.182
-B/+L	-96.08
Eur Call	53.104
Δ_{OPT}	1.000
β_{OPT}	2.809
ROR_S	4.081%
ROR_Opt	4.081%
Prob	30.42%

Stock	100.000
-B/+L	-43.25
Eur Call	11.732
Δ_{OPT}	0.550
β_{OPT}	4.687
ROR_S	4.081%
ROR_Opt	4.081%
Prob	49.47%

Stock	67.032
-B/+L	0.00
Eur Call	0.000
Δ_{OPT}	0.000
β_{OPT}	0.000
ROR_S	4.081%
ROR_Opt	0.000%
Prob	20.11%

Node 3 (terminal nodes):

3	3
Stock	182.212
-B/+L	N/A
Eur Call	82.212
Δ_{OPT}	N/A
β_{OPT}	N/A
ROR_S	N/A
ROR_Opt	N/A
Prob	16.78%

Stock	122.140
-B/+L	N/A
Eur Call	22.140
Δ_{OPT}	N/A
β_{OPT}	N/A
ROR_S	N/A
ROR_Opt	N/A
Prob	40.92%

Stock	81.873
-B/+L	N/A
Eur Call	0.000
Δ_{OPT}	N/A
β_{OPT}	N/A
ROR_S	N/A
ROR_Opt	N/A
Prob	33.28%

Stock	54.881
-B/+L	N/A
Eur Call	0.000
Δ_{OPT}	N/A
β_{OPT}	N/A
ROR_S	N/A
ROR_Opt	N/A
Prob	9.02%

The Black-Scholes-Merton (BSM) model even throws in a bonus value for free. $N(d_2)$ equals the *risk-neutral* probability that the call option expires in the money ($S_E > K$). From Figure 4.4, d_2 equals 0.1732 and $N(0.1732)$ equals 0.5688 or 56.88%. For the binomial, we would have to add up the discrete probabilities of every terminal node with $S_E > K$ at expiration. With only four terminal nodes (and only two expiring in the money), the calculation is simple. The comparable binomial probability equals 57.70% (16.78% + 40.92%), which is surprisingly close to the BSM value.

Finding the replicating portfolio for the call option is also much easier when using the BSM model. In fact, the BSM equation is set up exactly like the replicating portfolio. The left-side of the equation represents the equity investment and the right-side of the equation represents the amount allocated to the risk-free investment (Figure 4.5 below).

$$C = SN(d_1) - Ke^{-rt}N(d_2)$$

Figure 4.5

You will recall that the Delta of the call option equals $N(d_1)$ in the BSM model, which we already determined equals 0.6983 for the three-year call option. The left-side of the BSM equation tells us that a purchase of 0.6983 shares of stock is required for the equity portion of the call replicating portfolio.

The entire right-side of the BSM equation represents the amount invested in the risk-free investment: $-Ke^{-rt}N(d_2)$. We calculated this value earlier in Figure 4.4 (-50.444). The negative value indicates borrowing at the risk-free interest rate, the same convention we used with the binomial model. The comparable amount invested at the risk-free rate for the three-year binomial was negative 46.73 (46.73 borrowed), resulting in a binomial error of 3.71. The error was due to the artificially constrained number of periods. All binomial values converge to the corresponding BSM values as the number of intervals becomes large.

BSM Put Option Formula

In this section, I will present the BSM formula for European put options. In the subsequent section, I will use the BSM formula to calculate the specific put option value, ancillary values, and risk metrics for the same three-year, risk-neutral put option that we evaluated with the binomial backward induction process in Chapter 3. The general form of the BSM formula for a European put option is shown below in Figure 4.6.

$$P = S(-N(-d_1)) + Ke^{-rt}N(-d_2)$$

$$d_1 = \frac{\ln\left(\frac{S}{K}\right) + \left(r + \frac{\sigma^2}{2}\right)t}{\sigma\sqrt{t}}$$

$$d_2 = d_1 - \sigma\sqrt{t}$$

Figure 4.6

We already calculated the values of d_1 and d_2 when we analyzed the BSM call option. However, the BSM formula for the put option requires the normal Cumulative Density Functions (CDF) of $N(-d_1)$ and $N(-d_2)$, *not* $N(d_1)$ and $N(d_2)$. I will explain this further when we review the put option BSM calculations for our three-year put option in the next section.

BSM: Three-Year, Risk-Neutral ATM Put Option

We will use the same input values from the three-year put option, risk-neutral example (Figure 3.7) in the last chapter: initial stock price (S_0) equal to 100, strike price (K) also equal to 100, time to expiration (t) equal to three-years (3.0), annualized standard deviation of the continuously compounded expected stock returns (σ) equal to 20%, annual risk-free rate of interest (r) equal to 4% (continuously compounded), and the Market Risk Premium (MRP) equal to 0% (risk neutral).

In Figure 4.7 below, I have entered each of the input values into the BSM formula for European put option from earlier in this chapter (Figure 4.6) and provided every step in the calculation of the value of the put option. The intermediate values shown in Figure 4.7 are rounded, but the full-precision of these values were used in the actual BSM put option calculation.

We have already calculated d_1 and d_2 for the call option, so we can immediately calculate the resulting normal CDF values for *negative* d_1 and *negative* d_2, $N(-0.5196)$ and $N(-0.1732)$, which equal 0.3017 and 0.4312 respectively.

$$P = 100.0\left(-N(-0.5196)\right) + 100.0e^{-0.04(3.0)}N(-0.1732)$$
$$P = 100.0(-(0.3017)) + 100.0(0.8869)(0.4312)$$
$$P = 100.0(-(0.3017)) + 38.248$$
$$P = 8.081$$

$$-d_1 = -0.5196$$

$$-d_2 = -0.1732$$

Figure 4.7

The resulting BSM value of the three-year put option is 8.081. This compares to a binomial value of the three-year call option in Chapter 3 of 8.960. To facilitate the comparisons of the BSM and BOM values, I have included the three-year, three-period, risk-neutral binomial lattice from Chapter 3 below (Figure 3.7).

The BOM value of the put option is overstated by 0.879 relative to the BSM value, which is the exact same error as the binomial call option. This is not a coincidence. Since Put/Call parity holds for the BOM and for the BSM model, if the BOM value call option value is overstated (or understated) relative to the BSM value, the BOM put value must also be overstated (or understated) by the same amount.

Figure 3.7 Risk Neutral

Cum R$_S$	12.750%
Cum R$_O$	12.750%

European Put Option

S$_0$	100.000
Rf (C)	4.000%
Rf EAR	4.081%
MRP (C)	0.000%
MRP EAR	0.000%
Strike	100.000
Time	3.000
Up	1.2214
Down	0.8187
Pru	55.152%
Prd	44.848%

Cum R$_S$	8.329%
Cum R$_O$	8.329%

Cum R$_S$	4.081%
Cum R$_O$	4.081%

Time 0 node

0	**0**
Stock	100.000
-B/+L	41.96
EUR Put	8.960
Δ$_{OPT}$	-0.330
β$_{OPT}$	-3.683
ROR$_S$	4.081%
ROR$_{Opt}$	4.081%
Prob	100.00%

Time 1 nodes

1	**1**
Stock	122.140
-B/+L	22.76
EUR Put	3.366
Δ$_{OPT}$	-0.159
β$_{OPT}$	-5.763
ROR$_S$	4.081%
ROR$_{Opt}$	4.081%
Prob	55.15%

Stock	81.873
-B/+L	69.39
EUR Put	16.655
Δ$_{OPT}$	-0.644
β$_{OPT}$	-3.166
ROR$_S$	4.081%
ROR$_{Opt}$	4.081%
Prob	44.85%

Time 2 nodes

2	**2**
Stock	149.182
-B/+L	0.00
EUR Put	0.000
Δ$_{OPT}$	0.000
β$_{OPT}$	0.000
ROR$_S$	4.081%
ROR$_{Opt}$	0.000%
Prob	30.42%

Stock	100.000
-B/+L	52.83
EUR Put	7.811
Δ$_{OPT}$	-0.450
β$_{OPT}$	-5.763
ROR$_S$	4.081%
ROR$_{Opt}$	4.081%
Prob	49.47%

Stock	67.032
-B/+L	96.08
EUR Put	29.047
Δ$_{OPT}$	-1.000
β$_{OPT}$	-2.308
ROR$_S$	4.081%
ROR$_{Opt}$	4.081%
Prob	20.11%

Time 3 nodes

3	**3**
Stock	182.212
-B/+L	N/A
EUR Put	0.000
Δ$_{OPT}$	N/A
β$_{OPT}$	N/A
ROR$_S$	N/A
ROR$_{Opt}$	N/A
Prob	16.78%

Stock	122.140
-B/+L	N/A
EUR Put	0.000
Δ$_{OPT}$	N/A
β$_{OPT}$	N/A
ROR$_S$	N/A
ROR$_{Opt}$	N/A
Prob	40.92%

Stock	81.873
-B/+L	N/A
EUR Put	18.127
Δ$_{OPT}$	N/A
β$_{OPT}$	N/A
ROR$_S$	N/A
ROR$_{Opt}$	N/A
Prob	33.28%

Stock	54.881
-B/+L	N/A
EUR Put	45.119
Δ$_{OPT}$	N/A
β$_{UVI}$	N/A
ROR$_S$	N/A
ROR$_{Opt}$	N/A
Prob	9.02%

We will use the same techniques we used above for the call option to calculate the BSM risk metrics (Delta and Beta) and the replicating portfolio for the three-year put option.

The BSM calculation of Delta for the put option is simple, but slightly different than the calculation for the call option. In the BSM formula, the Delta of the put option equals *negative* N(-d$_1$). If you refer to Figure 4.7, negative d$_1$ equals negative 0.5196 (-0.5196). Negative one multiplied by N(-

0.5196) equals negative 0.3017 (-0.3017).

Remember the normal CDF of any number is positive and the Delta of a put option is always negative. The BSM Deltas of the call option (0.6983) and put option (-0.3017) are related through Put/Call Parity. The Delta of the call option (0.6983), minus the Delta of the put option (-0.3017), must equal the Delta of the underlying stock (+1.0). This explains why we use $N(d_1)$ and $N(-d_1)$ in the respective BSM call and put option formulas. By definition, $N(d_1)$ and $N(-d_1)$ sum to 1.0, which again ensures Delta Put/Call Parity. The BSM put option Delta of -0.3017 compares to a Delta of -0.330 for the BOM.

The Black-Scholes-Merton (BSM) *risk-neutral* probability of the put option expiring in the money ($S_E < K$) equals $N(-d_2)$. From Figure 4.7, negative d_2 equals -0.1732 and $N(-0.1732)$ equals 0.4312 or 43.12%. As we would expect, the BSM probability of the call option expiring in the money ($N(d_2)$: 56.88%), plus the BSM probability of the put option expiring in the money ($N(-d_2)$: 43.12%) must equal 100%.

To find the comparable probability for the binomial, we have to add up the discrete probabilities of every terminal node with $S_E < K$ at expiration. The comparable binomial probability equals 42.30% (33.28% + 9.02%), which is surprisingly close to the BSM value of 43.12%.

Finding the replicating portfolio for the put option is also much easier when using the BSM model. As was the case with the call option, the BSM put equation is set up exactly like the replicating portfolio. The left-side of the equation represents the equity investment and the right-side of the equation represents the amount invested in the risk-free investment (Figure 4.8 below).

$$P = S(-N(-d_1)) + Ke^{-rt}N(-d_2)$$

Figure 4.8

You will recall that the Delta of the put option equals $-N(-d_1)$ in the BSM model, which we already determined equals -0.3017 for the three-year put option. The left-side of the BSM equation tells is that a *sale* of 0.3017 shares of stock is required for the equity portion of the put replicating portfolio.

The entire right-side of the BSM equation represents the amount invested in the risk-free investment: $+Ke^{-rt}N(-d_2)$. We calculated this value earlier in Figure 4.7 (+38.248). The positive value implies investing (not borrowing) at the risk-free interest rate. The comparable amount invested at the risk-free rate for the three-year binomial was 41.96, resulting in a binomial error of 3.71.

While the BSM formulas for the call and put options are not immediately intuitive, the BSM model does have a number of advantages over the more computationally intensive BOM. It is simpler to use and much faster to calculate. In addition, the ancillary values and risk metrics are all represented directly in the formulas and do not need to be calculated separately. The BSM is also more accurate than the BOM, unless the BOM uses a sufficient number of intervals.

However, the discrete nature of the BOM allows exercise decisions to be made at any node, allowing the BOM to calculate the value of American options, which is not possible with the BSM. Finally, the discrete nodes and intervals used in the BOM allows us to calculate precise intermediate values of options and risk metrics at any point in the lattice. This makes it possible to use the BOM values for simulation and for optimization – an enormous practical advantage for the Binomial Options Model (BOM) over the Black-Scholes Merton (BSM) model.

Invalid and Inconsistent BSM Assumptions

While the BSM and BOM represent important contributions to the field of finance, both models have serious deficiencies. All of their underlying assumptions are violated in practice. Since the BOM converges to the BSM as the number of binomial intervals approaches infinity, the BSM and BOM assumptions are very similar, as are the implications when the assumptions are violated in practice. A detailed discussion of every BSM/BOM assumption is included in every derivatives textbook, so I will not include a comprehensive list of those assumptions here.

Many of the requisite assumptions relate to efficient markets, which support the use of hedged and replicating portfolios, as well as riskless borrowing and lending in the BSM and BOM. While these assumptions are not entirely valid in practice, violations of the market-efficiency assumptions do not seriously compromise the results from the Black-Scholes-Merton (BSM) model and the Binomial Options Model (BOM). Unfortunately, the same is *not* true for violations of the constant interest rate and constant volatility assumptions.

The BOM and BSM both assume that volatility and interest rates will be constant over the life of every option. These assumptions are internally inconsistent and are violated in practice for interest rates and for volatility. In fact, these assumptions are notoriously inaccurate, especially for volatility.

In reality, market forces (supply and demand) continuously interact through financial markets to determine *different* equilibrium risk-free interest rates and *different* levels of expected volatility *for each future period.* This results in an ever-evolving term structure of unique interest rates and term structure of unique volatilities.

To be theoretically correct and internally consistent, the *same* interest rate and *same* expected volatility should apply to the *same* future period and *different* interest rates and *different* expected volatilities should apply to *different* future periods. Due to their constant interest rate and volatility assumptions, the BOM and BSM implicitly apply *different* interest rates and *different* implied volatilities to the *same* period, and apply the *same* interest rates and *same* expected volatilities to *different* periods.

This means that current and future option values calculated by the BOM and BSM are incorrect and inconsistent, as are the current and future Greek values (risk metrics), which are derived from these invalid assumptions!

In the next chapter, I will explain how the Johnson Aggregation Framework (JAF) corrects for the deficiencies inherent in the BOM and BSM.

5) JOHNSON AGGREGATION FRAMEWORK (JAF)

As explained in the final section of Chapter 4, the BOM and BSM have fundamental flaws, which lead to invalid and inconsistent option values and Greeks for both models. The Johnson Aggregation Framework (JAF) corrects the serious deficiencies of the BSM and BOM by eliminating the invalid constant interest rate and constant volatility assumptions, allowing us to solve for and use the complete term structure of unique interest rates and term structure of unique volatilities. This chapter will explain: the objective of the JAF, the components and implementation of the JAF, and the advantages of the JAF.

JAF Objective:
Design an objective framework that employs a user-specified Market Risk Premium in conjunction with the complete term structure of unique interest rates and the complete term structure of unique volatilities to calculate theoretically sound and internally consistent: current and future option values, current and future Greeks, and current and future volatility index (VIX) values.

JAF Components & Implementation

Several tools and algorithms are required to implement the JAF. A list of the individual JAF components is outlined below as a road map for this section. Each of these components will be reviewed in detail, including an explanation of all JAF formulas. When formulas are provided, simple numerical examples will also be presented for demonstration purposes. *Intermediate values in all numerical examples will typically be rounded, but the final values will include the full precision available for all values in each formula.* Sufficient documentation will be included in this chapter to allow the dedicated reader to implement the JAF in practice.

JAF Components:
1) Formula to aggregate and disaggregate forward rates
2) Formula to aggregate and disaggregate expected forward volatilities
3) Algorithm to use aggregated and disaggregated forward rates and forward volatilities to solve for current and future values of options and volatility index futures
4) Algorithm to use aggregated and disaggregated forward rates and forward volatilities to solve for current and future option Greeks

Simplified Time-Period Assumption

To facilitate the use of interest rates and volatilities in specific examples, the following sections will assume that all monthly options expire at the close on the last trade-day of the month and that there are exactly 21 trade days in every month. Given this assumption, interest rates, volatilities, and option expiration dates will all coincide perfectly with calendar months. This will allow us to discuss hypothetical interest rates and volatilities for specific calendar month examples, without any confusion regarding whether we are referring to the period before or after the standard monthly option expiration date on the third Friday of the month. *Note: this assumption is only included to avoid confusion and is NOT required for the JAF, which can accommodate any number of periods, each with a variable number of trade days.*

Interest Rate Aggregation Formula

The risk-free interest rate is an important input parameter in all valuation models, including the BSM and BOM. However, in reality, there is not a single risk-free interest rate, which means that there should not be a single input parameter for the risk-free rate. Instead, there are different risk-free rates that apply to different time periods; together, they represent the term structure of interest rates.

A full primer on interest rates and the time value of money is beyond the scope of this book. If you are interested in a comprehensive review of the time value of money, this information is widely available for free online, and several chapters are typically devoted to this topic in every finance textbook. Fortunately, a basic understanding of spot and forward rates is the only requirement to understand the use of risk-free interest rates in the JAF. I will begin with some basic definitions to provide the foundation for the interest rate aggregation formula.

This book uses continuously compounded annual interest rates exclusively. This helps avoid confusion when comparing discrete (BOM) and continuous models (BSM), and it also helps highlight the similarities in both models. The math for working with continuously compounded rates is much simpler, which further warrants the use of continuously compounded returns in all formulas. Note: this not a limitation. Every continuously compounded return can be expressed as an effective annual return and vice versa. Continuously compounded simply means that interest is compounded continuously, rather than at discrete intervals. Below are the standard time-value-of-money formulas for continuously compounded interest rates.

Present Value of $1: e^{-rt}
Future Value of $1: e^{rt}
Effective Annual Rate: $e^r - 1$

Before evaluating the interest rate aggregation formula, we have to review forward and spot rates. A forward rate is the interest rate (risk-free in our case) applicable to a specific period in the future. It could also be interpreted as the expected interest rate for a specific period in the future.

Let's assume it is the last trade day of December at the market close. Let's also assume that the risk-free forward rates for January, February, and March are 4%, 5%, and 6%, respectively. That implies that we could invest in a risk-free investment today and earn a continuously compounded annual rate of 4% in January, 5% in February, and 6% in March. It also implies that the market expects the risk-free rate to be 5% in February and 6% in March.

If we were discounting cash flows to be received in the future at the prevailing risk-free forward rates, we would discount a cash flow received at the end of March by the continuously compounded annual rate of 6% in March, by 5% in February, and by 4% in January. Note, different risk-free interest rates are used in different periods.

Spot rates represent the average rate over multiple forward rate periods. In other words, they represent the average rate earned over the several forward rate periods or the average discount rate applied over several forward rate periods.

In our simplified monthly example (all months with the same number of trade days: 21), the spot rate for cash flows invested from the end of December to the end of March would equal 5% (arithmetic average of 4%, 5%, and 6%). The spot rate for cash flows invested from the end of December to the end of February would equal 4.5% (arithmetic average of 4% and 5%). The spot rate for cash flows invested from the end of

December to the end of January would equal 4.0% (single period – no averaging required). The formula to aggregate continuously compounded annual forward rates of the same length is a simple arithmetic average. Even if the forward rate periods are of different lengths, the formula is a simple arithmetic *weighted-average*. This is the advantage of using continuously compounded rates. The aggregate interest rate formulas for discrete compounding periods are much more complex and far less intuitive.

The general spot rate formula for periods of the same length is shown below, where SR represents the continuously compounded annual Spot Rate and FR represents the continuously compounded annual forward rates. N represents the number of forward rate periods of equal length.

$$\text{SR}_{0,N} = [\text{FR}_{0,1} + \text{FR}_{1,2} + \dots \text{FR}_{N-1,N}]/N$$
$$\text{SR}_{0,3} = [4\% + 5\% + 6\%]/3.0 = 5.0\%$$

Similarly, we can use a variation of the same formula to calculate the expected spot rate *after any number of time periods in the future*. Using the above example, the expected Spot rate at the end of *January* would equal 5.5% (arithmetic average of 5% for February and 6% for March). Note: the forward rate of 4% applies specifically to the month of January and we are calculating the expected spot rate at the end of January, which means the forward rate for January would no longer be relevant. The term structure of interest rates ages over time and we drop off rates that are applicable to periods that have passed.

The general formula for the *expected* future continuously compounded annual spot rate (for periods of the same length) is shown below, where ESR represents the continuously compounded annual Expected Spot Rate and FR represents the continuously compounded annual forward rates. N and n are used to designate the forward rate periods applicable to the specific future cash flow (at the end of March in the above example). As you can see in this specific example, the expected future spot rate at the end of January only uses the forward rates for February and March.

$$\text{ESR}_{n,N} = [\text{FR}_{n,n+1} + \text{FR}_{n+1,n+2} + \dots \text{FR}_{N-1,N}]/(N - n)$$
$$\text{ESR}_{1,3} = [\text{FR}_{1,2} + \text{FR}_{2,3}]/(3 - 1)$$
$$\text{ESR}_{1,3} = [5.0\% + 6.0\%]/2.0 = 5.5\%$$

The two general interest rate aggregation formulas above demonstrated that we can aggregate forward rates now and at any chosen time in the future. We can also use algebraic variants of the above general spot rate formulas to solve for implied forward rates.

For example, if we knew the March (5.0%) spot rate and the February (4.5%) spot rate (or the spot rate for any shorter period), we could calculate the forward rate from the end of the earlier period to the end of the longer period (the March forward rate in this case, which represents the period from the end of February to the end of March).

$$\mathbf{FR_{N-n,N} = [SR_{0,N} *N - SR_{0,n} * n]/(N - n)}$$
$$FR_{2,3} = [SR_{0,3}*(3) - SR_{0,2}* (2.0)]/(3.0 - 2.0)$$
$$FR_{2,3} = [5.0\%*(3) - 4.5\%* (2.0)]/(1.0)$$
$$FR_{2,3} = [5.0\%*(3) - 4.5\%* (2.0)]/(1.0) = 6.0\%$$

The disaggregation formula above (or any variation thereof) allows us to derive each of the forward rates directly from the observed spot rates (or even from the prices of zero-coupon US Treasury securities or T-Bills). It also allows us to solve for any missing forward rate if we know the appropriate spot rate and the remaining forward rates. *This framework allows us to solve for all current and future expected spot and forward rates.*

The aggregation formula above is an example of a simple bootstrapping technique. It is relatively easy to apply in practice. As an investment professional, I used more sophisticated non-linear forward rate estimation algorithms (cubic spline and iterative regression using forward rate return sensitivities) based on all US Treasury securities, including notes and bonds with interim cash flows.

As I mentioned earlier, the JAF accommodates any number of forward rate periods of varying length. Below are the corresponding aggregation and disaggregation formulas for periods of varying length. The specific numerical examples are the same as the ones used above in the general case. The only difference is that the number of trade days for each forward rate period is included in the calculations.

$$\mathbf{SR_{0,N} = [NTD_{0,1} (FR_{0,1}) + NTD_{1,2} (FR_{1,2}) + ... NTD_{N-1,N} (FR_{N-1,N})]}$$
$$\mathbf{/[NTD_{0,N}]}$$
$$SR_{0,N} = [NTD_{0,1} (FR_{0,1}) + NTD_{1,2} (FR_{1,2}) + NTD_{2,3} (FR_{2,3})]/[NTD_{0,3}]$$
$$SR_{0,3} = [21 (4.0\%) + 21 (5.0\%) + 21 (6.0\%)]/[63]$$
$$SR_{0,3} = [315\%]/[63] = 5.0\%$$
$$NTD_{n,N} = \text{Number of Trade Days from period n to period N}$$

The formula below allows for any number of periods of varying length to solve for the expected future spot rate. In this case, I am using the more flexible formula below to confirm our earlier calculation of the expected future spot rate at the end of January. Note that the new formula uses the actual number of trade days in February and March, in addition to the forward rates for February and March.

$$\mathbf{ESR_{n,N}} = [\mathbf{NTD_{n,n+1}(FR_{n,n+1})} + \mathbf{NTD_{n+1,n+2}} (\mathbf{FR_{n+1,n+2}}) + \dots \mathbf{NTD_{N-1,N}} (\mathbf{FR_{N-1,N}})] / (\mathbf{NTD_{n,N}})$$
$$ESR_{1,3} = [NTD_{1,2}(FR_{1,2}) + NTD_{2,3}(FR_{2,3})] / (NTD_{1,3})$$
$$ESR_{1,3} = [21(5.0\%) + 21(6.0\%)] / (42)$$
$$ESR_{1,3} = [231\%] / (42) = 5.5\%$$

The final formula below allows the user to use any number of periods and periods of any length to solve for the forward rates, directly from spot rates. We will use the more flexible formula below to confirm our earlier calculation of the March forward rate, given the March (5.0%) spot rate and the February (4.5%) spot rate. As was the case in the general example, we could calculate the forward rate from the end of any earlier period to the end of the longer period.

$$\mathbf{FR_{N-n,N}} = [\mathbf{NTD_{0,N}(SR_{0,N})} - \mathbf{NTD_{0,n}(SR_{0,n})}] / (\mathbf{NTD_{0,N}} - \mathbf{NTD_{0,n}})$$
$$FR_{2,3} = [NTD_{0,3}(SR_{0,3}) - NTD_{0,2}(SR_{0,2})] / (NTD_{0,3} - NTD_{0,2})$$
$$FR_{2,3} = [63(5.0\%) - 42(4.5)] / (63 - 42)$$
$$FR_{2,3} = [126\%] / (21) = 6.0\%$$

The more flexible formulas above generated the exact same results as the general formulas for periods of equal length. However, the more flexible interest rate aggregation and disaggregation formulas work for any number of user-specified, variable length periods. The interest rate aggregation and disaggregation formulas are required, because the objective of the JAF is to calculate *current* and *future* derivative values and Greeks using the entire term structure of interest rates.

Continuously compounded returns and natural logarithms have been around since the 1600s, so I cannot take any credit for the above formulas - other than developing an algorithm to integrate the interest rate aggregation and disaggregation formulas into the JAF, which was required to utilize the complete term structure of interest rates to value derivative instruments and calculate their risk metrics or Greeks. I will present those JAF algorithms later in this chapter.

The JAF allows the user to enter any number of periods, each with a user-specified length. The JAF requires a risk-free interest rate for each period.

Bootstrapping or non-linear estimation techniques like those above could be used to find market-implied forward rates, or interest rate forecasting models could be used to estimate forward rates instead. Either way, the JAF will use the forward rate estimates to calculate option values that are theoretically sound and consistent with the entire term structure of interest rates - as specified by the user.

Johnson Volatility Aggregation Formula (JVAF)

Volatility is arguably the single most important input parameter in all option valuation models, far more important than interest rates in practice. As was the case with interest rates, there is not one single volatility, which means that there should not be a single input parameter for the volatility. Instead, there are different volatilities that apply to different time periods; together, they represent the term structure of volatilities.

I provided a detailed volatility primer in Chapter 1 and we have used volatility extensively in the BOM and BSM models in Chapters 2 and 3. As a result, we have a solid foundation for aggregating and disaggregating different expected levels of volatility over different time periods in the future.

Before evaluating the Johnson Volatility Aggregation Formula (JFAV), we have to review forward volatilities and how they relate to implied volatility. A forward volatility is the expected level of volatility applicable to a specific period in the future.

Let's assume it is the last trade day of December at the market close. Let's also assume that the expected or forward (annualized) volatilities for January, February, and March are 10%, 15%, and 20%, respectively.

Just as spot rates represent the equivalent average rate over multiple forward rate periods, we also need to be able to calculate an equivalent aggregate volatility over multiple forward volatility periods. In order to determine the value of an ATM option expiring at the end of March, we would need to be able to aggregate the forward volatilities for January (10%), February (15%), and March (20%).

Note we will be using the JAF to solve for the at-the-money (ATM) term structure of volatilities and the values of ATM options almost exclusively. Extending the JAF to include the vertical skew (OTM and ITM options) and/or a stochastic volatility process to value options would require another book to explain the modified JAF process.

If calculated correctly (and options were efficiently priced), the resulting aggregate 3-month volatility would be equivalent to the *implied volatility* of the ATM option expiring at the end of March. *The key to calculating theoretically sound current and future derivative values and risk metrics, using the entire term structure of volatilities, is the Johnson Aggregate Volatility Formula (JVAF).*

I first introduced an early version of the JVAF in my June 2011 *Active Trader* article titled "Modeling Implied Volatility," which applied the formula to earnings events. I refined this approach in my subsequent book, *Exploiting Earnings Volatility*, published in 2015. Both of these publications applied the JVAF to earnings events. To avoid confusion, I will not reproduce the versions of the JVAF that are specific to earnings volatility. If you are interested in the topic, *Exploiting Earnings Volatility* is available on Amazon. In that book, I foreshadowed future applications of the JVAF: *"We could even use this formula to estimate the forward volatilities implicit in the term structure of volatilities, otherwise known as the horizontal skew."*

The JVAF will allow us to exactly aggregate and disaggregate forward and implied volatilities, just as the aggregate interest rate formula allowed us to aggregate and disaggregate forward and spot rates. Unlike the interest rate aggregation formula for continuously compounded rates, the JVAF is not linear.

Instead, the aggregate *variance* over the entire period equals the weighted-average of the forward *variances* over each forward volatility period. After calculating the weighted-average aggregate variance, we need to calculate the square root of the aggregate variance to find the aggregate volatility. When the length of the forward volatility periods is the same, we can calculate the simple arithmetic-average of the forward variances. For variable length periods, we need to calculate the weighted-average of the forward variances. When using actual market data, remember that the Root-Mean-Square (RMS) of the periodic continuously compounded returns is preferable to the standard deviation.

In our simplified monthly example (all months with the same number of trade days: 21), the aggregate volatility (derived with the JVAF) from the end of December to the end of March equals 15.546%. Note that 15.546% does *not* equal the arithmetic-average of the forward volatilities for January, February, and March (10%, 15%, and 20%). The resulting JVAF aggregate volatility from the end of December to the end of February equals 12.748% and the JVAF aggregate volatility from the end of December to the end of January equals 10.0% (single period – no aggregation required).

The JVAF *for periods of the same length* is shown below, where IV represents the annualized aggregate level of volatility over multiple periods and FV represents the annualized expected or forward volatility over a period in the future. N represents the number of forward volatility periods of equal length. The IV for the December to March period is used for a numerical example below.

$$IV_{0,N} = ([(FV_{0,1})^2 + (FV_{1,2})^2 + \ldots (FV_{N-1,N})^2]/N)^{(1/2)}$$
$$IV_{0,3} = ([(FV_{0,1})^2 + (FV_{1,2})^2 + (FV_{2,3})^2]/3)^{(1/2)}$$
$$IV_{0,3} = ([(10\%)^2 + (15\%)^2 + (20\%)^2]/3)^{(1/2)}$$
$$IV_{0,3} = [2.417\%]^{(1/2)} = 15.546\%$$

Similarly, we can use a variation of the JVAF to calculate the expected aggregate or implied volatility *after any number of time periods in the future*. Using the above example, the expected aggregate volatility for the period from the end of *January* through the end of March would equal 17.678% (derived from the expected forward volatilities of 15% in February and 20% in March). Note: the forward volatility of 10% applies specifically to the month of January and we are calculating the expected aggregate volatility at the end of January, which means the forward volatility for January would no longer be relevant.

The term structure of volatilities ages over time and we drop off volatilities that are applicable to periods that have passed. This is exactly the same methodology that we used when aging the term structure of interest rates. Note, the process for aging *stochastic* term structures of interest rates and volatilities is more complex than the process described above and is beyond the scope of this book.

The general formula for the *expected* future aggregate volatility (for periods of the same length) is shown below, where EIV represents the annualized Expected Implied Volatility and FV represents the annualized forward volatilities. N and n are used to designate the forward volatility periods applicable to the specific option expiration date (at the end of March in the above example). As you can see in this specific example, the expected future aggregate implied volatility at the end of January only uses the forward volatilities for February and March.

$$EIV_{n,N} = ([(FV_{n,n+1})^2 + (FV_{n+1,n+2})^2 + \ldots (FV_{N-1,N})^2]/(N - n))^{(0.5)}$$
$$EIV_{1,3} = ([(FV_{1,2})^2 + (FV_{2,3})^2]/(3 - 1))^{(0.5)}$$
$$EIV_{1,3} = ([(15\%)^2 + (20)^2]/(2))^{(0.5)}$$
$$EIV_{1,3} = (3.125\%)^{(1/2)} = 17.678\%$$

The two general interest rate aggregation formulas above demonstrated that we can aggregate forward volatilities now and at any chosen time in the future. We can also use algebraic variants of the above general spot rate formulas to solve for implied forward volatilities.

For example, if we knew the March aggregate or implied volatility (15.546%) and the February aggregate implied volatility (12.748%), or the IV for any shorter period, we could calculate the forward volatility from the end of the earlier period to the end of the longer period (the March forward volatility in this case, which represents the expected volatility from the end of February to the end of March).

$$FV_{N-n,N} = ([N(IV_{0,N})^2 - n(IV_{0,n})^2]/(N - n))^{(0.5)}$$
$$FV_{2,3} = ([3(IV_{0,3})^2 - 2(IV_{0,2})^2]/(3 - 2))^{(0.5)}$$
$$FV_{2,3} = ([3(15.546\%\%)^2 - 2(12.748\%)^2]/(3 - 2))^{(0.5)}$$
$$FV_{2,3} = (4.0\%)^{(0.5)} = 20.0\%$$

The JVAF formula above (or any variation thereof) allows us to derive each of the forward volatilities directly from the observed ATM implied volatilities from the option chain. It also allows us to solve for any missing forward volatilities if we know the appropriate implied volatilities and the remaining forward volatilities. *This framework allows us to solve for all current and future expected implied volatilities and forward volatilities.*

As I mentioned earlier, the JVAF accommodates any number of forward volatility periods of varying length. Below are the corresponding volatility aggregation and disaggregation versions of the JVAF for periods of *varying* length. The specific numerical examples are the same as the ones used above in the general case. The only difference is that the number of trade days for each forward volatility period is included in the calculations.

$$IV_{0,N} = ([NTD_{0,1}(FV_{0,1})^2 + NTD_{1,2}(FV_{1,2})^2 + ... NTD_{N-1,N}(FV_{N-1,N})^2]/NTD_{0,N})^{(1/2)}$$
$$IV_{0,3} = ([NTD_{0,1}(FV_{0,1})^2 + NTD_{1,2}(FV_{1,2})^2 + NTD_{2,3}(FV_{2,3})^2]/NTD_{0,3})^{(1/2)}$$
$$IV_{0,3} = ([21(10\%)^2 + 21(15\%)^2 + 21(20\%)^2]/63)^{(1/2)}$$
$$IV_{0,3} = ([152.25\%]/63)^{(1/2)}$$
$$IV_{0,3} = (2.417\%)^{(1/2)} = 15.546\%$$
$$NTD_{n,N} = \text{Number of Trade Days from period n to period N}$$

The formula below allows for any number of periods of varying length to solve for the expected future aggregate or implied volatility. In this case, I am using the more flexible formula below to confirm our earlier calculation of the expected future aggregate volatility from the end of January to the end of March. Note that the new formula uses the actual number of trade days in February and March, in addition to the forward volatilities for February and March.

$$\mathbf{EIV_{n,N}} = (\mathbf{[NTD_{n,n+1}} (\mathbf{FV_{n,n+1}})^2 + \mathbf{NTD_{n+1,n+2}} (\mathbf{FV_{n+1,n+2}})^2 + \ldots \mathbf{NTD_{N-1,N}}$$
$$(\mathbf{FV_{N-1,N}})^2] / (\mathbf{NTD_{n,N}}))^{(0.5)}$$

$$EIV_{1,3} = ([NTD_{1,2} (FV_{1,2})^2 + NTD_{2,3} (FV_{2,3})^2] / (NTD_{1,3}))^{(0.5)}$$
$$EIV_{1,3} = ([21 (15\%)^2 + 21 (20\%)^2] / (42))^{(0.5)}$$
$$EIV_{1,3} = (131.25\%] / (42))^{(0.5)} = 17.678\%$$

The final formula below allows the user to use any number of periods and periods of any length to solve for the forward volatilities, directly from implied or aggregate volatilities. We will use the more flexible formula below to confirm our earlier calculation of the March forward volatility, given the March (15.546%) implied volatility and the February (12.748%) implied volatility. As was the case in the general example, we could calculate the forward volatility from the end of any earlier period to the end of the longer period.

$$\mathbf{FV_{N-n,N}} = (\mathbf{[NTD_{0,N}} (\mathbf{IV_{0,N}})^2 - \mathbf{NTD_{0,n}} (\mathbf{IV_{0,n}})^2] / (\mathbf{NTD_{0,N}} - \mathbf{NTD_{0,n}}))^{(0.5)}$$

$$FV_{2,3} = ([NTD_{0,3} (IV_{0,3})^2 - NTD_{0,2} (IV_{0,2})^2] / (NTD_{0,3} - NTD_{0,2}))^{(0.5)}$$
$$FV_{2,3} = ([63 (15.546\%)^2 - 42 (12.748\%)^2] / (63 - 42))^{(0.5)}$$
$$FV_{2,3} = ([84\%] / (21))^{(0.5)} = 20.00\%$$

The more flexible versions of the JVAF above generated the exact same results as the general JVAF for periods of equal length. However, the more flexible versions of the JVAF work for any number of user-specified, variable length periods. The aggregation and disaggregation of volatilities are required, because the objective of the JAF is to calculate current and future derivative values and Greeks using the entire term structure of volatilities.

The JAF allows the user to enter any number of periods, each with a user-specified length. The JAF requires a unique risk-free forward rate and a unique forward volatility for each period. These forward rates and forward volatilities can be derived from market prices, or they can be forecasted with sophisticated, non-linear, modeling techniques (including AI). Forward rates and forward volatilities are the building blocks of the term structure of interest rates and the term structure of volatilities.

Included with this book is an Excel spreadsheet that uses ATM implied volatilities and volatility index prices to solve for the market-implied forward volatilities. The spreadsheet then uses the resulting *market-implied* forward volatilities to calculate the relative values of ATM options and corresponding volatility futures across the entire term structure of volatilities. Chapter 9 provides an overview of how to use this spreadsheet.

If *market-implied* forward rates and forward volatilities are used in the JAF, the resulting model prices would quantify the relative values or pricing anomalies (degree of overvaluation or undervaluation) of ATM options and volatility futures – but only in the context of the market.

If *models are used to forecast* forward rates and forward volatilities for use in the JAF, the resulting model prices would again quantify the relative value or pricing anomalies of ATM options and volatility futures. However, the resulting pricing anomalies would include additional value-added opportunities derived from the predictive power of the forecasting models.

Either way, the JAF will use the forward rate and forward volatility estimates to calculate current and future option values and volatility futures values that are theoretically sound and consistent with the entire term structure of interest rates and the entire term structure of volatilities. The following section explains how the JAF Valuation Algorithm calculates these values.

JAF Valuation Algorithm

The next two sections will explain the JAF algorithms in detail and will introduce a few new formulas used in the JAF. Numerical examples will be provided for each new formula, but results validating that the JAF will not be included in the current chapter. Instead, Chapter 6 will document a partial sample of results validating the JAF valuation framework. Chapter 8 will review a subset of results validating the JAF Greeks framework. Chapters 6 and 8 will only include a handful of the validation analysis I performed for the JAF.

Unfortunately, the full analysis is too long to include in this book, with over 70 pages of analysis and 180 tables of validation results. As a result, I created a comprehensive supplement that includes all of the validation results, which is available exclusively to readers of this book. Please see the Resources chapter at the end of this book for the link address and passwords required to download and open the PDF.

Given the aforementioned deficiencies in the BOM and BSM, how can we calculate the theoretically sound and internally consistent, current and future expected stock, option, and volatility futures values (and expected returns) in risk-neutral and risk-averse environments – all while using the complete term structure of interest rates and the complete term structure of volatilities? The JVAF and interest rate aggregation formulas provide the key.

The breakthrough is that we can use the aggregation formulas introduced in this chapter to aggregate risk-free forward rates and forward volatilities as needed, and use the resulting average spot rates and aggregate or implied volatilities in a *strategic combination or hybrid of the BOM and BSM models* to calculate theoretically sound and internally consistent current and future expected values of options, by *exploiting the computational advantage of the BSM and the discrete nature of the BOM.*

In other words, valuation becomes a two-step process. First, use the JVAF and interest rate aggregation formulas to calculate the precise spot rate and aggregate volatility that is theoretically correct and consistent with the forward risk-free rates and volatilities. Second, use the resulting spot rate and aggregate volatilities in a strategic combination of the BOM and BSM models.

The creative combination of the BOM and BSM models will depend on whether we are calculating current or future expected option values and whether the expected future time period occurs prior to the expiration date of the option. I will explain each of the required frameworks below.

Before I explain how the JAF strategically combines the BOM and BSM models, I need to introduce a few new formulas for using the BSM and BOM in the JAF.

JAF Valuation Algorithm: BSM Formulas

To test the validity of the JAF, we will need to be able to calculate the expected future value (and returns) of the underlying stock, the call option, and the put option under the BSM model. We can use the Sprenkle (1961) formulas in Figure 5.1 below to calculate the expected call and put option values at expiration.

$$Sprenkle:$$
$$E(C) = Se^{(\mu + \sigma^2/2)t}N(b_1) - KN(b_2)$$
$$E(P) = E(C) + K - Se^{(\mu + \sigma^2/2)t}$$

$$b_1 = \frac{\ln\left(\frac{S}{K}\right) + (\mu + \sigma^2)t}{\sigma\sqrt{t}}$$

$$b_2 = b_1 - \sigma\sqrt{t}$$

Figure 5.1

The Sprenkle formulas above calculate the expected values of the call and put options ($E(C)$ and $E(P)$) at expiration. Upon close inspection, it should be evident that the expected value of the put option is derived using Put/Call Parity at option expiration. The formulas use the same input parameters as the BSM, but require one new value: mu or μ, the expected rate of return on the underlying stock.

As a practitioner, I prefer to derive μ from the CAPM input values (the risk-free rate and the Market Risk Premium (MRP)), rather than specify μ directly. I find this approach much more intuitive. While the CAPM does not adequately explain equity returns in practice, it is a logical framework that generates consistent and comparable results for the BOM and BSM. Since we are deriving μ from the CAPM input values, we will not focus on the intermediate value of μ. Instead, we will focus on the expected future values and returns that are generated from the formulas.

However, we need the value of μ for our expected future value formulas. The required formula for μ is shown below. *Note: the values of σ and r in the formula for μ below must first be derived using the JVAF and aggregate interest rate formulas presented in this chapter.* The sample calculation of μ uses the risk-free rate (4.0%) and Market-Risk-Premium (MRP) values from the examples in the BOM and BSM chapters.

μ = r + MRP - 0.5 * (σ ** 2)
Risk-Neutral μ = 0.04 + 0.00 - 0.5 * (0.20 ** 2) = 2.00%
Risk-Averse μ = 0.04 + 0.05 - 0.5 * (0.20 ** 2) = 7.00%

We can use the above values of μ in the Sprenkle formulas to calculate the expected values at expiration of the one-year call and put options that we have been using in all of our examples: (S_0) equal to 100, strike price (K) also equal to 100, time to expiration (t) equal to one-year (1.0), annualized standard deviation of the continuously compounded expected stock returns (σ) equal to 20%, and the annual risk-free rate of interest (r) equal to 4% (continuously compounded). The stock Beta is assumed to be equal to 1.0.

Sprenkle Calculation (Risk-neutral):

$$E(C) = 100e^{\left(0.02 + \frac{0.2^2}{2}\right)1}0.6179 - 100(0.5398) = 10.330$$

$$E(P) = 10.330 + 100 - 100e^{\left(0.02 + \frac{0.2^2}{2}\right)1} = 6.249$$

$$b_1 = \frac{\ln\left(\frac{100}{100}\right) + (0.02 + 0.20^2)1}{0.2\sqrt{1}} = 0.30$$

$$b_2 = 0.30 - 0.20\sqrt{1} = 0.10$$

Figure 5.2

Sprenkle Calculation (Risk-Averse):

$$E(C) = 100e^{\left(0.07 + \frac{0.2^2}{2}\right)1}0.7088 - 100(0.6368) = 13.876$$

$$E(P) = 13.876 + 100 - 100e^{\left(0.07 + \frac{0.2^2}{2}\right)1} = 4.459$$

$$b_1 = \frac{\ln\left(\frac{100}{100}\right) + (0.07 + 0.20^2)1}{0.2\sqrt{1}} = 0.55$$

$$b_2 = 0.55 - 0.20\sqrt{1} = 0.35$$

Figure 5.3

The initial BSM values of the call and put options were 9.925 and 6.004, respectively (BSM calculations not shown). We can use the expected risk-neutral and risk-averse expected values and the initial values to calculate the one-year expected risk-neutral and risk-averse returns for the call and put options.

ER(C) = E(C) / C$_0$ - 1
Risk-Neutral ER(C) = 10.330 / 9.925 – 1 = 4.081%
Risk-Averse ER(C) = 13.876 / 9.925 – 1 = 39.812%

ER(P) = E(P) / P$_0$ - 1
Risk-Neutral ER(P) = 6.249 / 6.004 – 1 = 4.081%
Risk-Averse ER(P) = 4.459 / 6.004 – 1 = - 25.733%

Hull provides the formula for calculating the expected rate of return of the underlying stock at any time (t years) into the future.

$E(S) = S_0e^{(\mu * t + ((\sigma ** 2) * t) / 2)}$
Risk-Neutral $E(S)$ = $100e^{(0.02 * 1 + ((0.20 ** 2) * 1.0) / 2)}$ = 104.081
Risk-Averse $E(S)$ = $100e^{(0.07 * 1 + ((0.20 ** 2) * 1.0) / 2)}$ = 109.417

We can then use the expected future values of the stock to calculate the expected return on the stock in the risk-free and risk-averse environments.

$ER(S) = E(S) / S_0 - 1$
Risk-Neutral $ER(S)$ = 104.081 / 100.000 – 1 = 4.081%
Risk-Averse $ER(S)$ = 109.417 / 100.000 – 1 = 9.417%

Given the stock Beta of 1.0, the expected or required annual continuously compounded return on the stock in the *risk-neutral* environment equals 4%. Note: the natural log of the (1 + 4.081%) equals 4%.

$R_S = R_f + \beta * (MRP)$
Risk-Neutral R_S = 0.04 + 1.0 * (0.0%) = 4.0% continuously compounded

The expected or required annual continuously compounded return on the stock in the *risk-averse* environment equals 9%. Note: the natural log of the (1 + 9.417%) equals 9%.

$R_S = R_f + \beta * (MRP)$
Risk-Averse R_S = 0.04 + 1.0 * (5.0%) = 9.0% continuously compounded

JAF Valuation Algorithm: BSM Python Functions

I wrote all of the JAF code in Python. I cannot include the Python code that I developed for all current and future JAF valuations and Greeks, but the Python code for all of the BSM expected return functions described above is included below.

BSM Python Function Code:

```python
import math

def CumDF(zscore):
    """ Calculates normal cumulative density function from z-score using math library
    """
    return (1+math.erf(zscore/math.sqrt(2.0)))/2.0

def expstockror(mu, v, t):
    """ Calculates expected return using Hull framework, derived from mu, annualized
    volatility,
    and time in years """
    sror = math.exp(mu * t + ((v ** 2) * t) / 2)
    return sror

def sprenkle(type, s, k, time, r, v, mu):
    """ #calculates Sprenkle expected future value of option  from Sprenkle (1961)
    formula"""
    v2 = v * v
    rt = r * time
    mut = mu * time
    v2t = v2 * time
    sqt = time ** 0.5
    vsqrtt = v * sqt
    d2 = (math.log(s / k) + mut) / vsqrtt
    d1 = d2 + vsqrtt
    nd1 = CumDF(d1)
    nd2 = CumDF(d2)
    h = math.exp(mut + v2t / 2)
    efv = h * s * nd1 - k * nd2
    if type == 'p':
        efv = efv + k - h * s
    return efv

def calcmu(r, mrp, v):
    """ Calculates mu (underlying security return) for use in Sprenkle and expstockror
    functions.
    Derived from r: annual continuously compounded risk-free rate,
    mrp: annual continuously compounded market risk premium from CAPM, and
```

v: annual volatility. All parameters are expressed in decimal form. For example 0.04 means 4%. """"

mu = r + mrp - **0.5** * (v ** **2**)
return mu

JAF Valuation Algorithm: BOM Formulas

The JAF uses a *strategic combination or hybrid of the BOM and BSM models*. As a result, to test the validity of the JAF, we will also need to be able to calculate the expected future value (and returns) of the underlying stock, the call option, and the put option under the BOM model. Fortunately, no additional formulas are required. I already demonstrated how to find the expected future value of the underlying stock or option using the binomial lattice: simply calculate the probability-weighted average of the stock or option across all nodes at a specified point in the future. The probabilities, expected future values, and expected returns will be different for the risk-neutral and risk-averse (CAPM) requirements, but the calculations are straightforward.

While it would be possible to use the Hull probabilities (PrU and PrD) and the UP (U) and DOWN (D) moves from Chapters 2 and 3 to populate the JAF binomial lattice, I elected to use an algebraic variation of binomial formulas published by Cox and Rubinstein (CR) instead. The resulting formulas for the JAF probabilities (PrU and PrD) and the UP (U) and DOWN (D) moves are shown below. I am using the Excel format for these formulas to facilitate experimentation by interested readers. The numerical example below uses the same input values as the risk-neutral and risk-averse, three-year binomial call lattices in Chapter 3 (as shown in Figures 3.5 and 3.6). *Note: the values of σ and r in the binomial formulas below must first be derived using the JVAF and aggregate interest rate formulas presented earlier in this chapter.*

U =EXP(σ*((T/NP)^0.5))
U =EXP(0.20*((3.00/3)^0.5)) = 1.22140

D =EXP(-σ*((T/NP)^0.5))
D =EXP(0.20*((3.00/3)^0.5)) = 0.81873

T = Time to expiration in years
NP = Number of binomial periods (intervals)

$Pr_U = 0.5 + 0.5*((r + MRP - 0.5*(\sigma^2))/\sigma)*((T/NP)^{0.5})$
$Pr_D = 1 - Pr_U$

Risk-Neutral Probabilities:
$Pr_U = 0.5 + 0.5*((0.04 + 0.0 - 0.5*(0.2^2))/0.2)*((3.0/3)^{0.5}) = 55.00\%$
$Pr_D = 1 - 0.55 = 45.00\%$

Risk-Averse Probabilities:
$Pr_U = 0.5 + 0.5*((0.04 + 0.05 - 0.5*(0.2^2))/0.2)*((3.0/3)^{0.5}) = 67.50\%$
$Pr_D = 1 - 0.55 = 32.50\%$

The resulting UP (U) and DOWN (D) moves for each interval are identical to those we calculated in the three-year risk-neutral and risk-averse Hull lattices in Chapter 3. However, the Cox-Rubinstein (CR) probabilities are slightly different. The CR risk-neutral probabilities are 55% and 45%, which are slightly different than the Hull probabilities from Chapter 3 (55.152% and 44.848%). The CR risk-averse probabilities (67.5% and 32.5%) are also slightly different from the Hull probabilities in Chapter 3 (68.404% and 31.596%).

The Hull probabilities are designed to generate one-period expected returns exactly consistent with the returns of the underlying equity investment in the risk-neutral and risk-averse environments. Cox and Rubinstein proved that their binomial valuation framework converged to the BSM as the number of nodes approached infinity.

The new formulas provided here are all that is required to calculate and validate current and future JAF values. We can now proceed with the JAF valuation algorithms for several different situations.

JAF Valuation Algorithm: Current

The JAF valuation algorithm uses *a strategic combination or hybrid of the BOM and BSM models* to calculate theoretically sound and internally consistent current and future expected values of options, by *exploiting the computational advantage of the BSM and the discrete nature of the BOM*. As a result, the specific algorithm for combining the BOM and BSM models to value options will vary, depending on the situation.

There are only three possible types of JAF valuation algorithms required: current, at option expiration, and interim. Risk-neutral and risk-averse valuations will be required for each specified time, but the general algorithms will work for both environments. Only the parameters will differ.

The steps required to implement the JAF algorithm to calculate the current values of the underlying stock, the call option, and the put option are listed below. However, the put option is not shown in the sample calculations.

JAF Valuation Algorithm: Current

1) Use non-linear estimation techniques (including Chapter 9 spreadsheet) OR forecasting models to solve for forward rates and forward volatilities for user-specified periods of varying length.

2) Use JVAF and interest rate aggregation formulas on forward rates and forward volatilities to derive average spot rate and aggregate volatility from the current date until the expiration date of the specific ATM option.

3) Use the resulting average spot rate and aggregate volatility, in conjunction with stock price, strike price, and time to expiration (determined from the number of trading days) in the Black-Scholes-Merton (BSM) model to solve for the option value.

4) Repeat steps 2 and 3 above for every option expiration date of interest – each will have a unique average spot rate and unique aggregate volatility, and all will be theoretically consistent with the entire term structure of interest rates and the entire term structure of volatilities.

The first two steps above will be identical in all three JAF valuation algorithms. The JVAF and interest rate aggregation formulas must always be used to ensure the resulting valuations are theoretically sound and internally consistent. The JAF Current Valuation algorithm is the simplest of the three. By definition, we already know the current underlying stock price. It is an input into the valuation model; it is not a derivative. As a result, we do not need a separate valuation formula for the current stock price.

We showed in Chapters 2 and 3 that the current values of call and put options must be the same in risk-neutral and risk-averse environments. The expected returns and expected future values will be different, but the current option values must be the same in both environments. We confirmed this using the binomial hedge framework, which demonstrated that call and put option values are independent of the probabilities of the UP and DOWN states.

So that leaves us with the BOM/BSM integration method. I will demonstrate this claim in Chapter 6 and in even more detail in the JAF Validation Supplement PDF download that accompanies this book, but the BOM and BSM will generate the same results, given a sufficiently large number of binomial intervals. As a result, we can substitute them or choose between them as desired, depending on their strengths and weaknesses in each situation.

In this case, discrete nodes are not required and I always prefer more efficient computation, so I elected to use the Black-Scholes-Option (BSM) model. Let's use the following example to demonstrate a simplified application of the three (current, expiration, and interim) JAF valuation algorithms: initial stock price (S_0) equal to 100, strike price (K) also equal to 100, time to option expiration (t) equal to two years (2.0), broken into two forward rate and forward volatility periods of equal length (252 trade days each), annualized forward volatilities in period one and two of 10% and 15% respectively, annual forward risk-free rates in forward periods one and two of 4% and 5% respectively, and a Market Risk Premium (MRP) equal to 0% in the risk-neutral environment and 5% in the risk-averse environment.

Example:
Step 2) Use JVAF and interest rate aggregation formulas on forward rates and forward volatilities to derive average spot rate and aggregate volatility from the current date until the expiration date of the specific ATM option.

$$IV_{0,N} = ([NTD_{0,1} (FV_{0,1})^2 + NTD_{1,2} (FV_{1,2})^2 + \ldots NTD_{N-1,N} (FV_{N-1,N})^2] / NTD_{0,N})^{(1/2)}$$
$$IV_{0,2} = ([252 (10\%)^2 + 252 (15)^2] / 504)^{(1/2)} = 12.74755\%$$

$$SR_{0,N} = [NTD_{0,1} (FR_{0,1}) + NTD_{1,2} (FR_{1,2}) + \ldots NTD_{N-1,N} (FR_{N-1,N})] / [NTD_{0,N}]$$
$$SR_{0,2} = [252 (4\%) + 252 (5\%)] / [504] = 4.500\%$$

Step 3) Use the resulting average spot rate and aggregate volatility, in conjunction with stock price, strike price, and time to expiration (determined from the number of trading days) in the Black-Scholes-Merton (BSM) model to solve for the current option value.

Current BSM Call Value = 12.0128
Current BOM Call Value = 12.0128

While we would only use the BSM in the JAF Current Valuation algorithm in practice due to its computational efficiency, I also included the BOM value (over 10,000 intervals) above to demonstrate that it converges to the BSM. The BOM value was calculated from the binomial lattice using the formulas presented earlier in this chapter. The BOM values for the call option are accurate to four decimal places.

JAF Valuation Algorithm: Expiration

The steps required to implement the JAF algorithm to calculate the expected future values of the underlying stock, the call option, and the put option at expiration are listed below. However, the put option is not shown in the sample calculations.

JAF Valuation Algorithm: Expiration

1) Use non-linear estimation techniques (including Chapter 9 spreadsheet) OR forecasting models to solve for forward rates and forward volatilities for user-specified periods of varying length.

2) Use JVAF and interest rate aggregation formulas on forward rates and forward volatilities to derive average spot rate and aggregate volatility from the current date until the expiration date of the specific ATM option.

3) Use the resulting average spot rate and aggregate volatility values to derive the value of mu (μ), which will allow us to calculate the expected future price of the option and the underlying stock.

4) Use the expected rate of return formulas for the underlying stock and for the option (Sprenkle) to calculate the expected future prices for the underlying stock, the call option, and the put option.

5) Repeat steps 2 - 4 above for every option expiration date of interest – each will have a unique average spot rate, unique aggregate volatility, unique value of mu (μ) - and all will be theoretically consistent with the entire term structure of interest rates and the entire term structure of volatilities.

Example:

Step 2) Use JVAF and interest rate aggregation formulas on forward rates and forward volatilities to derive average spot rate and aggregate volatility from the current date until the expiration date of the specific ATM option.

$$IV_{0,N} = ([NTD_{0,1} (FV_{0,1})^2 + NTD_{1,2} (FV_{1,2})^2 + \dots NTD_{N-1,N} (FV_{N-1,N})^2] / NTD_{0,N})^{(1/2)}$$

$$IV_{0,2} = ([252 (10\%)^2 + 252 (15)^2] / 504)^{(1/2)} = 12.74755\%$$

$$SR_{0,N} = [NTD_{0,1} (FR_{0,1}) + NTD_{1,2} (FR_{1,2}) + \dots NTD_{N-1,N} (FR_{N-1,N})] / [NTD_{0,N}]$$

$$SR_{0,2} = [252 (4\%) + 252 (5\%)] / [504] = 4.500\%$$

3) Use the resulting average spot rate and aggregate volatility values to derive the value of mu (μ), which will allow us to calculate the expected future price of the option and the underlying stock.

Risk-Neutral:
$\mu = r + MRP - 0.5 * (\sigma ** 2)$
Risk-Neutral $\mu = 0.045 + 0.00 - 0.5 * (0.1274755 ** 2) = 3.6875\%$

Risk-Averse:
$\mu = r + MRP - 0.5 * (\sigma ** 2)$
Risk-Averse $\mu = 0.04 + 0.05 - 0.5 * (0.1274755 ** 2) = 8.6875\%$

4) Use the expected rate of return formulas for the underlying stock and for the option (Sprenkle) to calculate the expected future prices for the underlying stock, the call option, and the put option (not shown in the example).

$E(S) = S_0 e^{(\mu * t + ((\sigma ** 2) * t) / 2)}$
Risk-Neutral $E(S) = 100e^{(0.036875 * 2 + ((0.1274755 ** 2) * 2.0) / 2)} = 109.417$
Risk-Averse $E(S) = 100e^{(0.086875 * 1 + ((0.20 ** 2) * 1.0) / 2)} = 120.925$

$ER(S) = E(S) / S_0 - 1$
Risk-Neutral $ER(S) = 109.417 / 100.000 - 1 = 9.417\% = 4.5\%$ (CC) for 2 years
Risk-Averse $ER(S) = 120.925 / 100.000 - 1 = 20.925\%$

While we would only use the BSM in the JAF Expiration Valuation algorithm in practice due to its computational efficiency, I also included the BOM value for the expected future value of the stock at option expiration (over 10,000 intervals) to demonstrate that it converges to the BSM model and to the corresponding expected value formula for the underlying stock (presented earlier in this chapter). You will recall that the expected future value of any asset using the binomial equals the probability-weighted future values of all nodes in the lattice. The risk-neutral and risk-averse probabilities will be different and are calculated from the formulas presented earlier in this chapter.

In practice, over 10,000 binomial intervals are not required, but I wanted to demonstrate that any degree of accuracy could be obtained by increasing the number of intervals in the binomial lattice. The resulting BOM values for the expected stock price at option expiration below are accurate to three decimal places.

BOM: Risk-Neutral E(S) = 109.417
BOM: Risk-Averse E(S) = 120.925

Given the stock Beta of 1.0, the expected or required annual continuously compounded return on the stock in the *risk-neutral* environment equals 4.5%. Note: the natural log of (1 + 9.41743%) divided by two years equals 4.5%, the average risk-free spot rate over the two distinct forward rate periods.

R$_S$ = R$_f$ + β * (MRP)
Risk-Neutral R$_S$ = 0.045 + 1.0 * (0.0%) = 4.50% continuously compounded

The expected or required annual continuously compounded return on the stock in the *risk-averse* environment equals 9.5%. Note: the natural log of (1 + 20.92496%) divided by two years equals 9.5%, the average annual required (risk-averse) return over the two distinct forward periods.

R$_S$ = R$_f$ + β * (MRP)
Risk-Averse R$_S$ = 0.045 + 1.0 * (5.0%) = 9.50% continuously compounded

Continuing with Step 4, we use Sprenkle to calculate the expected values of the call option at expiration in the risk-neutral and risk-averse environments, based on the average spot rate and aggregate volatility over the two future one-year periods (Figures 5.4 and 5.5 below).

Sprenkle Calculation 2-yr JAF (Risk-Neutral):

$$E(C) = 100e^{\left(0.036875 + \frac{0.1274755^2}{2}\right)2}0.7222 - 100(0.6588) = 13.144$$

$$b_1 = \frac{\ln\left(\frac{100}{100}\right) + \left(0.036875 + 0.1274755^2\right)2}{0.1274755\sqrt{2}} = 0.5894$$

$$b_2 = 0.5894 - 0.1274755\sqrt{2} = 0.4091$$

Figure 5.4

Sprenkle Calculation 2-yr JAF(Risk-Averse):

$$E(C) = 100e^{\left(0.086875 + \frac{0.1274755^2}{2}\right)2}0.8737 - 100(0.8324) = 22.410$$

$$b_1 = \frac{\ln\left(\frac{100}{100}\right) + (0.086875 + 0.1274755^2)2}{0.1274755\sqrt{2}} = 1.1441$$

$$b_2 = 1.1441 - 0.1274755\sqrt{2} = 0.9638$$

Figure 5.5

From the JAF Current Valuation Algorithm, we know that the current value of the 2-year call option is 12.0128. That allows us to calculate the expected returns for the call option in the risk-neutral and risk-averse environments.

ER(C) = E(C) / C$_0$ - 1
Risk-Neutral ER(C) = 13.144 / 12.0128 – 1 = 9.4167% = 4.50% (CC) for 2 years
Risk-Averse ER(C) = 22.410 / 12.0128 – 1 = 86.547% = 31.12% (CC) for 2 years

As we would expect, the annual continuously compounded return of the call option in the risk-neutral environment exactly equals the risk-free spot rate over the two-year period. In addition, the required or expected return on the call option is much higher in the risk-averse environment due to the high Beta of the call option. However, since the model is continuous and Beta changes continuously (and I have not provided a formula for the average Beta of the call option in the BSM), we cannot confirm the risk-averse return of the call option with the CAPM formula. However, I will further validate the JAF results in the risk-neutral and risk-averse environments in Chapter 6 and in the JAF Validation Supplement PDF.

While we would only use the BSM in the JAF Expiration Valuation algorithm in practice due to its computational efficiency, I also included the BOM value for the expected future value of the call option at expiration (over 10,000 intervals) to demonstrate that it converges to the BSM model and to the corresponding Sprenkle expected value. You will recall that the expected future value of any asset using the binomial equals the probability-weighted future values of all nodes in the lattice. The risk-neutral and risk-averse probabilities will be different and are calculated from the formulas presented earlier in this chapter. The resulting BOM expected values of the call option at expiration are accurate to three decimal places.

BOM: Risk-Neutral E(C) = 13.144
BOM: Risk-Averse E(C) = 22.410

JAF Valuation Algorithm: Interim

The steps required to implement the JAF algorithm to calculate the values of the underlying stock, the call option, and the put option *on any interim date* (before option expiration) are listed below. However, the put option is not shown in the sample calculations. Due to the unique nature of calculating interim values before option expiration with different forward volatilities and forward risk-free rates, the JAF Interim Valuation Algorithm will require a hybrid combination of the BOM and BSM models.

JAF Valuation: Interim
1) Use non-linear estimation techniques (including Chapter 9 spreadsheet) OR forecasting models to solve for forward rates and forward volatilities for user-specified periods of varying length.
2) Use JVAF and interest rate aggregation formulas on forward rates and forward volatilities to derive average spot rates and aggregate volatilities *for two periods*: 1) from the current date until the desired interim valuation date, and 2) from the desired interim valuation date to the expiration date of the specific ATM option.
3) Use the resulting average spot rate and aggregate volatility values for the *first* period and the BOM formulas from this chapter to generate the future stock prices and probabilities for each terminal node of the binomial lattice (ending on the interim date).
4) For each terminal node of the binomial lattice (at the interim date), use the BOM stock price from the lattice and the resulting average spot rate and aggregate volatility values for the *second* period to calculate the *Black-Scholes Merton (BSM)* value of the option.
5) Use the resulting *BSM* option values for each terminal node of the binomial lattice (at the interim date) and the *BOM* probabilities at each terminal node to calculate the probability-weighted values of the stock and the option.
6) Repeat steps 2 - 5 above for every option expiration date of interest.

The JAF interim valuation algorithm is more complex. Calculating interim values requires average spot rates and aggregate volatilities for *both* periods, because we will be applying valuation models to both periods. Due to the use of average spot rates and aggregate volatilities in both periods, we need to use the discrete *BOM* for the *first* period. That is the only way we can integrate two different valuation models for the two distinct periods (before and after the interim date).

Fortunately, we can still use the more computationally efficient *BSM* in the *second* period. This ensures that we only need to run the less efficient BOM once for each option. In my extreme example, we would need to run the BSM 10,000 times (once for each BOM terminal node on the interim date), but the algorithm still runs almost instantaneously on my high-powered laptop. It would not be practical to run the BOM 10,000 times for each option.

Note, we will never need to use more than two periods to calculate the expected value of any stock or option on any interim date. Even if we had 24 monthly forward rates and forward volatilities over the two-year period, we would still be able to calculate the average spot rate and aggregate volatilities for the periods before and after the interim date.

Let's proceed with the same example to demonstrate a simplified application of the JAF Interim Valuation algorithm: initial stock price (S_0) equal to 100, strike price (K) also equal to 100, time to option expiration (t) equal to two years (2.0), broken into two forward rate and forward volatility periods of equal length (252 trade days each), annualized forward volatilities in period one and two of 10% and 15% respectively, annual forward risk-free rates in forward periods one and two of 4% and 5% respectively, and a Market Risk Premium (MRP) equal to 0% in the risk-neutral environment and 5% in the risk-averse environment. Note: changing the MRP does not affect the current value of the any of the instruments (Stock, Call, or Put), so we can use the easier risk-neutral valuation framework exclusively.

Due to the large numbers of nodes, numerical examples will not be shown for most formulas in this section. Instead, the results from the JAF Python code will be provided.

Example:
2) Use JVAF and interest rate aggregation formulas on forward rates and forward volatilities to derive average spot rates and aggregate volatilities *for two periods*: 1) from the current date until the desired interim valuation date, and 2) from the desired interim valuation date to the expiration date of the specific ATM option.

In the example below, the aggregation formulas are not necessary, because there are two forward periods and two valuation periods. However, if we had more forward period than valuation periods, we would use the JVAF and interest rate aggregation formulas to calculate the average spot rates and aggregate volatilities for each of the two valuation periods.

$$ESR_{n,N} = [NTD_{n,n+1}(FR_{n,n+1}) + NTD_{n+1,n+2} (FR_{n+1,n+2})+ ... NTD_{N-1,N} (FR_{N-1,N})]/(NTD_{n,N})$$

$ESR_{0,1} = 4.00\%$

$ESR_{1,2} = 5.00\%$

$$EIV_{n,N} = ([NTD_{n,n+1} (FV_{n,n+1})^2 + NTD_{n+1,n+2} (FV_{n+1,n+2})^2 + ... NTD_{N-1,N} (FV_{N-1,N})^2]/(NTD_{n,N}))^{(0.5)}$$

$IV_{0,1} = 10.00\%$

$IV_{1,2} = 15.00\%$

3) Use the resulting average spot rate and aggregate volatility values for the *first* period and the BOM formulas from this chapter to generate the future stock prices and probabilities for each terminal node of the binomial lattice (ending on the interim date).

4) For each terminal node of the binomial lattice (at the interim date), use the BOM stock price from the lattice and the resulting average spot rate and aggregate volatility values for the *second* period to calculate the *BSM* value of the option.

5) Use the resulting *BSM* option values for each terminal node of the binomial lattice (at the interim date) and the *BOM* probabilities at each terminal node to calculate the probability-weighted values of the stock and the option.

JAF Interim Valuation: Stock

As I explained above, due to the large numbers of interim nodes, numerical examples will not be shown for steps 3 – 5 above. Instead, the results from the JAF Interim Valuation Python code are provided for the risk-neutral and risk-averse interim stock and call option values at the end of one year.

Since we needed the stock prices and probabilities at each terminal node on the interim date to calculate the future option value, I used the same values to calculate the probability-weighted future value of the stock on the interim valuation date. If we had derived μ for the JAF Interim Valuation algorithm, we could have used the continuous formula instead:

$$E(S) = S_0 e^{(\mu \, * \, t \, + \, ((\sigma \, ** \, 2) \, * \, t) \, / \, 2)}$$
Risk-Neutral $E(S_1)$ = 104.081
Risk-Averse $E(S_1)$ = 109.417

JAF Interim Returns: Stock Period 1
$ER(S_1) = E(S_1) / S_0 - 1$
Risk-Neutral $ER(S_1)$ = 104.081 / 100.000 − 1 = 4.081% = 4.0% (cc)
Risk-Averse $ER(S_1)$ = 109.417 / 100.000 − 1 = 9.417% = 9.0% (cc)

Given the stock Beta of 1.0, the expected or required annual continuously compounded return on the stock in the *risk-neutral* environment equals 4.0% *in the first period*. Note: the natural log of (1 + 4.081%) equals 4.0%, the average continuously compounded risk-free rate in the first forward period.

$R_S = R_f + \beta * (MRP)$
Risk-Neutral R_S = 0.040 + 1.0 * (0.0%) = 4.00% continuously compounded

The expected or required annual continuously compounded return on the stock in the *risk-averse* environment equals 9.0% *in the first period*. Note: the natural log of (1 + 9.417%) equals 9.0%, the average continuously compounded annual required (risk-averse) return in the first forward period.

$R_S = R_f + \beta * (MRP)$
Risk-Averse R_S = 0.040 + 1.0 * (5.0%) = 9.00% continuously compounded

JAF Interim Returns: Stock Period 2
Since we already used the JAF Expiration Algorithm above to calculate the expected values of the stock at expiration, we can use these values to calculate the expected returns on the stock in the *second period* as well. The *second period* begins on the interim date and ends on the expiration date, which corresponds exactly to the second forward period in our example. The resulting returns will be enlightening.

$ER(S_2) = E(S_2) / S_1 - 1$
Risk-Neutral $ER(S_2)$ = 109.417 / 104.081 − 1 = 5.127% = 5.0% (cc)
Risk-Averse $ER(S_2)$ = 120.925 / 109.417 − 1 = 10.518% = 10.0% (cc)

Given the stock Beta of 1.0, the expected or required annual continuously compounded return on the stock in the *risk-neutral* environment equals 5.0% *in the second period*. Note: the natural log of (1 + 5.127%) equals 5.0%, the average continuously compounded risk-free rate in the *second* forward period.

$R_S = R_f + \beta * (MRP)$
Risk-Neutral R_S = 0.050 + 1.0 * (0.0%) = 5.00% continuously compounded

The expected or required annual continuously compounded return on the stock in the *risk-averse* environment equals 10.0% *in the second period*. Note: the natural log of (1 + 10.518%) equals 10.0%, the average continuously compounded annual required (risk-averse) return in the *second* forward period.

$R_S = R_f + \beta * (MRP)$
Risk-Averse R_S = 0.050 + 1.0 * (5.0%) = 10.00% continuously compounded

The JAF Interim Valuation algorithm produces expected risk-neutral and risk-averse stock values that are exactly consistent with CAPM, using forward term structures with different rates and volatilities in both periods.

JAF Interim Valuation: Call Option
Risk-Neutral $E(C_1)$ = 12.503
Risk-Averse $E(C_1)$ = 16.593

JAF Interim Returns: Call Option Period 1
$ER(C_1) = E(C_1) / C_0 - 1$
Risk-Neutral $ER(C_1)$ = 12.503 / 12.013 – 1 = 4.081% = 4.00% (cc)
Risk-Averse $ER(C_1)$ = 16.593 / 12.013 – 1 = 38.123% = 32.30% (cc)

As we would expect, the annual continuously compounded return of the call option in the risk-neutral environment exactly equals the risk-free spot rate over the first period (4%). In addition, the required or expected return on the call option is much higher in the risk-averse environment due to the high Beta of the call option. Due to the continuously changing Beta of the call option, I will not use CAPM to evaluate the call option returns in the first period.

JAF Interim Returns: Call Option Period 2

Since we already used the JAF Expiration Algorithm above to calculate the expected values of the call option at expiration, we can use these values to calculate the expected returns on the call option in the *second period* as well. The *second period* begins on the interim date and ends on the expiration date, which corresponds exactly to the second forward period in our example.

$ER(C_2) = E(C_2) / C_1 - 1$
Risk-Neutral $ER(C_2)$ = 13.144 / 12.503 – 1 = 5.127% = 5.000% (cc)
Risk-Averse $ER(C_2)$ = 22.410 / 16.593 – 1 = 35.060% = 30.056% (cc)

As we would expect, the annual continuously compounded return of the call option in the risk-neutral environment exactly equals the risk-free spot rate over the second period (5%). In addition, the required or expected return on the call option is much higher in the risk-averse environment due to the high Beta of the call option. Due to the continuously changing Beta of the call option, I will not use CAPM to evaluate the call option returns in the first period.

The JAF Interim Valuation algorithm produces expected risk-neutral and risk-averse interim call values that are exactly consistent with the entire term structure of forward rates and forward volatilities.

JAF Greek Algorithm

The option Greeks are the primary risk management tools employed in option trading. An understanding of the Greeks is a prerequisite for efficiently designing, evaluating, and adjusting option strategies and is often the key to success as an option trader.

So, what are the Greeks and how can we calculate the corresponding JAF Greek metrics - given the unique integration of the forward term structures of interest rates and volatilities in the JAF? The Greeks are sensitivity measures that quantify how much one value of interest changes in response to a standardized change in an explanatory variable. There are many different Greeks, but I will limit the JAF formulas and numerical examples to the principal Greeks used in option trading: Delta, Gamma, Theta, Vega, and Rho. However, *the JAF Option Greeks algorithm presented in this section can be applied to calculate any of the Greek metrics.*

I have written about the Greeks extensively in all of my previous books, so my introduction here will be brief. Delta represents the change in the price of the option in response to a one-unit change (increase) in the price of the underlying stock. Gamma represents the change in the Delta of an option for the same one-unit change (increase) in the price of the underlying stock. Theta is slightly different. Theta represents the change in the price of the option for a one day *decrease* in the time remaining to expiration. I always use trade days in all of my volatility and risk metric calculations and Theta is no exception.

Vega is typically expressed as the change in the value of the option for a *one-percent* (not one unit) change in the annualized volatility. Evaluating a *one-unit* change in the annualized volatility would not be useful in practice (e.g., from 20% to 120%) Similarly, Rho is typically expressed as the change in the value of the option for a *one-percent* (not one unit) change in the annualized, continuously compounded risk-free rate. Again, a *one-unit* change in the risk-free interest rate (e.g., from 4% to 104%) would be completely unrealistic and the resulting value of Rho would be useless as a practical risk measure.

The Black-Scholes-Merton (BSM) model is continuous and is continuously differentiable. For those of you who are familiar with calculus, the BSM Greeks are *similar* to partial derivatives of the BSM valuation equations for call and put options. I used the word *similar* because Theta is typically expressed as the change in the value of the option for a *one-day* decrease in the time to expiration.

Partial derivatives are interpreted as the change in value for an instantaneous *increase* in the explanatory variable, holding all other explanatory variables constant. As I explained above, the BSM actual partial derivatives for Vega and Rho are expressed per *one-unit* change in the annualized volatility or risk-free rate, not the typical *one-percent* change used in practice. As a result, the BSM partial derivatives need to be scaled accordingly. The JAF Greeks require a similar scaling factor.

Before I continue, please note that all of the Greeks can be calculated for the underlying stock, the riskless investment, riskless borrowing, as well as for call and put options as described above. Put/Call parity holds for valuation as well as for Greeks, which can be verified using the results from applying the JAF Greeks algorithm.

As I described in the preceding section, Step 2 of the JAF Current Valuation algorithm first requires us to use the JVAF and interest rate aggregation formulas on forward rates and forward volatilities to derive average spot rate and aggregate volatility from the current date until the expiration date of the specific ATM option. Step 3 of the JAF Current Valuation algorithm then requires us to use resulting average spot rate and aggregate volatility, in conjunction with stock price, strike price, and time to expiration (determined from the number of trading days) in the Black-Scholes-Merton (BSM) model to solve for the option value.

To calculate the *current* Greeks for the JAF, we are interested in the changes in *current* values, hence our interest in the JAF *Current* Valuation algorithm. Even though the JAF Current Valuation algorithm eventually uses the continuous BSM model, the addition of the JVAF and interest rate aggregation step effectively changes this problem from continuous to discrete. So, how do we calculate Greeks for a discrete valuation process?

The key insight is that a partial derivative simply represents the slope or rate-of-change of a function. A slope can be expressed as the change in the variable of interest in the numerator, divided by the change in the explanatory variable in the denominator. The resulting formulas for the JAF Greeks are shown below for call options, put options, and for the underlying stock. All formulas are properly scaled to be consistent with the practical conventions described above.

Call Option Greeks:

$Delta_C = (C_U - C_D)/(S_U - S_D)$

$Gamma_C = (Delta_{CU} - Delta_{CD})/(S_U - S_D)$

$Theta_C = - (C_0 - C_D)/(NTD_0 - NTD_D)$ *Note the negative sign*

$Vega_C = [(C_U - C_D)/(\sigma_U - \sigma_D)]/100$

$Rho_C = [(C_U - C_D)/(r_U - r_D)]/100$

Put Option Greeks:

$Delta_P = (P_U - P_D)/(S_U - S_D)$

$Gamma_P = (Delta_{PU} - Delta_{PD})/(S_U - S_D)$

$Theta_P = - (P_0 - P_D)/(NTD_0 - NTD_D)$

$Vega_P = [(P_U - P_D)/(\sigma_U - \sigma_D)]/100$

$Rho_P = [(P_U - P_D)/(r_U - r_D)]/100$

Stock Greeks:

$Delta_S = (S_U - S_D)/(S_U - S_D) = 1.0$

$Gamma_S = (Delta_{SU} - Delta_{SD})/(S_U - S_D) = 0.0$

$Theta_S = - (S_0 - S_D)/(NTD_0 - NTD_D) = 0.0$ *per independence assumption*

$Vega_S = [(S_U - S_D)/(\sigma_U - \sigma_D)]/100 = 0.0$ *per independence assumption*

$Rho_S = [(S_U - S_D)/(r_U - r_D)]/100 = 0.0$ *per independence assumption*

Rather than provide numerical examples with the formulas above, I will provide tables later in this section that will include the respective UP and DOWN values in the numerator and denominator for each JAF Greek calculation, as well as the resulting JAF Greek value and BSM Greek value for comparison purposes.

The steps required to implement the JAF algorithm to calculate the current JAF Greeks values for the call option and the put option are listed below.

JAF Greek Algorithm: Current

1) Use non-linear estimation techniques (including Chapter 9 spreadsheet) OR forecasting models to solve for forward rates and forward volatilities for user-specified periods of varying length.

2) Use JVAF and interest rate aggregation formulas on forward rates and forward volatilities to derive average spot rate and aggregate volatility from the current date until the expiration date of the specific ATM option, and modify these values as required for the UP and DOWN moves in the numerator and denominator of each JAF Greek formula described above.

3) Use the resulting average spot rate and aggregate volatility, in conjunction with stock price, strike price, and time-to-expiration in the Black-Scholes-Merton (BSM) model to solve for UP and DOWN values required for the JAF Greek formulas provided above.

4) Repeat steps 2 and 3 above for every option expiration date of interest – each will have a unique average spot rate and unique aggregate volatility, and all will be theoretically consistent with the entire term structure of interest rates and the entire term structure of volatilities.

Let's proceed with the same example used throughout this chapter to demonstrate a simplified application of the JAF Greeks algorithm: initial stock price (S_0) equal to 100, strike price (K) also equal to 100, time to option expiration (t) equal to two years (2.0), broken into two forward rate and forward volatility periods of equal length (252 trade days each), annualized forward volatilities in period one and two of 10% and 15% respectively, annual forward risk-free rates in forward periods one and two of 4% and 5% respectively, and a Market Risk Premium (MRP) equal to 0% in the risk neutral environment and 5% in the risk-averse environment. Note: changing the MRP does not affect the current value of the any of the instruments (Stock, Call, or Put) and therefore does not change the JAF Greeks.

The JAF Greek tables for the call and put options derived from the above example are shown below in Figures 5.6 and 5.7 respectively. There are a number of items to note in Figures 5.6 and 5.7. For each Greek calculation, the change in the item of interest is always in the numerator and is derived using the JAF Greeks Algorithm described above. In the case of Delta,

Theta, Vega, and Rho, the item of interest will be the change in the *value of the option*. In the case of Gamma, the variable of interest will be the change in *Delta*. However, for Theta, the change will be one-directional, so the UP value will represent the current value of the option.

The denominator in all of the JAF Greek formulas represents the change in the *explanatory variable* that causes the change in the item of interest in the numerator. For Delta and Gamma, the explanatory variable will be the underlying stock price, which will reflect a plus (UP) and minus (DOWN) one-unit (one dollar) change.

The denominators of the JAF Vega and Rho formulas represent the change in the annualized volatility and annualized risk-free rate respectively. Each reflect a 1% UP move and a 1% DOWN move rather than a one-unit change. This is the reason both JAF Greek formulas require the 1/100 scaling factor.

The UP and DOWN values for the numerator and denominator (for each of the Greek formulas) are provided in the tables below, as are the resulting JAF and BSM Greek metrics.

	Call Option	Delta	Gamma	Theta*	Vega(1)	Vega(2)	Vega(1&2)	Rho(1)	Rho(2)	Rho(1&2)
Greeks	JAF Greek	0.722	0.019	-0.013	0.186	0.279	0.465	0.602	0.602	1.203
Greeks	BSM Greek	0.722	0.019	-0.017	NA	NA	0.474	NA	NA	1.204
Numerator	UP*	12.744	0.740	12.013	12.206	12.296	12.483	12.621	12.621	13.241
Numerator	DOWN	11.300	0.703	12.000	11.834	11.738	11.553	11.417	11.417	10.835
Denominator	UP*	101.00	101.00	252	11.000%	16.000%	13.748%	5.000%	6.000%	5.500%
Denominator	DOWN	99.00	99.00	251	9.000%	14.000%	11.748%	3.000%	4.000%	3.500%

Figure 5.6

	Put Option	Delta	Gamma	Theta*	Vega(1)	Vega(2)	Vega(1&2)	Rho(1)	Rho(2)	Rho(1&2)
Greeks	JAF Greek	-0.278	0.019	0.001	0.186	0.279	0.465	-0.312	-0.312	-0.625
Greeks	BSM Greek	-0.278	0.019	0.000	NA	NA	0.474	NA	NA	-0.624
Numerator	UP*	3.137	-0.260	3.406	3.599	3.689	3.876	3.105	3.105	2.825
Numerator	DOWN	3.693	-0.297	3.407	3.227	3.132	2.946	3.729	3.729	4.074
Denominator	UP*	101.00	101.00	252	11.000%	16.000%	13.748%	5.000%	6.000%	5.500%
Denominator	DOWN	99.00	99.00	251	9.000%	14.000%	11.748%	3.000%	4.000%	3.500%

Figure 5.7

Technically, the BSM Greek calculations above require the JVAF aggregate volatility and average spot rate values to be derived first from the respective forward term structures. I used the resulting aggregate volatility and spot rates in the BSM Greeks calculations above. As you can see in the tables, the Delta and Gamma values for the JAF match the corresponding BSM Greeks. However, the JAF Theta of the call option (-0.013) is materially different from the BSM Theta (-0.017). This may appear to be a small error, but these Greek values are on a per share (not per contract basis). The magnitude of the BSM Theta is overstated by over 30%! Note: the BSM value is incorrect, not the JAF value. The BSM Theta assumes that interest rates are constant over the life of each option. Hence, the BSM Theta calculations for all options are incorrect and inconsistent.

Remember, the *same* interest rate and *same* expected volatility should apply to the *same* future period, and *different* interest rates and *different* expected volatilities should apply to *different* future periods (JAF). Due to their constant interest rate and volatility assumptions, the BOM and BSM implicitly apply *different* interest rates and *different* implied volatilities to the *same* period, and apply the *same* interest rates and *same* expected volatilities to *different* periods.

In the JAF Greek tables above, note that there are three different Vega calculations: Vega(1), Vega(2), and Vega(12). There are also three different Rho calculations: Rho(1), Rho(2), and Rho(12). All three values are derived using the multi-step JAF Greek algorithm described above. Vega(1) and Rho(1) represent the changes in the values of the options per 1% change in the annualized *forward* volatility and *forward* rate for the *first* period alone. Similarly, Vega(2) and Rho(2) represent the changes in the values of the options per 1% change in the annualized *forward* volatility and *forward* rate for the *second* period alone.

For the first time, the JAF Greek algorithm allows us to calculate all of the *partial-Greeks* for Vega and Rho, for any number of forward periods of varying length. All of these new *partial-Greek* measures are theoretically correct and internally consistent. They each quantify the instantaneous change in the option value for a 1% change in the annualized forward volatility or forward rate for a single forward period, holding all other forward volatilities and forward rates constant.

In Chapter 7, I will expand the partial-Vega calculations to compute True Vega, which accounts for the fact that all forward volatilities do not change by the same amount in practice – due to time-dependent sensitivities to mean-reversion. I developed the mean reversion sensitivity model using over 15 years of daily option volatility data for the SPX, NDX, and RUT. In Chapter 7, I will demonstrate how I integrated the resulting mean-reversion model with the JVAF partial Vega algorithm to calculate one of the most accurate and practical measures of True Vega to date.

Finally, Vega(1&2) and Rho(1&2) represent the changes in the values of the options for simultaneous 1% changes in the annualized *forward* volatilities and *forward* rates in *both the first and second periods*. Vega(1&2) and Rho(1&2) are therefore comparable to the typical BSM measures of sensitivity to changes in the annualized volatility (Vega) and interest rates (Rho) *over the life of the option*. In practice, the above BSM Vega(1&2) and

Rho(1&2) Greeks require the JVAF and JAF interest rate aggregation formulas to be applied first, but I still included the BSM values to allow comparison with the JAF Greeks.

I will provide more JAF Greek examples in Chapter 8 (JAF: Abridged Greek Results). More comprehensive JAF Valuation and Greek results are available in the JAF Validation Supplement PDF (see Resource Chapter for download link address).

JAF VIX Algorithm

One part of the JAF objective is to use the complete term structure of unique volatilities to calculate theoretically sound and internally consistent, current and future volatility index (VIX) values. So far, this chapter has been devoted to options. Fortunately, we can use the same JVAF formulas we used throughout this chapter to calculate the current value of any volatility index and the current value of any VIX futures contract. As was the case with JAF option valuation, we could use market-implied forward volatilities or volatilities derived from forecasting models to estimate the value of any VIX instrument.

The first JVAF formula below (IV) is used to solve for the current value of any volatility index. The second formula below (EIV) is used to solve for the value of any VIX futures contract and represents the expected aggregate volatility on the expiration date of the VIX futures contract.

$$IV_{0,N} = ([NTD_{0,1} (FV_{0,1})^2 + NTD_{1,2} (FV_{1,2})^2 + \ldots NTD_{N-1,N} (FV_{N-1,N})^2] / NTD_{0,N})^{(1/2)}$$

$$EIV_{n,N} = ([NTD_{n,n+1} (FV_{n,n+1})^2 + NTD_{n+1,n+2} (FV_{n+1,n+2})^2 + \ldots NTD_{N-1,N} (FV_{N-1,N})^2] / (NTD_{n,N}))^{(0.5)}$$

The use of the JVAF formulas ensures the resulting VIX derivative values are theoretically correct and consistent with the term structure of volatilities used to value ATM options. However, there is one slight addition necessary to value VIX derivatives. As noted throughout this chapter, the JVAF uses ATM forward volatilities, which means that I did not include a model of the vertical skew for use in the JAF option valuation. That topic is beyond the scope of this book.

However, I did model the effects of the vertical skew in the JAF calculation of VIX derivatives. As I mentioned earlier, *included with this book is an Excel spreadsheet that uses ATM implied volatilities and volatility index prices to solve for the market-implied forward volatilities.* The spreadsheet then uses the resulting *market-implied* forward volatilities to calculate the relative values of ATM options and corresponding volatility futures across the entire term structure of volatilities. Chapter 9 provides an overview of how to use this spreadsheet. In that spreadsheet, I modeled and integrated the effects of the vertical skew on the VIX calculations. I will explain this further in Chapter 9.

JAF Advantages

The Johnson Aggregation Framework (JAF) corrects the serious deficiencies of the BSM and BOM by eliminating the invalid constant interest rate and constant volatility assumptions, allowing us to solve for and use the complete term structure of unique interest rates and the complete term structure of unique volatilities. I have restated the JAF Objective below, followed by a list of the JAF Advantages that have been demonstrated throughout this chapter.

JAF Objective:
Design an objective framework that employs a user-specified Market Risk Premium in conjunction with the complete term structure of unique interest rates and the complete term structure of unique volatilities to calculate theoretically sound and internally consistent: current and future option values, current and future Greeks, and current and future volatility index (VIX) values.

JAF Advantages:
1) Theoretically sound and internally consistent framework
2) Utilizes the complete term structure of unique interest rates
    - Accommodates forward rates estimated from market prices or forecasted with a model
        - Accommodates user-specified number of periods
        - Accommodates periods of variable length
3) Utilizes the complete term structure of unique volatilities
    - Accommodates volatilities estimated from market prices or forecasted with a model
        - Accommodates user-specified number of periods
        - Accommodates periods of variable length
4) Accommodates a user-specified Market Risk Premium (MRP): risk-neutral or risk-averse

5) Calculates current and future option and VIX valuations and Greeks
6) Computationally efficient/practical

JAF Summary

Market forces (supply and demand) continuously interact through financial markets to determine *different* equilibrium risk-free interest rates and *different* levels of expected volatility *for each future period*. This results in an ever-evolving term structure of unique interest rates and term structure of unique volatilities.

To be theoretically correct and internally consistent, the *same* interest rate and *same* expected volatility should apply to the *same* future period and *different* interest rates and *different* expected volatilities should apply to *different* future periods. Due to their constant interest rate and volatility assumptions, the BOM and BSM implicitly apply *different* interest rates and *different* implied volatilities to the *same* period, and apply the *same* interest rates and *same* expected volatilities to *different* periods.

This means that current and future option values calculated by the BOM and BSM are incorrect and inconsistent, as are the current and future Greek values (risk metrics), which are derived from these invalid assumptions!

This chapter fully explained the Johnson Aggregation Framework (JAF), the JAF Objective, the JAF advantages, and the JAF principal components:

- Interest Rate Aggregation Formula
- Johnson Volatility Aggregation Formula (JVAF)
- JAF Valuation Algorithm: BSM Formulas
- JAF Valuation Algorithm: BSM Python Functions
- JAF Valuation Algorithm: BOM Formulas
- JAF Valuation Algorithm: Current
- JAF Valuation Algorithm: Expiration
- JAF Valuation Algorithm: Interim
- JAF Greek Algorithm
- JAF VIX Algorithm

The JAF corrects the most serious deficiencies of the BSM and BOM by eliminating the invalid constant interest rate and constant volatility assumptions, allowing us to solve for and use the complete term structure of unique interest rates and the complete term structure of unique volatilities. The resulting current and future option values, VIX values, and Greeks are all theoretically sound and internally consistent. This chapter is very detailed and includes all of the algorithms and formulas with sufficient documentation to allow the dedicated reader to implement the JAF in practice.

6) JAF: ABRIDGED VALUATION RESULTS

This chapter will provide an abridged version of the JAF valuation (and rate of return) results. Before we can review the JAF abridged Greek results in Chapter 8, I will need to introduce True Vega and partial Greeks in Chapter 7. Comprehensive JAF Valuation and Greek results are available in the JAF Validation Supplement PDF (see Resource Chapter for download link address). The purpose of the JAF Validation Supplement is to provide a complete, logical progression of test cases that demonstrate the validity of the JAF. All of the values in the JAF supplement and in this book are actual output values from a Python application of the JAF algorithm - exported to Excel for formatting purposes.

The JAF Validation Supplement is divided into nine sections, each with multiple groups of exhibits. The first seven sections are covered in this chapter and the last two sections are included in Chapter 8. Each of the validation sections in this book will include the objective or objectives of the section, plus one or more validation exhibits from the JAF Validation supplement (with the same numbering system). For each of the validation exhibits included in this book, I will explain how the validation results fit into the context of the JAF Validation plan, referencing specific values when it would be instructive.

As was the case in the last chapter, the validation results assume that all monthly options expire at the close on the last trade-day of the month and that there are exactly 21 trade days in every month. Given this assumption, interest rates, volatilities, and option expiration dates will all coincide perfectly with calendar months. This will allow us to discuss hypothetical interest rates and volatilities for specific calendar month examples, without any confusion regarding whether we are referring to the period before or after the standard monthly option expiration date on the third Friday of the month. *Note: this assumption is only included to avoid confusion and is NOT required for the JAF, which can accommodate any number of periods, each with a variable number of trade days.*

JAF Validation Plan

The JAF validation plan is designed to demonstrate that the JAF satisfies every element of its objective.

JAF Objective:

Design an objective framework that employs a user-specified Market Risk Premium in conjunction with the complete term structure of unique interest rates and the complete term structure of unique volatilities to calculate theoretically sound and internally consistent: current and future option values, current and future Greeks, and current and future volatility index (VIX) values.

Each of the validation sections is designed to demonstrate one or more of the following elements:

Validation Plan Elements (VPE): (Multiple forward interest rate and volatility periods)

1) Demonstrate that aggregate input values derived from the Interest Rate Aggregation Formula and the Johnson Volatility Aggregation Formula (JVAF), applied to multiple forward periods, generate theoretically correct and consistent results when used with the BOM, BSM, and the JAF combined BOM & BSM model.

2) Demonstrate that the BOM converges to the BSM as the number of intervals is increased and that the resulting BOM error can be made arbitrarily small by increasing the number of binomial intervals as desired.

3) Demonstrate that the JAF current, interim, and expiration valuation algorithms generate theoretically correct and internally consistent current, interim, and expiration *values*.

4) Demonstrate that the values derived from the JAF current, interim, and expiration valuation algorithms generate theoretically correct and internally consistent *rates of return*.

5) Demonstrate that the values derived from the JAF current, interim, and expiration valuation algorithms generate theoretically correct and internally consistent current and future *Greeks*.

JAF Validation: Section I

Section I Objectives:
1) The first objective of Section I is to demonstrate that the option present values, option future values, stock present value, stock future value, option returns, and stock returns derived from the discrete BOM all converge to the corresponding BSM (continuous lognormal) model values, for both risk-neutral and risk-averse environments, as the number of binomial intervals increases.

2) The second objective of Section I is to demonstrate that for a sufficiently large number of binomial intervals, the above BOM values are almost identical to the corresponding BSM values over a wide range of: stock prices, implied volatilities, interest rates, and risk premiums.

Section I: Comparison of Binomial to BSM - Single Period Analysis; various: number of intervals, stock prices, volatilities, interest rates, and risk premiums
Group 1) Binomial Risk-Neutral: Even intervals converge to BSM present value & future value as number of intervals increases

Group 2) Binomial Risk-Neutral: Odd intervals converge to BSM present value & future value as number of intervals increases

Group 3) Binomial Risk-Neutral: N & N+1 intervals converge to BSM present value & future value as number of intervals increases, errors partially offset

Group 4) Binomial Risk-Premium: 5%, 8192 N & N+1 intervals converge to BSM present value & future value as number of intervals increases, errors partially offset

Group 5) Binomial Risk-Neutral: 8192 N & N+1 intervals converge to BSM for range of stock price & strike price values (1000 – 2875)

Group 6) Binomial Risk-Neutral: 8192 N & N+1 intervals converge to BSM for range of implied volatilities (20% to 80%)

Group 7) Binomial Risk-Neutral: 8192 N & N+1 intervals converge to BSM for range of interest rates (4% to 19%)

Group 8) Binomial Risk-Neutral: 8192 N & N+1 intervals converge to BSM for range of risk premiums (0% to 7.5%)

Section I: Group and Exhibit Structure

The complete set of validation groups and exhibits from Section I is available in the JAF Validation Supplement. One or more *select* exhibits will be included in each section to highlight a few key elements of the validation process. All groups and exhibits from Section I of the JAF Validation Supplement are described below, so please pay particular attention to the descriptions of the *select* sample exhibits examined in this section: Exhibits 3.1, 3.5, 4.2, 4.6, 6.1, and 6.5.

There are eight groups of exhibits in Section I, each with a different set of input values, assumptions, and validation objectives. The first three validation groups compare the risk-neutral BOM to the risk-neutral BSM results over a range of binomial intervals, and demonstrates the effectiveness of combining the results from an odd and even number of binomial intervals. Group 4 validates the BOM - BSM convergence for a *risk-averse* environment. Validation groups 5-8 demonstrate the BOM - BSM convergence for a wide range of: stock prices, implied volatilities, interest rates, and risk premiums, respectively.

Each validation group in Section I includes the same six exhibits. Exhibit 1 provides the BOM and BSM present and future values of a call option and the corresponding errors (differences between the BOM and BSM models). Exhibits 2 and 3 provide the same information for the put option and for the underlying stock. As a side note, the BOM and BSM models were *not* used to calculate the current value of the stock. Instead, the actual input value was used. Both models were used to generate the future values and rates of return for all instruments. This applies to all exhibits in all sections.

Exhibit 4 presents the BOM stock returns in Period 1, Period 2, Periods 1 & 2 combined, plus the BSM stock returns in Periods 1 & 2 combined, and the BOM error for the combined Periods 1 & 2. Exhibits 5 and 6 present the same return information for the call and put options, respectively.

All of the exhibits in Section I are one-year, one-period examples. As a result, the rates of return in Period 2 were all zero by definition. The second period data were included to maintain consistency with the format of exhibits in other sections.

Section I: Sample Exhibits

Exhibit 3 - Model Assumptions / Input Values:
One-Period Example, Stock Price = 1000, Strike Price = 1000, Time to Expiration = 1.0 years, Annual IV = 20% lognormal, Risk-Free Rate = 4% annual continuously compounded, annual risk premium = 0% (risk-neutral), *Combined or average of results for N and N+1 BOM intervals*

The complete set of model assumptions and input values for all Group 3 Exhibits is provided above. Exhibit 3.1 compares the Binomial and BSM present and future values of an ATM call option in a risk-neutral environment.

There is an obscure phenomenon in the BOM; the errors (deviations from the continuous BSM model) alternate positive and negative signs for successive numbers of intervals in the lattice. For example, if the BOM error for 16 intervals was positive, then the BOM error for 17 paths would be negative. The JAF exploits this phenomenon by creating two Binomial lattices, one for N intervals and the next for N+1 intervals – and then calculates the average of the results. This is more efficient than simply doubling the number of intervals. For example, the row with 16 intervals actually creates two lattices, one with 16 intervals *and* another with 17 intervals - and then calculates the average of the resulting values. The Binomial values in all sample exhibits in this book reflect the average of N & N+1 intervals.

As is evident in Exhibit 3.1, the BOM present and future values of the ATM call option converge to the BSM as the number of intervals increases. The process used to calculate the present and future values was described in the preceding Binomial (2&3), BSM(4), and JAF(5) chapters. For 1,024 intervals and above, the values are all accurate to the nearest 0.001.

For our initial scenario of 20% volatility and a 4% risk-free interest rate, Exhibit 3.1 demonstrates that the BOM converges to the BSM as the number of intervals is increased and that the resulting BOM error can be made arbitrarily small by increasing the number of binomial intervals as desired (Validation Plan Element (VPE) #2). In addition, Exhibit 3.1 also demonstrates that the JAF current, interim, and expiration valuation algorithms generate theoretically correct and internally consistent current, interim, and expiration *values* (VPE #3).

Exhibit 3.1: Call Option Values (Risk-Neutral) - Bin. Intervals (n & n+1)						
Number of Intervals	Binomial Present Value	BSM Present Value	Binomial PV Error	Binomial Future Value	BSM Future Value	Binomial FV Error
2	97.672	99.251	-1.578	101.659	103.301	-1.643
4	98.633	99.251	-0.617	102.659	103.301	-0.642
8	99.010	99.251	-0.240	103.051	103.301	-0.250
16	99.151	99.251	-0.099	103.198	103.301	-0.103
32	99.207	99.251	-0.044	103.256	103.301	-0.045
64	99.230	99.251	-0.020	103.280	103.301	-0.021
128	99.241	99.251	-0.010	103.291	103.301	-0.010
256	99.246	99.251	-0.005	103.296	103.301	-0.005
512	99.248	99.251	-0.002	103.299	103.301	-0.002
1,024	99.249	99.251	-0.001	103.300	103.301	-0.001
2,048	99.250	99.251	-0.001	103.300	103.301	-0.001
4,096	99.250	99.251	0.000	103.301	103.301	0.000
8,192	99.250	99.251	0.000	103.301	103.301	0.000
16,384	99.250	99.251	0.000	103.301	103.301	0.000
32,768	99.251	99.251	0.000	103.301	103.301	0.000
65,536	99.251	99.251	0.000	103.301	103.301	0.000

Exhibit 3.5 compares the Binomial and BSM returns of the same ATM call option described above in a risk-neutral environment. All of the exhibits in Section I are one-year, one-period examples. As a result, the rates of return in Period 2 were all zero by definition. The second period data were included to maintain consistency with the format of exhibits in other sections.

As is evident in Exhibit 3.5, the BOM one-year, one-period returns of the ATM call option are exactly equal to the BSM one-period returns. Perhaps more important, the BOM and BSM returns are also equal to the effective return on a risk-free asset. You will recall we are assuming a risk-neutral environment, and that the continuously compounded risk-free interest rate is 4%. Earning 4% continuously compounded for one year generates an effective return of 4.081% ($e^{0.04(1.0)} - 1 = 4.081\%$), exactly equal to the BOM and BSM returns of the call option in Exhibit 3.5. This is a major advantage of validating model results in a risk-neutral environment: being able to compare the returns of all assets directly to the effective risk-free return earned over the period.

For our initial scenario of 20% volatility and a 4% risk-free interest rate, Exhibit 3.5 demonstrates that the BOM converges to the BSM as the number of intervals is increased and that the resulting BOM error can be made arbitrarily small by increasing the number of binomial intervals as desired (VPE #2). In addition, Exhibit 3.5 also demonstrates that the values derived from the JAF current, interim, and expiration valuation algorithms generate theoretically correct and internally consistent *rates of return* (VPE #4).

	Binomial Call Option Return Period 1	Binomial Call Option Return Period 2	Binomial Call Option Return Per 1 & 2	BSM Call Option Return Per 1 & 2	Binomial Call Option Return Error 1&2
Exhibit 3.5: Call Option Return (Risk-Neutral) - Bin. Intervals (n & n+1)					
Number of Intervals					
2	4.081%	0.000%	4.081%	4.081%	0.000%
4	4.081%	0.000%	4.081%	4.081%	0.000%
8	4.081%	0.000%	4.081%	4.081%	0.000%
16	4.081%	0.000%	4.081%	4.081%	0.000%
32	4.081%	0.000%	4.081%	4.081%	0.000%
64	4.081%	0.000%	4.081%	4.081%	0.000%
128	4.081%	0.000%	4.081%	4.081%	0.000%
256	4.081%	0.000%	4.081%	4.081%	0.000%
512	4.081%	0.000%	4.081%	4.081%	0.000%
1,024	4.081%	0.000%	4.081%	4.081%	0.000%
2,048	4.081%	0.000%	4.081%	4.081%	0.000%
4,096	4.081%	0.000%	4.081%	4.081%	0.000%
8,192	4.081%	0.000%	4.081%	4.081%	0.000%
16,384	4.081%	0.000%	4.081%	4.081%	0.000%
32,768	4.081%	0.000%	4.081%	4.081%	0.000%
65,536	4.081%	0.000%	4.081%	4.081%	0.000%

Exhibit 4 - Model Assumptions / Input Values:

One-Period Example, Stock Price = 1000, Strike Price = 1000, Time to Expiration = 1.0 years, Annual IV = 20% lognormal, Risk-Free Rate = 4% annual continuously compounded, annual continuously compounded *risk premium = 5% (risk-averse or CAPM), Combined or average of results for N and N+1 BOM intervals.*

The complete set of model assumptions and input values for all Group 4 Exhibits is provided above. Exhibit 4.2 compares the Binomial and BSM present and future values of an ATM put option in a risk-averse (CAPM) environment, with a 5% risk-premium.

As is evident in Exhibit 4.2, the BOM present and future values of the ATM put option converge to the BSM as the number of intervals increases. The process used to calculate the present and future values was described in the preceding Binomial (2&3), BSM(4), and JAF(5) chapters. For 2,048 intervals and above, the values are all accurate to the nearest 0.001.

For our initial scenario of 20% volatility and a 4% risk-free interest rate,

Exhibit 4.2 demonstrates that the BOM converges to the BSM as the number of intervals is increased and that the resulting BOM error can be made arbitrarily small by increasing the number of binomial intervals as desired (Validation Plan Element (VPE) #2). In addition, Exhibit 4.2 also demonstrates that the JAF current, interim, and expiration valuation algorithms generate theoretically correct and internally consistent current, interim, and expiration *values* (VPE #3).

Exhibit 4.2: Put Option Values (Risk Prem: 5%) - Bin. Intervals (n & n+1)						
Number of Intervals	Binomial Present Value	BSM Present Value	Binomial PV Error	Binomial Future Value	BSM Future Value	Binomial FV Error
2	58.709	60.040	-1.331	42.384	44.590	-2.206
4	59.557	60.040	-0.483	43.621	44.590	-0.969
8	59.870	60.040	-0.170	44.165	44.590	-0.425
16	59.977	60.040	-0.063	44.396	44.590	-0.194
32	60.015	60.040	-0.025	44.498	44.590	-0.091
64	60.029	60.040	-0.011	44.546	44.590	-0.044
128	60.035	60.040	-0.005	44.568	44.590	-0.022
256	60.038	60.040	-0.002	44.579	44.590	-0.011
512	60.039	60.040	-0.001	44.585	44.590	-0.005
1,024	60.039	60.040	-0.001	44.587	44.590	-0.003
2,048	60.040	60.040	0.000	44.589	44.590	-0.001
4,096	60.040	60.040	0.000	44.589	44.590	-0.001
8,192	60.040	60.040	0.000	44.590	44.590	0.000
16,384	60.040	60.040	0.000	44.590	44.590	0.000
32,768	60.040	60.040	0.000	44.590	44.590	0.000
65,536	60.040	60.040	0.000	44.590	44.590	0.000

Exhibit 4.6 compares the Binomial and BSM returns of the same ATM put option described above in a *risk-averse* environment.

As is evident in Exhibit 4.6, the BOM one-year, one-period returns of the ATM put option converge to the BSM one-period returns, as the number of BOM intervals is increased. As you will note, the returns of the put option do not (and should not) converge to the return of the risk-free asset in a *risk-averse* environment. In fact, the expected one-year return of the ATM put option in a risk-averse environment is negative and quite large (-25.733%).

In later exhibits, I will provide some additional validation of the put option returns in a risk-averse environment. For now, it is important to recognize that ATM put options have a negative Delta, and contain implicit leverage. This results in a large negative Beta, which generates a negative expected and required return under CAPM. Why would any investor purchase an asset with a negative expected return? In a risk-averse environment, negative Beta assets have value as hedging vehicles, which allow investors to purchase alternative investments with higher levels of systematic risk and higher expected returns.

For our initial risk-averse scenario of 20% volatility, a 4% risk-free interest rate, and a 5% risk-premium, Exhibit 4.6 demonstrates that the BOM converges to the BSM as the number of intervals is increased and that the resulting BOM error can be made arbitrarily small by increasing the number of binomial intervals as desired (VPE #2). In addition, Exhibit 4.6 also demonstrates that the values derived from the JAF current, interim, and expiration valuation algorithms generate theoretically correct and internally consistent *rates of return* (VPE #4).

Exhibit 4.6: Put Option Return (Risk Prem:5%) - Bin. Intervals (n & n+1)					
Number of Intervals	Binomial Put Option Return Period 1	Binomial Put Option Return Period 2	Binomial Put Option Return Per 1 & 2	BSM Put Option Return Per 1 & 2	Binomial Put Option Return Error 1&2
2	-27.807%	0.000%	-27.807%	-25.733%	-2.074%
4	-26.757%	0.000%	-26.757%	-25.733%	-1.024%
8	-26.233%	0.000%	-26.233%	-25.733%	-0.500%
16	-25.978%	0.000%	-25.978%	-25.733%	-0.245%
32	-25.854%	0.000%	-25.854%	-25.733%	-0.121%
64	-25.793%	0.000%	-25.793%	-25.733%	-0.060%
128	-25.763%	0.000%	-25.763%	-25.733%	-0.030%
256	-25.748%	0.000%	-25.748%	-25.733%	-0.015%
512	-25.740%	0.000%	-25.740%	-25.733%	-0.007%
1,024	-25.737%	0.000%	-25.737%	-25.733%	-0.004%
2,048	-25.735%	0.000%	-25.735%	-25.733%	-0.002%
4,096	-25.734%	0.000%	-25.734%	-25.733%	-0.001%
8,192	-25.733%	0.000%	-25.733%	-25.733%	0.000%
16,384	-25.733%	0.000%	-25.733%	-25.733%	0.000%
32,768	-25.733%	0.000%	-25.733%	-25.733%	0.000%
65,536	-25.733%	0.000%	-25.733%	-25.733%	0.000%

Exhibit 6 - Model Assumptions / Input Values:
One-Period Example, Stock Price = 1000, Strike Price = 1000, Time to Expiration = 1.0 years, Risk-Free Rate = 4% annual continuously compounded, annual risk premium = 0% (risk neutral), *8192 binomial intervals, all BOM values are average of N and N+1 BOM intervals, over Range of Implied Volatilities.*

The complete set of model assumptions and input values for all Group 6 Exhibits is provided above. Exhibit 6.1 compares the Binomial and BSM present and future values of an ATM call option in a risk-neutral environment, over a wide range of annual volatilities. In the first few examples, we assumed a constant 20% volatility and a constant 4% risk-free interest rate. While these are plausible and realistic assumptions, a much wider set of assumptions is required for validation purposes. A comprehensive set of tests is provided in the JAF Validation Supplement; the select examples presented in the book are not exhaustive, but they are representative.

For Exhibit 6.1 and remaining sample exhibits in this book, 8,192 N & N+1 intervals will be used. In practice, it would not be necessary to use this many intervals. However, the purpose of this exercise is to validate the results of the JAF. As a result, additional precision is required. Using 8,192 N & N+1 intervals is generally sufficient to reduce the magnitude of JAF valuation and return errors to 0.001 and 0.001% respectively. If greater validation accuracy was desired, more intervals could be used.

As is evident in Exhibit 4.2, the BOM present and future values of the ATM call option are all within 0.001 of the corresponding BSM value for annual volatilities ranging from 20% to 80%. Similar validation tests are provided in the Supplement for wide ranges of risk-free rates, risk-premiums, stock prices, etc.

For a range of volatilities from 20% to 80% and a 4% risk-free interest rate, Exhibit 6.1 demonstrates that the BOM converges to the BSM as the number of intervals is increased and that the resulting BOM error can be made arbitrarily small by increasing the number of binomial intervals as desired (Validation Plan Element (VPE) #2). In addition, Exhibit 6.1 also demonstrates that the JAF current, interim, and expiration valuation algorithms generate theoretically correct and internally consistent current, interim, and expiration *values* (VPE #3).

Exhibit 6.1: Call Option Values (Risk-Neutral) - 8192 Intervals (n & n+1)						
Implied Volatility	Binomial Present Value	BSM Present Value	Binomial PV Error	Binomial Future Value	BSM Future Value	Binomial FV Error
20.0%	99.250	99.251	0.000	103.301	103.301	0.000
24.0%	114.541	114.541	0.000	119.215	119.215	0.000
28.0%	129.867	129.867	0.000	135.167	135.167	0.000
32.0%	145.196	145.196	0.000	151.121	151.122	0.000
36.0%	160.506	160.506	0.000	167.057	167.057	0.000
40.0%	175.783	175.783	0.000	182.957	182.957	0.000
44.0%	191.014	191.014	0.000	198.809	198.809	0.000
48.0%	206.189	206.189	0.000	214.604	214.604	0.000
52.0%	221.301	221.301	0.000	230.332	230.333	0.000
56.0%	236.341	236.341	0.000	245.986	245.987	0.000
60.0%	251.302	251.303	-0.001	261.558	261.559	-0.001
64.0%	266.179	266.180	-0.001	277.042	277.043	-0.001
68.0%	280.964	280.965	-0.001	292.431	292.431	-0.001
72.0%	295.652	295.653	-0.001	307.718	307.719	-0.001
76.0%	310.237	310.239	-0.001	322.898	322.900	-0.001
80.0%	324.714	324.716	-0.002	337.966	337.967	-0.002

Exhibit 6.5 compares the Binomial and BSM one-period returns of the same ATM call option described above in a risk-neutral environment, over a wide range of annual volatilities.

As is evident in Exhibit 6.5, the BOM one-year, one-period returns of the ATM call option are exactly equal to the BSM one-period returns. The BOM and BSM returns are also equal to the effective return on a risk-free asset. Earning 4% continuously compounded for one year generates an effective return of 4.081% ($e^{0.04(1.0)} - 1 = 4.081\%$), exactly equal to the BOM and BSM returns of the call option in Exhibit 6.5. This is a major advantage of validating model results in a risk-neutral environment: being able to compare the returns of all assets directly to the effective risk-free return earned over the period.

For a range of volatilities from 20% to 80% and a 4% risk-free interest rate, Exhibit 6.5 demonstrates that the BOM converges to the BSM as the number of intervals is increased and that the resulting BOM error can be made arbitrarily small by increasing the number of binomial intervals as desired (VPE #2). In addition, Exhibit 3.5 also demonstrates that the values derived from the JAF current, interim, and expiration valuation algorithms generate theoretically correct and internally consistent *rates of return* (VPE #4).

Exhibit 6.5: Call Option Return (Risk-Neutral) - 8192 Intervals (n & n+1)					
Implied Volatility	Binomial Call Option Return Period 1	Binomial Call Option Return Period 2	Binomial Call Option Return Per 1 & 2	BSM Call Option Return Per 1 & 2	Binomial Call Option Return Error 1&2
20.0%	4.081%	0.000%	4.081%	4.081%	0.000%
24.0%	4.081%	0.000%	4.081%	4.081%	0.000%
28.0%	4.081%	0.000%	4.081%	4.081%	0.000%
32.0%	4.081%	0.000%	4.081%	4.081%	0.000%
36.0%	4.081%	0.000%	4.081%	4.081%	0.000%
40.0%	4.081%	0.000%	4.081%	4.081%	0.000%
44.0%	4.081%	0.000%	4.081%	4.081%	0.000%
48.0%	4.081%	0.000%	4.081%	4.081%	0.000%
52.0%	4.081%	0.000%	4.081%	4.081%	0.000%
56.0%	4.081%	0.000%	4.081%	4.081%	0.000%
60.0%	4.081%	0.000%	4.081%	4.081%	0.000%
64.0%	4.081%	0.000%	4.081%	4.081%	0.000%
68.0%	4.081%	0.000%	4.081%	4.081%	0.000%
72.0%	4.081%	0.000%	4.081%	4.081%	0.000%
76.0%	4.081%	0.000%	4.081%	4.081%	0.000%
80.0%	4.081%	0.000%	4.081%	4.081%	0.000%

JAF Validation: Section II

Section II Objectives:
1) The first objective of Section II is to demonstrate that the *two-period* option present values, option future values, stock present value, stock future value, option returns, and stock returns derived from the JAF Combined Binomial & BSM model all converge to the corresponding BSM (continuous lognormal) model values, for both risk-neutral and risk-averse environments, as the number of binomial intervals increases.

2) The second objective of Section II is to demonstrate that for a sufficiently large number of binomial intervals, the above JAF combined BOM / BSM values are almost identical to the corresponding BSM values.

Section II: JAF Combined Binomial & BSM (Constant) – Two Period
Analysis, risk-neutral and risk-averse, various number of intervals, *constant* interest rates, volatilities and risk premiums in periods one and two.

Group 9) JAF Combined two-period risk-neutral Binomial & BSM, converge to BSM as number of paths increases

Group 10) JAF Combined two-period risk-premium 5%, Binomial & BSM, converge to BSM as number of paths increases

Section II: Group and Exhibit Structure

The complete set of validation groups and exhibits from Section II is available in the JAF Validation Supplement. All groups and exhibits from Section II of the JAF Validation Supplement are described below, so please pay particular attention to the descriptions of the *select* sample exhibits examined in this section: Exhibits 9.1, 9.5, 10.2, and 10.6.

There are only two groups of exhibits in Section II, each with a different set of input values, assumptions, and validation objectives. Group 9 validates the convergence of the *risk-neutral* JAF combined BOM/BSM values to the risk-neutral BSM results over a range of binomial intervals, using the same N & N+1 interval methodology described in Section I. Group 10 validates the convergence of the *risk-averse (risk premium 5%)* JAF combined BOM/BSM values to the risk-averse BSM results over a range of binomial intervals.

Each validation group in Section II includes the same six exhibits as Section I. Exhibit 1 provides the JAF combined BOM / BSM and BSM present and future values of a call option and the corresponding errors (differences between the JAF combined BOM / BSM and BSM models). Exhibits 2 and 3 provide the same information for the put option and for the underlying stock. The columns labeled JAF were generated using the JAF method of combining the BOM in Period 1 with the BSM in Period 2.

Exhibit 4 presents the JAF combined BOM / BSM stock returns in Period 1, Period 2, and Periods 1 & 2 combined, plus the BSM stock returns in Periods 1 & 2 combined, and the JAF combined BOM / BSM error for the combined Periods 1 & 2. Exhibits 5 and 6 present the same return information for the call and put options, respectively.

All of the exhibits in Section II are one-year, *two-period* examples (126 trade days each). Unlike Section I, the rates of return in Period 2 are no longer zero. Instead, the returns for all securities in Period 1, Period 2, and in the combined Periods 1 & 2 are consistent with the risk-neutral and risk-averse environments under CAPM.

Section II: Sample Exhibits

Exhibit 9 - Model Assumptions / Input Values: *Two-Period Examples:* JAF = BOM in first period and BSM in second half of period. *Risk-Neutral,* Stock

Price = 1000, Strike Price = 1000, Time to Expiration = 1.0 years, Annual IV = 20% lognormal, Risk-Free Rate = 4% annual continuously compounded, annual risk premium = 0% (*risk neutral*), *over range of intervals.* All BOM values are an average of N and N+1 intervals.

The complete set of model assumptions and input values for all Group 9 Exhibits is provided above. Exhibit 9.1 compares the *two-period* call option present and future values derived from the JAF Combined Binomial & BSM model to the corresponding BSM (continuous lognormal) model values in a risk-neutral environment, as the number of binomial intervals increases (average of N & N+1 intervals).

As is evident in Exhibit 9.1, the JAF combined BOM/BSM present and future values of the ATM call option converge to the BSM as the number of intervals increases. For 1,024 intervals and above, the values are all accurate to the nearest 0.001.

For our simple two-period scenario with 20% volatility and 4% risk-free interest rates in both periods, Exhibit 9.1 demonstrates that the JAF current, interim, and expiration valuation algorithms generate theoretically correct and internally consistent current, interim, and expiration *values* (VPE #3).

Exhibit 9.1: Call Option Values (Risk-Neutral) - Bin. Intervals (n & n+1)						
Number of Intervals	JAF Present Value	BSM Present Value	JAF PV Error	JAF Future Value	BSM Future Value	JAF FV Error
2	99.858	99.251	0.607	103.933	103.301	0.632
4	99.561	99.251	0.311	103.624	103.301	0.323
8	99.408	99.251	0.158	103.465	103.301	0.164
16	99.330	99.251	0.080	103.384	103.301	0.083
32	99.291	99.251	0.040	103.343	103.301	0.042
64	99.271	99.251	0.020	103.322	103.301	0.021
128	99.261	99.251	0.010	103.311	103.301	0.010
256	99.256	99.251	0.005	103.306	103.301	0.005
512	99.253	99.251	0.003	103.304	103.301	0.003
1,024	99.252	99.251	0.001	103.302	103.301	0.001
2,048	99.251	99.251	0.001	103.302	103.301	0.001
4,096	99.251	99.251	0.000	103.301	103.301	0.000
8,192	99.251	99.251	0.000	103.301	103.301	0.000
16,384	99.251	99.251	0.000	103.301	103.301	0.000
32,768	99.251	99.251	0.000	103.301	103.301	0.000
65,536	99.251	99.251	0.000	103.301	103.301	0.000

Exhibit 9.5 compares the *two-period* call option returns derived from the JAF Combined Binomial & BSM model to the corresponding BSM

(continuous lognormal) model values in a risk-neutral environment, as the number of binomial intervals increases (average of N & N+1 intervals).

As is evident in Exhibit 9.5, the JAF one-year, two-period returns of the ATM call option are exactly equal to the BSM one-year (periods 1 & 2) returns. In addition, the returns derived from the JAF combined BOM/BSM model are equal to the effective return on a risk-free asset in each period and over both periods. You will recall we are assuming a risk-neutral environment, and that the continuously compounded risk-free interest rate is 4%. Earning 4% continuously compounded for one year generates an effective return of 4.081% ($e^{0.04(1.0)} - 1 = 4.081\%$), exactly equal to the JAF and BSM returns of the call option in Exhibit 9.5. Earning 4% continuously compounded for half of the year (126/252 trade days) generates an effective return of 2.02% ($e^{0.04(0.5)} - 1 = 2.02\%$), exactly equal to the JAF Period 1 and Period 2 returns of the call option in Exhibit 9.5.

For our simple two-period scenario with 20% volatility and 4% risk-free interest rates in both periods, Exhibit 9.5 demonstrates that the JAF combined BOM/BSM model converges to the BSM as the number of intervals is increased and that the resulting JAF error can be made arbitrarily small by increasing the number of binomial intervals as desired (VPE #2). In addition, Exhibit 9.5 also demonstrates that the values derived from the JAF current, interim, and expiration valuation algorithms generate theoretically correct and internally consistent *rates of return* (VPE #4).

Exhibit 9.5: Call Option Return (Risk-Neutral) - Bin. Intervals (n & n+1)				
Number of Intervals	JAF Call Option Return Period 1	JAF Call Option Return Period 2	JAF Call Option Return Per 1 & 2	BSM Call Option Return Per 1 & 2	JAF Call Option Return Error 1&2
2	2.020%	2.020%	4.081%	4.081%	0.000%
4	2.020%	2.020%	4.081%	4.081%	0.000%
8	2.020%	2.020%	4.081%	4.081%	0.000%
16	2.020%	2.020%	4.081%	4.081%	0.000%
32	2.020%	2.020%	4.081%	4.081%	0.000%
64	2.020%	2.020%	4.081%	4.081%	0.000%
128	2.020%	2.020%	4.081%	4.081%	0.000%
256	2.020%	2.020%	4.081%	4.081%	0.000%
512	2.020%	2.020%	4.081%	4.081%	0.000%
1,024	2.020%	2.020%	4.081%	4.081%	0.000%
2,048	2.020%	2.020%	4.081%	4.081%	0.000%
4,096	2.020%	2.020%	4.081%	4.081%	0.000%
8,192	2.020%	2.020%	4.081%	4.081%	0.000%
16,384	2.020%	2.020%	4.081%	4.081%	0.000%
32,768	2.020%	2.020%	4.081%	4.081%	0.000%
65,536	2.020%	2.020%	4.081%	4.081%	0.000%

Exhibit 10 - Model Assumptions / Input Values: *Two-Period Example*: JAF = BOM in first period and BSM in second half of period. *Risk-Premium: 5%*, Stock Price = 1000, Strike Price = 1000, Time to Expiration = 1.0 years, Annual IV = 20% lognormal, Risk-Free Rate = 4% annual continuously compounded, annual risk premium = 5% (*risk-averse*), *over range of intervals*. All BOM values are average of N and N+1 intervals.

The complete set of model assumptions and input values for all Group 10 Exhibits is provided above. Exhibit 10.2 compares the *two-period* put option present and derived from JAF Combined Binomial & BSM model to the corresponding BSM (continuous lognormal) model values in a risk-averse (5% risk premium) environment, as the number of binomial intervals increases (average of N & N+1 intervals).

As is evident in Exhibit 10.2, the JAF combined BOM/BSM present and future values of the ATM put option converge to the BSM as the number of intervals increases. For 1,024 intervals and above, the values are all accurate to the nearest 0.001.

For our simple risk-averse scenario, with 20% volatility, a 4% risk-free interest rate, and a 5% risk-premium in both periods, Exhibit 10.2 demonstrates that the JAF current, interim, and expiration valuation algorithms generate theoretically correct and internally consistent current, interim, and expiration *values* (VPE #3).

Exhibit 10.2: Put Option Values (Risk Prem: 5%) - Bin. Intervals (n & n+1)						
Number of Intervals	JAF Present Value	BSM Present Value	JAF PV Error	JAF Future Value	BSM Future Value	JAF FV Error
2	60.709	60.040	0.669	45.008	44.590	0.418
4	60.384	60.040	0.344	44.803	44.590	0.213
8	60.215	60.040	0.175	44.698	44.590	0.108
16	60.129	60.040	0.089	44.644	44.590	0.054
32	60.085	60.040	0.045	44.617	44.590	0.027
64	60.062	60.040	0.022	44.604	44.590	0.014
128	60.051	60.040	0.011	44.597	44.590	0.007
256	60.046	60.040	0.006	44.593	44.590	0.003
512	60.043	60.040	0.003	44.592	44.590	0.002
1,024	60.041	60.040	0.001	44.591	44.590	0.001
2,048	60.041	60.040	0.001	44.590	44.590	0.000
4,096	60.040	60.040	0.000	44.590	44.590	0.000
8,192	60.040	60.040	0.000	44.590	44.590	0.000
16,384	60.040	60.040	0.000	44.590	44.590	0.000
32,768	60.040	60.040	0.000	44.590	44.590	0.000
65,536	60.040	60.040	0.000	44.590	44.590	0.000

Exhibit 10.6 compares the *two-period* put option returns derived from JAF Combined Binomial & BSM model to the corresponding BSM (continuous lognormal) model values in a risk-averse (5% risk premium) environment, as the number of binomial intervals increases (average of N & N+1 intervals).

As is evident in Exhibit 10.6, the JAF combined BOM/BSM two-period returns of the ATM put option converge to the BSM as the number of intervals increases. For 256 intervals and above, the values are all accurate to the nearest 0.001%. In addition, the JAF is also able to calculate theoretically correct and internally consistent interim values and returns for each sub-period in a risk-averse environment.

In later exhibits, I will provide some additional validation of the put option returns in a risk-averse environment. As we noted in the one-period risk-averse put option example, ATM put options have a negative Delta, and contain implicit leverage. This results in a large negative Beta, which generates a negative expected and required return under CAPM. However, the returns in Periods 1 and 2 are not equal. Even assuming no change in the stock price, the characteristics (Delta & Beta) of the put option are not constant over the life of the option. As a result, in a risk-averse environment, the expected and required returns under CAPM will change over time.

For our simple risk-averse scenario, with 20% volatility, a 4% risk-free interest rate, and a 5% risk-premium in both periods, Exhibit 10.6 demonstrates that the JAF converges to the BSM as the number of intervals is increased and that the resulting JAF error can be made arbitrarily small by increasing the number of binomial intervals as desired (VPE #2). In addition, Exhibit 10.6 also demonstrates that the values derived from the JAF current, interim, and expiration valuation algorithms generate theoretically correct and internally consistent *rates of return* (VPE #4).

Exhibit 10.6: Put Opt. Return (Risk Prem:5%) - Bin. Intervals (n & n+1)					
Number of Intervals	JAF Put Option Return Period 1	JAF Put Option Return Period 2	JAF Put Option Return Per 1 & 2	BSM Put Option Return Per 1 & 2	JAF Put Option Return Error 1&2
2	-13.792%	-14.003%	-25.863%	-25.733%	-0.130%
4	-13.606%	-14.118%	-25.803%	-25.733%	-0.070%
8	-13.507%	-14.179%	-25.770%	-25.733%	-0.037%
16	-13.454%	-14.210%	-25.752%	-25.733%	-0.019%
32	-13.428%	-14.225%	-25.743%	-25.733%	-0.010%
64	-13.414%	-14.233%	-25.738%	-25.733%	-0.005%
128	-13.407%	-14.237%	-25.735%	-25.733%	-0.002%
256	-13.404%	-14.239%	-25.734%	-25.733%	-0.001%
512	-13.402%	-14.240%	-25.734%	-25.733%	-0.001%
1,024	-13.401%	-14.241%	-25.733%	-25.733%	0.000%
2,048	-13.401%	-14.241%	-25.733%	-25.733%	0.000%
4,096	-13.400%	-14.241%	-25.733%	-25.733%	0.000%
8,192	-13.400%	-14.241%	-25.733%	-25.733%	0.000%
16,384	-13.400%	-14.241%	-25.733%	-25.733%	0.000%
32,768	-13.400%	-14.241%	-25.733%	-25.733%	0.000%
65,536	-13.400%	-14.241%	-25.733%	-25.733%	0.000%

JAF Validation: Section III

Section III Objective:
The objective of Section III is to demonstrate that the option present values, option future values, stock present value, stock future value, option returns, and stock returns derived from the *two-period* JAF Combined Binomial & BSM model are almost identical to the corresponding BSM (continuous lognormal) model values, for both risk-neutral and risk-averse environments - over extreme random variations in interest rates, volatilities, and risk premiums in periods one and two.

Section III: JAF Combined Binomial & BSM (Random) – Two Period Analysis, 8192 intervals N & N+1, extreme & *random:* interest rates, volatilities, and risk premiums in periods one and two.

Group 11) JAF Combined Binomial and BSM model results are almost exactly the same as the BSM (continuous lognormal) model values over a wide range of extreme random selection of implied volatilities and risk-free interest rates in periods one and two (risk-neutral).

Group 12) JAF Combined Binomial and BSM results are almost exactly the same as the BSM (continuous lognormal) model values over a wide range of extreme random selection of implied volatilities, risk-free interest rates, *and risk premiums* in periods one and two.

Section III: Group and Exhibit Structure

The complete set of validation groups and exhibits from Section III is available in the JAF Validation Supplement. All groups and exhibits from Section III of the JAF Validation Supplement are described below, so please pay particular attention to the descriptions of the *select* sample exhibits examined in this section: Exhibits 11.2 and 12.2.

There are only two groups of exhibits in Section III, each with a different set of input values, assumptions, and validation objectives. Group 11 validates the convergence of the *risk-neutral* JAF combined BOM/BSM values to the risk-neutral BSM results for a large number (8,192) of binomial intervals, using the same N & N+1 interval methodology described in Section I. Validation Group 11 uses a wide range of extreme random selection of implied volatilities and risk-free interest rates in periods one and two. Group 12 validates the convergence of the *risk-averse* JAF combined BOM/BSM values to the risk-averse BSM results for a large number (8192) of binomial intervals. Group 12 uses a wide range of extreme random selection of implied volatilities, risk-free interest rates, and risk premiums in periods one and two.

Each validation group in Section III includes the same three exhibits. The left-side of Exhibit 1 presents the random volatility and risk-free rate scenarios for Period 1, Period 2, and Periods 1 & 2 combined. The right-side of Exhibit 1 compares the JAF combined BOM / BSM present and future option values to the corresponding BSM values. The left-side of Exhibit 2 presents the random volatility and risk-free rate scenarios for Period 1, Period 2, and Periods 1 & 2 combined. The right-side of Exhibit 2 compares the JAF combined BOM / BSM option returns in Period 1, Period 2, and

Periods 1 & 2 combined to the corresponding BSM returns. Exhibit 3 is identical to Exhibit 2, except for presenting the stock returns instead of the option returns.

All of the exhibits in Section III are one-year, *two-period* examples (126 trade days each). Unlike Section I, the rates of return in Period 2 are no longer zero. Instead, the returns for all securities in Period 1, Period 2, and in the combined Periods 1 & 2 are consistent with the risk-neutral and risk-averse environments under CAPM.

It is important to reiterate that the standard BOM and BSM models both assume constant volatilities and constant interest rates. It is not possible to use the standard BOM or BSM model with multiple risk-free rates or volatilities. All of the multi-period examples in this document use the Johnson Volatility Aggregation Formula (JVAF) and the Interest Rate Aggregation Formula to calculate the aggregate volatility and aggregate interest rate for use in the BOM and BSM models. Without the JAF, it would not be possible to use the BSM model for comparison purposes with multiple volatilities and interest rates.

Section III: Sample Exhibits

Exhibit 11 - Model Assumptions / Input Values:
Two-Period Example, Stock Price = 1000, Strike Price = 1000, Time to Expiration = 1.0 years, JAF = 0.5-year BOM, followed by 0.5-year BSM, Extreme Random Annual IV values in Periods 1 & 2, Extreme random annual Risk-Free Rates in Periods 1 & 2, *Risk-Neutral.* 8192 binomial intervals, all BOM values are an average of N and N+1 intervals.

The complete set of model assumptions and input values for all Group 11 Exhibits is provided above. Exhibit 11.2 compares the *two-period* call and put option returns derived from the JAF Combined Binomial & BSM model to the corresponding BSM (continuous lognormal) model values, *using extreme, random* volatilities and risk-free rates, in a risk-neutral environment, for a large number of intervals (8,192 average of N & N+1).

Unlike previous examples, all scenarios in Section III assume *different* volatilities and *different* risk-free interest rates in each sub-period. In fact, the random volatilities and interest rates in both periods are intended to be extreme (and unrealistic) – to provide a rigorous validation test of the JAF. Due to the variable volatilities and interest rates in both periods, the JVAF and interest rate aggregation formulas are now both required. In addition, the JAF current, interim, and expiration algorithms will also be essential to calculate returns in both sub-periods.

As is evident in Exhibit 11.2, the JAF one-year, two-period returns of the ATM call and put option are exactly equal to the BSM one-year (periods 1 & 2) returns. In addition, the call and put returns derived from the JAF combined BOM/BSM model are equal to the effective return on a risk-free asset in each period and over both periods. You will recall we are assuming a risk-neutral environment. In the second scenario below (Rows 3 & 4), the volatility in Periods 1 & 2 were 13% and 60%, respectively. The risk-free rates in Periods 1 & 2 were 17% and 1%, respectively. Earning 17% continuously compounded for half of the year (126/252 trade days) generates an effective return of 8.872% ($e^{0.17(0.5)} - 1 = 8.872\%$), exactly equal to the JAF Period 1 returns of the call and put option in Exhibit 11.2.

Earning 1% continuously compounded for half of the year (126/252 trade days) generates an effective return of 0.501% ($e^{0.01(0.5)} - 1 = 0.501\%$), exactly equal to the JAF Period 2 returns of the call and put option in Exhibit 11.2.

Finally, earning 9% continuously compounded for the combined one-year period (252/252 trade days) generates an effective return of 9.417% ($e^{0.09(1.0)} - 1 = 9.417\%$), exactly equal to the JAF Period 1 & 2 returns of the call and put option in Exhibit 11.2.

For our extreme, random two-period scenarios in a risk-neutral environment, Exhibit 11.2 demonstrates that aggregate input values derived from the Interest Rate Aggregation Formula and the Johnson Volatility Aggregation Formula (JVAF), applied to multiple forward periods, generate theoretically correct and consistent results when used with the BOM, BSM, and the JAF combined BOM & BSM model. (VPE#1).

In addition, Exhibit 11.2 demonstrates that the JAF current, interim, and expiration valuation algorithms generate theoretically correct and internally consistent current, interim, and expiration *values* (VPE#3). Finally, Exhibit 11.2 demonstrates that the values derived from the JAF current, interim, and expiration valuation algorithms generate theoretically correct and internally consistent *rates of return* (VPE#4).

							Risk	JAF Option	JAF Option	JAF Option	BSM Option	JAF Option
Type	IV 1	IV 2	IV 1&2	Rf 1	Rf 2	Rf 1&2	Premium	ROR 1	ROR 2	ROR 1&2	ROR 1&2	ROR Error
Call	33.00%	79.00%	60.54%	10.00%	12.00%	11.00%	0.00%	5.127%	6.184%	11.628%	11.628%	0.000%
Put	33.00%	79.00%	60.54%	10.00%	12.00%	11.00%	0.00%	5.127%	6.184%	11.628%	11.628%	0.000%
Call	13.00%	60.00%	43.41%	17.00%	1.00%	9.00%	0.00%	8.872%	0.501%	9.417%	9.417%	0.000%
Put	13.00%	60.00%	43.41%	17.00%	1.00%	9.00%	0.00%	8.872%	0.501%	9.417%	9.417%	0.000%
Call	15.00%	27.00%	21.84%	19.00%	18.00%	18.50%	0.00%	9.966%	9.417%	20.322%	20.322%	0.000%
Put	15.00%	27.00%	21.84%	19.00%	18.00%	18.50%	0.00%	9.966%	9.417%	20.322%	20.322%	0.000%
Call	50.00%	76.00%	64.33%	19.00%	12.00%	15.50%	0.00%	9.966%	6.184%	16.766%	16.766%	0.000%
Put	50.00%	76.00%	64.33%	19.00%	12.00%	15.50%	0.00%	9.966%	6.184%	16.766%	16.766%	0.000%
Call	58.00%	52.00%	55.08%	5.00%	2.00%	3.50%	0.00%	2.532%	1.005%	3.562%	3.562%	0.000%
Put	58.00%	52.00%	55.08%	5.00%	2.00%	3.50%	0.00%	2.532%	1.005%	3.562%	3.562%	0.000%
Call	29.00%	11.00%	21.93%	8.00%	12.00%	10.00%	0.00%	4.081%	6.184%	10.517%	10.517%	0.000%
Put	29.00%	11.00%	21.93%	8.00%	12.00%	10.00%	0.00%	4.081%	6.184%	10.517%	10.517%	0.000%
Call	35.00%	63.00%	50.96%	6.00%	20.00%	13.00%	0.00%	3.045%	10.517%	13.883%	13.883%	0.000%
Put	35.00%	63.00%	50.96%	6.00%	20.00%	13.00%	0.00%	3.045%	10.517%	13.883%	13.883%	0.000%

Exhibit 11.2: Option Returns - Two-Period, Random: IV & Risk-Free Rate. Risk Premium = 0.0% (8192 Intevals)

The complete set of model assumptions and input values for all Group 12 Exhibits is provided above. Exhibit 12.2 compares the *two-period* call and put option returns derived from the JAF Combined Binomial & BSM model to the corresponding BSM (continuous lognormal) model values, *using extreme, random* volatilities, risk-free rates, and *risk-premiums*, for a large number of intervals (8,192 average of N & N+1).

Exhibit 12.2 assumes *different* volatilities, *different* risk-free interest rates, and *different* risk-premiums in each sub-period. The random volatilities, interest rates, and risk-premiums in both periods are intended to be extreme (and unrealistic) – to provide a rigorous validation test of the JAF. Due to the variable volatilities, interest rates, and risk-premiums in both periods, the JVAF and interest rate aggregation formulas are now both required. In addition, the JAF current, interim, and expiration algorithms will also be essential to calculate returns in both sub-periods.

As is evident in Exhibit 12.2, the JAF one-year, two-period returns of the ATM call and put option are exactly equal to the BSM one-year (periods 1 & 2) returns. However, in a risk-averse environment, the call and put option returns are no longer equal, nor are they equal to the effective return earned on the riskless asset. In later exhibits, I will provide some additional validation of the put option returns in a risk-averse environment.

For our extreme, random two-period scenarios, with variable volatilities, risk-free rates, and risk premiums, Exhibit 12.2 demonstrates that aggregate input values derived from the Interest Rate Aggregation Formula and the Johnson Volatility Aggregation Formula (JVAF), applied to multiple forward periods, generate theoretically correct and consistent results when used with the BOM, BSM, and the JAF combined BOM & BSM model. (VPE#1).

In addition, Exhibit 12.2 demonstrates that the JAF current, interim, and expiration valuation algorithms generate theoretically correct and internally consistent current, interim, and expiration *values*. (VPE#3). Finally, Exhibit 12.2 demonstrates that the values derived from the JAF current, interim, and expiration valuation algorithms generate theoretically correct and internally consistent *rates of return* (VPE#4).

Type	IV 1	IV 2	IV 1&2	Rf 1	Rf 2	Rf 1&2	Risk Premium	JAF Option ROR 1	JAF Option ROR 2	JAF Option ROR 1&2	BSM Option ROR 1&2	JAF Option ROR Error
Call	44.00%	21.00%	34.47%	20.00%	3.00%	11.50%	10.00%	31.857%	19.906%	58.105%	58.105%	-0.001%
Put	44.00%	21.00%	34.47%	20.00%	3.00%	11.50%	10.00%	-8.893%	-17.448%	-24.789%	-24.789%	0.000%
Call	25.00%	25.00%	25.00%	7.00%	5.00%	6.00%	7.00%	22.752%	20.351%	47.734%	47.734%	0.000%
Put	25.00%	25.00%	25.00%	7.00%	5.00%	6.00%	7.00%	-13.868%	-15.776%	-27.456%	-27.456%	0.000%
Call	18.00%	23.00%	20.65%	17.00%	13.00%	15.00%	8.00%	30.973%	26.501%	65.682%	65.682%	0.000%
Put	18.00%	23.00%	20.65%	17.00%	13.00%	15.00%	8.00%	-21.321%	-24.907%	-40.918%	-40.916%	-0.001%
Call	39.00%	67.00%	54.82%	9.00%	17.00%	13.00%	9.00%	17.291%	21.667%	42.704%	42.705%	0.000%
Put	39.00%	67.00%	54.82%	9.00%	17.00%	13.00%	9.00%	-4.881%	-1.409%	-6.221%	-6.221%	0.000%
Call	57.00%	40.00%	49.24%	3.00%	18.00%	10.50%	1.00%	2.958%	10.971%	14.254%	14.254%	0.000%
Put	57.00%	40.00%	49.24%	3.00%	18.00%	10.50%	1.00%	0.336%	8.144%	8.507%	8.507%	0.000%
Call	54.00%	77.00%	66.50%	7.00%	4.00%	5.50%	1.00%	4.785%	3.222%	8.161%	8.161%	0.000%
Put	54.00%	77.00%	66.50%	7.00%	4.00%	5.50%	1.00%	2.792%	1.258%	4.085%	4.085%	0.000%
Call	79.00%	44.00%	63.94%	8.00%	9.00%	8.50%	6.00%	11.721%	12.152%	25.297%	25.297%	0.000%
Put	79.00%	44.00%	63.94%	8.00%	9.00%	8.50%	6.00%	-0.895%	-0.528%	-1.418%	-1.418%	0.000%

Exhibit 12.2: Option Returns - Two-Period, Random: IV, Risk-Free Rate, & Risk Premium (8192 Intervals)

JAF Validation: Section IV

Section IV Objective:

The objective of Section IV is to design three plausible, but relatively extreme, multi-period (15), base cases for use throughout the remainder of the validation testing. Each case will reflect a different type of economic and market environment.

Section IV: Base Case Scenarios – Define forward rates and forward volatilities for three, multi-period, base case scenarios: flat term structure, normal (upward sloping) term structure, and inverted term structure.

Group 13) Base-Case Scenarios (Flat, Normal, and Inverted Term Structures)

Section IV: Group and Exhibit Structure

The complete set of validation groups and exhibits from Section IV is available in the JAF Validation Supplement. All groups and exhibits from Section IV of the JAF Validation Supplement are described below, so please pay particular attention to the descriptions of the *select* sample exhibits examined in this section: Exhibits 13.1, 13.3, and 13.5.

The first case is consistent with an inflection point in the economy and has a flat (constant) term structure of volatilities (20%) and a flat or constant term structure of interest rates (4%). The second case is consistent with a typical economic expansion, with a "normal" or upward-sloping term structure of volatilities, beginning at 10% at the front end of the curve and increasing to 24% in the final period. The "normal" scenario also has an upward-sloping term structure of interest rates, beginning at 4% at the front end of the curve and increasing to 5.4% in the final period. The last case is consistent with a market in turmoil, with an expectation of entering a prolonged recession, accompanied by accommodative monetary policy. The third case or scenario has an inverted or downward-sloping term structure of volatilities, beginning at 80% at the front end of the curve and decreasing to 10% in the final period. The inverted scenario also has a downward-sloping term structure of interest rates, beginning at 10% at the front end of the curve and decreasing to 3.0% in the final period.

The above term structures of volatilities and interest rates will be used to calculate the current option values and Greeks for a wide range of option expirations. I will also present the results after aging both term structures by 21 trading days. Risk-neutral and risk-averse environments will both be evaluated.

There is only one group of exhibits in Section IV. Group 13 provides the forward volatilities and forward risk-free rates, for each of the 15 forward periods, in each of the three base cases.

Validation Group 13 includes six Exhibits. Exhibit 1 presents the *current* term structure of volatilities and term structure of interest rates for the first base case (Flat). The left-side of Exhibit 1 documents the number of trade days in each period and the cumulative trade days through the end of each period. The center section of Exhibit 1 lists the forward volatilities and forward risk-free rates for each forward period. The right-side of Exhibit 1 shows the aggregate volatility (JVAF) and aggregate interest rate from time zero to the end of each forward period. The table format for all six exhibits is the same.

Exhibit 2 presents the *aged (+21 Trade Days)* term structure of volatilities and term structure of interest rates for the first base case (Flat). Exhibits 3 and 4 present the *current and aged (+21 Trade Days)* term structures of volatilities and term structures of interest rates for the second base case (Normal). Exhibits 5 and 6 present the *current and aged (+21 Trade Days)* term structures of volatilities and term structures of interest rates for the third base case (Inverted).

Section IV: Sample Exhibits

Exhibit 13: Sections I - III used the JAF to demonstrate the convergence of the Binomial, the JAF combined BOM/BSM, and the BSM in single and multiple periods, over a wide range of interest rates, volatilities, and risk premiums. Going forward, we will evaluate the JAF with 15 different options, with expirations ranging from one week (5 TD) to one year (252 TD), over the three plausible, but extreme base case scenarios described above and documented below. We will also examine the JAF results from aging the term structures by 21 trading days.

As I explained earlier, the following sections will assume that all monthly options expire at the close on the last trade-day of the month and that there are exactly 21 trade days in every month. Given this assumption, interest rates, volatilities, and option expiration dates will all coincide perfectly with calendar months. This will allow us to discuss hypothetical interest rates and volatilities for specific calendar month examples, without any confusion regarding whether we are referring to the period before or after the standard monthly option expiration date on the third Friday of the month. *Note: this assumption is only included to avoid confusion and is NOT required for the JAF, which can accommodate any number of periods, each with a variable number of trade days.*
The forward volatilities, forward risk-free rates, JVAF aggregate volatilities, and average risk-free rates are provided for each period, for each of the three base cases below.

Exhibit 13.1: Flat Term Structures of Volatility & Interest Rates					
Trade Days in Period	Cumulative Trade Days	Forward Period Volatility	Forward Period Risk-Free Rate	Average Implied Volatility	Average Risk-Free Rate
5	5	20.00%	4.00%	20.000%	4.000%
5	10	20.00%	4.00%	20.000%	4.000%
5	15	20.00%	4.00%	20.000%	4.000%
6	21	20.00%	4.00%	20.000%	4.000%
21	42	20.00%	4.00%	20.000%	4.000%
21	63	20.00%	4.00%	20.000%	4.000%
21	84	20.00%	4.00%	20.000%	4.000%
21	105	20.00%	4.00%	20.000%	4.000%
21	126	20.00%	4.00%	20.000%	4.000%
21	147	20.00%	4.00%	20.000%	4.000%
21	168	20.00%	4.00%	20.000%	4.000%
21	189	20.00%	4.00%	20.000%	4.000%
21	210	20.00%	4.00%	20.000%	4.000%
21	231	20.00%	4.00%	20.000%	4.000%
21	252	20.00%	4.00%	20.000%	4.000%

Exhibit 13.3 below documents the forward volatility and risk-free rate values used in the "normal" term structure or "normal" base case. Both term structures are upward sloping. Let me provide an example, to demonstrate how to interpret the table. I will use Row 5 as an example.

The fifth forward period is 21 trade days in length and occurs 21 trade days in the future (after the cumulative number of trade days in forward period #4). The annualized forward volatility in the fifth period is 14% and the average volatility from time zero through the end of period 5 equals 12.868%. This value was derived by applying the JVAF to the forward volatilities in Periods 1 – 5 (10%, 11%, 12%, 13%, and 14%). You will recall that the JVAF is non-linear and is applied using the actual number of trade days in each period.

The annualized risk-free rate in the fifth period is 4.4% and the average risk-free rate from time zero through the end of period 5 equals 4.279%. This value was derived by applying the aggregate interest rate formula to the forward risk-free rates in Periods 1 – 5 (4.0%, 4.1%, 4.2%, 4.3%, and 4.4%).

Exhibit 13.3: Normal Term Structures of Volatility & Interest Rates					
Trade Days in Period	Cumulative Trade Days	Forward Period Volatility	Forward Period Risk-Free Rate	Average Implied Volatility	Average Risk-Free Rate
5	5	10.00%	4.00%	10.000%	4.000%
5	10	11.00%	4.10%	10.512%	4.050%
5	15	12.00%	4.20%	11.030%	4.100%
6	21	13.00%	4.30%	11.627%	4.157%
21	42	14.00%	4.40%	12.868%	4.279%
21	63	15.00%	4.50%	13.616%	4.352%
21	84	16.00%	4.60%	14.249%	4.414%
21	105	17.00%	4.70%	14.840%	4.471%
21	126	18.00%	4.80%	15.412%	4.526%
21	147	19.00%	4.90%	15.974%	4.580%
21	168	20.00%	5.00%	16.531%	4.632%
21	189	21.00%	5.10%	17.085%	4.684%
21	210	22.00%	5.20%	17.639%	4.736%
21	231	23.00%	5.30%	18.191%	4.787%
21	252	24.00%	5.40%	18.744%	4.838%

Exhibit 13.5 below documents the forward volatility and risk-free rate values used in the downward-sloping term structure or "Inverted" base case. Both term structures are downward sloping.

Exhibit 13.5: Inverted Term Structures of Volatility & Interest Rates					
Trade Days in Period	Cumulative Trade Days	Forward Period Volatility	Forward Period Risk-Free Rate	Average Implied Volatility	Average Risk-Free Rate
5	5	80.00%	10.00%	80.000%	10.000%
5	10	75.00%	9.50%	77.540%	9.750%
5	15	70.00%	9.00%	75.111%	9.500%
6	21	65.00%	8.50%	72.366%	9.214%
21	42	60.00%	8.00%	66.471%	8.607%
21	63	55.00%	7.50%	62.881%	8.238%
21	84	50.00%	7.00%	59.921%	7.929%
21	105	45.00%	6.50%	57.248%	7.643%
21	126	40.00%	6.00%	54.752%	7.369%
21	147	35.00%	5.50%	52.389%	7.102%
21	168	30.00%	5.00%	50.140%	6.839%
21	189	25.00%	4.50%	48.001%	6.579%
21	210	20.00%	4.00%	45.975%	6.321%
21	231	15.00%	3.50%	44.068%	6.065%
21	252	10.00%	3.00%	42.291%	5.810%

Not only will these term structure scenarios be used in the remaining validation exhibits, each of these exhibits will examine multiple call and put options (with expiration dates at the end of each forward period).

JAF Validation: Section V

Section V Objective:
The objective of Section V is to demonstrate that the option present values, option future values, stock present values, stock future values, option returns, and stock returns derived from the one-period Binomial & BSM model (using the JAVF and the interest rate aggregation formula) are almost identical to the corresponding BSM (continuous lognormal) model values, for both risk-neutral and risk-averse environments, over all three base cases, for all option expirations, using a large number of BOM intervals (8192, N & N+1).

Section V: Base Case Binomial and BSM Comparison – Compares risk-neutral and risk-averse JAF current values, expiration values, and expiration returns for Binomial and BSM models, for all three base cases, for a range of option expirations.

Group 14) Base Case BOM and BSM Comparison: Calls & Puts, Flat, Risk-Neutral

Group 15) Base Case BOM and BSM Comparison: Calls & Puts, Normal, Risk-Neutral

Group 16) Base Case BOM and BSM Comparison: Calls & Puts, Inverted, Risk-Neutral

Group 17) Base Case BOM and BSM Comparison: Calls & Puts, Flat, Risk-Premium: 5%

Group 18) Base Case BOM and BSM Comparison: Calls & Puts, Normal, Risk-Premium: 5%

Group 19) Base Case BOM and BSM Comparison: Calls & Puts, Inverted, Risk-Premium: 5%

Section V: Group and Exhibit Structure

The complete set of validation groups and exhibits from Section V is available in the JAF Validation Supplement. All groups and exhibits from Section V of the JAF Validation Supplement are described below, so please pay particular attention to the descriptions of the *select* sample exhibits examined in this section: Exhibits 15.1 and 19.2.

There are six groups of exhibits in Section V, each with a different set of input values, assumptions, and validation objectives. All aggregate volatility and average risk-free rates were derived using the JAF. Group 14 validates the accuracy of the JAF BOM relative to the BSM for the *Flat* base case, in a risk-neutral environment, across all option expirations. Validation Groups 15 and 16 document the same JAF BOM and BSM validation analysis for the *Normal* and *Inverted* base cases, both in risk-neutral environments. Groups 17-19 provide the JAF BOM and BSM validation results for the *Flat, Normal, and Inverted* base cases in a *risk-averse* (5% risk premium) environment.

Each validation group in Section V includes the same two exhibits: Exhibit 1 for calls and Exhibit 2 for puts. The format of Exhibits 1 and 2 are identical. The left-sides of Exhibits 1 & 2 present the number of trade days until option expiration for all 15 options, plus the aggregate volatility and average risk-free rate from time zero until option expiration (using the JAF). From left to right, the next pair of columns compares the BOM and BSM option *present* values. The following pair of columns compares the BOM and BSM option *future* values. The final pair of columns provides the BOM returns from time zero to option expiration. All of this data is provided for every option expiration, ranging from five trade days (one week) to 252 trade days (one year). The corresponding stock values are shown in the bottom row of all exhibits. All of the exhibits in Section V are one-year, *one-period* examples.

It is important to reiterate that the standard BOM and BSM models both assume constant volatilities and constant interest rates. It is not possible to use the standard BOM or BSM model with multiple risk-free rates or volatilities. All of the multi-period examples in this document use the Johnson Volatility Aggregation Formula (JVAF) and the Interest Rate Aggregation Formula to calculate the aggregate volatility and aggregate interest rate for use in the BOM and BSM models. Without the JAF, it would not be possible to use the BSM model for comparison purposes with multiple volatilities and interest rates.

Section V: Sample Exhibits

Exhibit 15 - Model Assumptions / Input Values: *One-Period Examples.* Stock Price = 1000, Strike Price = 1000, Time to Expiration = various, **Normal term structure, risk-neutral.** 8192 binomial intervals, all BOM values are an average of N and N+1 intervals.

The complete set of model assumptions and input values for all Group 15 Exhibits is provided above. Exhibit 15.1 compares the call option present values, call option future values, stock present values, stock future values, call option returns, and stock returns derived from the *one-period* Binomial & BSM model (using the JAVF and the interest rate aggregation formula) to the corresponding BSM (continuous lognormal) model values, in a risk-neutral environment, for the Normal Term Structure, for all option expirations, using a large number of BOM intervals (8192, N & N+1).

As is evident in Exhibit 15.1, the present and future values of the BOM and BSM models (using the JAF) are almost identical for call options, across all option expirations. All values are accurate to the nearest 0.001 and all returns are accurate (consistent with the effective return earned on the riskless asset to the nearest 0.001%).

For example, the two-month return of the February call option is 0.716%, which equates to a continuously compounded annualized return of 4.279%. This is exactly equal to the average continuously compounded annualized 42-trade-day risk-free rate for the "normal" term structure (shown in Exhibit 13.3).

Using the JVAF and interest rate aggregation formulas, the call option returns for all expiration dates are theoretically correct and internally consistent, even when using 15 different forward periods of varying length, with extreme, but plausible unique volatilities and risk-free rates in each period.

Exhibit 15.1 demonstrates that aggregate input values derived from the Interest Rate Aggregation Formula and the Johnson Volatility Aggregation Formula (JVAF), applied to multiple forward periods, generate theoretically correct and consistent results when used with the BOM, BSM, and the JAF combined BOM & BSM model (VPE#1). Exhibit 15.1 further demonstrates that the BOM converges to the BSM as the number of intervals is increased and that the resulting BOM error can be made arbitrarily small by increasing the number of binomial intervals as desired (VPE#2). Exhibit 15.1 also demonstrates that the JAF current, interim, and expiration valuation algorithms generate theoretically correct and internally consistent current, interim, and expiration *values* (VPE#3). Finally, Exhibit 15.1 demonstrates that the values derived from the JAF current, interim, and expiration valuation algorithms generate theoretically correct and internally consistent *rates of return* (VPE#4).

Exhibit 15.1: Call Option Values - Normal Term Structure (Risk Premium: 0%)								
Opt.Expire (TD)	Annualized Implied Volatility	Annualized Risk-Free Rate	Binomial Present Value	BSM Present Value	Binomial Future Value	BSM Future Value	Binomial ROR	Annualized ROR (CC)
JAN W1 (5)	10.000%	4.000%	6.023	6.023	6.028	6.028	0.079%	4.000%
JAN W2 (10)	10.512%	4.050%	9.175	9.175	9.189	9.189	0.161%	4.050%
JAN W3 (15)	11.030%	4.100%	11.985	11.985	12.015	12.015	0.244%	4.100%
JAN W4 (21)	11.627%	4.157%	15.167	15.167	15.219	15.219	0.347%	4.157%
FEB (42)	12.868%	4.279%	24.626	24.626	24.803	24.803	0.716%	4.279%
MAR (63)	13.616%	4.352%	32.763	32.763	33.121	33.121	1.094%	4.352%
APR (84)	14.249%	4.414%	40.394	40.394	40.993	40.993	1.482%	4.414%
MAY (105)	14.840%	4.471%	47.791	47.792	48.690	48.690	1.881%	4.471%
JUN (126)	15.412%	4.526%	55.079	55.080	56.340	56.340	2.289%	4.526%
JUL (147)	15.974%	4.580%	62.326	62.326	64.013	64.014	2.707%	4.580%
AUG (168)	16.531%	4.632%	69.571	69.571	71.753	71.753	3.136%	4.632%
SEP (189)	17.085%	4.684%	76.840	76.841	79.588	79.588	3.576%	4.684%
OCT (210)	17.639%	4.736%	84.150	84.150	87.537	87.537	4.025%	4.736%
NOV (231)	18.191%	4.787%	91.510	91.510	95.615	95.615	4.486%	4.787%
DEC (252)	18.744%	4.838%	98.928	98.928	103.832	103.832	4.957%	4.838%
STOCK	N/A	4.838%	1,000.000	1,000.000	1,049.570	1,049.570	4.957%	4.838%

Exhibit 19 - Model Assumptions / Input Values: *One-Period Examples.* Stock Price = 1000, Strike Price = 1000, Time to Expiration = various, **Inverted term structure, risk-premium 5%.** 8192 binomial intervals, all BOM values are an average of N and N+1 intervals.

The complete set of model assumptions and input values for all Group 19 Exhibits is provided above. Exhibit 19.2 compares the put option present values, put option future values, stock present values, stock future values, put option returns, and stock returns derived from the *one-period* Binomial & BSM model (using the JAVF and the interest rate aggregation formula) to the corresponding BSM (continuous lognormal) model values, in a *risk-averse* environment, for the *Inverted* Term Structure, for all option expirations, using a large number of BOM intervals (8192, N & N+1).

As is evident in Exhibit 19.2, the present and future values of the BOM and BSM models (using the JAF) are almost identical for put options, across all option expirations. All values are accurate to the nearest 0.001. In later exhibits, I will provide some additional validation of the put option returns in a risk-averse environment.

Using the JVAF and interest rate aggregation formulas, the put option returns for all expiration dates are theoretically correct and internally consistent, even when using 15 different forward periods of varying length, with extreme, but plausible unique volatilities and risk-free rates in each period.

Exhibit 19.2 demonstrates that aggregate input values derived from the Interest Rate Aggregation Formula and the Johnson Volatility Aggregation Formula (JVAF), applied to multiple forward periods, generate theoretically correct and consistent results when used with the BOM, BSM, and the JAF combined BOM & BSM model (VPE#1). Exhibit 19.2 further demonstrates that the BOM converges to the BSM as the number of intervals is increased and that the resulting BOM error can be made arbitrarily small by increasing the number of binomial intervals as desired (VPE#2). Exhibit 19.2 also demonstrates that the JAF current, interim, and expiration valuation algorithms generate theoretically correct and internally consistent current, interim, and expiration *values* (VPE#3). Finally, Exhibit 19.2 demonstrates that the values derived from the JAF current, interim, and expiration valuation algorithms generate theoretically correct and internally consistent *rates of return* (VPE#4).

Exhibit 19.2: Put Option Values - Inverted Term Structure (Risk Premium: 5%)								
Opt.Expire (TD)	Annualized Implied Volatility	Annualized Risk-Free Rate	Binomial Present Value	BSM Present Value	Binomial Future Value	BSM Future Value	Binomial ROR	Annualized ROR (CC)
JAN W1 (5)	80.000%	10.000%	43.903	43.903	43.524	43.524	-0.863%	-43.699%
JAN W2 (10)	77.540%	9.750%	59.531	59.531	58.851	58.851	-1.142%	-28.944%
JAN W3 (15)	75.111%	9.500%	70.014	70.014	69.068	69.068	-1.351%	-22.854%
JAN W4 (21)	72.366%	9.214%	79.102	79.102	77.861	77.861	-1.569%	-18.979%
FEB (42)	66.471%	8.607%	100.188	100.188	98.077	98.077	-2.107%	-12.778%
MAR (63)	62.881%	8.238%	113.711	113.711	110.888	110.888	-2.483%	-10.057%
APR (84)	59.921%	7.929%	122.889	122.889	119.411	119.411	-2.830%	-8.612%
MAY (105)	57.248%	7.643%	129.150	129.150	125.018	125.018	-3.199%	-7.804%
JUN (126)	54.752%	7.369%	133.304	133.304	128.482	128.482	-3.617%	-7.368%
JUL (147)	52.389%	7.102%	135.880	135.880	130.310	130.310	-4.099%	-7.175%
AUG (168)	50.140%	6.839%	137.257	137.258	130.868	130.869	-4.655%	-7.150%
SEP (189)	48.001%	6.579%	137.731	137.731	130.446	130.446	-5.290%	-7.246%
OCT (210)	45.975%	6.321%	137.545	137.545	129.285	129.286	-6.005%	-7.431%
NOV (231)	44.068%	6.065%	136.912	136.912	127.605	127.605	-6.798%	-7.680%
DEC (252)	42.291%	5.810%	136.030	136.030	125.607	125.607	-7.663%	-7.972%
STOCK	N/A	5.810%	1,000.000	1,000.000	1,114.153	1,114.154	11.415%	10.810%

JAF Validation: Section VI

Section VI Objective:

The objective of Section VI is to demonstrate that the cumulative returns, periodic returns, and continuously compounded periodic returns derived from the *two-period* JAF combined Binomial & BSM model are consistent with the complete term structure of interest rates and the complete term structure of volatilities, in a *risk-neutral* environment, for all option expirations, in all three base cases, using a large number of BOM intervals (8192, N & N+1).

Section VI: Cumulative, Periodic, and Annualized Periodic Returns –

JAF *risk-neutral* period returns, cumulative returns, and annualized period returns, for a range of option expirations, in every base case: flat, normal, and inverted.

Group 20) Returns: Calls, Flat, Risk-Premium: 0%
Group 21) Returns: Puts, Flat, Risk-Premium: 0%
Group 22) Returns: Calls, Normal, Risk-Premium: 0%
Group 23) Returns: Puts, Normal, Risk-Premium: 0%
Group 24) Returns: Calls, Inverted, Risk-Premium: 0%
Group 25) Returns: Puts, Inverted, Risk-Premium: 0%

Section VI: Group and Exhibit Structure

The complete set of validation groups and exhibits from Section VI is available in the JAF Validation Supplement. All groups and exhibits from Section VI of the JAF Validation Supplement are described below, so please pay particular attention to the descriptions of the *select* sample exhibits examined in this section: Exhibits 22.2 and 22.3.

There are six groups of exhibits in Section VI, each with a different set of input values, assumptions, and validation objectives. All aggregate volatility and average risk-free rates were derived using the JAF. All six Groups assume a risk-neutral environment. Group 20 validates the accuracy of the JAF combined BOM /BSM call option returns for all option expirations, in the *Flat* base case, relative to the risk-free interest rate in each forward period. Group 21 performs the same validation analysis for put options in the *Flat* base case. Groups 22 & 23 provide the same validation return data for calls and puts in the *Normal* base case. Finally, Groups 24 & 25 validate the accuracy of the JAF combined BOM /BSM option returns for all option expirations, in the *Inverted* base case, relative to the risk-free interest rate in each forward period.

Each validation group in Section VI includes the same three exhibits: Exhibit 1 for cumulative returns, Exhibit 2 for periodic returns, and Exhibit 3 for periodic annualized continuously compounded returns. The cumulative returns were calculated directly by the JAF Python code. The periodic returns were derived from the cumulative returns using standard time-value-of-money formulas. The format of all exhibits is identical. The top five rows of each exhibit summarize the market environment. Row 1 shows the annualized volatility for each forward period. Row 2 shows the aggregate volatility from time zero through the end of each forward period. Rows 3 and 4 show the forward risk-free rate in each forward period and the average risk-free rate from time zero through the end of each forward period. Row 5 shows the number of trade days in each forward period. Row six provides the forward period for analysis.

The left-hand column shows the expiration date of each option, followed by its return data for each forward period, either cumulative or periodic. All option expirations are shown in each exhibit. Options expiring at the end of the first period (one-week) will only have one forward return period. Options expiring at the end the year will have 15 return periods, one for each forward period. All of the exhibits in Section VI are *two-period* examples. The first period is always from time zero to the interim date of interest (end of first period, end of second period, etc.). The second period is always from the interim date until option expiration. The JAF is used to calculate the aggregate volatility and average risk-free rate for each of the two periods (derived from the volatilities and risk-free rates in all 15 of the forward periods).

Section VI: Sample Exhibits

Exhibit 22 - Model Assumptions / Input Values: *Two-Period Call Option Examples.* JAF = BOM in Period 1 and BSM in Period 2. Stock Price = 1000, Strike Price = 1000, Time to Expiration = various, Normal term structure, risk-premium 0%. 8,192 binomial intervals, all BOM values are an average of N and N+1 intervals.

The comprehensive set of Exhibits in *Section V demonstrated* that the option present values, option future values, stock present values, stock future values, option returns, and stock returns derived from the one-period Binomial & BSM model (using the JAVF and the interest rate aggregation formula) are almost identical to the corresponding BSM (continuous lognormal) model values, for both risk-neutral and risk-averse environments, over all three base cases, for all option expirations, using a large number of BOM intervals (8192, N & N+1). As a result, we can now turn our attention to the periodic returns of the JAF model.

The complete set of model assumptions and input values for all Group 22 Exhibits is provided above. Exhibit 22.2 provides the call option returns for each option in each period, derived from the JAF Combined Binomial & BSM model, using *"normal" upward-sloping term structures* of volatilities and risk-free rates, in a risk-neutral environment, for a large number of intervals (8,192 average of N & N+1).

Section VI exhibits assume *different* volatilities and *different* risk-free interest rates in each of 15 sub-periods. Due to the variable volatilities and interest rates in a multiple period of varying length, the JVAF and interest rate aggregation formulas are both required. In addition, the JAF current, interim, and expiration algorithms will also be essential to calculate returns in both sub-periods.

As is evident in Exhibit 22.2, the JAF Combined Binomial & BSM model returns of all call options are exactly the same in each period. In addition, the call and put returns derived from the JAF combined BOM/BSM model are equal to the effective return on a risk-free asset in each period.

Let's look at the October returns for illustration purposes. You will recall we are assuming a risk-neutral environment. The options with expiration dates prior to October do not have an expected or required return in October by definition. The call options expiring in October, November, and December all have expected or required returns in October of 0.434%, which is consistent with the forward risk-free rate in October ($e^{0.052(21/252)} - 1$ = 0.434%).

The risk-neutral JAF expected returns for all assets in the *same* period are the *same*, and the JAF returns for all assets in *different* periods are *different*. In all forward periods, the risk-neutral JAF returns on all assets (calls, puts, & stock) equal the return earned on the risk-free asset in the forward period. This demonstrates that the JAF valuation algorithms and the resulting returns are theoretically correct and internally consistent with the complete term structure of unique forward rates and the complete term structure of unique forward volatilities.

Conversely, without applying the JAF, the BOM and BSM models would generate *different* risk-neutral returns for all assets in the *same* period, and the *same* returns for each asset in *different* periods, which is exactly the opposite of what is required.

Exhibit 22.2: JAF Call Option Period Returns (Risk Premium: 0%, Normal Term Structure)														
Annualized	10.000%	11.000%	12.000%	13.000%	14.000%	15.000%	16.000%	17.000%	18.000%	19.000%	20.000%	21.000%	22.000%	23.000%	24.000%
Volatility	10.000%	10.512%	11.030%	11.627%	12.868%	13.616%	14.249%	14.840%	15.412%	15.974%	16.531%	17.085%	17.639%	18.191%	18.744%
Risk Free	4.000%	4.100%	4.200%	4.300%	4.400%	4.500%	4.600%	4.700%	4.800%	4.900%	5.000%	5.100%	5.200%	5.300%	5.400%
Interest Rate	4.000%	4.050%	4.100%	4.157%	4.279%	4.352%	4.414%	4.471%	4.526%	4.580%	4.632%	4.684%	4.736%	4.787%	4.838%
Trade Days	5	5	5	6	21	21	21	21	21	21	21	21	21	21	21
Period / Opt.Expire (TD)	JAN W1	JAN W2	JAN W3	JAN W4	FEB	MAR	APR	MAY	JUN	JUL	AUG	SEP	OCT	NOV	DEC
JAN W1 (5)	0.079%														
JAN W2 (10)	0.079%	0.081%													
JAN W3 (15)	0.079%	0.081%	0.083%												
JAN W4 (21)	0.079%	0.081%	0.083%	0.102%											
FEB (42)	0.079%	0.081%	0.083%	0.102%	0.367%										
MAR (63)	0.079%	0.081%	0.083%	0.102%	0.367%	0.376%									
APR (84)	0.079%	0.081%	0.083%	0.102%	0.367%	0.376%	0.384%								
MAY (105)	0.079%	0.081%	0.083%	0.102%	0.367%	0.376%	0.384%	0.392%							
JUN (126)	0.079%	0.081%	0.083%	0.102%	0.367%	0.376%	0.384%	0.392%	0.401%						
JUL (147)	0.079%	0.081%	0.083%	0.102%	0.367%	0.376%	0.384%	0.392%	0.401%	0.409%					
AUG (168)	0.079%	0.081%	0.083%	0.102%	0.367%	0.376%	0.384%	0.392%	0.401%	0.409%	0.418%				
SEP (189)	0.079%	0.081%	0.083%	0.102%	0.367%	0.376%	0.384%	0.392%	0.401%	0.409%	0.418%	0.426%			
OCT (210)	0.079%	0.081%	0.083%	0.102%	0.367%	0.376%	0.384%	0.392%	0.401%	0.409%	0.418%	0.426%	0.434%		
NOV (231)	0.079%	0.081%	0.083%	0.102%	0.367%	0.376%	0.384%	0.392%	0.401%	0.409%	0.418%	0.426%	0.434%	0.443%	
DEC (252)	0.079%	0.081%	0.083%	0.102%	0.367%	0.376%	0.384%	0.392%	0.401%	0.409%	0.418%	0.426%	0.434%	0.443%	0.451%
STOCK	0.079%	0.081%	0.083%	0.102%	0.367%	0.376%	0.384%	0.392%	0.401%	0.409%	0.418%	0.426%	0.434%	0.443%	0.451%

Exhibit 22.3 provides the continuously compounded annualized returns for each call option in each period, derived from the JAF Combined Binomial & BSM model, using *"normal" upward-sloping term structures* of volatilities and risk-free rates, in a risk-neutral environment, for a large number of intervals (8,192 average of N & N+1).

This makes the comparison to the forward risk-free rate much easier for all forward periods. As you can see in Exhibit 22.3, the JAF returns of all call options are accurate (consistent with the annualized continuously compounded return earned on the riskless asset) to the nearest 0.001%.

Exhibit 22.2 & 22.3 demonstrate that aggregate input values derived from the Interest Rate Aggregation Formula and the Johnson Volatility Aggregation Formula (JVAF), applied to multiple forward periods, generate theoretically correct and consistent results when used with the BOM, BSM, and the JAF combined BOM & BSM model (VPE#1). Exhibits 22.2 & 22.3 also demonstrate that the JAF current, interim, and expiration valuation algorithms generate theoretically correct and internally consistent current, interim, and expiration *values* (VPE#3). Finally, Exhibit 22.2 & 22.3 demonstrate that the values derived from the JAF current, interim, and expiration valuation algorithms generate theoretically correct and internally consistent *rates of return* (VPE#4).

Exhibit 22.3: JAF Call Option Annualized Period Returns (CC) (Risk Premium: 0%, Normal Term Structure)															
Annualized	10.000%	11.000%	12.000%	13.000%	14.000%	15.000%	16.000%	17.000%	18.000%	19.000%	20.000%	21.000%	22.000%	23.000%	24.000%
Volatility	10.000%	10.512%	11.030%	11.627%	12.868%	13.616%	14.249%	14.840%	15.412%	15.974%	16.531%	17.085%	17.639%	18.191%	18.744%
Risk Free	4.000%	4.100%	4.200%	4.300%	4.400%	4.500%	4.600%	4.700%	4.800%	4.900%	5.000%	5.100%	5.200%	5.300%	5.400%
Interest Rate	4.000%	4.050%	4.100%	4.157%	4.279%	4.352%	4.414%	4.471%	4.526%	4.580%	4.632%	4.684%	4.736%	4.787%	4.838%
Trade Days	5	5	5	6	21	21	21	21	21	21	21	21	21	21	21
Period / Opt.Expire (TD)	JAN W1	JAN W2	JAN W3	JAN W4	FEB	MAR	APR	MAY	JUN	JUL	AUG	SEP	OCT	NOV	DEC
JAN W1 (5)	4.000%														
JAN W2 (10)	4.000%	4.100%													
JAN W3 (15)	4.000%	4.100%	4.200%												
JAN W4 (21)	4.000%	4.100%	4.200%	4.300%											
FEB (42)	4.000%	4.100%	4.200%	4.300%	4.400%										
MAR (63)	4.000%	4.100%	4.200%	4.300%	4.400%	4.500%									
APR (84)	4.000%	4.100%	4.200%	4.300%	4.400%	4.500%	4.600%								
MAY (105)	4.000%	4.100%	4.200%	4.300%	4.400%	4.500%	4.600%	4.700%							
JUN (126)	4.000%	4.100%	4.200%	4.300%	4.400%	4.500%	4.600%	4.700%	4.800%						
JUL (147)	4.000%	4.100%	4.200%	4.300%	4.400%	4.500%	4.600%	4.700%	4.800%	4.900%					
AUG (168)	4.000%	4.100%	4.200%	4.300%	4.400%	4.500%	4.600%	4.700%	4.800%	4.900%	5.000%				
SEP (189)	4.000%	4.100%	4.200%	4.300%	4.400%	4.500%	4.600%	4.700%	4.800%	4.900%	5.000%	5.100%			
OCT (210)	4.000%	4.100%	4.200%	4.300%	4.400%	4.500%	4.600%	4.700%	4.800%	4.900%	5.000%	5.100%	5.200%		
NOV (231)	4.000%	4.100%	4.200%	4.300%	4.400%	4.500%	4.600%	4.700%	4.800%	4.900%	5.000%	5.100%	5.200%	5.300%	
DEC (252)	4.000%	4.100%	4.200%	4.300%	4.400%	4.500%	4.600%	4.700%	4.800%	4.900%	5.000%	5.100%	5.200%	5.300%	5.400%
STOCK	4.000%	4.100%	4.200%	4.300%	4.400%	4.500%	4.600%	4.700%	4.800%	4.900%	5.000%	5.100%	5.200%	5.300%	5.400%

JAF Validation: Section VII

Section VII Objective:
The objective of Section VII is to demonstrate that the cumulative returns, periodic returns, and continuously compounded periodic returns derived from the *two-period* JAF combined Binomial & BSM model are consistent with the complete term structure of interest rates and the complete term structure of volatilities, in a *risk-averse (CAPM)* environment, for all option expirations, in all three base cases, using a large number of BOM intervals (8192, N & N+1).

Section VII: Cumulative, Periodic, and Annualized Periodic Returns
– JAF *risk-averse* period returns, cumulative returns, and annualized period returns, for a range of option expirations, in every base case: flat, normal, and inverted.

Group 26) Returns: Calls, Flat, Risk-Premium: 5%
Group 27) Returns: Puts, Flat, Risk-Premium: 5%
Group 28) Returns: Calls, Normal, Risk-Premium: 5%
Group 29) Returns: Puts, Normal, Risk-Premium: 5%
Group 30) Returns: Calls, Inverted, Risk-Premium: 5%
Group 31) Returns: Puts, Inverted, Risk-Premium: 5%

Section VII: Group and Exhibit Structure

The complete set of validation groups and exhibits from Section VII is available in the JAF Validation Supplement. All groups and exhibits from

Section VII of the JAF Validation Supplement are described below, so please pay particular attention to the descriptions of the *select* sample exhibits examined in this section: Exhibits 31.2, 31.3, 31.4, and 31.5.

There are six groups of exhibits in Section VII, each with a different set of input values, assumptions, and validation objectives. All aggregate volatility and average risk-free rates were derived using the JAF. All six Groups assume a *risk-averse* (5% risk premium) environment. Group 26 validates the accuracy of the JAF combined BOM /BSM call option returns for all option expirations, in the *Flat* base case, relative to the risk-free interest rate in each forward period, plus the effects of CAPM. Group 27 performs the same validation analysis for put options in the *Flat* base case. Groups 28 & 29 provide the same validation return data for calls and puts in the *Normal* base case. Finally, Groups 30 & 31 validate the accuracy of the JAF combined BOM /BSM option returns for all option expirations, in the *Inverted* base case.

Each validation group in Section VII includes the same three exhibits as Section VI: Exhibit 1 for cumulative returns, Exhibit 2 for periodic returns, and Exhibit 3 for periodic annualized continuously compounded returns. In addition, Section IV includes two additional exhibits that are specific to the risk-averse (CAPM) environment: Exhibit 4 for the implied Beta of each option in each period and Exhibit 5 for the implied Delta of each option in each period.

The cumulative returns in Exhibit 1 were calculated directly by the JAF Python code. The periodic returns in Exhibits 2 & 3 were derived from the cumulative returns using standard time-value-of-money formulas. The format of all five exhibits is identical, except that Exhibits 1-3 provide return data, and Exhibits 4 & 5 provide implied Beta and Implied Delta values for each option in each period. The top five rows of Exhibits 1-5 summarize the market environment. Row 1 shows the annualized volatility for each forward period. Row 2 shows the aggregate volatility from time zero through the end of each forward period. Rows 3 and 4 show the forward risk-free rate in each forward period and the average risk-free rate from time zero through the end of each forward period. Row 5 shows the number of trade days in each forward period. Row 6 provides the forward period for analysis.

The left-hand column shows the expiration date of each option, followed by its return, implied Beta, or implied Delta data for each forward period. All option expirations are shown in each exhibit. Options expiring at the end of the first period (one-week) will only have one forward period. Options expiring at the end of the year will have data for 15 forward periods. All of the exhibits in Section VII are *two-period* examples. The first period is always from time zero to the interim date of interest (end of first period, end of second period, etc.). The second period is always from the interim date until option expiration. The JAF is used to calculate the aggregate volatility and average risk-free rate for each of the two periods (derived from the volatilities and risk-free rates in all 15 of the forward periods).

Unlike the risk-neutral environment, the period returns of each instrument are not identical and cannot be compared directly to the risk-free forward rate. That is the reason for including the two additional exhibits (Exhibits 4 & 5). We can use the following formulas to derive the implied Beta and implied Delta in each period, for each option.

$$R_i = R_f + \beta_i * (MRP)$$
$$\text{Implied } \beta_i = (R_i - R_f) / MRP$$
$$\text{Implied Delta}_i = (\text{Price}_i * \beta_i) / S_0$$

After calculating the implied Betas and implied Deltas of each option in each period, we can use our understanding of Beta and Delta to validate the JAF returns relative to CAPM.

Section VII: Sample Exhibits

Exhibit 31 - Model Assumptions / Input Values: *Two-Period Put Option Examples.* JAF = BOM in Period 1 and BSM in Period 2. Stock Price = 1000, Strike Price = 1000, Time to Expiration = various, **Inverted term structure, risk-premium 5%.** 8,192 binomial intervals, all BOM values are an average of N and N+1 intervals.

The complete set of model assumptions and input values for all Group 31 Exhibits is provided above. Exhibit 31.2 provides the put option returns for each option in each period, derived from the JAF Combined Binomial & BSM model, using *"Inverted" downward-sloping term structures* of volatilities and risk-free rates, in a risk-averse (5% risk premium) environment, for a large number of intervals (8,192 average of N & N+1).

Section VII exhibits assume *different* volatilities and *different* risk-free interest rates in each of 15 sub-periods. Due to the variable volatilities and interest rates in a multiple period of varying length, the JVAF and interest rate aggregation formulas are both required. In addition, the JAF current, interim, and expiration algorithms will also be essential to calculate returns in both sub-periods.

As is evident in Exhibit 31.2, the JAF Combined Binomial & BSM model risk-averse returns of all put option are no longer the same in each period, nor are the returns the same as the effective return on a risk-free asset in each period - although they are related through CAPM.

	Exhibit 31.2: JAF Put Option Period Returns (Risk Premium: 5%, Inverted Term Structure)														
Annualized	80.000%	75.000%	70.000%	65.000%	60.000%	55.000%	50.000%	45.000%	40.000%	35.000%	30.000%	25.000%	20.000%	15.000%	10.000%
Volatility	80.000%	77.540%	75.111%	72.366%	66.471%	62.881%	59.921%	57.248%	54.752%	52.389%	50.140%	48.001%	45.975%	44.068%	42.291%
Risk Free	10.000%	9.500%	9.000%	8.500%	8.000%	7.500%	7.000%	6.500%	6.000%	5.500%	5.000%	4.500%	4.000%	3.500%	3.000%
Interest Rate	10.000%	9.750%	9.500%	9.214%	8.607%	8.238%	7.929%	7.643%	7.369%	7.102%	6.839%	6.579%	6.321%	6.065%	5.810%
Trade Days	5	5	5	6	21	21	21	21	21	21	21	21	21	21	21
Period / Opt.Expire (TD)	JAN W1	JAN W2	JAN W3	JAN W4	FEB	MAR	APR	MAY	JUN	JUL	AUG	SEP	OCT	NOV	DEC
JAN W1 (5)	-0.863%														
JAN W2 (10)	-0.567%	-0.579%													
JAN W3 (15)	-0.441%	-0.452%	-0.464%												
JAN W4 (21)	-0.358%	-0.369%	-0.381%	-0.470%											
FEB (42)	-0.223%	-0.233%	-0.244%	-0.306%	-1.116%										
MAR (63)	-0.161%	-0.172%	-0.182%	-0.231%	-0.854%	-0.906%									
APR (84)	-0.126%	-0.136%	-0.147%	-0.188%	-0.705%	-0.755%	-0.805%								
MAY (105)	-0.104%	-0.114%	-0.124%	-0.162%	-0.611%	-0.660%	-0.709%	-0.758%							
JUN (126)	-0.089%	-0.100%	-0.110%	-0.144%	-0.550%	-0.598%	-0.646%	-0.694%	-0.742%						
JUL (147)	-0.080%	-0.090%	-0.100%	-0.133%	-0.509%	-0.557%	-0.605%	-0.652%	-0.700%	-0.748%					
AUG (168)	-0.073%	-0.084%	-0.094%	-0.125%	-0.483%	-0.530%	-0.578%	-0.625%	-0.673%	-0.720%	-0.768%				
SEP (189)	-0.070%	-0.080%	-0.090%	-0.121%	-0.466%	-0.514%	-0.561%	-0.609%	-0.656%	-0.703%	-0.751%	-0.798%			
OCT (210)	-0.068%	-0.078%	-0.088%	-0.118%	-0.458%	-0.505%	-0.552%	-0.600%	-0.647%	-0.694%	-0.741%	-0.788%	-0.836%		
NOV (231)	-0.067%	-0.077%	-0.087%	-0.117%	-0.454%	-0.502%	-0.549%	-0.596%	-0.643%	-0.690%	-0.738%	-0.785%	-0.832%	-0.879%	
DEC (252)	-0.067%	-0.077%	-0.087%	-0.117%	-0.455%	-0.502%	-0.549%	-0.596%	-0.643%	-0.691%	-0.738%	-0.785%	-0.832%	-0.879%	-0.926%
STOCK	0.298%	0.288%	0.278%	0.322%	1.089%	1.047%	1.005%	0.963%	0.921%	0.879%	0.837%	0.795%	0.753%	0.711%	0.669%

Given that the asset returns are no longer equal in a risk-averse environment, we must look at the pattern and consistency of returns for validation. I promised earlier to examine the risk-averse returns of the put options more closely. Exhibits 31.3 through 31.5 will offer additional insight.

Exhibit 31.3 provides the continuously compounded *annualized* returns for each put option (and for the underlying stock) in each period, derived from the JAF Combined Binomial & BSM model, using *"Inverted" downward-sloping term structures* of volatilities and risk-free rates, in a risk-averse (5% risk-premium) environment, for a large number of intervals (8,192 average of N & N+1).

Using annualized returns standardizes the return comparisons across all forward periods. As you can see in Exhibit 31.3, the JAF returns of the put options tends to decline (becomes more negative as we move forward in time). This is partly due to the inverted term structure of interest rates in this specific scenario. Forward risk-free rates decline from 10% to 3% in this example, and the risk-free rate is a component of CAPM. All else being equal, we would expect the returns to decline as we move forward in time.

Also evident in Exhibit 31.3 is that the JAF returns of all put options become less negative as the time to expiration increases.

Exhibit 31.3: JAF Put Option Annualized Period Returns (CC) (Risk Premium: 5%, Inverted Term Structure)

Annualized	80.000%	75.000%	70.000%	65.000%	60.000%	55.000%	50.000%	45.000%	40.000%	35.000%	30.000%	25.000%	20.000%	15.000%	10.000%
Volatility	80.000%	77.540%	75.111%	72.366%	66.471%	62.881%	59.921%	57.248%	54.752%	52.389%	50.140%	48.001%	45.975%	44.068%	42.291%
Risk Free	10.000%	9.500%	9.000%	8.500%	8.000%	7.500%	7.000%	6.500%	6.000%	5.500%	5.000%	4.500%	4.000%	3.500%	3.000%
Interest Rate	10.000%	9.750%	9.500%	9.214%	8.607%	8.238%	7.929%	7.643%	7.369%	7.102%	6.839%	6.579%	6.321%	6.065%	5.810%
Trade Days	5	5	5	6	21	21	21	21	21	21	21	21	21	21	21
Period / Opt.Expire (TD)	JAN W1	JAN W2	JAN W3	JAN W4	FEB	MAR	APR	MAY	JUN	JUL	AUG	SEP	OCT	NOV	DEC
JAN W1 (5)	-43.699%														
JAN W2 (10)	-28.634%	-29.254%													
JAN W3 (15)	-22.269%	-22.854%	-23.439%												
JAN W4 (21)	-18.088%	-18.654%	-19.219%	-19.792%											
FEB (42)	-11.241%	-11.780%	-12.319%	-12.862%	-13.468%										
MAR (63)	-8.125%	-8.654%	-9.184%	-9.716%	-10.294%	-10.918%									
APR (84)	-6.349%	-6.874%	-7.398%	-7.924%	-8.489%	-9.091%	-9.694%								
MAY (105)	-5.234%	-5.755%	-6.276%	-6.799%	-7.357%	-7.946%	-8.535%	-9.126%							
JUN (126)	-4.502%	-5.022%	-5.541%	-6.062%	-6.614%	-7.196%	-7.778%	-8.359%	-8.943%						
JUL (147)	-4.018%	-4.536%	-5.055%	-5.574%	-6.123%	-6.700%	-7.276%	-7.853%	-8.430%	-9.009%					
AUG (168)	-3.705%	-4.222%	-4.739%	-5.258%	-5.805%	-6.378%	-6.952%	-7.525%	-8.099%	-8.673%	-9.249%				
SEP (189)	-3.513%	-4.030%	-4.547%	-5.065%	-5.611%	-6.182%	-6.753%	-7.325%	-7.896%	-8.468%	-9.040%	-9.614%			
OCT (210)	-3.410%	-3.927%	-4.443%	-4.962%	-5.506%	-6.076%	-6.646%	-7.216%	-7.787%	-8.357%	-8.928%	-9.499%	-10.072%		
NOV (231)	-3.371%	-3.887%	-4.404%	-4.922%	-5.466%	-6.035%	-6.605%	-7.174%	-7.744%	-8.314%	-8.884%	-9.455%	-10.025%	-10.598%	
DEC (252)	-3.373%	-3.890%	-4.406%	-4.924%	-5.468%	-6.037%	-6.606%	-7.176%	-7.745%	-8.315%	-8.885%	-9.455%	-10.026%	-10.596%	-11.169%
STOCK	15.000%	14.500%	14.000%	13.500%	13.000%	12.500%	12.000%	11.500%	11.000%	10.500%	10.000%	9.500%	9.000%	8.500%	8.000%

This is due to the fact that the Beta of the put option is less negative for longer-dated options. I have used the implied Beta formula to derive the Beta of every put option (and the underlying stock) in each period. The resulting implied Betas are shown in Exhibit 31.4.

Implied $\beta_i = (R_i - R_f) / MRP$

You will recall that the implied leverage of an option is less for longer-dated options (due to their higher relative price), which reduces the magnitude of the negative Beta, which results in higher (less negative) expected returns under CAPM. Notice the consistent decline in the magnitude in put option Betas in each forward period, as the time to expiration increases.

Exhibit 31.4: JAF Put Option Implied Beta (Risk Premium: 5%, Inverted Term Structure)

Annualized	80.000%	75.000%	70.000%	65.000%	60.000%	55.000%	50.000%	45.000%	40.000%	35.000%	30.000%	25.000%	20.000%	15.000%	10.000%
Volatility	80.000%	77.540%	75.111%	72.366%	66.471%	62.881%	59.921%	57.248%	54.752%	52.389%	50.140%	48.001%	45.975%	44.068%	42.291%
Risk Free Interest	10.000%	9.500%	9.000%	8.500%	8.000%	7.500%	7.000%	6.500%	6.000%	5.500%	5.000%	4.500%	4.000%	3.500%	3.000%
Rate	10.000%	9.750%	9.500%	9.214%	8.607%	8.238%	7.929%	7.643%	7.369%	7.102%	6.839%	6.579%	6.321%	6.065%	5.810%
Trade Days	5	5	5	6	21	21	21	21	21	21	21	21	21	21	21
Period / Opt.Expire (TD)	JAN W1	JAN W2	JAN W3	JAN W4	FEB	MAR	APR	MAY	JUN	JUL	AUG	SEP	OCT	NOV	DEC
JAN W1 (5)	-10.74														
JAN W2 (10)	-7.73	-7.75													
JAN W3 (15)	-6.45	-6.47	-6.49												
JAN W4 (21)	-5.62	-5.63	-5.64	-5.66											
FEB (42)	-4.25	-4.26	-4.26	-4.27	-4.29										
MAR (63)	-3.63	-3.63	-3.64	-3.64	-3.66	-3.68									
APR (84)	-3.27	-3.27	-3.28	-3.28	-3.30	-3.32	-3.34								
MAY (105)	-3.05	-3.05	-3.06	-3.06	-3.07	-3.09	-3.11	-3.13							
JUN (126)	-2.90	-2.90	-2.91	-2.91	-2.92	-2.94	-2.96	-2.97	-2.99						
JUL (147)	-2.80	-2.81	-2.81	-2.81	-2.82	-2.84	-2.86	-2.87	-2.89	-2.90					
AUG (168)	-2.74	-2.74	-2.75	-2.75	-2.76	-2.78	-2.79	-2.81	-2.82	-2.83	-2.85				
SEP (189)	-2.70	-2.71	-2.71	-2.71	-2.72	-2.74	-2.75	-2.76	-2.78	-2.79	-2.81	-2.82			
OCT (210)	-2.68	-2.69	-2.69	-2.69	-2.70	-2.72	-2.73	-2.74	-2.76	-2.77	-2.79	-2.80	-2.81		
NOV (231)	-2.67	-2.68	-2.68	-2.68	-2.69	-2.71	-2.72	-2.73	-2.75	-2.76	-2.78	-2.79	-2.81	-2.82	
DEC (252)	-2.67	-2.68	-2.68	-2.68	-2.69	-2.71	-2.72	-2.74	-2.75	-2.76	-2.78	-2.79	-2.81	-2.82	-2.83
STOCK	1.00	1.00	1.00	1.00	1.00	1.00	1.00	1.00	1.00	1.00	1.00	1.00	1.00	1.00	1.00

We can gain even more validation insight by examining the implied Deltas of the put options in each period. I have used the implied Delta formula to derive the Delta of every put option (and the underlying stock) in each period.

Implied Delta$_i$ = (Price$_i$ * β_i) / S$_0$

The resulting implied Deltas are shown in Exhibit 31.5. Notice the consistency of the implied Deltas for the same option over time, and for options with increasing time to expiration in each period. As the time to expiration increases (for a given period), the Delta of the each put option becomes slightly less negative, or more out of the money. Why more out of the money? Because the stock price is expected to increase over time.

Given the extreme changes in forward volatilities and interest rates in this scenario, it would be difficult to fully and succinctly summarize the pattern of Deltas across time and expirations, but the results are remarkably consistent and appear to fully support CAPM.

Exhibit 31.5: JAF Put Option Implied Delta (Risk Premium: 5%, Inverted Term Structure)

Annualized Volatility		80.000%	75.000%	70.000%	65.000%	60.000%	55.000%	50.000%	45.000%	40.000%	35.000%	30.000%	25.000%	20.000%	15.000%	10.000%
		80.000%	77.540%	75.111%	72.366%	66.471%	62.881%	59.921%	57.248%	54.752%	52.389%	50.140%	48.001%	45.975%	44.068%	42.291%
Risk Free Interest Rate		10.000%	9.500%	9.000%	8.500%	8.000%	7.500%	7.000%	6.500%	6.000%	5.500%	5.000%	4.500%	4.000%	3.500%	3.000%
		10.000%	9.750%	9.500%	9.214%	8.607%	8.238%	7.929%	7.643%	7.369%	7.102%	6.839%	6.579%	6.321%	6.065%	5.810%
Trade Days		5	5	5	6	21	21	21	21	21	21	21	21	21	21	21
Option Value	Period / Opt.Expire	JAN W1	JAN W2	JAN W3	JAN W4	FEB	MAR	APR	MAY	JUN	JUL	AUG	SEP	OCT	NOV	DEC
43.903	JAN W1 (5)	-0.47														
59.531	JAN W2 (10)	-0.46	-0.46													
70.014	JAN W3 (15)	-0.45	-0.45	-0.45												
79.102	JAN W4 (21)	-0.44	-0.45	-0.45	-0.45											
100.188	FEB (42)	-0.43	-0.43	-0.43	-0.43	-0.43										
113.711	MAR (63)	-0.41	-0.41	-0.41	-0.41	-0.42	-0.42									
122.889	APR (84)	-0.40	-0.40	-0.40	-0.40	-0.41	-0.41	-0.41								
129.150	MAY (105)	-0.39	-0.39	-0.39	-0.40	-0.40	-0.40	-0.40	-0.40							
133.304	JUN (126)	-0.39	-0.39	-0.39	-0.39	-0.39	-0.39	-0.39	-0.40	-0.40						
135.880	JUL (147)	-0.38	-0.38	-0.38	-0.38	-0.38	-0.39	-0.39	-0.39	-0.39	-0.39					
137.257	AUG (168)	-0.38	-0.38	-0.38	-0.38	-0.38	-0.38	-0.38	-0.39	-0.39	-0.39	-0.39				
137.731	SEP (189)	-0.37	-0.37	-0.37	-0.37	-0.37	-0.38	-0.38	-0.38	-0.38	-0.39	-0.39	-0.39			
137.545	OCT (210)	-0.37	-0.37	-0.37	-0.37	-0.37	-0.37	-0.38	-0.38	-0.38	-0.38	-0.38	-0.39	-0.39		
136.912	NOV (231)	-0.37	-0.37	-0.37	-0.37	-0.37	-0.37	-0.37	-0.37	-0.38	-0.38	-0.38	-0.38	-0.38	-0.39	
136.030	DEC (252)	-0.36	-0.36	-0.36	-0.37	-0.37	-0.37	-0.37	-0.37	-0.37	-0.38	-0.38	-0.28	0.30	-0.38	-0.39
1000.00	STOCK	1.00	1.00	1.00	1.00	1.00	1.00	1.00	1.00	1.00	1.00	1.00	1.00	1.00	1.00	1.00

Exhibits 31.2 through 31.5 demonstrate that aggregate input values derived from the Interest Rate Aggregation Formula and the Johnson Volatility Aggregation Formula (JVAF), applied to multiple forward periods, generate theoretically correct and consistent results when used with the BOM, BSM, and the JAF combined BOM & BSM model (VPE#1). Exhibits 31.2 – 31.5 also demonstrate that the JAF current, interim, and expiration valuation algorithms generate theoretically correct and internally consistent current, interim, and expiration *values* (VPE#3). Finally, Exhibits 31.2 – 31.5

demonstrate that the values derived from the JAF current, interim, and expiration valuation algorithms generate theoretically correct and internally consistent *rates of return* (VPE#4).

Summary

This chapter provided an abridged version of the JAF valuation (and rate of return) results. Comprehensive JAF Valuation and Greek results are available in the JAF Validation Supplement PDF (see Resource Chapter for download link address). All of the values in the JAF supplement and in this chapter are actual output values from a Python application of the JAF algorithm - exported to Excel for formatting purposes.

This chapter included a select group of sample exhibits from the first seven sections of the JAF Validation supplement. Each section of examples validated one or more of the Validation Plan Exhibits below and provided compelling evidence that the JAF is able to employ a user-specified Market Risk Premium in conjunction with the complete term structure of unique interest rates and the complete term structure of unique volatilities to calculate theoretically sound and internally consistent current and future option values and rates of return in risk-neutral and risk-averse environments. This has profound implications for generating excess returns and for customized option simulation and strategy optimization in user-specified environments.

Review of JAF Objective:
Design an objective framework that employs a user-specified Market Risk Premium in conjunction with the complete term structure of unique interest rates and the complete term structure of unique volatilities to calculate theoretically sound and internally consistent: current and future option values, current and future Greeks, and current and future volatility index (VIX) values.

Review of Validation Plan Elements (VPE): (Multiple forward interest rate and volatility periods)
1) Demonstrate that aggregate input values derived from the Interest Rate Aggregation Formula and the Johnson Volatility Aggregation Formula (JVAF), applied to multiple forward periods, generate theoretically correct and consistent results when used with the BOM, BSM, and the JAF combined BOM & BSM model.

2) Demonstrate that the BOM converges to the BSM as the number of intervals is increased and that the resulting BOM error can be made arbitrarily small by increasing the number of binomial intervals as desired.

3) Demonstrate that the JAF current, interim, and expiration valuation algorithms generate theoretically correct and internally consistent current, interim, and expiration *values*.

4) Demonstrate that the values derived from the JAF current, interim, and expiration valuation algorithms generate theoretically correct and internally consistent *rates of return*.

5) Demonstrate that the values derived from the JAF current, interim, and expiration valuation algorithms generate theoretically correct and internally consistent current and future *Greeks*.

Validation Plan Element #5 (Greeks) is the only VPE that was not addressed in this chapter.

I will provide the necessary foundation for the JAF abridged Greek results in Chapter 8 by introducing True Vega and partial Greeks in Chapter 7.

7) JAF: TRUE VEGA

The purpose of this chapter is to provide the requisite background in True Vega and partial Greeks for evaluating the JAF Greek results presented in Chapter 8. Vega is one of the most important Greek metrics, and the BSM Vega calculation has serious deficiencies. In the BSM model, Vega represents the change in the value of an option or option strategy in response to an instantaneous one unit change in implied volatility, holding all of the other variables constant. For practical purposes, Vega is typically scaled to a 1% change in implied volatility for all options, regardless of the time remaining until expiration.

In practice, volatilities are mean-reverting. In other words, extremely low and extremely high levels of volatility eventually revert to a more typical or average level of volatility. This is true for all securities across all markets. In my 30+ years as an investment professional, I have never discovered any asset with a term structure of volatilities that does not reflect mean reversion. Discrete shocks to the market (economic events, elections, terrorist strikes, political turmoil, conflicts, wars, etc.), have a much larger effect on near-term option volatilities and diminishing effects on longer-term option volatilities – since most events and the associated uncertainty will eventually be resolved. As a result, the implied volatilities of short-term options change more than the implied volatilities of longer-term options. This is true regardless of the initial shape of the term structure of volatilities: flat, normal (positively sloped), or inverted.

Fortunately, we can move beyond the limitations of traditional Vega; we do *not* need to assume that all implied volatilities change by the same amount when calculating the JAF True Vega. Instead, we can assume a 1% change in the *reference volatility* (the implied volatility of an ATM option with 21 trade days remaining until expiration), and derive exact and internally consistent changes in implied volatilities for all other options and volatility index futures contracts as a function of their time to expiration. The resulting volatility multipliers can be used to calculate JAF "True" Vega. I use the term "True" Vega because it quantifies the *actual or True* price behavior of options and is not limited by the artificial BSM assumptions.

I have written about True Greeks in several of my other books. In my 2015 book *Exploiting Earnings Volatility*, I published a True Vega model derived from daily implied volatility data for a range of expiration dates, across a broad spectrum of diverse securities. The underlying securities included stocks, ETFs, commodities, currencies, bonds, and indices. At the time, I modeled the volatility multipliers as a function of time to expiration. The model was a significant improvement over the standard BSM Vega metric, and I used a variation of this model in my proprietary research and trading for a number of years – but I recently developed a much more sophisticated and accurate methodology, which is used to calculate JAF True Vega.

I originally derived the Johnson Volatility Aggregation Formula (JVAF) as an exact means of aggregating and disaggregating non-earnings and earnings volatility. I first introduced the formula in my June 2011 *Active Trader* article titled "Modeling Implied Volatility" and wrote extensively about the application of the JVAF in *Exploiting Earnings Volatility*. In my joint research for this book and for the AI Volatility Edge model, I used the JVAF to derive a methodology for calculating an *exact, deterministic, and objective (not estimated)* measure of True Vega that is internally consistent for all ATM options and volatility index futures contracts.

As was the case in the last two chapters, the examples in this chapter assume that all monthly options expire at the close on the last trade-day of the month and that there are exactly 21 trade days in every month. Given this assumption, interest rates, volatilities, and option expiration dates will all coincide perfectly with calendar months. This will allow us to discuss hypothetical interest rates and volatilities for specific calendar month examples, without any confusion regarding whether we are referring to the period before or after the standard monthly option expiration date on the third Friday of the month. *Note: this assumption is only included to avoid confusion and is NOT required for the JAF, or for the calculation of True Vega, both of which can accommodate any number of periods, each with a variable number of trade days.*

True Vega Volatility Multiplier Methodology

There are only four steps required to calculate the True Vega Volatility Multiplier for any option and any volatility index futures contract.

True Vega Volatility Multiplier Methodology:
1) Calculate the *Daily Volatility Multipliers* (DVM) for all future trade days
2) Calculate the *Aggregate Volatility Multiplier* (AVM) for the reference volatility (21-TD)
3) Calculate the *Aggregate Volatility Multiplier* (AVM) for the security of

interest

4) Calculate the Security *True Vega Volatility Multiplier* (TVVM)

TVVM = (AVM Security **/ AVM** Reference**)**

The resulting *True Vega Volatility Multiplier* (TVVM) represents the percentage change in the aggregate volatility over a specified time interval for a given 1% change in the reference volatility (21 Trade Day ATM option). For example, a TVVM of 1.319 for an ATM option with 10 trade days remaining until expiration would mean that aggregate (implied) volatility of the ATM 10-trade-day option would change by 1.319%, for a 1% change in the reference volatility. *If the volatility is constant over the entire forward interval*, the JAF True Vega equals the constant 1% Vega multiplied by the True Vega Volatility Multiplier (TVVM) for each security. This multiplicative relationship only holds *if the volatility is constant over the forward period*. If the volatility is *not* constant over the forward period, it is still possible to use the general JAF Greek algorithm and the JVAF to calculate precise JAF True Vegas and partial True Vegas.

In general, the components of the TVVM (JVAF$_{+dV}$ and JVAF$_{-dV}$) for each security are used in the JAF Greek Algorithm from Chapter 5 to calculate the JAF True Vega.

Vega$_C$ = [(C$_U$ – C$_D$)/(σ_U – σ_D)]/100
Vega$_P$ = [(P$_U$ – P$_D$)/(σ_U – σ_D)]/100

The JAF True Vega formulas below first use the JVAF to derive the aggregate volatilities for a 1% increase and decrease in volatility (dV), adjusted for mean reversion via the Daily Volatility Multiplier (DVM). The resulting JVAF aggregate volatilities are then used in the JAF Greek Algorithm to calculate the sensitivity of the price of the option to a change in volatility. The final step is to divide the resulting price sensitivity by the Average Volatility Multiplier (AVM) for the 21-day reference volatility. This standardizes the resulting JAF True Vega calculation relative to the reference volatility. Each element of this calculation will be described in this chapter.

JAF True Vega$_C$ = {[(C$_{+dV}$ – C$_{dV}$)/(JVAF$_{+dV}$ – JVAF$_{-dV}$)]/100}
/ AVM Reference
JAF True Vega$_P$ = {[(P$_{+dV}$ – P$_{dV}$)/(JVAF$_{+dV}$ – JVAF$_{-dV}$)]/100}
/ AVM Reference

Daily Volatility Multiplier (DVM)

Steps 2 - 4 of the True Vega Volatility Multiplier Methodology above are objective, deterministic, and exact, but the Daily Volatility Multiplier or mean reversion model (applied in Step 1) must still be estimated from actual daily volatility market data. The precise Aggregate Volatility Multiplier and True Vega Volatility Multiplier formulas were both used in the DVM model estimation process to ensure the Daily Volatility Multipliers were internally consistent with the JVAF across all securities.

The Daily Volatility Multiplier (DVM) represents the change in the expected daily volatility (on a single trade day), as a function of how far in the future each trade day occurs. The DVM model was estimated using over 15 years of daily ATM implied volatilities for the entire option matrices for the SPX, NDX, and RUT indices (over 170,000 daily data observations). I recognize that individual forward daily volatilities multipliers are not observable directly, but they can be aggregated using the JVAF. I will explain how the DVMs are aggregated in the following sections.

The resulting Python code for calculating the DVM is included below. The value of TD represents the number of trade days in the future. For example, passing in a value of TD of 10 would generate a DVM of 0.879. This indicates the expected annualized volatility on the 10th trade day in the future would change by 0.879% in response to a 1% change in volatility (dV). There are four constants used in the formula (a, b, c, and d). The values of these constants are provided in the Python code below. After cleaning the data for pricing errors, the resulting Root Mean Square Error (RMSE) of the DVM mean-reversion model was 0.386% (across all 15 years of daily data, all three indices, and all ATM options in the matrices). Note: a single DVM or mean-reversion model is used for all three equity indices. Mean reversion is a fundamental concept, applicable to all markets. It is not necessary or even desirable to estimate different DVM functions for most markets.

Python DVM Function
```python
def DVM(TD):
    a = 12.7524497577126
    b = 0.239021016250414
    c = -0.0987378460389707
    d = 0.462862829394134
    DVolMult = (a * b + c * TD ** d) / (b + TD ** d)
    return DVolMult
```

For those with very limited experience with writing or reading code, below is the DVM formula and the associated coefficient values:

DVM = (a * b + c * TD ** d) / (b + TD ** d)

TD = Number of Trade Days in the future
a = 12.7524497577126
b = 0.239021016250414
c = -0.0987378460389707
d = 0.462862829394134

Figure 7.1 is a plot of the individual daily DVM values for trade day 1 to trade day 252 in the future (Step 1). Note: these are *not* average values. The DVM values represent the multiplier for a single trade day – a specified number of trade days into the future. While the graph in Figure 7.1 only shows DVM values for day 1 through day 252, weekly, monthly, quarterly, and LEAP data values were all used in the model estimation. The resulting DVM model can be applied to all exchange-traded index option expiration dates. Notice how rapidly the DVM values decline as a result of mean reversion. This presages the problems of using BSM Vega as a risk measure.

In the next two sections, I will explain how these Daily Volatility Multipliers will be used as building blocks (with the JVAF) to calculate *exact, deterministic, and objective* JAF True Vega Volatility Multipliers that are internally consistent for all ATM options and volatility index futures contracts.

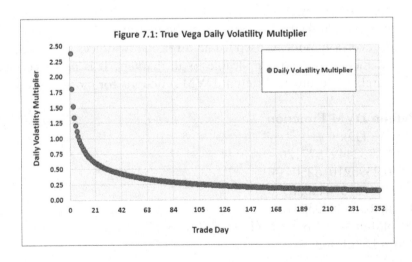

Figure 7.1: True Vega Daily Volatility Multiplier

Average Volatility Multiplier (AVM)

To be practical, we need to calculate the Aggregate Volatility Multiplier (AVM) for all option and volatility index futures contracts, from the appropriate DVM values. So, what are the "appropriate" DVM values? For an option that expires 21 trade days in the future, the answer is straightforward. The DVM values for the first 21 trade days should be used in the AVM calculation. For an option expiring 42 trade days in the future, the DVM values for the first trade days would be used, and so on. With respect to partial Vega calculations (introduced later in this chapter) and volatility index futures contracts, the answer is less obvious.

Let's assume we are interested in calculating the AVM of a VIX futures contract that expires in 10 trade days. Continuing our generic calendar month assumptions, we will also assume that there are 21 trade days in the 30 calendar-day VIX index calculation period at expiration of the VIX futures contract (*any number of trade days could be accommodated by the JAF True Vega methodology in practice*). In this scenario, the DVM values for the first 10 trade days would be irrelevant. They are not applicable to the calculation of the Aggregate Forward Volatility (10 trade days in the future). As a result, we would only use the DVM values for trade days 11 through 31 in the AVM calculation for the VIX futures contract.

After one additional trade day passes, we would use the DVM values for trade days 10 through 30, then 9 through 29, followed by 8 through 28, etc. (all periods have 21 trade days). So, what would happen to the Average Volatility Multiplier (AVM) of the VIX futures contract as time passes? It would increase, just as we see in practice. As time passes, the time until each forward trade day included in the 30-day VIX calculation window declines. Due to mean reversion, near-term trade days have higher DVMs than longer-term trade days. As a result, the AVM increases as time passes. We would see the same effect on the AVM of all options as time passes as well.

While I have not reviewed the AVM calculation yet, it is a deterministic function of the appropriate DVM values used in the calculation of each option and volatility index futures contract. While a DVM mean reversion model is required, the AVM calculation is exact and the same DVM values are used in the calculation of AVM values for all option and volatility index futures contracts.

For example, the specific DVM for the 20th trade day in the future would be used in the AVM calculation for an option expiring in 42 trade days (DVMs 1-42), and would also be used in the AVM calculation for the VIX futures contract expiring 10 trade days in the future (DVMs 11-31). Using the same DVM values for all securities ensures that all AVM values are internally consistent. While a DVM mean-reversion model is still required, the AVM and True Vega Volatility Multiplier formulas are both structural and exact.

Average Volatility Multiplier (AVM): Reference Volatility

The key to designing a robust, internally consistent, and theoretically accurate True Vega model is to use the same DVM values for all ATM options and volatility index futures. It would be tempting to use a simple arithmetic average of the DVM values when calculating the AVM. While the simple arithmetic average would be in the ballpark, the actual AVM formula is more complicated.

As I demonstrated with the Johnson Volatility Aggregation Formula (JVAF), aggregating and disaggregating volatilities is a non-linear problem. As a result, aggregating Daily Volatility Multipliers (DVMs) is also a non-linear problem, which requires a non-linear solution. Fortunately, we can use the JVAF to calculate the Aggregate Volatility Multiplier (AVM) for all securities and/or forward volatility periods.

Figure 7.2 illustrates how to calculate the AVM Reference Volatility (21 TD ATM Option), which is Step 2 of the True Vega Volatility Multiplier Methodology. This example uses the Flat 20% term structure of volatilities base case introduced in Chapter 6. The DVM for each of the first 21 trade days is provided in the center column of Figure 7.2. The two columns on the right-side of Figure 7.2 represent the forward volatilities for each trade day, after applying the Daily Volatility Multiplier (DVM) for each trade day to a 1% increase and a 1% decrease in volatility (dV). For example, the forward volatility for the first trade day after a 1% *increase* in volatility (dV) would equal 22.380% (20.00% + 2.380 x 1%) and the forward volatility for the first trade day after a 1% *decrease* in volatility (dV) would equal 17.620% (20.00% + 2.380 x -1%).

After repeating the calculations of the up and down forward volatilities for each of the required trade days, we use the JVAF to calculate the aggregate up (JVAF$_{+dV}$: 21.004%) and aggregate down (JVAF$_{-dV}$: 19.006%) volatilities for the 21-trade-day period. The JVAF values for the up and down cases are shown in the last data row of Figure 7.2.

The AVM for the 21-day ATM option equals 0.999, which is also the AVM of the reference volatility in this specific scenario. This AVM reference volatility is also shown in the last data row of Figure 7.2.

The following general formula is used to calculate the AVM for all securities:

AVM = (JVAF$_{+dV}$ - JVAF$_{-dV}$) / (+dV − (-dV))
AVM = (JVAF$_{+dV}$ - JVAF$_{-dV}$) / (2dV)
AVM = (21.004% - 19.006%) / (2 x 1%) = 0.999

A dV of 1% is always used in the JAF True Vega Calculation. While any reasonable value could be used in practice, the average historical daily change in the ATM volatility of an option expiring in 21 trade days is remarkably close to 1%. In addition, using a dV of 1% is consistent with the standard Vega calculation.

Figure 7.2 Flat Term Structure (1-21)			+dV	-dV
TD	Forward Volatility	Daily Vol. Multiplier	1.00%	-1.00%
1	20.00%	2.380	22.380%	17.620%
2	20.00%	1.801	21.801%	18.199%
3	20.00%	1.516	21.516%	18.484%
4	20.00%	1.338	21.338%	18.662%
5	20.00%	1.211	21.211%	18.789%
6	20.00%	1.115	21.115%	18.885%
7	20.00%	1.039	21.039%	18.961%
8	20.00%	0.976	20.976%	19.024%
9	20.00%	0.924	20.924%	19.076%
10	20.00%	0.879	20.879%	19.121%
11	20.00%	0.840	20.840%	19.160%
12	20.00%	0.805	20.805%	19.195%
13	20.00%	0.775	20.775%	19.225%
14	20.00%	0.747	20.747%	19.253%
15	20.00%	0.722	20.722%	19.278%
16	20.00%	0.700	20.700%	19.300%
17	20.00%	0.679	20.679%	19.321%
18	20.00%	0.660	20.660%	19.340%
19	20.00%	0.642	20.642%	19.358%
20	20.00%	0.626	20.626%	19.374%
21	20.00%	0.610	20.610%	19.390%
Aggregate Multiplier (1-21)		0.999	21.004%	19.006%
			JVAF$_{+dV}$	JVAF$_{-dV}$

True Vega Multiplier (1-10)

We are now ready to proceed to Steps 3 and 4 of the True Vega Volatility Multiplier Methodology:
3) Calculate the *Aggregate Volatility Multiplier* (AVM) for the security of interest
4) Calculate the Security *True Vega Volatility Multiplier* (TVVM)

In this example, we will calculate the AVM of an ATM option expiring 10 trade days into the future, in the same Flat term structure base case. Figure 7.3 illustrates the calculation of the AVM, using the DVM for the first 10 trade days. Note that the DVMs and the increases and decreases in the daily forward volatilities are identical to those we used in the 21-trade-day reference AVM calculation in Figure 7.2. However, the JVAF$_{+dv}$ (21.323%) and JVAF$_{-dv}$ (18.687%) values are different and the AVM is higher (1.318), because we are only using the first 10 trade day in the calculation. The forward volatilities for the next 11 trade days occur after the expiration of the option and do not affect the AVM calculation of an option expiring in 10 trade days.

The last step (Step 4) is to calculate the True Vega Volatility Multiplier for the ATM option expiring in 10 trade days. This standardizes the True Vega Volatility Multiplier (TVVM), relative to the AVM of the Reference Volatility. The resulting TVVM will always represent the percentage change in the aggregate volatility over a specified time interval for a given 1% change in the reference volatility (21 Trade Day ATM option).

TVVM = (AVM Security / AVM Reference)
TVVM (1-10) Flat = (1.318 / 0.999) = 1.319

It might seem unnecessary to complete the final step (Step 4). After all, the Aggregate Volatility Multiplier (AVM) of the Reference volatility is almost exactly equal to one (0.999). I constrained the AVM of the reference volatility to be very close to 1.0 during the DVM estimation process, but the AVM is not constant. Instead, *the AVM is a function of the level and shape of the term structure of volatilities.* This is the same non-linear volatility aggregation problem that consistently requires application of the JVAF.

The JAF and JVAF are not approximations; they are exact functions. As a result, I wanted to use the same level of precision in the JAF True Vega Multiplier methodology and did not want to compromise the TVVM results by using an approximation.

Figure 7.3 Flat Term Structure (1-10)			+dV	-dV
TD	Forward Volatility	Daily Vol. Multiplier	1.00%	-1.00%
1	20.00%	2.380	22.380%	17.620%
2	20.00%	1.801	21.801%	18.199%
3	20.00%	1.516	21.516%	18.484%
4	20.00%	1.338	21.338%	18.662%
5	20.00%	1.211	21.211%	18.789%
6	20.00%	1.115	21.115%	18.885%
7	20.00%	1.039	21.039%	18.961%
8	20.00%	0.976	20.976%	19.024%
9	20.00%	0.924	20.924%	19.076%
10	20.00%	0.879	20.879%	19.121%
Aggregate Multiplier (1-10)		1.318	21.323%	18.687%
Aggregate Multiplier (1-21)		0.999	21.004%	19.006%
True Vega Multiplier (1-10)		1.319	JVAF$_{+dV}$	JVAF$_{-dV}$

Figure 7.4 illustrates how to calculate the AVM Reference Volatility (21 TD ATM Option), which is Step 2 of the True Vega Volatility Multiplier Methodology. This example uses the Inverted term structure of volatilities base case introduced in Chapter 6. The DVM for each of the first 21 trade days is provided in the center column of Figure 7.4. The two columns on the right side of Figure 7.2 represent the forward volatilities for each trade day, after applying the Daily Volatility Multiplier (DVM) for each trade day to a 1% increase and a 1% decrease in volatility (dV). For example, the forward volatility for the first trade day after a 1% *increase* in volatility (dV) would equal 82.380% (80.00% + 2.380 x 1%) and the forward volatility for the first trade day after a 1% *decrease* in volatility (dV) would equal 77.620% (80.00% + 2.380 x -1%).

After repeating the calculations of the up and down forward volatilities for each of the required trade days, we use the JVAF to calculate the aggregate up (JVAF$_{+dV}$: 73.392%) and aggregate down (JVAF$_{-dV}$: 71.343%) volatilities for the 21-trade-day period. The JVAF values for the up and down cases are shown in the last data row of Figure 7.4.

The AVM for the 21-day ATM option equals 1.024, which is also the AVM of the reference volatility in this specific scenario. This AVM reference volatility is also shown in the last data row of Figure 7.4. Note that this value is still close to 1.0, but it is different from the earlier reference AVM in the Flat term structure example (0.999).

AVM = (JVAF$_{+dV}$ - JVAF$_{-dV}$) / (2dV)
AVM = (73.392% - 71.343%) / (2 x 1%) = 1.024

Figure 7.4 Inverted Term Structure (1-21)			+dV	-dV
TD	Forward Volatility	Daily Vol. Multiplier	1.00%	-1.00%
1	80.00%	2.380	82.380%	77.620%
2	80.00%	1.801	81.801%	78.199%
3	80.00%	1.516	81.516%	78.484%
4	80.00%	1.338	81.338%	78.662%
5	80.00%	1.211	81.211%	78.789%
6	75.00%	1.115	76.115%	73.885%
7	75.00%	1.039	76.039%	73.961%
8	75.00%	0.976	75.976%	74.024%
9	75.00%	0.924	75.924%	74.076%
10	75.00%	0.879	75.879%	74.121%
11	70.00%	0.840	70.840%	69.160%
12	70.00%	0.805	70.805%	69.195%
13	70.00%	0.775	70.775%	69.225%
14	70.00%	0.747	70.747%	69.253%
15	70.00%	0.722	70.722%	69.278%
16	65.00%	0.700	65.700%	64.300%
17	65.00%	0.679	65.679%	64.321%
18	65.00%	0.660	65.660%	64.340%
19	65.00%	0.642	65.642%	64.358%
20	65.00%	0.626	65.626%	64.374%
21	65.00%	0.610	65.610%	64.390%
Aggregate Multiplier (1-21)		1.024	73.392%	71.343%
			JVAF$_{+dV}$	JVAF$_{-dV}$

We are now ready to proceed to Steps 3 and 4 of the True Vega Volatility Multiplier Methodology for the Inverted base case:

3) Calculate the *Aggregate Volatility Multiplier* (AVM) for the security of interest

4) Calculate the Security *True Vega Volatility Multiplier* (TVVM)

In this example, we will calculate the AVM of an ATM option expiring 10 trade days into the future, in the same Inverted term structure base case. Figure 7.5 illustrates the calculation of the AVM, using the DVM for the first 10 trade days. The DVMs and the increases and decreases in the daily forward volatilities are identical to those we used in the 21-trade-day reference AVM calculation in Figure 7.3. However, the JVAF$_{+dv}$ (78.869%) and JVAF$_{-dv}$ (76.214%) values are different and the AVM is higher (1.328).

The last step (Step 4) is to calculate the True Vega Volatility Multiplier for the ATM option expiring in 10 trade days.

TVVM = (AVM Security **/ AVM** Reference**)**
TVVM (1-10) Inverted = (1.328 / 1.024) = 1.297

The TVVM of the option expiring in 10 trade days in the Inverted term structure (1.297) is similar to the TVVM of the same 10-day option in the Flat term structure (1.319), but they are slightly different. Given the importance of the True Vega risk metric, the additional precision of using the exact JAF True Vega formulation is warranted.

Figure 7.5 Inverted Term Structure (1-10)			+dV	-dV
TD	Forward Volatility	Daily Vol. Multiplier	1.00%	-1.00%
1	80.00%	2.380	82.380%	77.620%
2	80.00%	1.801	81.801%	78.199%
3	80.00%	1.516	81.516%	78.484%
4	80.00%	1.338	81.338%	78.662%
5	80.00%	1.211	81.211%	78.789%
6	75.00%	1.115	76.115%	73.885%
7	75.00%	1.039	76.039%	73.961%
8	75.00%	0.976	75.976%	74.024%
9	75.00%	0.924	75.924%	74.076%
10	75.00%	0.879	75.879%	74.121%
Aggregate Multiplier (1-10)		1.328	78.869%	76.214%
Aggregate Multiplier (1-21)		1.024	73.392%	71.343%
True Vega Multiplier (1-10)		1.297	JVAF$_{+dV}$	JVAF$_{-dV}$

Partial Volatility Multipliers (6-10) - Flat

We can use the JVAF to go beyond True Vega and calculate JAF partial True Vegas. Partial True Vegas represent the change in the value of an option for a *change in aggregate volatility over a specific forward volatility period*, in response to *a 1% change in an ATM option with exactly 21 trade days until expiration (the reference volatility)*. To calculate partial Vegas, we need to calculate *partial* Aggregate Volatility Multipliers (AVMs) for each forward volatility period of interest. For example, if we were interested in calculating the partial AVM for the 6-10 forward trade day period (the second week in the Chapter 6 validation examples), we would use the same AVM calculation, but limit the AVM calculation to DVMs in the 6-10 trade day forward volatility period.

Figure 7.6 illustrates the AVM calculation for the 6-10 trade day forward volatility period in the Flat term structure base case. *Note ALL options expiring on or after 10 trade days in the future would be exposed to this volatility multiplier and would be affected by a change in the 6-10 trade day aggregate volatility.* The partial volatility multipliers would be used to calculate the partial Vegas and the partial True Vegas for all forward volatility periods. Detailed examples of partial Vegas and partial True Vegas will be provided in the next chapter and in the JAF Validation Supplement.

The DVMs and the increases and decreases in the daily 6-10 trade day forward volatilities are identical to those we used in the earlier 21-trade-day reference AVM calculation in Figure 7.2. However, the $JVAF_{+dV}$ (20.987%) and $JVAF_{-dV}$ (19.014%) values are different and the AVM is lower (0.987).

The last step (Step 4) is to calculate the True Vega Volatility Multiplier for the 6-10 trade day forward volatility period. Notice that the 6-10 trade day partial TVVM is lower than the 1-10 trade day TVVM due to mean reversion.

TVVM = (AVM Security **/ AVM** Reference**)**
TVVM (6-10) Flat = (0.987 / 0.999) = 0.988

Figure 7.6 Flat Term Structure (6-10)			+dV	-dV
TD	Forward Volatility	Daily Vol. Multiplier	1.00%	-1.00%
6	20.00%	1.115	21.115%	18.885%
7	20.00%	1.039	21.039%	18.961%
8	20.00%	0.976	20.976%	19.024%
9	20.00%	0.924	20.924%	19.076%
10	20.00%	0.879	20.879%	19.121%
Aggregate Multiplier (6-10)		0.987	20.987%	19.014%
Aggregate Multiplier (1-21)		0.999	21.004%	19.006%
True Vega Multiplier (6-10)		0.988	$JVAF_{+dV}$	$JVAF_{-dV}$

Partial Volatility Multipliers (6-10) - Inverted

Figure 7.7 illustrates the AVM calculation for the 6-10 trade day forward volatility period in the *Inverted term structure base case*. The DVMs and the increases and decreases in the daily 6-10 trade day forward volatilities are identical to those we used in the 21-trade-day reference AVM calculation in Figure 7.4. However, the $JVAF_{+dV}$ (75.987%) and $JVAF_{-dV}$ (74.013%) values are different and the AVM is lower (0.987).

The last step (Step 4) is to calculate the True Vega Volatility Multiplier for the 6-10 trade day forward volatility period. Notice that the 6-10 trade-day partial TVVM is lower than the 1-10 trade-day TVVM due to mean reversion.

TVVM = (AVM Security **/ AVM** Reference**)**
TVVM (6-10) Inverted = (0.987 / 1.024) = 0.963

Figure 7.7 Inverted Term Structure (6-10)		+dV	-dV
TD	Forward Volatility	Daily Vol. Multiplier	1.00%	-1.00%
6	75.00%	1.115	76.115%	73.885%
7	75.00%	1.039	76.039%	73.961%
8	75.00%	0.976	75.976%	74.024%
9	75.00%	0.924	75.924%	74.076%
10	75.00%	0.879	75.879%	74.121%
Aggregate Multiplier (6-10)		0.987	75.987%	74.013%
Aggregate Multiplier (1-21)		1.024	73.392%	71.343%
True Vega Multiplier (6-10)		0.963	JVAF$_{+dV}$	JVAF$_{-dV}$

Figure 7.8 is a graphical example of the Daily Volatility Multipliers (DVMs) (Circles), the True Vega Volatility Multipliers (TVVMs) for a series of ATM SPX options (Squares), and the TVVMs for a series of VIX futures contracts (Diamonds). The Flat 20% term structure of volatilities was used to calculate all of the volatility multipliers. The TVVMs will vary with the level and shape of term structure of volatilities, but the values in the graph are representative. A full year of volatility multipliers is included in the graph.

Since the DVM mean reversion graph is downward sloping, the DVM for a specific trade day will always be below the options and VIX futures TVVMs. This is because the options and futures TVVMs both represent the aggregation of shorter-term DVMs, which will always exceed the DVM of the final trade day.

For example, the DVM of the 42nd trade day in the future equals 0.4293. The AVM for the ATM option that expires 42 trade days into the future aggregates DVMs 1-42. The standardized TVVM for the 42-trade-day ATM option equals 0.7489, well above the DVM of the 42nd trade day. The AVM for the VIX futures contract that expires 21 trade days into the future aggregates DVMs 22-42, and has an X-coordinate in the graph of 42 (the final trade day used in the VIX contract volatility period). The resulting TVVM for the VIX futures contract expiring 21 trade days into the future equals 0.4980, which is also above the DVM of the 42nd trade day (0.4293).

As we would expect, the TVVM of the option is higher than the TVVM of the VIX futures contract, which is higher than the DVM for the final trade day in the period. This pattern is evident for all periods. However, the effect for long-term periods is more muted due to the more modest slope of the DVM function for distant trade days. As options and volatility futures contracts age, their TVVMs will increase.

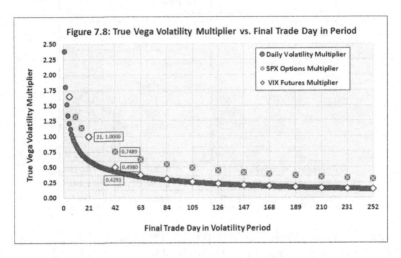

Conclusion

This chapter provided a detailed explanation of the process used to calculate the JAF True Vegas and partial True Vegas. To review, the following steps are required to calculate the True Vega Volatility Multipliers for all securities.

True Vega Volatility Multiplier Methodology:
1) Calculate the *Daily Volatility Multipliers* (DVM) for all future trade days
2) Calculate the *Aggregate Volatility Multiplier* (AVM) for the reference volatility (21-TD)
3) Calculate the *Aggregate Volatility Multiplier* (AVM) for the security of interest
4) Calculate the Security *True Vega Volatility Multiplier* (TVVM)

TVVM = (AVM $_{Security}$ / AVM $_{Reference}$)

The resulting *True Vega Volatility Multiplier* (TVVM) represents the percentage change in the aggregate volatility over a specified time interval for a given 1% change in the reference volatility (21 Trade Day ATM option). *If the volatility is constant over the entire forward interval*, the JAF True Vega equals the constant 1% Vega multiplied by the True Vega Volatility Multiplier

(TVVM) for each security. This multiplicative relationship only holds *if the volatility is constant over the forward period*. If the volatility is *not* constant over the forward period, it is still possible to use the general JAF Greek algorithm and the JVAF to calculate precise JAF True Vegas and partial True Vegas.

In general, the components of the TVVM (JVAF$_{+dV}$ and JVAF$_{-dV}$) for each security are used in the JAF Greek Algorithm from Chapter 5 to calculate the JAF True Vega.

Vega$_C$ = [(C$_U$ – C$_D$)/(σ_U – σ_D)]/100
Vega$_P$ = [(P$_U$ – P$_D$)/(σ_U – σ_D)]/100

JAF True Vega$_C$ = {[(C$_{+dV}$ – C$_{dV}$)/(JVAF$_{+dV}$ – JVAF$_{-dV}$)]/100}/ AVM
Reference
JAF True Vega$_P$ = {[(P$_{+dV}$ – P$_{dV}$)/(JVAF$_{+dV}$ – JVAF$_{-dV}$)]/100}/ AVM
Reference

The first step in the methodology requires the application of the DVM mean reversion model:

DVM = (a * b + c * TD ** d) / (b + TD ** d)

TD = Number of Trade Days in the future
a = 12.7524497577126
b = 0.239021016250414
c = -0.0987378460389707
d = 0.462862829394134

The coefficients for the above DVM model were estimated from over 15 years of daily implied volatility data for the SPX, NDX, and RUT indices. Since the *True Vega Volatility Multiplier* (TVVM) represents the percentage change in the aggregate volatility over a specified time interval for a given 1% change in the reference volatility (21 Trade Day ATM option), the first step in the model estimation process was to calculate the closing reference volatilities for SPX, NDX, and RUT options.

Since it was rare that an ATM option would be available with exactly 21 trade days remaining until expiration, it was necessary to derive the reference volatility from ATM options with expiration dates that bracketed 21 trade days. This requires the disaggregation and aggregation of forward volatilities, which again requires the JVAF. Unfortunately, many practitioners and option analytics vendors use a simple linear interpolation when solving for similar interim volatilities for a desired date.

An example is the easiest way to understand the magnitude of the interpolation error. Let's assume we observe the implied volatilities of two ATM options, one with 10 trade days remaining until expiration (10.00%) and the second with 31 trade days remaining until expiration (15.00%). A simple linear interpolation of the two volatilities would generate an ATM implied volatility of 12.62% for the option with 21 trade days remaining until expiration. The linear weights would be 47.62% for option one and 52.38% for option two; using the same weights would generate a linear weighted-average of 21 trade days.

The correct methodology requires the JVAF. The first step is to use the JVAF to solve for the forward volatility between the 10th and 31st trade day. I have demonstrated the JVAF several times, so I will not include the formulas here, but the annualized forward volatility equals 16.868%. We then use the JVAF again to aggregate the 10.000% volatility for the first 10 trade days and the 16.868% volatility for the next 11 trade days to find the JVAF aggregate volatility for the hypothetical option with 21 trade days remaining until expiration. The resulting JVAF aggregate volatility for the 21-day option equals 14.023%.

In this example, the error from the linear interpolation equals 1.403%, which is almost four times as large as the error of the DVM model. To make matters worse, the magnitude of the linear interpolation error is not constant over time. It fluctuates with the term structure of volatilities and with the width of the trade-day bracket around the desired 21 trade day reference period.

The resulting daily changes in the ATM reference volatilities were used as the explanatory variable in the DVM estimation model. The non-linear optimization process identified the DVM coefficients that minimized the sum of the squared errors of the DVM mean reversion model. Since daily DVM values cannot be observed directly, the process described in this chapter used the DVM model coefficients to solve for the daily Average Volatility Multipliers (AVMs) and True Vega Volatility Multipliers (TVVMs) for each ATM option in the matrix (over 170,000 observations). This was a massive non-linear optimization problem. After cleaning the data for pricing errors, the resulting Root Mean Square Error (RMSE) of the DVM mean-reversion model was 0.386% (across all 15 years of daily data, all three indices, and all ATM options in the matrices).

The resulting DVM model was used with the JVAF to demonstrate the calculations of Aggregate Volatility Multipliers (AVMs) and standardized True Vega Volatility Multipliers (TVVMs) for several periods (including partial forward periods), using two different term structures of volatilities.

If the volatility is constant over the entire forward interval, the JAF True Vega equals the constant 1% Vega multiplied by the True Vega Volatility Multiplier (TVVM) for each security. This multiplicative relationship only holds *if the volatility is constant over the forward period.* If the volatility is *not* constant over the forward period, it is still possible to use the general JAF Greek algorithm and the JVAF to calculate precise JAF True Vegas and partial True Vegas.

In general, the components of the TVVM (JVAF$_{+dV}$ and JVAF$_{-dV}$) for each security are used in the JAF Greek Algorithm from Chapter 5 to calculate the JAF True Vega.

Vega$_C$ = [(C$_U$ − C$_D$)/(σ$_U$ − σ$_D$)]/100
Vega$_P$ = [(P$_U$ − P$_D$)/(σ$_U$ − σ$_D$)]/100

The JAF True Vega formulas below first use the JVAF to derive the aggregate volatilities for a 1% increase and decrease in volatility (dV), adjusted for mean reversion via the Daily Volatility Multiplier (DVM). The resulting JVAF aggregate volatilities are then used in the JAF Greek Algorithm to calculate the sensitivity of the price of the option to a change in volatility. The final step is to divide the resulting price sensitivity by the Average Volatility Multiplier (AVM) for the 21-day reference volatility. This standardizes the resulting JAF True Vega calculation relative to the reference volatility.

JAF True Vega$_C$ = {[(C$_{+dV}$ − C$_{dV}$)/(JVAF$_{+dV}$ − JVAF$_{-dV}$)]/100}
/ AVM Reference
JAF True Vega$_P$ = {[(P$_{+dV}$ − P$_{dV}$)/(JVAF$_{+dV}$ − JVAF$_{-dV}$)]/100}
/ AVM Reference

The resulting JAF True Vega values and partial True Vega values are much more accurate and realistic than the standard BSM Vega values. The use of the JVAF in the calculation of AVM and TVVM ensures that all of the True Vega values are consistent across all options and volatility futures contracts. A selection of JAF Greek exhibits will be included in Chapter 8, including partial Vega, True Vega, partial True Vega, partial Rho, and Theta. The JAF Greeks correct the invalid constant interest rate and volatility assumptions of the BSM.

In Chapter 8, JAF partial Greeks are provided for Vega, True Vega, and for Rho. Partial Rho is similar to partial Vega, except the option price sensitivity is calculated with respect to a 1% change in the forward *risk-free rate*, instead of the forward *volatility*. The JAF partial Greeks offer a new and unprecedented level of risk management insight and control in option trading. Please see the JAF Validation supplement for a comprehensive set of JAF Greek validation examples.

8) JAF: ABRIDGED GREEK RESULTS

This chapter will provide an abridged version of the JAF Greek results. The JAF Greek Algorithm presented in Chapter 5 is flexible enough to calculate all of the Greeks, including the more obscure second or third-order Greeks. In addition, the JAF Greek Algorithm uses pairs of discrete values, which means that the independence assumption implicit in the BSM partial derivatives can be relaxed to calculate "True" Greeks. For example, "True" Delta and "True" Gamma can be calculated by integrating a volatility model with the JAF Greek Algorithm. I have discussed True Greeks extensively in my earlier books and articles, so I will not revisit True Delta and True Gamma here.

Instead, I will limit the JAF Greek validation results in this chapter and in the JAF Validation Supplement to the JAF Greeks that are affected by eliminating the invalid constant interest rate and volatility assumptions of the BSM: Vega, Partial Vega, True Vega, Partial True Vega, Rho, Partial Rho, and Theta.

Comprehensive JAF Valuation and Greek results are available in the JAF Validation Supplement PDF (see Resource Chapter for download link address). The JAF Validation Supplement is divided into nine sections, each with multiple groups of exhibits. Abridged samples from the first seven sections were presented in Chapter 6 and samples from the last two sections are included in this chapter. Each of the validation sections in this book include the objective or objectives of the section, plus one or more validation exhibits from the JAF Validation supplement (with the same numbering system). For each of the validation exhibits included in this book, I will explain how the validation results fit into the context of the JAF Validation plan, referencing specific values when it would be instructive.

As was the case in the last few chapters, the validation results assume that all monthly options expire at the close on the last trade-day of the month and that there are exactly 21 trade days in every month. Given this assumption, interest rates, volatilities, and option expiration dates will all coincide perfectly with calendar months. This will allow us to discuss hypothetical interest rates and volatilities for specific calendar month examples, without any confusion regarding whether we are referring to the period before or after the standard monthly option expiration date on the third Friday of the month. *Note: this assumption is only included to avoid confusion and is NOT required for the JAF, which can accommodate any number of periods, each with a variable number of trade days.*

JAF Validation Plan

The JAF validation plan is designed to demonstrate that the JAF satisfies every element of its objective. For ease of reference, I have repeated the JAF Objective and Validation Plan Elements below.

JAF Objective:
Design an objective framework that employs a user-specified Market Risk Premium in conjunction with the complete term structure of unique interest rates and the complete term structure of unique volatilities to calculate theoretically sound and internally consistent: current and future option values, current and future Greeks, and current and future volatility index (VIX) values.

Each of the validation sections is designed to demonstrate one or more of the following elements:

Validation Plan Elements (VPE): (Multiple forward interest rate and volatility periods)
1) Demonstrate that aggregate input values derived from the Interest Rate Aggregation Formula and the Johnson Volatility Aggregation Formula (JVAF), applied to multiple forward periods, generate theoretically correct and consistent results when used with the BOM, BSM, and the JAF combined BOM & BSM model.
2) Demonstrate that the BOM converges to the BSM as the number of intervals is increased and that the resulting BOM error can be made arbitrarily small by increasing the number of binomial intervals as desired.
3) Demonstrate that the JAF current, interim, and expiration valuation algorithms generate theoretically correct and internally consistent current, interim, and expiration *values.*
4) Demonstrate that the values derived from the JAF current, interim, and expiration valuation algorithms generate theoretically correct and internally consistent *rates of return.*
5) Demonstrate that the values derived from the JAF current, interim, and expiration valuation algorithms generate theoretically correct and internally consistent current and future *Greeks.*

Note: the above validation plan elements are not independent. For example, the JAF Greek Algorithm requires the use of the JVAF and Interest Rate Aggregation Formulas, plus the JAF Current, Interim, and Expiration Valuation Algorithms. As a result, validating the results of the JAF Greek Algorithm also indirectly validates the JAF aggregation formulas, the JAF Valuation Algorithms, and the resulting JAF risk-neutral and risk-averse returns.

The *BSM* Greeks are derived from continuous functions which assume that interest rates and volatilities are constant and consistent for all options across all expiration dates. It is widely known and understood that this *BSM* assumption is invalid, which means the continuous *BSM* Greek values are not theoretically consistent and are in fact incorrect. As a result, the objective of the JAF Greek algorithm is <u>NOT</u> to reproduce the invalid and internally inconsistent BSM Greeks.

Instead, the objective of the JAF Greek Algorithm is to demonstrate that the values derived from the JAF current, interim, and expiration valuation algorithms generate theoretically correct and internally consistent current and future Greeks, derived from a user-specified complete term structure of unique interest rates and a complete term structure of unique forward volatilities.

While the sample Exhibits in this chapter include the BSM Greeks (using the JVAF and Interest Rate Aggregation formulas) for comparison purposes, any BSM deviation from the JAF Greeks reflects the errors in the *BSM* Greeks - due to their invalid and limiting assumptions.

JAF Validation: Section VIII

Section VIII Objective:
The objective of Section VIII is to demonstrate that the JAF Greek algorithm produces highly accurate *current* Partial Vega, Partial True Vega, Partial Rho, and Theta for all option expirations, in all three bases cases, by eliminating the errors from the invalid constant interest rate and constant volatility assumptions of the BOM and BSM.

Section VIII: JAF Current Greeks – JAF *Current* Partial Vega, Partial True Vega, Partial Rho, and Theta for all three base case scenarios: flat, normal, and inverted.

Group 32) JAF Greeks (Partial Vega, Partial True Vega, Partial Rho, Theta): Calls, Flat

Group 33) JAF Greeks (Partial Vega, Partial True Vega, Partial Rho,

Theta): Puts, Flat

Group 34) JAF Greeks (Partial Vega, Partial True Vega, Partial Rho, Theta): Calls, Normal

Group 35) JAF Greeks (Partial Vega, Partial True Vega, Partial Rho, Theta): Puts, Normal

Group 36) JAF Greeks (Partial Vega, Partial True Vega, Partial Rho, Theta): Calls, Inverted

Group 37) JAF Greeks (Partial Vega, Partial True Vega, Partial Rho, Theta): Puts, Inverted

Section VIII: Group and Exhibit Structure

The complete set of validation groups and exhibits from Section VIII is available in the JAF Validation Supplement. All groups and exhibits from Section VIII of the JAF Validation Supplement are described below, so please pay particular attention to the descriptions of the *select* sample exhibits examined in this section: Exhibits 37.1, 37.2, 37.3, and 37.4.

There are six groups of exhibits in Section VIII, each with a different set of input values, assumptions, and validation objectives. All aggregate volatility and average risk-free rates were derived using the JAF and the resulting values were used with the BSM model to calculate the required price sensitivities (Greeks). This process is described in detail in Chapter 5. All Groups in this section compare the sum of the JAF Partial Vegas and Partial Rhos (all forward volatilities or rates change individually), the JAF Vega and Rho (all forward volatilities or rates change at the same time), and the standard BSM Vega and Rho (calculated using the JAVF and aggregate interest rate formulas).

JAF Vega calculations assume a constant 1% change in forward volatility; BSM Vega calculations assume a constant 1% change in aggregate volatility (derived with the JAVF); JAF True Vega assumes a 1% change in the 21-trade-day ATM volatility with corresponding (non-constant) forward volatility changes derived from the JAF True Vega mean reversion model (explained in Chapter 7). All Groups in this section also compare the JAF Theta to the BSM standard Theta. Groups 32 & 33 present the Greek analysis for calls and puts in the *Flat* base case. Groups 34 & 35 present the Greek analysis for calls and puts in the *Normal* base case. Finally, Groups 36 & 37 perform the same Greek analysis for calls and puts in the *Inverted* base case.

Each validation group in Section VIII includes the same four exhibits: Exhibit 1 for constant Partial Vega, Exhibit 2 for Partial True Vega, Exhibit

3 for Partial Rho, and Exhibit 4 for Theta. Each exhibit compares the JAF values to the BSM standard Greeks. The BSM Greeks are derived from continuous functions which assume that interest rates and volatilities are constant and consistent for all options across all expiration dates. It is widely known and understood that this BSM assumption is invalid, which means the continuous BSM Greek values are not theoretically consistent and are, in fact, incorrect.

The JAF allows us to calculate partial and total Vega, True Vega, Rho, and Theta values which are theoretically consistent and accurate for all term structures of interest rates and volatilities. In addition, the partial Greeks provide much more information about the price sensitivity of each option to the entire forward term structures of interest rates and volatilities. These partial risk metrics have never been available for options in the past and are only possible in practice using the JAF. The Partial True Vegas are highly accurate given their use of market-derived volatility multipliers for the entire term structure of volatilities. The True Vega model used in the JAF was estimated using over 15 years of daily ATM IVs for the entire SPX, NDX, and RUT indices. The JAF True Vega model is described in detail in Chapter 7.

The formats of Exhibits 1 and 3 are identical. The top four rows of each exhibit summarize the market environment. Row 1 shows the annualized volatility for each forward period. Row 2 shows the *aggregate* volatility from time zero through the end of each forward period. Rows 3 and 4 show the forward risk-free rate in each forward period and the *average* risk-free rate from time zero through the end of each forward period. Row 5 in Exhibits 1 and 3 show the number of trade days in each forward period.

The format of Exhibit 2 is the same as Exhibits 1 and 3, except for two additional rows inserted (Rows 5 and 6). The new Rows 5 and 6 provide the True Vega Volatility Multiplier (TVVM) for each forward period and for the period from time zero through the end of each forward period. For example, a hypothetical value of 0.75 would indicate that the forward volatility in that period would only increase by 0.75% in response to a 1% change in the reference (21 TD) aggregate volatility. *If the forward volatilities are constant for an entire period*, it is possible to multiply the Partial Vegas in each period by the forward volatility multiplier for that period to calculate the Partial True Vega for each period.

The left-hand column in all four exhibits shows the expiration date of each option, followed by its Vega, True Vega, Rho, or Theta values. All option expirations are shown in each exhibit.

Section VIII: Sample Exhibits

Exhibit 37 - Model Assumptions / Input Values: Stock Price = 1000, Strike Price = 1000, Time to Expiration = various, Inverted term structure, risk-premium N/A.

The complete set of model assumptions and input values for all Group 37 Exhibits is provided above. Exhibit 37.1 provides the put option partial Vegas for each option in each forward volatility period, derived from the JAF Combined Binomial & BSM model, using *"Inverted" downward-sloping term structures* of volatilities and risk-free rates, for a large number of intervals (8,192 average of N & N+1). Since current option values are independent of the risk environment (neutral or averse), and the Greek metrics quantify changes in these current values, the Greeks are also independent of the risk environment. The sums of the partial Vegas are also included in Exhibit 37.1, as are the BSM Vegas for all put options.

Section VIII exhibits assume *different* volatilities and *different* risk-free interest rates in each of 15 sub-periods. Due to the variable volatilities and interest rates in a multiple period of varying length, the JVAF and interest rate aggregation formulas are both required. In addition, the JAF current, interim, and expiration algorithms will also be essential to calculate returns in both sub-periods.

The partial Vegas In Exhibit 37.1 measure the change in the value of the option per 1% change in the *forward volatility* in each forward period. By definition, the sum of the partial Vegas assume that all forward volatilities change individually by a constant or uniform 1%.

As discussed extensively in Chapter 7, the constant 1% change in all forward volatilities is grossly inaccurate for all assets. Volatility is mean-reverting for all asset-classes and is priced accordingly in all options and volatility futures markets. I only included the *constant 1%* partial Vegas to provide a realistic comparison with the BSM Vega. As explained in Chapter 7, Partial *True* Vega and *True* Vega should always be used in practice.

There are a number of interesting observations we can make from examining Exhibit 37.1. First, every put option is not exposed to a change in every forward volatility. For example, a 1% change in the expected forward volatility in the month of February would have no impact on any of the put options expiring in January, which is consistent with their JAF partial Vegas of zero. All put options with expirations in February or a later month would be affected by a change in the expected forward volatility in February.

Interestingly, the JAF February partial Vegas of these longer-dated options are not the same. In addition, the JAF partial Vegas for March, April, May, etc. continue to decline. This is not a function of time; instead, it is a function of the unique forward volatilities. In addition, if we compare the sum of the JAF partial Vegas for the December put option to the BSM Vega for the same option, we find that the BSM Vega is overstated by more than 11% (3.754 versus 3.381). All of these effects are due to using the unique term structure of forward volatilities. *The only time the BSM values will match the sum of the JAF partial Vegas is if all of the forward volatilities are exactly the same.* This would require that every option of every maturity would have the same implied volatility. In all other cases, the BSM will be incorrect, and the partial Vegas will be different for each option and for each forward period.

In Chapter 6 and in the JAF Validation Supplement, I demonstrated that the JAF valuation algorithms (which are used to derive the JAF Greeks) incorporate the complete unique term structures of interest rates and volatilities *exactly* – provided a sufficient number of intervals are used in the calculation. The aggregate volatilities are therefore a function of the forward volatilities and can be derived using the JVAF.

I will not go into the math here, but the BSM Vega formula assumes that all implied volatilities change by exactly 1%. Mathematically, this requires a different set of changes in the forward volatilities for every forward volatility curve. In addition, it also requires different changes in each forward volatility, or a shift in the slope and shape of the term structure of volatilities – which is illogical.

Out of curiosity, I calculated the required changes in the term structure of volatilities for the Inverted base case, under the level 1% BSM Vega assumption (calculations not shown). In the Inverted term structure example, the BSM constant 1% change in all *aggregate* volatilities would require the longest *forward* volatilities to decline by over 2.5 times the magnitude of the change in the shortest *forward* volatility. Even the resulting increases and decreases in forward volatilities would be asymmetric under the BSM assumptions!

Aggregate volatilities are derived from forward volatilities. The BSM assumption of constant changes in aggregate volatilities results in unrealistic and inconsistent changes in forward volatilities, and these unrealistic and inconsistent changes would be dependent on the level and shape of the forward volatility curve. The resulting BSM Vega values are incorrect, and the premise of constant 1% changes in aggregate volatilities is not practical.

Conversely, the JAF partial Vegas represent the change in the value of an option for a 1% change in each *forward volatility*. The JAF is theoretically correct and can be applied accurately to any forward volatility curve, and used in conjunction with any term structure of unique forward rates.

Exhibit 37.1: JAF Put Option Partial Vega (Inverted Term Structure)

	JAN W1	JAN W2	JAN W3	JAN W4	FEB	MAR	APR	MAY	JUN	JUL	AUG	SEP	OCT	NOV	DEC	Sum JAF Partials	JAF Vega	BSM Vega
Annualized	80.000%	75.000%	70.000%	65.000%	60.000%	55.000%	50.000%	45.000%	40.000%	35.000%	30.000%	25.000%	20.000%	15.000%	10.000%			
Volatility	80.000%	77.540%	75.111%	72.366%	66.471%	62.881%	59.921%	57.248%	54.752%	52.389%	50.140%	48.001%	45.975%	44.068%	42.291%	42.291%	42.291%	42.291%
Risk Free	10.000%	9.500%	9.000%	8.500%	8.000%	7.500%	7.000%	6.500%	6.000%	5.500%	5.000%	4.500%	4.000%	3.500%	3.000%			
Interest Rate	10.000%	9.750%	9.500%	9.214%	8.607%	8.238%	7.929%	7.643%	7.369%	7.102%	6.839%	6.579%	6.321%	6.065%	5.810%	5.810%	5.810%	5.810%
Trade Days	5	5	5	6	21	21	21	21	21	21	21	21	21	21	21	252	252	252
Period / Opt.Expire (TD)	JAN W1	JAN W2	JAN W3	JAN W4	FEB	MAR	APR	MAY	JUN	JUL	AUG	SEP	OCT	NOV	DEC			
JAN W1 (5)	0.560	0.000	0.000	0.000	0.000	0.000	0.000	0.000	0.000	0.000	0.000	0.000	0.000	0.000	0.000	0.560	0.560	0.560
JAN W2 (10)	0.408	0.382	0.000	0.000	0.000	0.000	0.000	0.000	0.000	0.000	0.000	0.000	0.000	0.000	0.000	0.790	0.790	0.791
JAN W3 (15)	0.343	0.322	0.300	0.000	0.000	0.000	0.000	0.000	0.000	0.000	0.000	0.000	0.000	0.000	0.000	0.965	0.965	0.966
JAN W4 (21)	0.300	0.281	0.263	0.293	0.000	0.000	0.000	0.000	0.000	0.000	0.000	0.000	0.000	0.000	0.000	1.137	1.137	1.140
FEB (42)	0.229	0.215	0.201	0.224	0.722	0.000	0.000	0.000	0.000	0.000	0.000	0.000	0.000	0.000	0.000	1.590	1.590	1.600
MAR (63)	0.196	0.184	0.172	0.192	0.619	0.567	0.000	0.000	0.000	0.000	0.000	0.000	0.000	0.000	0.000	1.930	1.930	1.946
APR (84)	0.177	0.166	0.155	0.173	0.559	0.512	0.466	0.000	0.000	0.000	0.000	0.000	0.000	0.000	0.000	2.209	2.209	2.233
MAY (105)	0.165	0.155	0.145	0.161	0.520	0.477	0.434	0.390	0.000	0.000	0.000	0.000	0.000	0.000	0.000	2.447	2.447	2.482
JUN (126)	0.157	0.147	0.137	0.153	0.494	0.453	0.412	0.371	0.329	0.000	0.000	0.000	0.000	0.000	0.000	2.653	2.653	2.706
JUL (147)	0.151	0.142	0.132	0.147	0.476	0.436	0.397	0.357	0.317	0.278	0.000	0.000	0.000	0.000	0.000	2.834	2.834	2.910
AUG (168)	0.147	0.138	0.129	0.143	0.463	0.425	0.386	0.348	0.309	0.270	0.232	0.000	0.000	0.000	0.000	2.991	2.991	3.099
SEP (189)	0.144	0.135	0.126	0.141	0.455	0.417	0.379	0.341	0.303	0.265	0.227	0.190	0.000	0.000	0.000	3.125	3.125	3.276
OCT (210)	0.143	0.134	0.125	0.139	0.449	0.412	0.374	0.337	0.300	0.262	0.225	0.187	0.150	0.000	0.000	3.236	3.236	3.443
NOV (231)	0.142	0.133	0.124	0.138	0.446	0.409	0.371	0.334	0.297	0.260	0.223	0.186	0.149	0.111	0.000	3.322	3.322	3.602
DEC (252)	0.141	0.132	0.123	0.137	0.444	0.407	0.370	0.333	0.296	0.259	0.222	0.185	0.148	0.111	0.074	3.381	3.381	3.754

As explained above, *True* Vega should always be used in practice. Exhibit 37.2 provides the put option partial True Vegas for each option in each forward volatility period, derived from the JAF Combined Binomial & BSM model, using *"Inverted" downward-sloping term structures* of volatilities and risk-free rates, for a large number of intervals (8,192 average of N & N+1). The sums of the partial True Vegas are also included in Exhibit 37.2, as are the BSM Vegas for all put options.

Unlike the conventional BSM Vega, the JAF True Vega uses the JAF Greek algorithm to calculate the change in the value of an option *for a 1% change in an ATM option with exactly 21 trade days until expiration (the reference volatility)*. This means that every option will experience a different change in volatility, instead of the constant 1% change assumed by the BSM. Similar to Exhibit 37.1, partial True Vegas are calculated for each forward period in Exhibit 37.2. Each partial True Vega is derived from two components: the partial (1% constant) Vega from Exhibit 37.1 and the partial True Vega Multiplier for the respective period.

For example, the partial (1% constant) February Vega for the February put option equals 0.722 (Exhibit 37.1), which indicates that the sensitivity of the February put option to a 1% change in the February forward volatility is +0.722. However, due to mean-reversion, the February forward volatility will not change by 1% in response to a 1% change in the 21-trade-day reference volatility. In fact, it will only change by 0.486% (from Row 5 of Figure 37.2). As a result, the JAF partial True Vega for the February forward volatility period equals 0.351 (0.722 x 0.486). This multiplicative relationship holds *if the volatility is constant over the forward period*. If the volatility is not constant over the forward period, it is still possible to calculate precise JAF True Vegas and partial True Vegas.

The partial True Vegas for all options in all forward periods are shown in Exhibit 37.2. In all cases, the JAF partial True Vega represents the sensitivity of the value of the option *to a 1% change in the 21-trade-day ATM reference volatility*. The JAF True Vega Volatility multiplier for each forward period automatically integrates the unique effects of mean-reversion for each specific forward volatility period.

The most obvious observation from Exhibit 37.2 is that the partial True Vegas decline much more sharply over time. Due to mean-reversion, near-term forward volatilities are much more sensitive to changes in the reference volatility than longer-term forward volatilities. The resulting near-term partial True Vegas are magnified and the longer-term partial True Vegas are diminished.

Perhaps the most important observation is the BSM Vega is not a reasonable risk metric. For the December put option, the BSM Vega is overstated by over 180% relative to the sum of the JAF partial True Vegas (3.754 versus 1.339)! While the JAF partial True Vegas do rely on a mean-reversion function, using *any* reasonable mean-reversion function would be much more accurate and useful than assuming all aggregate volatilities change by a constant amount.

Exhibit 37.2: JAF Put Option Partial True Vega (Inverted Term Structure)

Annualized Volatility	80.000%	75.000%	70.000%	65.000%	60.000%	55.000%	50.000%	45.000%	40.000%	35.000%	30.000%	25.000%	20.000%	15.000%	10.000%			
Volatility	80.000%	77.540%	75.111%	72.366%	66.471%	62.881%	59.921%	57.248%	54.752%	52.389%	50.140%	48.001%	45.975%	44.068%	42.291%	42.29%	42.291%	42.29%
Risk Free Interest Rate	10.000%	9.500%	9.000%	8.500%	8.000%	7.500%	7.000%	6.500%	6.000%	5.500%	5.000%	4.500%	4.000%	3.500%	3.000%			
	10.000%	9.750%	9.500%	9.214%	8.607%	8.238%	7.929%	7.643%	7.369%	7.102%	6.889%	6.579%	6.321%	6.065%	5.810%	5.81%	5.810%	5.81%
Volatility Multiplier	1.610	0.963	0.759	0.637	0.486	0.365	0.301	0.258	0.228	0.204	0.185	0.170	0.157	0.145	0.136			
	1.610	1.297	1.128	1.000	0.764	0.645	0.570	0.518	0.479	0.449	0.424	0.403	0.386	0.371	0.357	0.357	0.357	0.357
Trade Days	5	5	5	6	21	21	21	21	21	21	21	21	21	21	21	252	252	252
Period / Opt.Expire (TD)	JAN W1	JAN W2	JAN W3	JAN W4	FEB	MAR	APR	MAY	JUN	JUL	AUG	SEP	OCT	NOV	DEC	Sum JAF Partials	JAF True Vega	BSM Vega
JAN W1 (5)	0.902	0.000	0.000	0.000	0.000	0.000	0.000	0.000	0.000	0.000	0.000	0.000	0.000	0.000	0.000	0.902	0.902	0.560
JAN W2 (10)	0.657	0.368	0.000	0.000	0.000	0.000	0.000	0.000	0.000	0.000	0.000	0.000	0.000	0.000	0.000	1.025	1.025	0.791
JAN W3 (15)	0.552	0.310	0.228	0.000	0.000	0.000	0.000	0.000	0.000	0.000	0.000	0.000	0.000	0.000	0.000	1.090	1.090	0.966
JAN W4 (21)	0.483	0.271	0.199	0.186	0.000	0.000	0.000	0.000	0.000	0.000	0.000	0.000	0.000	0.000	0.000	1.140	1.140	1.140
FEB (42)	0.369	0.207	0.152	0.142	0.351	0.000	0.000	0.000	0.000	0.000	0.000	0.000	0.000	0.000	0.000	1.222	1.222	1.600
MAR (63)	0.316	0.177	0.131	0.122	0.301	0.207	0.000	0.000	0.000	0.000	0.000	0.000	0.000	0.000	0.000	1.254	1.254	1.946
APR (84)	0.286	0.160	0.118	0.110	0.271	0.187	0.140	0.000	0.000	0.000	0.000	0.000	0.000	0.000	0.000	1.273	1.273	2.233
MAY (105)	0.266	0.149	0.110	0.103	0.253	0.174	0.130	0.101	0.000	0.000	0.000	0.000	0.000	0.000	0.000	1.286	1.286	2.482
JUN (126)	0.253	0.142	0.104	0.097	0.240	0.166	0.124	0.096	0.075	0.000	0.000	0.000	0.000	0.000	0.000	1.296	1.296	2.706
JUL (147)	0.243	0.136	0.100	0.094	0.231	0.159	0.119	0.092	0.072	0.057	0.000	0.000	0.000	0.000	0.000	1.305	1.305	2.910
AUG (168)	0.237	0.133	0.098	0.091	0.225	0.155	0.116	0.090	0.070	0.055	0.043	0.000	0.000	0.000	0.000	1.314	1.314	3.059
SEP (189)	0.233	0.130	0.096	0.090	0.221	0.152	0.114	0.088	0.069	0.054	0.042	0.032	0.000	0.000	0.000	1.322	1.322	3.276
OCT (210)	0.230	0.129	0.095	0.089	0.218	0.151	0.113	0.087	0.068	0.053	0.042	0.032	0.023	0.000	0.000	1.329	1.329	3.443
NOV (231)	0.228	0.128	0.094	0.088	0.217	0.149	0.112	0.086	0.068	0.053	0.041	0.032	0.023	0.016	0.000	1.335	1.335	3.602
DEC (252)	0.227	0.127	0.094	0.088	0.216	0.149	0.111	0.086	0.067	0.053	0.041	0.031	0.023	0.016	0.010	1.339	1.339	3.754

The problems with BSM Vega are most evident when evaluating time spreads, including calendars and diagonals. Let's use the same Inverted Term Structure example to look at a 10 put contract FEB-JAN calendar spread. Figure 8.1 below shows the JAF partial True Vegas, the sum of the partial True Vegas, and the BSM Vegas on a per share basis for the JAN and FEB options, and for the 10-contract calendar spread.

Note the glaring difference between the sum of the JAF True Vegas (81.46) and the BSM Vega (459.76) in Figure 8.1. The BSM calendar spread

Vega is overstated by over 464%. In addition, note that the long calendar spread has *negative* partial True Vegas for all forward volatility periods in January, and a *positive* partial True Vega for the forward volatility period in February. The net True Vega is positive, but the negative and positive partials illustrate an important point. There are many different forward volatilities and the JAF partial True Vegas are able to quantify the risk exposures with respect to each forward volatility period. This allows the option trader much more control when designing option strategies. The JAF partial Greeks can even be used to provide an unprecedented level of risk management when using optimization and simulation tools to construct option strategies.

Figure 8.1: JAF True Vega 10 Put Contract FEB-JAN Calendar Spread (Inverted)							
Period / Opt.Expire (TD)	JAN W1	JAN W2	JAN W3	JAN W4	FEB	Sum Partials	BSM Vega
JAN W4 (21)	0.483	0.271	0.199	0.186	0.000	1.140	1.140
FEB (42)	0.369	0.207	0.152	0.142	0.351	1.222	1.600
+ 10 Calendars	-114.13	-64.01	-47.10	-44.04	350.74	81.46	459.76

Figure 8.2 below shows the JAF partial True Vegas, the sum of the partial True Vegas, and the BSM Vegas for the same 10-contract calendar spread above - but in the *Normal Term Structure* base case. The magnitude of the BSM error (1170%) is even larger in the Normal term structure scenario (464.06 versus 36.55). In addition, note that the sum of the JAF partial Vegas in the Normal based case (36.55) is much different than the sum of the JAF partial Vegas in the Inverted case (81.46). This demonstrates the importance of using the JAF Greek algorithm with the complete term structure of unique forward volatilities when calculating partial True Vegas. Simply applying a mean-reversion model is not sufficient.

Figure 8.2: JAF True Vega 10 Put Contract FEB-JAN Calendar Spread (Normal)							
Period / Opt.Expire (TD)	JAN W1	JAN W2	JAN W3	JAN W4	FEB	Sum Partials	BSM Vega
JAN W4 (21)	0.402	0.265	0.228	0.249	0.000	1.143	1.143
FEB (42)	0.256	0.168	0.145	0.158	0.453	1.180	1.607
+ 10 Calendars	-146.63	-96.58	-83.08	-90.63	453.47	36.55	464.06

Exhibit 37.3 provides the put option JAF partial Rhos for each option in each forward interest rate period, derived from the JAF Combined Binomial & BSM model, using *"Inverted" downward-sloping term structures* of volatilities and risk-free rates, for a large number of intervals (8,192 average of N & N+1). The sums of the partial Rhos are also included in Exhibit 37.3, as are

the BSM Rhos for all put options.

The JAF Rho results presented in Exhibit 37.3 are less interesting than the Vega results presented earlier. The JAF partial Rho values in each period are approximately the same for all put options and the JAF partial Rho values for different forward periods are a direct function of the number of trade days in each forward period. Similarly, the sums of the JAF partial Rho values are almost identical to the corresponding BSM Rho values. This is because the aggregate interest rate formula is linear (for continuously compounded rates), while the JVAF is non-linear. However, note that the JAF Aggregate Interest Rate Formula is still required to calculate the appropriate average risk-free rate for each option for use in the BSM Rho formula.

The partial Rhos are approximately equal because we are assuming European options with no dividend payments. This means that there are no interim cash flows. The partial Rhos would be very different if there were interim cash flows, as is the case for similar risk metrics applied to fixed income portfolios. In the 1980s, I developed a similar parametric or partial derivative approach for quantifying yield curve (forward rate) and sector exposures (return sensitivities) in fixed income portfolios. I used the resulting custom risk metrics, in conjunction with proprietary valuation models and a large linear program (optimizer) to manage over $13 billion in assets for institutional clients. The JAF partial Greeks described above could be used with the latest optimization tools to similar advantage in managing option portfolios.

The JAF partial Rho calculations could be integrated with a mean-reversion model to calculate Partial True Rho metrics – similar to the Partial True Vegas calculated above. If the Federal Reserve's unprecedented expansionary monetary policy resurrects the inflationary pressures of the 1970s and early 1980s, implementing a mean reversion model for interest rates and calculating Partial True Rho values would be a very worthwhile exercise. With interest rates under 2%, there are more pressing concerns. However, the JAF partial Rho metrics and the JAF Greek Algorithm make this possible.

Exhibit 37.3: JAF Put Option Partial Rho (Inverted Term Structure)

Period / Opt.Expire (TD)	JAN W1	JAN W2	JAN W3	JAN W4	FEB	MAR	APR	MAY	JUN	JUL	AUG	SEP	OCT	NOV	DEC	Sum JAF Partials	JAF Rho	BSM Rho
Annualized	80.000%	75.000%	70.000%	65.000%	60.000%	55.000%	50.000%	45.000%	40.000%	35.000%	30.000%	25.000%	20.000%	15.000%	10.000%			
Volatility	80.000%	77.540%	75.111%	72.366%	66.471%	62.881%	59.921%	57.248%	54.752%	52.389%	50.140%	48.001%	45.975%	44.068%	42.291%	42.29%	42.29%	42.29%
Risk Free	10.000%	9.500%	9.000%	8.500%	8.000%	7.500%	7.000%	6.500%	6.000%	5.500%	5.000%	4.500%	4.000%	3.500%	3.000%			
Interest Rate	10.000%	9.750%	9.500%	9.214%	8.607%	8.238%	7.929%	7.643%	7.369%	7.102%	6.839%	6.579%	6.321%	6.065%	5.810%	5.81%	5.81%	5.81%
Trade Days	5	5	5	6	21	21	21	21	21	21	21	21	21	21	21	252	252	252
JAN W1 (5)	-0.102	0.000	0.000	0.000	0.000	0.000	0.000	0.000	0.000	0.000	0.000	0.000	0.000	0.000	0.000	-0.102	-0.102	-0.102
JAN W2 (10)	-0.103	-0.103	0.000	0.000	0.000	0.000	0.000	0.000	0.000	0.000	0.000	0.000	0.000	0.000	0.000	-0.206	-0.206	-0.206
JAN W3 (15)	-0.103	-0.103	-0.103	0.000	0.000	0.000	0.000	0.000	0.000	0.000	0.000	0.000	0.000	0.000	0.000	-0.310	-0.310	-0.310
JAN W4 (21)	-0.104	-0.104	-0.104	-0.125	0.000	0.000	0.000	0.000	0.000	0.000	0.000	0.000	0.000	0.000	0.000	-0.436	-0.436	-0.436
FEB (42)	-0.104	-0.104	-0.104	-0.125	-0.438	0.000	0.000	0.000	0.000	0.000	0.000	0.000	0.000	0.000	0.000	-0.876	-0.876	-0.876
MAR (63)	-0.104	-0.104	-0.104	-0.125	-0.438	-0.438	0.000	0.000	0.000	0.000	0.000	0.000	0.000	0.000	0.000	-1.314	-1.314	-1.314
APR (84)	-0.104	-0.104	-0.104	-0.125	-0.437	-0.437	-0.437	0.000	0.000	0.000	0.000	0.000	0.000	0.000	0.000	-1.748	-1.748	-1.748
MAY (105)	-0.104	-0.104	-0.104	-0.124	-0.435	-0.435	-0.435	-0.435	0.000	0.000	0.000	0.000	0.000	0.000	0.000	-2.177	-2.177	-2.177
JUN (126)	-0.103	-0.103	-0.103	-0.124	-0.433	-0.433	-0.433	-0.433	-0.433	0.000	0.000	0.000	0.000	0.000	0.000	-2.598	-2.598	-2.598
JUL (147)	-0.102	-0.102	-0.102	-0.123	-0.430	-0.430	-0.430	-0.430	-0.430	-0.430	0.000	0.000	0.000	0.000	0.000	-3.013	-3.013	3.013
AUG (168)	-0.102	-0.102	-0.102	-0.122	-0.428	-0.428	-0.428	-0.428	-0.428	-0.428	-0.428	0.000	0.000	0.000	0.000	-3.422	-3.422	-3.422
SEP (189)	-0.101	-0.101	-0.101	-0.121	-0.425	-0.425	-0.425	-0.425	-0.425	-0.425	-0.425	-0.425	0.000	0.000	0.000	-3.823	-3.823	-3.823
OCT (210)	-0.100	-0.100	-0.100	-0.121	-0.422	-0.422	-0.422	-0.422	-0.422	-0.422	-0.422	-0.422	-0.422	0.000	0.000	-4.219	-4.219	-4.219
NOV (231)	-0.100	-0.100	-0.100	-0.120	-0.419	-0.419	-0.419	-0.419	-0.419	-0.419	-0.419	-0.419	-0.419	-0.419	0.000	-4.609	-4.609	-4.609
DEC (252)	-0.099	-0.099	-0.099	-0.119	-0.416	-0.416	-0.416	-0.416	-0.416	-0.416	-0.416	-0.416	-0.416	-0.416	-0.416	-4.996	-4.996	-4.996

Exhibit 37.4 provides the JAF Theta for each put option, derived from the JAF Combined Binomial & BSM model, using *"Inverted" downward-sloping term structures* of volatilities and risk-free rates, for a large number of intervals (8,192 average of N & N+1). The BSM Rhos for all put options are also included.

The BSM Theta is an instantaneous measure of the change in the value of an option due to the passage of time. The BSM Theta is typically scaled to one calendar day or one trade day in practice. The values in the table below are scaled to one trade day. The JVAF and Interest Rate Aggregation formulas are both required to calculate the aggregate volatility and average risk-free rate in all BSM calculations, including the BSM Theta calculation.

Unfortunately, due to the limitations of the BSM assumptions and the continuous nature of the BSM model, the BSM model implicitly uses different risk-free rates in the same forward rate intervals and the same rates in different intervals. This is incorrect and results in Theta values that are inconsistent with the underlying term structure of interest rates and are grossly inaccurate, misleading, and theoretically incorrect. Conversely, the JAF uses the same rates in the same intervals, and different rates in different intervals. The resulting JAF Theta is theoretically correct and can be calculated for any term structure of unique interest rates and any term structure of unique volatilities.

In the Inverted term structure example (Exhibit 37.4), the BSM Theta values are overstated (less negative) by 0.25 to 0.73 per share. The BSM Theta for the December option is overstated by over 78%. Exhibits 37.1 through 37.4 directly or indirectly validate all five of the Validation Plan Elements.

Exhibit 37.4: JAF Put Theta (Inverted TS)		
Period / Opt.Expire (TD)	JAF Theta	BSM Theta
JAN W1 (5)	-4.531	-4.279
JAN W2 (10)	-3.150	-2.864
JAN W3 (15)	-2.592	-2.222
JAN W4 (21)	-2.230	-1.773
FEB (42)	-1.642	-1.087
MAR (63)	-1.374	-0.799
APR (84)	-1.219	-0.631
MAY (105)	-1.121	-0.518
JUN (126)	-1.055	-0.436
JUL (147)	-1.009	-0.373
AUG (168)	-0.978	-0.323
SEP (189)	-0.958	-0.283
OCT (210)	-0.945	-0.250
NOV (231)	-0.937	-0.223
DEC (252)	-0.933	-0.200

JAF Validation: Section IX

Section IX Objective:

The objective of Section IX is to demonstrate that the JAF Greek algorithm produces highly accurate *forward* Partial Vega, Partial True Vega, Partial Rho, and Theta for all option expirations, in all three bases cases, by eliminating the errors from the invalid constant interest rate and constant volatility assumptions of the BOM and BSM.

Section IX: JAF Forward/Aged (+ 21 TD) Greeks – JAF *Forward*

Partial Vega, Partial True Vega, Partial Rho, and Theta for all three base case scenarios: flat, normal, and inverted.

Group 38) JAF Forward (Age 21 TD) Greeks (Partial Vega, Partial True Vega, Partial Rho, Theta): Calls, Flat

Group 39) JAF Forward (Age 21 TD) Greeks (Partial Vega, Partial True Vega, Partial Rho, Theta): Puts, Flat

Group 40) JAF Forward (Age 21 TD) Greeks (Partial Vega, Partial True Vega, Partial Rho, Theta): Calls, Normal

Group 41) JAF Forward (Age 21 TD) Greeks (Partial Vega, Partial True Vega, Partial Rho, Theta): Puts, Normal

Group 42) JAF Forward (Age 21 TD) Greeks (Partial Vega, Partial True Vega, Partial Rho, Theta): Calls, Inverted

Group 43) JAF Forward (Age 21 TD) Greeks (Partial Vega, Partial True Vega, Partial Rho, Theta): Puts, Inverted

Section IX: Group and Exhibit Structure

The complete set of validation groups and exhibits from Section IX is available in the JAF Validation Supplement. All groups and exhibits from Section IX of the JAF Validation Supplement are described below, so please pay particular attention to the descriptions of the *select* sample exhibits examined in this section: Exhibits 43.1, 43.2, 43.3, and 43.4.

There are six groups of exhibits in Section IX, each with a different set of input values, assumptions, and validation objectives. All aggregate volatility and average risk-free rates were derived using the JAF and the resulting values were used with the BSM model to calculate the required price sensitivities (Greeks). The JAF incorporates the entire term structures of interest rates and volatilities, so it is possible to calculate forward Greeks that are theoretically correct and internally consistent. *All of the validation Groups in Section IX calculate Greeks 21 trade days into the future.*

All Groups in this section compare the sum of the JAF Partial Vegas and Rhos (all forward volatilities or rates change individually), the JAF Vega and Rho (all forward volatilities or rates change at the same time), and the standard BSM Vega and Rho (calculated using the JAVF and aggregate interest rate formulas).

JAF forward Vega calculations assume a constant 1% change in forward volatility; BSM Vega calculations assume a constant 1% change in aggregate volatility (derived with the JAVF); JAF True Vega assumes a 1% change in the 21-trade-day ATM volatility with corresponding (non-constant) forward volatility changes derived from the JAF True Vega mean reversion model (explained in Chapter 7). *All of these changes occur after aging the term structures of interest rates and volatilities by 21 trade days.* All Groups in this section also compare the JAF Theta to the BSM standard Theta. Groups 38 & 39 present the forward Greek analysis for calls and puts in the *Flat* base case. Groups 40 & 41 present the forward Greek analysis for calls and puts in the *Normal* base case. Finally, Groups 42 & 43 perform the same forward Greek analysis for calls and puts in the *Inverted* base case.

Each validation group in Section IX includes the same four exhibits: Exhibit 1 for constant Partial Vega, Exhibit 2 for Partial True Vega, Exhibit 3 for Partial Rho, and Exhibit 4 for Theta. Each exhibit compares the JAF values to the BSM standard Greeks, 21 trade days into the future. The BSM Greeks are derived from continuous functions which assume that interest rates and volatilities are constant and consistent for all options across all expiration dates. It is widely known and understood that this BSM assumption is invalid, which means the continuous BSM Greek values are not theoretically consistent and are, in fact, incorrect.

The JAF allows us to calculate forward (aged) partial and total Vega, True Vega, Rho, and Theta values which are theoretically consistent and accurate for all term structures of interest rates and volatilities. In addition, the partial Greeks provide much more information about the price sensitivity of each option to the entire forward term structures of interest rates and volatilities. These partial risk metrics have never been available for options in the past and are only possible in practice using the JAF. The Partial True Vegas are highly accurate given their use of market-derived volatility multipliers for the entire term structure of volatilities. The True Vega model used in the JAF was estimated using over 15 years of daily ATM IVs for the entire SPX, NDX, and RUT indices. The JAF True Vega model is described in detail in Chapter 7.

The formats of Exhibits 1 and 3 are identical. The top four rows of each exhibit summarize the market environment. Row 1 shows the annualized volatility for each forward period. Row 2 shows the *aggregate* volatility from time zero through the end of each forward period. Rows 3 and 4 show the forward risk-free rate in each forward period and the *average* risk-free rate from time zero through the end of each forward period. Row 5 in Exhibits 1 and 3 show the number of trade days in each forward period.

The format of Exhibit 2 is the same as Exhibits 1 and 3, except for two additional rows inserted (Rows 5 and 6). The new Rows 5 and 6 provide the True Vega Volatility Multiplier (TVVM) for each forward period and for the period from time zero through the end of each forward period. For example, a hypothetical value of 0.75 would indicate that the forward volatility in that period would only increase by 0.75% in response to a 1% change in the reference (21 TD) aggregate volatility. *If the forward volatilities are constant for an entire period*, it is possible to multiply the Partial Vegas in each period by the forward volatility multiplier for that period to calculate the Partial True Vega for each period.

The left-hand column in all four exhibits shows the expiration date of each option, followed by its Vega, True Vega, Rho, or Theta values. All option expirations are shown in each exhibit.

Section IX: Sample Exhibits

Exhibit 43 - Model Assumptions / Input Values: Stock Price = 1000, Strike Price = 1000, Time to Expiration = various, Inverted term structure, risk-premium N/A. Forward 21 TD in the future.

The complete set of model assumptions and input values for all Group 43 Exhibits is specified above. Exhibit 43.1 provides the put option *forward (+21 TD)* partial Vegas for each option in each forward volatility period, derived from the JAF Combined Binomial & BSM model, using *"Inverted" downward-sloping term structures* of volatilities and risk-free rates, for a large number of intervals (8,192 average of N & N+1). The sums of the *forward* partial Vegas are also included in Exhibit 43.1, as are the BSM Vegas for all put options. While it is always useful to review current risk metrics, it is also necessary to evaluate the Greeks of option strategies in the future - due to the dynamic, non-linear behavior of options. The *forward* Greeks in this section are derived by aging the term structures of interest rates and volatilities by 21 trade days, holding all other variables constant, including the price of the underlying stock. Aging the term structure by 21 trade days (one calendar month) requires dropping off the interest rates and volatilities for all forward periods in the month of January.

The *forward* partial Vegas in Exhibit 43.1 measure the change in the value of the option (21 trade days in the future), per 1% change in the *forward volatility* in each forward period. By definition, the sum of the forward partial Vegas assumes that all forward volatilities change by a constant or uniform 1% (21 trade days in the future). As I explained earlier, I only included the *constant 1%* partial Vegas to provide a realistic comparison with the BSM Vega. Partial *True* Vega and *True* Vega should always be used in practice.

There are several observations we can make from examining Exhibit 43.1. First, every put option is not exposed to a change in every forward volatility. All of the options with expiration dates in January would have already expired, so all of their forward partial Vegas are zero. Similarly, the forward partial Vegas for all forward periods in January are zero for all options, because the month of January would have already passed.

The remaining observations for forward JAF Vegas are the same as the observations we noted for the *current* JAF Vegas in Exhibits 37.1. The JAF forward February partial Vegas of these longer-dated options are not the same. In addition, the JAF forward partial Vegas for March, April, May, etc. continue to decline. This is a function of the unique forward volatilities. The BSM forward Vega is still overstated (3.628 versus 3.306). All of these effects are due to using the unique term structure of forward volatilities. *The only time the forward BSM values will match the sum of the JAF forward partial Vegas is if all of the forward volatilities are exactly the same.*

The BSM assumption of constant changes in aggregate volatilities results in unrealistic and inconsistent changes in forward volatilities, and these unrealistic and inconsistent changes would be dependent on the level and shape of the forward volatility curve. The resulting BSM Vega values are incorrect, and the premise of constant 1% changes in aggregate volatilities is not practical.

Conversely, the JAF forward partial Vegas represent the change in the value of an option for a 1% change in each *forward volatility (21 trade days into the future).* The JAF is theoretically correct and can be applied accurately to any forward volatility curve, and used in conjunction with any term structure of unique forward rates, now or in the future.

Exhibit 43.1: JAF Put Option Partial Vega (Inverted Term Structure); Age 21 TD																		
Annualized Volatility	80.000% 0.000%	75.000% 0.000%	70.000% 0.000%	65.000% 0.000%	60.000% 60.000%	55.000% 57.554%	50.000% 55.151%	45.000% 52.797%	40.000% 50.498%	35.000% 48.261%	30.000% 46.098%	25.000% 44.017%	20.000% 42.032%	15.000% 40.156%	10.000% 38.406%	38.406%	38.406%	38.406%
Risk Free Interest Rate	10.000% 0.000%	9.500% 0.000%	9.000% 0.000%	8.500% 0.000%	8.000% 8.000%	7.500% 7.750%	7.000% 7.500%	6.500% 7.250%	6.000% 7.000%	5.500% 6.750%	5.000% 6.500%	4.500% 6.250%	4.000% 6.000%	3.500% 5.750%	3.000% 5.500%	5.500%	5.500%	5.500%
Trade Days	5	5	5	6	21	21	21	21	21	21	21	21	21	21	21	252	252	252
Period / Opt.Expire (TD)	JAN W1	JAN W2	JAN W3	JAN W4	FEB	MAR	APR	MAY	JUN	JUL	AUG	SEP	OCT	NOV	DEC	Sum JAF Partials	JAF Vega	BSM Vega
JAN W1 (X)	0.000	0.000	0.000	0.000	0.000	0.000	0.000	0.000	0.000	0.000	0.000	0.000	0.000	0.000	0.000	0.000	0.000	0.000
JAN W2 (X)	0.000	0.000	0.000	0.000	0.000	0.000	0.000	0.000	0.000	0.000	0.000	0.000	0.000	0.000	0.000	0.000	0.000	0.000
JAN W3 (X)	0.000	0.000	0.000	0.000	0.000	0.000	0.000	0.000	0.000	0.000	0.000	0.000	0.000	0.000	0.000	0.000	0.000	0.000
JAN W4 (X)	0.000	0.000	0.000	0.000	0.000	0.000	0.000	0.000	0.000	0.000	0.000	0.000	0.000	0.000	0.000	0.000	0.000	0.000
FEB (21)	0.000	0.000	0.000	0.000	1.143	0.000	0.000	0.000	0.000	0.000	0.000	0.000	0.000	0.000	0.000	1.143	1.143	1.143
MAR (42)	0.000	0.000	0.000	0.000	0.836	0.767	0.000	0.000	0.000	0.000	0.000	0.000	0.000	0.000	0.000	1.603	1.603	1.605
APR (63)	0.000	0.000	0.000	0.000	0.708	0.649	0.590	0.000	0.000	0.000	0.000	0.000	0.000	0.000	0.000	1.947	1.948	1.953
MAY (84)	0.000	0.000	0.000	0.000	0.637	0.584	0.531	0.478	0.000	0.000	0.000	0.000	0.000	0.000	0.000	2.230	2.230	2.242
JUN (105)	0.000	0.000	0.000	0.000	0.593	0.543	0.494	0.445	0.395	0.000	0.000	0.000	0.000	0.000	0.000	2.470	2.470	2.494
JUL (126)	0.000	0.000	0.000	0.000	0.564	0.517	0.470	0.423	0.376	0.329	0.000	0.000	0.000	0.000	0.000	2.677	2.677	2.720
AUG (147)	0.000	0.000	0.000	0.000	0.544	0.499	0.453	0.408	0.363	0.317	0.272	0.000	0.000	0.000	0.000	2.857	2.857	2.927
SEP (168)	0.000	0.000	0.000	0.000	0.531	0.487	0.443	0.398	0.354	0.310	0.266	0.221	0.000	0.000	0.000	3.011	3.011	3.118
OCT (189)	0.000	0.000	0.000	0.000	0.523	0.479	0.436	0.392	0.349	0.305	0.261	0.218	0.174	0.000	0.000	3.138	3.138	3.297
NOV (210)	0.000	0.000	0.000	0.000	0.518	0.475	0.432	0.388	0.345	0.302	0.259	0.216	0.173	0.129	0.000	3.237	3.237	3.467
DEC (231)	0.000	0.000	0.000	0.000	0.515	0.472	0.429	0.386	0.343	0.301	0.258	0.215	0.172	0.129	0.086	3.306	3.306	3.628

Exhibit 43.2 provides the put option *forward (+21 TD)* partial True Vegas for each option in each forward volatility period, derived from the JAF Combined Binomial & BSM model, using *"Inverted" downward-sloping term structures* of volatilities and risk-free rates, for a large number of intervals (8,192 average of N & N+1). The sums of the *forward* partial True Vegas are also included in Exhibit 43.2, as are the BSM forward Vegas for all put options.

Unlike the conventional BSM Vega, the JAF *forward* True Vega uses the JAF Greek algorithm to calculate the change in the value of an option *for a 1% change in an ATM option with exactly 21 trade days until expiration (the reference volatility), occurring 21 trade days in the future.* This means that every option will experience a different change in volatility, instead of the constant 1% change assumed by the BSM. Similar to Exhibit 43.1, *forward* partial True Vegas are calculated for each forward period in Exhibit 43.2. Each *forward* partial True

Vega is derived from two components: the *forward* partial (1% constant) Vega from Exhibit 43.1 and the *forward* partial True Vega Multiplier for the respective period.

For example, the *forward* partial (1% constant) March Vega for the March put option equals 0.767 (Exhibit 43.1), which indicates that the sensitivity of the March put option to a 1% change in the March forward volatility (21 trade days in the future) is +0.767. However, due to mean-reversion, the March forward volatility will not change by 1% in response to a 1% change in the 21-trade-day reference volatility. In fact, it will only change by 0.498% (from Row 5 of Figure 43.2). As a result, the JAF *forward* partial True Vega for the March forward volatility period equals 0.382 (0.767 x 0.498). This multiplicative relationship holds *if the volatility is constant over the forward period.* If the volatility is not constant over the forward period, it is still possible to calculate precise JAF True Vegas and partial True Vegas. Note, the values in this aged term structure example are very similar to those I presented in Exhibit 37.2, but they not identical. They are slightly different due to the different forward volatilities in February and March.

The *forward* partial True Vegas for all options in all forward periods are shown in Exhibit 43.2. In all cases, the JAF forward partial True Vega represents the sensitivity of the value of the option *to a 1% change in the 21-trade-day ATM reference volatility (21 days in the future).* The JAF *forward* True Vega Volatility multiplier for each forward period automatically integrates the unique effects of mean-reversion for each specific forward volatility period.

As was the case with the current JAF True Vegas in Exhibit 37.2, the *forward* partial True Vegas decline sharply over time. Due to mean-reversion, near-term forward volatilities are much more sensitive to changes in the reference volatility than longer-term forward volatilities. The resulting near-term partial True Vegas are magnified and the longer-term partial True Vegas are diminished.

The BSM Vega is not a reasonable risk metric, now or in the future. For the December put option, the *forward* BSM Vega is overstated by over 168% relative to the sum of the JAF *forward* partial True Vegas (3.628 versus 1.349)! While the JAF *forward* partial True Vegas do rely on a mean-reversion function, using *any* reasonable mean-reversion function would be much more accurate and useful than assuming all aggregate volatilities change by a constant amount.

Exhibit 43.2: JAF Put Option Partial True Vega (Inverted Term Structure); Age 21 TD

	JAN W1	JAN W2	JAN W3	JAN W4	FEB	MAR	APR	MAY	JUN	JUL	AUG	SEP	OCT	NOV	DEC			
Annualized Volatility	80.000%	75.000%	70.000%	65.000%	60.000%	55.000%	50.000%	45.000%	40.000%	35.000%	30.000%	25.000%	20.000%	15.000%	10.000%			
	0.000%	0.000%	0.000%	0.000%	60.000%	57.554%	55.151%	52.797%	50.498%	48.261%	46.098%	44.017%	42.082%	40.156%	38.406%	38.41%	38.406%	38.41%
Risk Free Interest Rate	10.000%	9.500%	9.000%	8.500%	8.000%	7.500%	7.000%	6.500%	6.000%	5.500%	5.000%	4.500%	4.000%	3.500%	3.000%			
	0.000%	0.000%	0.000%	0.000%	8.000%	7.750%	7.500%	7.250%	7.000%	6.750%	6.500%	6.250%	6.000%	5.750%	5.500%	5.50%	5.500%	5.50%
Volatility Multiplier	0.000	0.000	0.000	0.000	1.000	0.498	0.375	0.308	0.265	0.233	0.209	0.190	0.174	0.161	0.149			
Trade Days	0.000	0.000	0.000	0.000	1.000	0.759	0.641	0.568	0.517	0.479	0.449	0.425	0.405	0.388	0.372	0.372	0.372	0.372
Trade Days	5	5	5	6	21	21	21	21	21	21	21	21	21	21	21	252	252	252
Period / Opt.Expire (TD)	JAN W1	JAN W2	JAN W3	JAN W4	FEB	MAR	APR	MAY	JUN	JUL	AUG	SEP	OCT	NOV	DEC	Sum JAF Partials	JAF True Vega	BSM Vega
JAN W1 (X)	0.000	0.000	0.000	0.000	0.000	0.000	0.000	0.000	0.000	0.000	0.000	0.000	0.000	0.000	0.000	0.000	0.000	0.000
JAN W2 (X)	0.000	0.000	0.000	0.000	0.000	0.000	0.000	0.000	0.000	0.000	0.000	0.000	0.000	0.000	0.000	0.000	0.000	0.000
JAN W3 (X)	0.000	0.000	0.000	0.000	0.000	0.000	0.000	0.000	0.000	0.000	0.000	0.000	0.000	0.000	0.000	0.000	0.000	0.000
JAN W4 (X)	0.000	0.000	0.000	0.000	0.000	0.000	0.000	0.000	0.000	0.000	0.000	0.000	0.000	0.000	0.000	0.000	0.000	0.000
FEB (21)	0.000	0.000	0.000	0.000	1.143	0.000	0.000	0.000	0.000	0.000	0.000	0.000	0.000	0.000	0.000	1.143	1.143	1.143
MAR (42)	0.000	0.000	0.000	0.000	0.836	0.382	0.000	0.000	0.000	0.000	0.000	0.000	0.000	0.000	0.000	1.218	1.218	1.605
APR (63)	0.000	0.000	0.000	0.000	0.708	0.323	0.221	0.000	0.000	0.000	0.000	0.000	0.000	0.000	0.000	1.252	1.252	1.953
MAY (84)	0.000	0.000	0.000	0.000	0.637	0.291	0.199	0.147	0.000	0.000	0.000	0.000	0.000	0.000	0.000	1.274	1.274	2.242
JUN (105)	0.000	0.000	0.000	0.000	0.593	0.271	0.185	0.137	0.105	0.000	0.000	0.000	0.000	0.000	0.000	1.290	1.290	2.494
JUL (126)	0.000	0.000	0.000	0.000	0.564	0.257	0.176	0.130	0.099	0.077	0.000	0.000	0.000	0.000	0.000	1.303	1.303	2.720
AUG (147)	0.000	0.000	0.000	0.000	0.544	0.248	0.170	0.126	0.096	0.074	0.057	0.000	0.000	0.000	0.000	1.315	1.315	2.927
SEP (168)	0.000	0.000	0.000	0.000	0.531	0.242	0.166	0.123	0.094	0.072	0.056	0.042	0.000	0.000	0.000	1.326	1.326	3.118
OCT (189)	0.000	0.000	0.000	0.000	0.523	0.239	0.163	0.121	0.092	0.071	0.055	0.041	0.030	0.000	0.000	1.336	1.336	3.297
NOV (210)	0.000	0.000	0.000	0.000	0.518	0.236	0.162	0.120	0.091	0.070	0.054	0.041	0.030	0.021	0.000	1.344	1.344	3.467
DEC (231)	0.000	0.000	0.000	0.000	0.515	0.235	0.161	0.119	0.091	0.070	0.054	0.041	0.030	0.021	0.013	1.349	1.349	3.628

Exhibit 43.3 provides the put option JAF *forward (+21 TD)* partial Rhos for each option in each forward interest rate period, derived from the JAF Combined Binomial & BSM model, using *"Inverted" downward-sloping term structures* of volatilities and risk-free rates, for a large number of intervals (8,192 average of N & N+1). The sums of the *forward* partial Rhos are also included in Exhibit 43.3, as are the *forward* BSM Rhos for all put options.

The JAF *forward* partial Rho values in each period are approximately the same for all put options, and the JAF *forward* partial Rho values for different forward periods are a direct function of the number of trade days in each forward period. Similarly, the sums of the JAF *forward* partial Rho values are almost identical to the corresponding *forward* BSM Rho values. This is because the aggregate interest rate formula is linear (for continuously compounded rates), while the JVAF is non-linear. However, note that the JAF Aggregate Interest Rate Formula is still required to calculate the appropriate average risk-free rate for each option for use in the BSM Rho formula.

Exhibit 43.3: JAF Put Option Partial Rho (Inverted Term Structure); Age 21 TD

	JAN W1	JAN W2	JAN W3	JAN W4	FEB	MAR	APR	MAY	JUN	JUL	AUG	SEP	OCT	NOV	DEC			
Annualized Volatility	80.000%	75.000%	70.000%	65.000%	60.000%	55.000%	50.000%	45.000%	40.000%	35.000%	30.000%	25.000%	20.000%	15.000%	10.000%			
	0.000%	0.000%	0.000%	0.000%	60.000%	57.554%	55.151%	52.797%	50.498%	48.261%	46.098%	44.017%	42.082%	40.156%	38.406%	38.41%	38.41%	38.41%
Risk Free Interest Rate	10.000%	9.500%	9.000%	8.500%	8.000%	7.500%	7.000%	6.500%	6.000%	5.500%	5.000%	4.500%	4.000%	3.500%	3.000%			
	0.000%	0.000%	0.000%	0.000%	8.000%	7.750%	7.500%	7.250%	7.000%	6.750%	6.500%	6.250%	6.000%	5.750%	5.500%	5.50%	5.50%	5.50%
Trade Days	5	5	5	6	21	21	21	21	21	21	21	21	21	21	21	252	252	252
Period / Opt.Expire (TD)	JAN W1	JAN W2	JAN W3	JAN W4	FEB	MAR	APR	MAY	JUN	JUL	AUG	SEP	OCT	NOV	DEC	Sum JAF Partials	JAF Rho	BSM Rho
JAN W1 (X)	0.000	0.000	0.000	0.000	0.000	0.000	0.000	0.000	0.000	0.000	0.000	0.000	0.000	0.000	0.000	0.000	0.000	0.000
JAN W2 (X)	0.000	0.000	0.000	0.000	0.000	0.000	0.000	0.000	0.000	0.000	0.000	0.000	0.000	0.000	0.000	0.000	0.000	0.000
JAN W3 (X)	0.000	0.000	0.000	0.000	0.000	0.000	0.000	0.000	0.000	0.000	0.000	0.000	0.000	0.000	0.000	0.000	0.000	0.000
JAN W4 (X)	0.000	0.000	0.000	0.000	0.000	0.000	0.000	0.000	0.000	0.000	0.000	0.000	0.000	0.000	0.000	0.000	0.000	0.000
FEB (21)	0.000	0.000	0.000	0.000	-0.430	0.000	0.000	0.000	0.000	0.000	0.000	0.000	0.000	0.000	0.000	-0.430	-0.430	-0.430
MAR (42)	0.000	0.000	0.000	0.000	-0.432	-0.432	0.000	0.000	0.000	0.000	0.000	0.000	0.000	0.000	0.000	-0.864	-0.864	-0.864
APR (63)	0.000	0.000	0.000	0.000	-0.432	-0.432	-0.432	0.000	0.000	0.000	0.000	0.000	0.000	0.000	0.000	-1.295	-1.295	-1.295
MAY (84)	0.000	0.000	0.000	0.000	-0.430	-0.430	-0.430	-0.430	0.000	0.000	0.000	0.000	0.000	0.000	0.000	-1.722	-1.722	-1.722
JUN (105)	0.000	0.000	0.000	0.000	-0.428	-0.428	-0.428	-0.428	-0.428	0.000	0.000	0.000	0.000	0.000	0.000	-2.142	-2.142	-2.142
JUL (126)	0.000	0.000	0.000	0.000	-0.426	-0.426	-0.426	-0.426	-0.426	-0.426	0.000	0.000	0.000	0.000	0.000	-2.555	-2.555	-2.555
AUG (147)	0.000	0.000	0.000	0.000	-0.423	-0.423	-0.423	-0.423	-0.423	-0.423	-0.423	0.000	0.000	0.000	0.000	-2.961	-2.961	-2.961
SEP (168)	0.000	0.000	0.000	0.000	-0.420	-0.420	-0.420	-0.420	-0.420	-0.420	-0.420	-0.420	0.000	0.000	0.000	-3.360	-3.360	-3.360
OCT (189)	0.000	0.000	0.000	0.000	-0.417	-0.417	-0.417	-0.417	-0.417	-0.417	-0.417	-0.417	-0.417	0.000	0.000	-3.752	-3.752	-3.752
NOV (210)	0.000	0.000	0.000	0.000	-0.414	-0.414	-0.414	-0.414	-0.414	-0.414	-0.414	-0.414	-0.414	-0.414	0.000	-4.138	-4.138	-4.138
DEC (231)	0.000	0.000	0.000	0.000	-0.411	-0.411	-0.411	-0.411	-0.411	-0.411	-0.411	-0.411	-0.411	-0.411	-0.411	-4.520	-4.520	-4.520

Exhibit 43.4 provides the JAF *forward (+21 TD)* Theta for each put option, derived from the JAF Combined Binomial & BSM model, using *"Inverted" downward-sloping term structures* of volatilities and risk-free rates, for a large number of intervals (8,192 average of N & N+1). The *forward* BSM Rhos for all put options are also included.

Due to the limitations of the BSM assumptions and the continuous nature of the BSM model, the BSM model implicitly uses different risk-free rates in the same forward rate intervals and the same rates in different intervals. This is incorrect and results in Theta values that are inconsistent with the underlying term structure of interest rates and are grossly inaccurate, misleading, and theoretically incorrect. This is true for current Greek metrics and forward Greek metrics. Conversely, the JAF uses the same rates in the same intervals, and different rates in different intervals. The resulting JAF Theta is theoretically correct and can be calculated for any term structure of unique interest rates and any term structure of unique volatilities.

In the *forward* Inverted term structure example (Exhibit 43.4), the BSM Theta values are overstated (less negative) by 0.02 to 0.38 per share. Exhibits 43.1 through 43.4 directly or indirectly validate all five of the Validation Plan Elements.

Exhibit 43.4: JAF Put Theta (Inverted TS) +21		
Period / Opt.Expire (TD)	JAF Theta	BSM Theta
JAN W1 (X)	0.000	0.000
JAN W2 (X)	0.000	0.000
JAN W3 (X)	0.000	0.000
JAN W4 (X)	0.000	0.000
FEB (21)	-1.489	-1.469
MAR (42)	-1.038	-0.940
APR (63)	-0.852	-0.701
MAY (84)	-0.750	-0.556
JUN (105)	-0.687	-0.457
JUL (126)	-0.646	-0.384
AUG (147)	-0.619	-0.328
SEP (168)	-0.601	-0.283
OCT (189)	-0.590	-0.248
NOV (210)	-0.584	-0.218
DEC (231)	-0.582	-0.194

Summary

This chapter provided an abridged version of the JAF Greek results. Comprehensive JAF Valuation and Greek results are available in the JAF Validation Supplement PDF (see Resource Chapter for download link address). All of the values in the JAF supplement and in this chapter are actual output values from a Python application of the JAF algorithm - exported to Excel for formatting purposes.

This chapter included a select group of sample Exhibits from Sections VIII and IX of the JAF Validation supplement. Each section of examples directly or indirectly validated all of the Validation Plan Exhibits below and provided compelling evidence that the JAF Valuation and Greek Algorithms are able to employ a user-specified Market Risk Premium in conjunction with the complete term structure of unique interest rates and the complete term structure of unique volatilities to calculate theoretically sound and internally consistent current and future option values and Greek metrics.

Review of JAF Objective:
Design an objective framework that employs a user-specified Market Risk Premium in conjunction with the complete term structure of unique interest rates and the complete term structure of unique volatilities to calculate theoretically sound and internally consistent: current and future option values, current and future Greeks, and current and future volatility index (VIX) values.

Review of Validation Plan Elements (VPE): (Multiple forward interest rate and volatility periods)
1) Demonstrate that aggregate input values derived from the Interest Rate Aggregation Formula and the Johnson Volatility Aggregation Formula (JVAF), applied to multiple forward periods, generate theoretically correct and consistent results when used with the BOM, BSM, and the JAF combined BOM & BSM model.
2) Demonstrate that the BOM converges to the BSM as the number of intervals is increased and that the resulting BOM error can be made arbitrarily small by increasing the number of binomial intervals as desired.
3) Demonstrate that the JAF current, interim, and expiration valuation algorithms generate theoretically correct and internally consistent current, interim, and expiration *values.*
4) Demonstrate that the values derived from the JAF current, interim, and expiration valuation algorithms generate theoretically correct and internally

consistent *rates of return.*

5) Demonstrate that the values derived from the JAF current, interim, and expiration valuation algorithms generate theoretically correct and internally consistent current and future *Greeks.*

The JAF Greek Algorithm requires the use of the JVAF and Interest Rate Aggregation Formulas, plus the JAF Current, Interim, and Expiration Valuation Algorithms. As a result, validating the results of the JAF Greek Algorithm also indirectly validates the JAF aggregation formulas, the JAF Valuation Algorithms, and the resulting JAF risk-neutral and risk-averse returns.

9) JAF: ESTIMATING FORWARD VOLATILITIES

The Johnson Aggregation Framework (JAF) goal is to design an objective framework that employs a user-specified Market Risk Premium in conjunction with the complete term structure of unique interest rates and the complete term structure of unique volatilities to calculate theoretically sound and internally consistent: current and future option values, current and future Greeks, and current and future volatility index (VIX) values.

The four preceding chapters introduced the Johnson Aggregation Framework (JAF), the Johnson Volatility Aggregation Formula (JVAF), the JAF Valuation and Greek Algorithms, the JAF True Vega, and validated the JAF valuations, returns, and Greeks. However, in order to apply the JAF in practice, it is necessary to estimate or forecast the entire term structures of interest rates and the entire term structure of volatilities. In other words, we either need to *estimate* the forward risk-free rates and forward volatilities (for our choice of forward intervals) from market prices, or we need to use a model to *forecast* them.

Forward rate estimation algorithms have been around for 40+ years and there is widespread literature available on various techniques. Interest rates are not the primary focus of this book. In addition, the current environment of very low and stable rates diminishes the importance of interest rates - at least relative to volatility. As a result, I will only provide a brief review of the 3-year forward rate estimation example from Chapter 5, before focusing on volatility.

The disaggregation formula below (or any variation thereof) allows us to derive each of the forward rates directly from the observed spot rates (or even from the prices of zero-coupon US Treasury securities or T-Bills). It also allows us to solve for any missing forward rate if we know the appropriate spot rate and the remaining forward rates. *This framework allows us to solve for all current and future expected spot and forward rates.* The aggregation formula above is an example of a simple bootstrapping technique. It is relatively easy to apply in practice.

In our simplified monthly interest rate example from Chapter 5 (all months with the same number of trade days: 21), the spot rate for cash flows invested from the end of December to the end of March would equal 5%

(arithmetic average of 4%, 5%, and 6%). The spot rate for cash flows invested from the end of December to the end of February would equal 4.5% (arithmetic average of 4% and 5%). The spot rate for cash flows invested from the end of December to the end of January would equal 4.0% (single period – no averaging required).

The formula to aggregate continuously compounded annual forward rates of the same length is a simple arithmetic average. Even if the forward rate periods are of different lengths, the formula is a simple arithmetic *weighted-average*. This is the advantage of using continuously compounded rates. The aggregate interest rate formulas for *discrete* compounding periods are much more complex and far less intuitive.

The general spot rate formula for periods of the same length is shown below, where SR represents the continuously compounded annual Spot Rate and FR represents the continuously compounded annual forward rates. N represents the number of forward rate periods of equal length.

$$FR_{N-n,N} = [SR_{0,N} * N - SR_{0,n} * n] / (N - n)$$
$$FR_{2,3} = [SR_{0,3}*(3) - SR_{0,2}* (2.0)] / (3.0 - 2.0)$$
$$FR_{2,3} = [5.0\%*(3) - 4.5\%* (2.0)] / (1.0)$$
$$FR_{2,3} = [5.0\%*(3) - 4.5\%* (2.0)] / (1.0) = 6.0\%$$

The final interest rate disaggregation formula below allows us to use any number of periods and periods of any length to solve for the forward rates, directly from spot rates. We will use the more flexible formula below to confirm our earlier calculation of the March forward rate, given the March (5.0%) spot rate and the February (4.5%) spot rate. As was the case in the previous example, we could calculate the forward rate from the end of any earlier period to the end of the longer period.

$$FR_{N-n,N} = [NTD_{0,N}(SR_{0,N}) - NTD_{0,n}(SR_{0,n})] / (NTD_{0,N} - NTD_{0,n})$$
$$FR_{2,3} = [NTD_{0,3}(SR_{0,3}) - NTD_{0,2}(SR_{0,2})] / (NTD_{0,3} - NTD_{0,2})$$
$$FR_{2,3} = [63(5.0\%) - 42(4.5)] / (63 - 42)$$
$$FR_{2,3} = [126\%] / (21) = 6.0\%$$

Readers who are interested in applying the JAF in practice could use the above technique, or any number of similar techniques to estimate risk-free forward rates for any choice of forward intervals. However, estimating forward volatilities requires the JVAF and is more challenging due to the non-linear nature of the aggregate volatility calculations. That is why I created a user-friendly Excel spreadsheet to estimate forward volatilities directly from a series of ATM implied volatilities for equity index options. The name of the spreadsheet is "TOV Estimate TSV 32.xlsb," and the TOV spreadsheet is included with the purchase of this book. Before introducing the spreadsheet, it is important to reexamine how the JVAF is used to estimate forward volatilities from ATM option volatilities.

As a result, I will review the 3-year JVAF forward volatility estimation example from Chapter 5. In our simplified monthly example (all months with the same number of trade days: 21), the aggregate volatility (derived with the JVAF) from the end of December to the end of March equals 15.546%. Note that 15.546% does *not* equal the arithmetic-average of the forward volatilities for January, February, and March (10%, 15%, and 20%). The resulting JVAF aggregate volatility from the end of December to the end of February equals 12.748% and the JVAF aggregate volatility from the end of December to the end of January equals 10.0% (single period – no aggregation required).

The general formula below allows us to use any number of periods and periods of any length to solve for the forward volatilities, directly from implied or aggregate volatilities. We will use the more flexible formula below to confirm our earlier calculation of the March forward volatility, given the March (15.546%) implied volatility and the February (12.748%) implied volatility. We could calculate the forward volatility from the end of any earlier period to the end of the longer period.

$$\mathbf{FV_{N\text{-}n,N}} = ([\mathbf{NTD_{0,N}}\,(\mathbf{IV_{0,N}})^2 - \mathbf{NTD_{0,n}}\,(\mathbf{IV_{0,n}})^2]/(\,\mathbf{NTD_{0,N}} - \mathbf{NTD_{0,n}}))^{(0.5)}$$

$$FV_{2,3} = ([NTD_{0,3}\,(IV_{0,3})^2 - NTD_{0,2}\,(IV_{0,2})^2]/(\,NTD_{0,3} - NTD_{0,2}))^{(0.5)}$$

$$FV_{2,3} = ([63\,(15.546\%)^2 - 42\,(12.748\%)^2]/(\,63 - 42))^{(0.5)}$$

$$FV_{2,3} = ([84\%]/(\,21))^{(0.5)} = 20.00\%$$

The more flexible versions of the JVAF work for any number of user-specified, variable length periods. The aggregation and disaggregation of volatilities are required, because the objective of the JAF is to calculate current and future derivative values and Greeks using the entire term structure of volatilities.

The JAF allows the user to enter any number of periods, each with a user-specified length. The JAF requires a unique risk-free forward rate and a unique forward volatility for each period. These forward rates and forward volatilities can be derived from market prices, or they can be forecasted with sophisticated, non-linear, modeling techniques (including AI). Forward rates and forward volatilities are the building blocks of the term structure of interest rates and the term structure of volatilities.

The remainder of this chapter will focus on the TOV Estimate TSV 32.xlsb spreadsheet, which *uses ATM implied volatilities and volatility index prices to solve for the market-implied forward volatilities*. Please see the Resources Chapter at the end of this book for instructions on how to download and access the accompanying spreadsheet. The TOV spreadsheet then uses the resulting *market-implied* forward volatilities to calculate the relative values of ATM options and corresponding volatility futures across the entire term structure of volatilities.

If *market-implied* forward rates and forward volatilities are used in the JAF, the resulting model prices would quantify the relative values or pricing anomalies (degree of overvaluation or undervaluation) of ATM options and volatility futures – *but only in the context of current market prices*.

If *models are used to forecast* forward rates and forward volatilities for use in the JAF, the resulting model prices would again quantify the relative value or pricing anomalies of ATM options and volatility futures. However, the resulting pricing anomalies would include additional value-added opportunities derived from the predictive power of the forecasting models, by comparing the current market environment in a historical context. The specific volatility forecasting tool I use for all volatility forecasts is the AI Volatility Edge (AIVE) Platform, which is explained in the Resources chapter at the end of this book.

The JAF will use the forward rate and forward volatility estimates (regardless how they are derived) to calculate current and future option values and volatility futures values that are theoretically sound and consistent with the entire term structure of interest rates and the entire term structure of volatilities.

TOV Spreadsheet

The TOV spreadsheet includes detailed instructions on how to enter data and how to run the macros. While I will briefly explain the process in general terms in this chapter, my primary focus will be to explain the purpose and practical applications of the TOV spreadsheet.

TOV Spreadsheet Functions:
1) Estimate the annualized forward volatility in each forward interval
2) Use the forward volatilities to calculate the JVAF estimated ATM IV for each equity index option
3) Use the forward volatilities to *project* the JVAF estimated ATM IV for each equity index option

4) Use the forward volatilities to calculate the JVAF estimated price of each volatility index future

5) Use the forward volatilities to calculate the JAF True Vega for each ATM equity index option

6) Use the forward volatilities to calculate the JAF True Vega for each volatility index future

7) Calculate the JAF True Vegas for ALL calendar spread pairs of ATM equity index options

8) Calculate the JAF True Vegas for ALL calendar spread pairs of volatility index futures

TOV Spreadsheet: ATM Equity Options

The TOV spreadsheet contains a lot of information, but is very easy to use. It requires minimal user input, and all functions are executed using push-button macros. Input data is limited to cells with a dark blue background and white text, or cells with blue text. All other cells and all worksheets are protected, to ensure the ongoing integrity of the spreadsheet calculations.

The first objective is to estimate the forward volatilities, which are used in all other calculations. All volatility estimation operations are performed on the "Estimate TSV" worksheet tab. The first step is to enter the "Analysis Date," which is used to populate a series of 25 monthly option expiration dates.

The Analysis Date and the resulting option expiration dates are used to determine the forward volatility intervals, and to calculate the number of trade days in each interval and the total number of trade days before the expiration date of each option. The user-specified dates in the "Holidays" worksheet tab are also used in the day count calculations. A secondary "Aged Date" allows the user to enter a future date (typically 30 calendar days after the Analysis date) to evaluate the projected term structure of volatilities. The TOV spreadsheet projects an arbitrage-free forward term structure of volatilities forward to the Aged Date. This allows the user to understand the arbitrage-free or expected term structure of volatilities on a specified future date.

Until this point in the book, I have treated volatility indices the same as ATM forward volatilities. This is not exactly the case. Volatility indices (such as the VIX index) are derived from multiple options with a range of strike prices, not from a single ATM option or from a single pair of options with strike prices that bracket the underlying stock price. As a result, the price of a volatility index will be slightly higher than the implied volatility of the ATM option. This is due to the non-linear vertical skew curve (the non-linear relationship between strike price and implied volatility).

The resulting volatility index price will therefore be equal to the JVAF forward volatility, *plus* the effect of the vertical skew. The TOV spreadsheet provides two different methods for incorporating the effects of the vertical skew on the prices of the volatility index futures contracts. The first is to estimate a single constant term (that is specific to the current market environment) during the forward volatility estimation process.

The second is to use (the included) historical models derived from 15+ years of daily ATM IV and VIX data to estimate the vertical skew spread for each volatility index futures contract. The resulting spread is not specific to the current environment. Instead, it is derived from the historical vertical skew relationship, which was modeled from the historical data. This choice of skew calculations is made by using a drop-down list selection, choosing either "Function" (model) or "Constant" (estimated). If "Function" is selected, the appropriate index must also be selected from a separate drop-down list with the following selections: SPX, NDX, or RUT. The vertical skew estimation functions are slightly different, due to the unique range of historical volatilities for each index.

The final step is to enter the ATM IV data (as of the Analysis Date) for all of the available equity option expiration dates. To ensure reliable forward volatility estimates, the ATM IV data is required for *all available options*, but ATM IV data will not be available for every date. The user may also choose to enter data for the corresponding volatility index futures contract (also as of the Analysis Date). I recommend using *both* ATM IV data *and* VIX futures data for SPX options. Unfortunately, as I write this, liquid and efficiently priced monthly volatility index futures contracts for the NDX and RUT are not yet available. However, the spreadsheet will accommodate them if that changes in the future.

The advantage of using both ATM IV and VIX futures prices is to help identify relative value between both markets, especially when using the "Function" model option. The "Function" option calculates the appropriate effect of the vertical skew from the historical model relationships, not from the current data snapshot alone. This can help identify pricing anomalies (often resulting from vertical skew anomalies), that could potentially be exploited.

If only ATM IV options are used to estimate the forward volatilities, the resulting volatility pricing errors would all approach zero. In other words, Solver would be able to calculate the forward volatilities very precisely. While the resulting forward volatilities are still required by the JAF and are still useful for comparative analysis, using ATM IVs exclusively to estimate forward volatilities does tend to preclude a relative value analysis.

Click on the "Solver" push-button macro to estimate the forward volatilities for the intervals determined by the populated expiration dates of the monthly equity index options. You will see the intermediate Solver results during processing at the bottom-left of the screen. When Solver is finished running, a dialog box will be displayed. Click OK to accept the solution and copy the forward volatilities into the appropriate cells of the spreadsheet. The resulting RMSE values are shown in the TOV spreadsheet. If Solver is unable to find a solution, consider manually *seeding* more appropriate values in the cells containing the forward volatilities (N6:N30). Note: the user is required to install the free Solver add-in in Microsoft Excel – prior to using the TOV spreadsheet.

It sounds more complicated than it is in practice. Once you have used the spreadsheet a few times, you will find it very straightforward. To recap, here are the abbreviated steps for estimating the forward volatilities:

TOV Estimating Forward Volatilities:
1) Enter Analysis Date
2) Enter Aged Date
3) Select Function or Constant
4) Select Index: SPX, NDX, or RUT
5) Enter ATM IV Data on Analysis Date
6) Enter Volatility Index Prices on Analysis Date
7) Run Solver Macro

The TOV spreadsheet uses the estimated forward volatilities to calculate the JVAF aggregate volatility, the difference between the actual market IV and the estimated aggregate IV (the error), and the Aged ATM IV for each ATM equity option. *Positive* differences (errors) indicate *overvalued* ATM options and *negative* errors indicate *undervalued* ATM options (in the context of the market). The resulting forward volatilities for each interval are also provided. The ATM IV section of the TOV Estimate TSV worksheet for 10/9/2020 is shown in Figure 9.1 below.

In general, the ATM equity options were slightly cheap (undervalued) on 10/9/2020. For example, the ATM option expiring on 9/17/2021 was undervalued by 1.48%. The ATM IV was 22.60%, compared to an estimated ATM IV of 24.08%. The TOV spreadsheet can be used with real-time data and with historical data. The AVM IV and volatility futures prices should always be simultaneous.

Analysis Date	Aged Date	VX Spread	Clear Input Data				Figure 9.1 - Trading Option Volatilities : Term Structure of Volatility Worksheet					
10/9/2020	11/9/2020	Function					Copyright © 2021 Trading Insights, LLC. All Rights Reserved.					
RMSE	RMSE wPenalty	Opt. Ex. Date	Set Chart Axis Min Max				ATM IV Count	Index Name	ATM IV RMSE	Penalty RMSE		
0.602%	0.602%	10/16/2020					11	SPX	0.640%	0.001%	Forward	Aged
Mo	Yr	SOLVER / EQ Index Options Expire	EQ Indx # TD	EQ Indx Tdif	VX FUT Tdif	VX FUT TD	10/09/20 EQ Index ATM Call & Put IV	10/09/20 Est. Index Option IV	10/09/20 Index ATM IV Error	10/09/20 Index ATM IV Penalty	10/09/20 Est ATM Option Forward IV Period	11/09/20 EST Aged Index Option IV
10	2020	10/16/2020	5	5	-5	22	17.50%	17.35%	0.15%	0.00%	17.35%	#N/A
11	2020	11/20/2020	30	25	2	21	21.90%	21.96%	-0.06%	0.00%	22.77%	22.77%
12	2020	12/18/2020	49	19	2	20	22.90%	23.23%	-0.33%	0.00%	25.12%	24.39%
1	2021	1/15/2021	67	18	-4	21	23.00%	23.43%	-0.43%	0.00%	23.94%	24.21%
2	2021	2/19/2021	90	23	2	22	23.00%	23.60%	-0.60%	0.00%	24.11%	24.18%
3	2021	3/19/2021	110	20	2	21	23.00%	23.72%	-0.72%	0.00%	24.26%	24.20%
4	2021	4/16/2021	129	19	-5	22		23.78%	0.00%	0.00%	24.10%	24.18%
5	2021	5/21/2021	154	25	2	21		23.78%	0.00%	0.00%	23.80%	24.11%
6	2021	6/18/2021	173	19	2	21	22.70%	23.75%	-1.05%	0.00%	23.46%	24.03%
7	2021	7/16/2021	192	19	-5	22		23.87%	0.00%	0.00%	24.98%	24.14%
8	2021	8/20/2021	217	25	2	21		24.00%	0.00%	0.00%	24.98%	24.25%
9	2021	9/17/2021	236	19	2	21	22.60%	24.08%	-1.48%	0.00%	24.98%	24.31%
10	2021	10/15/2021	256	20	-5	22		23.41%	0.00%	0.00%	13.09%	23.57%
11	2021	11/19/2021	281	25	2	21		22.68%	0.00%	0.00%	13.09%	22.77%
12	2021	12/17/2021	300	19	-5	19	22.20%	22.20%	0.00%	0.00%	13.09%	22.24%
1	2022	1/21/2022	322	22	2	22		22.56%	0.00%	0.00%	26.98%	22.62%
2	2022	2/18/2022	342	20	2	21		22.84%	0.00%	0.00%	26.98%	22.92%
3	2022	3/18/2022	361	19	3	22		23.08%	0.00%	0.00%	26.98%	23.17%
4	2022	4/14/2022	380	19	-5	22		23.29%	0.00%	0.00%	26.98%	23.38%
5	2022	5/20/2022	405	25	2	21		23.53%	0.00%	0.00%	26.98%	23.63%
6	2022	6/17/2022	424	19	2	21	23.70%	23.70%	0.00%	0.00%	26.98%	23.80%
7	2022	7/15/2022	443	19	-5	22		23.77%	0.00%	0.00%	25.41%	23.88%
8	2022	8/19/2022	468	25	2	21		23.86%	0.00%	0.00%	25.41%	23.97%
9	2022	9/16/2022	487	19	-5	22		23.93%	0.00%	0.00%	25.41%	24.03%
10	2022	10/21/2022	512	25			24.00%	24.00%	0.00%	0.00%	25.41%	24.10%

TOV Spreadsheet: ATM Equity Options

The forward volatilities and skew functions were already derived in the Solver estimation process described above. The TOV spreadsheet uses the estimated forward volatilities to calculate the estimated price of each volatility index futures contract (derived from the JVAF and the vertical skew function), and the difference between the actual volatility index futures price and the estimated futures price (the error). *Positive* differences (errors) indicate *overvalued* volatility futures contracts and *negative* errors indicate *undervalued* volatility futures contracts (in the context of the market). The volatility index futures section of the TOV Estimate TSV worksheet for 10/9/2020 are shown in Figure 9.2 below.

In general, the volatility index futures contracts were slightly rich (overvalued) on 10/9/2020. For example, the VIX futures contract expiring on 10/21/2020 was overvalued by 0.92%. The actual VIX futures price was 26.8%, compared to an estimated VIX futures price of 25.88%. The fact that equity options were generally undervalued and VIX futures were generally overvalued is primarily due to skew anomalies on 10/9/2020 (relative to the historical vertical skew relationship).

Figure 9.2 - Trading Option Volatilities : Term Structure of Volatility Worksheet

Copyright © 2021 Trading Insights, LLC. All Rights Reserved.

Fut. Ex. Date	VIX Spread	Futures Count		VX RMSE
10/14/2020	2.50%	9		0.553%

VX Futures Contract Matures	10/09/20 Est. VX Spread	10/09/20 VX Futures	10/09/20 Est. VX Futures	10/09/20 VX Futures Error
10/21/2020	3.12%	26.80%	25.88%	0.92%
11/18/2020	3.36%	29.05%	28.26%	0.79%
12/16/2020	3.24%	27.95%	27.30%	0.65%
1/20/2021	3.23%	27.91%	27.35%	0.56%
2/17/2021	3.23%	27.87%	27.47%	0.40%
3/17/2021	3.20%	27.58%	27.32%	0.26%
4/21/2021	3.16%	27.25%	26.96%	0.29%
5/19/2021	3.12%	26.82%	26.61%	0.21%
6/16/2021	3.31%	28.60%	28.15%	0.45%
7/21/2021	3.22%		28.20%	0.00%
8/18/2021	3.22%		28.20%	0.00%
9/15/2021	3.22%		17.80%	0.00%
10/20/2021	3.22%		16.31%	0.00%
11/17/2021	3.22%		16.31%	0.00%
12/22/2021	3.22%		30.20%	0.00%
1/19/2022	3.22%		30.20%	0.00%
2/16/2022	3.22%		30.20%	0.00%
3/15/2022	3.22%		30.20%	0.00%
4/20/2022	3.22%		30.20%	0.00%
5/18/2022	3.22%		30.20%	0.00%
6/15/2022	3.22%		28.78%	0.00%
7/20/2022	3.22%		28.63%	0.00%
8/17/2022	3.22%		28.63%	0.00%
9/21/2022	3.22%		28.63%	0.00%

TOV Spreadsheet: Graphical Term Structures of Volatilities

Figure 9.3 provides a 10/9/2020 graphical analysis of actual and estimated ATM IV data, actual and estimated VIX futures data, the forward volatilities for each forward period, and the aged or projected ATM IVs for all index options.

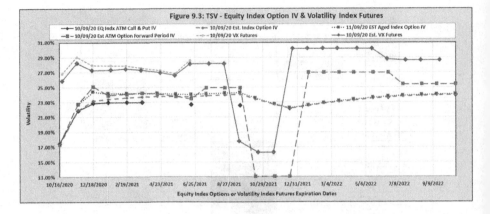

Figure 9.4 only shows the 10/9/2020 data related to equity index options: actual and estimated ATM IVs, the forward volatilities for each forward period, and the aged or projected ATM IVs.

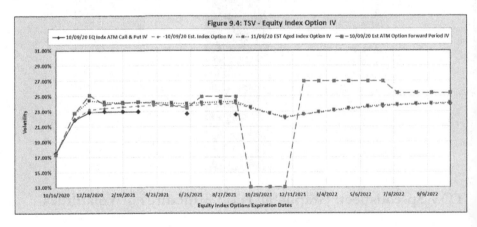

Figure 9.5 only shows the 10/9/2020 data related to volatility index futures: actual and estimated VIX futures prices, and the forward volatilities for each forward period.

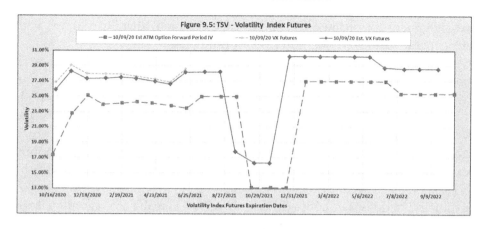

Figure 9.5: TSV - Volatility Index Futures

What is the most notable feature of all three charts? The sharp decline in forward volatilities in late 2021. The longest data available for the VIX futures contracts was for the June 2021 contract, so the sharp decline in forward volatilities is due entirely to the ATM IV data. There was also a gap in the expiration dates of equity options (with available data) from 9/17/2021 to 12/17/2021. The estimation process uses a penalty function to force forward volatilities with no interim data to be the same. This makes the forward volatilities (with no available interim data) more consistent and easier to evaluate.

In this case, the estimated forward volatility from 9/17/2021 to 12/17/2021 was only 13.09%, which was down sharply from the estimated forward volatilities immediately preceding (24.98%) and immediately following (26.98%) that three-month forward period (see Figure 9.1). What could explain the sharp decline to 13.09% in the interim three-month period? It is actually consistent with the data and is not a fluke of the estimation process (which is typically very reliable with accurate data). The most likely explanation is the market's perception of a decline in seasonal volatility around the year-end holidays.

Integrating Seasonal Volatility Research

While there is strong evidence of seasonality in historical volatility data, I personally prefer *not* to incorporate seasonal variables directly in my general volatility models – including the AI Volatility Edge platform. The main reason is that seasonal volatility is not constant and is heavily influenced by specific conditions in each market environment. However, it is still very important to quantify and understand the historical patterns in seasonal volatility. As a result, I prefer to model seasonal volatility independently and use judgment to integrate the quantifiable seasonal volatility patterns with my general volatility model forecasts or estimates.

To that end, I have included the results of my seasonal volatility research study that calculated the SPY average annualized realized volatilities and average VIX volatilities for all monthly index option expiration periods (Figure 9.6 and Graph 9.6). For example, the average annualized realized volatility (from 1/2000 to 1/2020) for the periods from each year's December option expiration date to the subsequent January option expiration date was 16.65%. Over the same *January* expiration periods, the VIX index averaged 21.33%. The resulting VIX spread over all *January* expiration periods was 4.68% (21.33 – 16.65%). The SPY average annualized realized volatility over *all* expiration periods was 18.91% and the average VIX over *all* expiration periods was 21.22%. The resulting VIX spread for *all* expiration periods was 2.31% (21.22% - 18.91%).

What can we conclude from the seasonal volatility study and how does that relate to the 10/9/2020 volatility estimates? First, the realized volatility for the January expiration periods (which includes the annual holiday season), was lower than the yearly average (consistent with the market's holiday volatility hypothesis). Surprisingly, the average VIX for the January expiration period was slightly higher than the annual average. As a result, the VIX spread was also higher in the January expiration period (4.68%) than the annual average (2.31%). While a portion of the VIX spread is attributable to the vertical skew function discussed earlier in this chapter, the data does suggest a slight advantage to Option Income Strategies (OIS) in the January expiration period.

So, does this explain the sharp decline in the 13.09% forward volatility for the 9/17/2021 to 12/17/2021, compared to estimated forward volatilities immediately preceding (24.98%) and immediately following (26.98%) that three-month forward period.

It does not! If you examine the historical seasonal results carefully, you will note that the period from 9/17/2021 to 12/17/2021 matches up to the October, November, and December expiration periods – *not* the January expiration period. The realized volatilities in October, November, and December expiration periods are all *higher* than the average realized volatility over all periods, in some cases materially *higher*.

As a result, the December 2021 equity index option appears to be materially mispriced, at least relative to the September 2021 equity index option. In other words, the ATM SPX September 2021 option was undervalued (error: -1.48%) relative to the ATM SPX December 2021 option (error: 0.00%) – from Figure 9.1.

Exp Month	Jan	Feb	Mar	Apr	May	Jun	Jul	Aug	Sep	Oct	Nov	Dec	Average
Realized Volatility	16.65%	17.86%	19.23%	18.10%	15.95%	15.39%	16.11%	19.26%	17.75%	25.05%	23.45%	19.60%	18.91%
VIX	21.33%	21.40%	21.59%	20.61%	19.37%	19.35%	19.14%	19.40%	20.72%	22.42%	24.93%	23.59%	21.22%
VIX Spread	4.68%	3.54%	2.36%	2.51%	3.42%	3.96%	3.03%	0.14%	2.97%	-2.63%	1.48%	3.99%	2.31%

Figure 9.6: SPY Realized Volatility vs. Average VIX (By Option Expiration Month) (1/2000 - 1/2020)

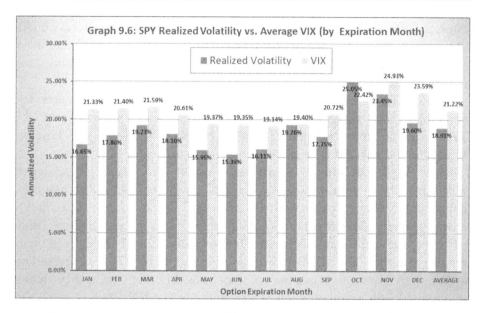

Graph 9.6: SPY Realized Volatility vs. Average VIX (by Expiration Month)

TOV Spreadsheet: JAF True Vega for ATM Options

Forward volatility estimates are required for the JAF Valuation and Greek Algorithms; evaluating the resulting forward volatility estimates can also generate unique relative value insights. To provide even greater value to the reader, I added a "True Vega" worksheet to the TOV Spreadsheet. The True Vega worksheet uses the forward volatility estimates from the "Estimate TSV" worksheet to calculate the JAF True Vega values for the same ATM equity options and volatility index futures contracts used in the Estimate TSV worksheet. As a result, *the forward volatilities on the Estimate TSV worksheet must always be estimated first – before proceeding to the True Vega worksheet.*

There are only two steps required to calculate the JAF True Vegas for all ATM equity options and all volatility index futures contracts: 1) Enter the average risk-free interest rate, and 2) click on the "JAF True Vega" macro button. The automated JAF True Vega macro will perform all related calculations and will populate the tables shown in Figures 9.7, 9.8, 9.10, and 9.11.

Note: the JAF is designed to use unique forward risk-free rates for each forward period. However, to make this spreadsheet as user-friendly as possible, I only required a single average risk-free rate for use in the JAF True Vega calculations for all options. In the current environment of very low, stable interest rates with a moderately sloped term structure of interest rates, the effects on True Vega will be minimal. However, the effects on JAF valuation and returns would be larger. As a result, the complete term structure of risk-free rates should always be used for JAF valuation and return simulation.

Figure 9.7 provides the descriptive characteristics, volatility estimates, and several JAF Vega metrics for each ATM equity option. Specifically, the JAF True Vega Volatility Multiplier (TVVM), the BSM Vega, the JAF Discrete Vega, and the JAF True Vega are all provided.

BSM Vega calculations assume a constant 1% change in aggregate volatility (derived with the JAVF), JAF Discrete Vega calculations assume a constant 1% change in forward volatility; JAF True Vega assumes a 1% change in the 21-trade-day ATM volatility with corresponding (non-constant) forward volatility changes derived from the JAF True Vega mean reversion model. The assorted Vega metrics in Figure 9.7 are expressed on a "Per Share" basis, not on a per contract basis. In other words, they are not multiplied by the standard equity index multiplier of 100.

As expected, the True Vega Volatility Multipliers decline as the time to expiration of the ATM options increases. Conversely, the BSM and JAF Discrete Vegas (which do not incorporate mean reversion) increase significantly as the time to expiration increases. The resulting JAF True Vega initially increases, then actually declines as the time to expiration increases beyond approximately one year. This result would surprise many option traders. In addition, the JAF True Vega calculations are dependent on the level and shape of the term structure of volatilities, so it is not advisable to attempt to draw general conclusions about the function of JAF True Vega relative to time to expiration.

Instead, it is advisable to derive JAF True Vegas directly from the unique term structure of forward volatilities in each specific market environment. True Vega is the primary risk management metric for managing volatility risk in option portfolios and it is vitally important to use accurate risk metrics when managing the critical exposure to changes in volatility.

Analysis Date	Index	RF-Rate	AVM (21)	JAF True Vega				
10/9/2020	SPX	0.10%	0.9544					

Figure 9.7

ATM Equity Index Options (Per "Share" - *NOT* Per Contract)

Equity Index Options Expiration Date	Interval #TD	End #TD	Annual Forward Volatility	10/09/20 Est. Index Option IV	Equity Index Option JAF TVVM	Equity Index Option BSM Vega	ATM Equity Index Option JAF Discrete Vega	ATM Equity Index Option JAF True Vega
10/16/2020	5	5	17.35%	17.35%	1.7274	0.562	0.562	0.971
11/20/2020	25	30	22.77%	21.96%	0.8676	1.375	1.370	1.193
12/18/2020	19	49	25.12%	23.23%	0.6945	1.757	1.748	1.220
1/15/2021	18	67	23.94%	23.43%	0.6053	2.053	2.046	1.243
2/19/2021	23	90	24.11%	23.60%	0.5283	2.378	2.371	1.256
3/19/2021	20	110	24.26%	23.72%	0.4797	2.627	2.621	1.260
4/16/2021	19	129	24.10%	23.78%	0.4438	2.843	2.838	1.262
5/21/2021	25	154	23.80%	23.78%	0.4064	3.104	3.099	1.262
6/18/2021	19	173	23.46%	23.75%	0.3833	3.288	3.284	1.261
7/16/2021	19	192	24.98%	23.87%	0.3622	3.462	3.457	1.254
8/20/2021	25	217	24.98%	24.00%	0.3385	3.678	3.673	1.245
9/17/2021	19	236	24.98%	24.08%	0.3230	3.833	3.828	1.238
10/15/2021	20	256	13.09%	23.41%	0.3126	3.991	3.954	1.247
11/19/2021	25	281	13.09%	22.68%	0.3008	4.180	4.109	1.257
12/17/2021	19	300	13.09%	22.20%	0.2925	4.318	4.224	1.263
1/21/2022	22	322	26.98%	22.56%	0.2779	4.470	4.374	1.242
2/18/2022	20	342	26.98%	22.84%	0.2662	4.603	4.506	1.225
3/18/2022	19	361	26.98%	23.08%	0.2561	4.726	4.629	1.210
4/14/2022	19	380	26.98%	23.29%	0.2470	4.845	4.748	1.197
5/20/2022	25	405	26.98%	23.53%	0.2361	4.997	4.901	1.180
6/17/2022	19	424	26.98%	23.70%	0.2286	5.110	5.014	1.168
7/15/2022	19	443	25.41%	23.77%	0.2221	5.220	5.126	1.160
8/19/2022	25	468	25.41%	23.86%	0.2142	5.360	5.269	1.148
9/16/2022	19	487	25.41%	23.93%	0.2086	5.464	5.374	1.140
10/21/2022	25	512	25.41%	24.00%	0.2017	5.598	5.510	1.129

TOV Spreadsheet: JAF True Vega for Volatility Futures

Figure 9.8 provides the descriptive characteristics, volatility estimates, and JAF True Vega for each volatility index futures contract. The calculation of Vega and especially True Vega probably seems strange to most traders. However, the concept of Vega can and should be applied to volatility futures, particularly if VIX futures are used for hedging purposes. The interpretation of JAF True Vega is no different for volatility index futures contracts.

In this case, JAF True Vega represents the change in the value of the volatility index futures contract in response to a 1% change in the reference volatility (aggregate volatility of a 21-trade-day ATM option). The JAF True Vegas in Figure 9.8 are expressed on a "Per Share" basis, not on a per contract basis. In other words, they are not multiplied by the VIX futures multiplier of 1000. These values are directly comparable to the JAF True

Vegas for ATM equity options.

As expected, the JAF True Vegas for futures contracts decline as the time to expiration of the volatility index futures contact increases. This is due to mean reversion. Unlike the True Vega of ATM equity options, there is no partially offsetting effect of increasing BSM Vega. As a result, the decline in JAF True Vega of futures contracts is more pronounced. It is also important to note that the JAF True Vega for all futures contracts will almost always be less than or equal to 1.0 (except in very rare cases for very near-term futures contracts with a unique number of holidays in the futures volatility window).

The futures contract will almost always have a forward volatility period longer than the 21-trade-day reference period. The resulting True Vega for the futures contract will be less than 1.0 due to mean reversion.

As was the case with the JAF True Vegas for ATM equity options, the JAF True Vega calculations for volatility futures are dependent on the level and shape of the term structure of volatilities. As a result, it is advisable to derive JAF True Vegas directly from the unique term structure of forward volatilities in each specific market environment.

It is also important to note that the True Vegas will change over time, especially for near-term options and volatility futures. It is critical to recalculate the JAF True Vegas in response to the passage of time and to changes in the level or shape of the term structure of volatilities.

While the Daily Volatility Multipliers (DVMs) are estimated from 15+ years of data, the JAF Vegas and Partial Vegas are structural, interrelated, and internally consistent. Day-to-day changes in actual ATM IVs and volatility futures prices will not match the JAF True Vegas exactly. However, actual changes in ATM IVs and volatility index futures prices that deviate significantly from the JAF True Vegas represent pricing anomalies that could potentially be exploited.

Figure 9.8					
VX Futures (Per "Share" - *NOT* Per Contract)					
Futures Contract Maturity Date	VX FUT Beg #TD	VX FUT End #TD	VX FUT #TD	10/09/20 Est. VX Futures	VX Futures JAF True Vega
10/21/2020	8	30	22	25.88%	0.693
11/18/2020	28	49	21	28.26%	0.466
12/16/2020	47	67	20	27.30%	0.374
1/20/2021	69	90	21	27.35%	0.308
2/17/2021	88	110	22	27.47%	0.269
3/17/2021	108	129	21	27.32%	0.240
4/21/2021	132	154	22	26.96%	0.212
5/19/2021	152	173	21	26.61%	0.195
6/16/2021	171	192	21	28.15%	0.180
7/21/2021	195	217	22	28.20%	0.164
8/18/2021	215	236	21	28.20%	0.153
9/15/2021	234	256	22	17.80%	0.140
10/20/2021	259	281	22	16.31%	0.133
11/17/2021	279	300	21	16.31%	0.126
12/22/2021	303	322	19	30.20%	0.118
1/19/2022	320	342	22	30.20%	0.112
2/16/2022	340	361	21	30.20%	0.107
3/15/2022	358	380	22	30.20%	0.102
4/20/2022	383	405	22	30.20%	0.096
5/18/2022	403	424	21	30.20%	0.092
6/15/2022	422	443	21	28.78%	0.088
7/20/2022	446	468	22	28.63%	0.083
8/17/2022	466	487	21	28.63%	0.079
9/21/2022	490	512	22	28.63%	0.075

TOV Spreadsheet: JAF True Vega
Interactive ATM Option Calendar Spreads

While the JAF True Vegas for each of the monthly equity option and volatility futures contracts are very useful, I also wanted to provide an interactive tool for calculating the JAF True Vegas for any pair of ATM equity options, and for the JAF True Vega for the resulting ATM calendar spread (Figure 9.9). The monthly option expiration dates that are automatically populated in the TOV spreadsheet do not include weekly options, which are very popular. As an alternative, the interactive tool allows the user to enter expiration dates for ATM options for weeklies, monthlies, quarterlies, or even LEAPs (with expiration dates less then 756 trade days).

To use the interactive tool, enter the dates for the pair of options and the resulting number of contracts long (positive) or short (negative). Then click on the "Interactive JAF True Vega ATM Calendar Spread" push-button macro. The macro will calculate the results and will populate the table in Figure 9.9. The JAF True Vegas for each option are expressed on a "Per Share" basis and the JAF True Vega for the Calendar Spread is expressed for the actual number of contracts – as specified by the user.

The calendar spread example shown in Figure 9.9 has a one-contract short position in the ATM equity option expiring on 10/16/2020 and a one-contract long position in the ATM equity option expiring on 11/20/2020. The estimated volatilities are shown for both options, as are their respective "Per Share" True Vegas. The resulting JAF True Vega for the one-contract long calendar spread equals 22.26, which indicates that the estimated linear change in the value of this one-contract calendar spread will increase by 22.26, in response to an instantaneous 1% increase in the 21-trade-day reference volatility.

Interactive JAF True Vega ATM Calendar Spread				
Figure 9.9				
Interactive ATM Calendar Spread JAF True Vega				
Contracts: Positive Long or Negative Short	Equity Index Options Expiration Date	End #TD	10/09/20 Est. Index Option IV	ATM Equity Index Option JAF True Vega
-1	10/16/2020	5	17.350%	0.971
1	11/20/2020	30	21.956%	1.193
ATM Calendar Spread True Vega (Actual # Contracts)				22.26

TOV Spreadsheet: JAF True Vega ATM Option Calendar Spread Pairs

Figure 9.10 lists the one-contract, long calendar spread JAF True Vegas for every pair of ATM monthly equity options. The long option expiration dates are shown in columns (horizontally) and the short option expiration dates are shown in rows (vertically). The single-cell intersection of each row and column contains the one-contract JAF True Vega for the specific ATM option calendar spread. Note the one-contract, calendar spread JAF True Vega in the top-left cell (22.26) is exactly the same as the one-contract, calendar spread in the interactive example (Figure 9.9). Both represent a calendar spread with a one-contract long position in the ATM equity option expiring on 11/20/2020 and a one-contract short position in the ATM equity option expiring on 10/16/2020.

Due to space limitations, the complete list of calendar spread pairs is not shown in Figure 9.10, but all ATM equity option calendar spread pairs are provided in the TOV spreadsheet. Due to the unique interrelationship of BSM Vega and mean reversion, the JAF True Vegas are *not* all positive – even for long calendar spreads. When the calendar spread JAF True Vegas are negative, the effects of mean reversion dominate the effects the effects of the longer time to option expiration.

The JAF True Vegas for ATM equity option calendar spreads are also dependent on the level and shape of the term structure of volatilities and they change over time. They should be calculated regularly.

Figure 9.10 - ATM Equity Index Option: Long Calendar Spread - JAF True Vega (Per Contract = 100x) – Derived from ESTIMATED FORWARD VOLATILITIES

| | Equity Index: Long ATM Option Expiration Date | | | | | | | | | | | | | |
	11/20/2020	12/18/2020	1/15/2021	2/19/2021	3/19/2021	4/16/2021	5/21/2021	6/18/2021	7/16/2021	8/20/2021	9/17/2021	10/15/2021	11/19/2021	12/17/2021
10/16/2020	22.26	24.94	27.21	28.55	28.97	29.11	29.10	28.99	28.32	27.42	26.73	27.68	28.66	29.27
11/20/2020		2.67	4.95	0.28	6.71	6.85	6.84	6.73	6.06	5.16	4.46	5.42	6.40	7.00
12/18/2020			2.28	3.61	4.04	4.18	4.17	4.06	3.38	2.48	1.79	2.75	3.72	4.33
1/15/2021				1.33	1.76	1.90	1.89	1.78	1.11	0.21	-0.49	0.47	1.45	2.05
2/19/2021					0.42	0.57	0.55	0.45	-0.23	-1.13	-1.82	-0.87	0.11	0.72
3/19/2021						0.14	0.13	0.02	-0.65	-1.55	-2.25	-1.29	-0.31	0.30
4/16/2021							-0.01	-0.12	-0.80	-1.69	-2.39	-1.43	-0.45	0.15
5/21/2021								-0.11	-0.78	-1.68	-2.38	-1.42	-0.44	0.17
6/18/2021									-0.67	-1.57	-2.27	-1.31	-0.33	0.27
7/16/2021										-0.90	-1.59	-0.64	0.34	0.95
8/20/2021											-0.69	0.26	1.24	1.85
9/17/2021												0.95	1.93	2.54
10/15/2021													0.98	1.59
11/19/2021														0.61
12/17/2021														
1/21/2022														
2/18/2022														
3/18/2022														
4/14/2022														
5/20/2022														
6/17/2022														
7/15/2022														
8/19/2022														
9/16/2022														

(Row labels: Equity Index: SHORT ATM Option Expiration Date)

TOV Spreadsheet: JAF True Vega Volatility Future Calendar Spread Pairs

Figure 9.11 provides the one-contract, long calendar spread JAF True Vegas for every pair of monthly volatility index futures contracts. The long futures expiration dates are shown in columns (horizontally) and the short futures expiration dates are shown in rows (vertically). The single-cell intersection of each row and column contains the one-contract JAF True Vega for the specific futures calendar spread. Due to space limitations, the complete list of calendar spread pairs is not shown in Figure 9.11, but all futures calendar spread pairs are provided in the TOV spreadsheet.

Due to the lack of an offsetting (increasing) BSM Vega in volatility futures, the effects of mean reversion result in negative JAF True Vegas for all long volatility index futures calendar spreads. Volatility calendar spreads can also be used for hedging purposes, but *the user should be very careful and intimately aware of the implicit exposure to volatilities in each unique forward volatility period.*

The JAF True Vegas for futures calendar spreads are also dependent on the level and shape of the term structure of volatilities and they change over time. They should be calculated regularly.

Figure 9.11 - VX Futures: Long Calendar Spread - JAF True Vega (Per Contract = 1000x) - Derived from ESTIMATED Forward Volatilities												
	VX Futures: LONG Contact Expiration Date											
	11/18/2020	12/16/2020	1/20/2021	2/17/2021	3/17/2021	4/21/2021	5/19/2021	6/16/2021	7/21/2021	8/18/2021	9/15/2021	10/20/2021
10/21/2020	-227.05	-318.74	-385.07	-423.68	-452.70	-480.62	-498.35	-512.97	-528.69	-539.45	-552.59	-559.60
11/18/2020		-91.69	-158.01	-196.63	-225.64	-253.57	-271.30	-285.91	-301.63	-312.39	-325.54	-332.55
12/16/2020			-66.32	-104.94	-133.95	-161.88	-179.61	-194.22	-209.94	-220.70	-233.85	-240.86
1/20/2021				-38.61	-67.63	-95.56	-113.28	-127.90	-143.62	-154.38	-167.52	-174.54
2/17/2021					-29.02	-56.94	-74.67	-89.29	-105.01	-115.76	-128.91	-135.92
3/17/2021						-27.93	-45.65	-60.27	-75.99	-86.75	-99.89	-106.91
4/21/2021							-17.73	-32.34	-48.06	-58.82	-71.97	-78.98
5/19/2021								-14.62	-30.34	-41.09	-54.24	-61.25
6/16/2021									-15.72	-26.48	-39.62	-46.64
7/21/2021										-10.76	-23.91	-30.92
8/18/2021											-13.15	-20.16
9/15/2021												-7.01
10/20/2021												
11/17/2021												
12/22/2021												
1/19/2022												
2/16/2022												
3/15/2022												
4/20/2022												
5/18/2022												
6/15/2022												
7/20/2022												
8/17/2022												

VX Futures: SHORT Contract Expiration Date (row axis label)

Trade Session Volatility – Counting Trade Days

I repeatedly make reference to the number of trade days for all calculations in this book, but all trade days are not created equal. While this concept is not directly applicable to the TOV spreadsheet, it is related to the title of this chapter: Estimating Forward Volatilities. The number of trade days is also required in the practical application of the JAF Valuation and Greek Algorithms – and in the application of all option valuation and Greek calculations.

When evaluating options, especially near-term options, it is critical to calculate the appropriate number of trade days remaining until option expiration. This seems simple on the surface, but we do not only calculate option values and Greeks at the close. We also need to calculate these values intra-day. In addition, the markets move during overnight sessions during the week and over the weekend and these movements are not uniform. The resulting "total" volatility is a function of the overnight volatility experienced during the week, over the weekend, and during the normal day sessions.

To better understand the relative contribution to volatility of these unique sessions, I did another volatility study on the SPY from 1/2000 to 1/2020 (intentionally avoiding the unique COVID environment). The results of this study are shown in Figure 9.12 below.

The annualized volatilities for each type of session are shown in the first row of the table. As you can see, the overnight sessions during the week experienced the lowest annualized volatility of 9.92%, followed by the weekend sessions with an annualized volatility of 12.06%. The "normal" or day sessions experienced the highest level of annualized volatility of 15.66%. The resulting "total" or close-to-close volatility for the SPY was 18.94%.

If we combine all non-day sessions together, the annualized volatility for all overnight sessions was 10.38%, which represents 30.5% of the total volatility (using the JVAF). Similarly, the normal or day session would contribute the remaining 69.5% of the overall volatility. In other words, if we did not differentiate between weekday and weekend overnight sessions, the number of trade days remaining at any open (after the preceding overnight session) would be reduced by 0.305 trade days.

If we did differentiate between weekend and weekday overnight sessions, the number of trade days remaining at the open on a *Monday* (after the overnight *weekend* session) would be reduced by 0.412 trade days. Similarly, the number of trade days remaining at the open on a *Tuesday through Friday* (after the overnight *weekday* session) would be reduced by 0.278 trade days.

Intra-day trade day calculations could be reduced proportionally, as a function of the number of hours remaining in the normal or day session. With the required intra-day price history, it would also be possible to calculate the relative volatility of each hour of the trading day. For traders of very short-term options, this could be beneficial. However, all trade day calculations should account for the relative volatility contribution of overnight weekday, weekend, and normal day sessions.

Figure 9.12: SPY Volatility by Trading Session (1/2000 - 1/2020)					
Trading Session	Weekday Overnight Sessions	Weekend Overnignt Sessions	All Overnight Sessions	"Normal" Day Sessions	Close to Close
Annualized Volatility	9.92%	12.06%	10.38%	15.66%	18.94%
Volatility Contribution (%)	41.2%	27.8%	30.5%	69.5%	100.0%

Summary

This chapter began with a review of forward rate and volatility disaggregation formulas, followed by an introduction to the TOV spreadsheet that accompanies this book. The spreadsheet introduction included a detailed example of estimating and interpreting forward volatilities using actual market data.

The resulting forward volatilities were used to evaluate the relative values of a series of ATM equity options and VIX futures contracts. To augment this analysis, the results from a 20-year seasonal volatility research study was provided and integrated into the analysis.

The spreadsheet introduction also explained how to use the True Vega worksheet to calculate the True Vega metrics for ATM equity options, volatility futures contracts, and for calendar spread pairs for both options and futures.

Finally, the results from a second volatility study were introduced to help quantify the volatility contributions of different types of trading sessions, which is crucial in the precise calculation of the fractional number of trade days remaining for all options and futures for all valuation and Greek calculations, particularly for near-term options.

10) GAMMA SCALPING & OPTION VALUATION

As an introduction to Gamma Scalping, let's begin by considering a hypothetical long ATM straddle (long ATM call & long ATM put), with 21 trade days remaining until expiration. Let's also assume the initial stock price equals 1000, the strike prices both equal 1000, the annualized implied volatility equals 20%, and the continuously compounded risk-free interest rate equals 4% (the Flat Base Case Scenario used earlier). Per the BSM model, the costs of the call option, put option, and the straddle would be 24.694, 21.366, and 46.059, rounded to three decimal places.

Here is the interesting question: if the stock price was exactly equal to the strike prices at expiration, how much would you gain or lose on the straddle over the 21 trade-day holding period? The vast majority of option traders would respond that both options would expire worthless and the straddle would lose all of its value, or 46.059 on a per share basis. A better answer to the question would be: "*it depends on how the straddle strategy is managed.*"

Would it surprise you to learn that you could employ a Gamma scalping strategy to profit from the above straddle, even in this potentially unfavorable scenario? I will fully explain and evaluate the results of this specific type of Gamma Scalping later in this chapter, but let's first examine the problems with the buy and hold trade management system for the long straddle.

Long Straddle: Held Until Expiration

When traders assume the straddle would lose all of its value in the above scenario, they are implicitly assuming that the straddle is held until expiration *and no adjustments are made during the holding period*. Using that approach, the price of the underlying stock would need to increase or decrease by more than 46.059 points during the holding period to make a profit. The resulting breakeven prices would be 1046.059 and 953.941, or a return of plus or minus 4.6059% on the underlying stock of the 21-trade-day holding period.

As most option traders are aware, option income strategies (net short options: negative Gamma, positive Theta, typically negative Vega) on equity indices have a demonstrated and proven edge historically. There are many different flavors of option income strategies and I have written extensively on this topic. The historical option income *advantage* translates into a historical *disadvantage* for long option strategies, particularly the long ATM straddle. This long-term bias creates an additional hurdle for straddles, but they can be a very powerful strategy. The key is how they are managed.

I used the 21-trade-day ATM IV data series I discussed earlier to study the performance of hypothetical 21-trade-day ATM straddles entered on a daily basis for the past 15+ years on the SPX, NDX, and RUT indices. I assumed each straddle was held until expiration – the same trade management strategy implied above. Over 62% of the 21-trade-day straddles lost money. The average return was -8.64%. Many traders can attest to the pain of trading straddles, especially when using the simple buy-and-hold approach. The pain of negative Theta, which grows over time, is like death by 1000 cuts.

While the buy-and-hold straddle performance in the 15+ year study was poor, the problem is *not* the straddle. The problem is trade management. Properly-weighted ATM straddles are Delta-neutral, and have positive Gamma, positive Vega, and negative Theta. The appropriate environment for buying ATM straddles is when options are cheap or undervalued. To be more specific, the above Greeks of the ATM straddle imply that the straddle buyer should have no opinion on market direction, but expects realized volatility over the holding period to exceed implied volatility, and expects implied volatility to increase (if the staddle is exited before expiration).

In this context, does buy-and-hold trade management make sense for the straddle? Definitely not. The price of the underlying stock changes continuously. If the price of the stock increased by 25 points on the first trade day, the Delta of the straddle would also increase and become positive (due to positive Gamma). The straddle would no longer be Delta-neutral. Instead, it would now be a bullish strategy – which directly contradicts the buyer's lack of directional insight. If the price of the underlying stock declined by the same 25 points the following trade day (returning to 1000), the decline in the price of the underlying stock would hurt the now bullish straddle. To make matters even worse, at the end of the second trade day, the straddle would be worth significantly less than it was at inception, due to negative Theta (assuming the implied volatility had not changed).

Let's recap; the initial *implied volatilities* of the ATM call and put options in the Delta-neutral straddle were both 20%. The annualized *realized volatility* of the underlying stock (RMS of the continuously compounded returns) over the two trade-day period was almost 40% (calculation not shown). The ATM straddle buyer expected realized volatility to exceed implied (which it did by almost 20%), and the straddle still would have lost money (assuming no change in implied volatility). Furthermore, the buy-and-hold trade management straddle would almost always have an undesired directional exposure throughout the entire holding period.

There are an infinite number of possible return paths of the underlying stock or equity index over any holding period. *For a given or specified level of realized volatility*, there are still an infinite number of possible return paths. Even if we assume that realized volatility will exceed implied volatility (as desired), only a select sample of the possible return paths will generate a profit for the buy-and-hold straddle – only those paths with a strong directional trend.

For example, alternating daily 2.5% (continuously compounded) price changes in the underlying security would leave the price of the underlying security unchanged at expiration (for an even number of trade days), resulting in a total loss for the buy-and-hold straddle. Conversely, daily positive or negative 2.5% price changes over the holding period would generate extraordinary profits for the buy-and-hold ATM straddle. The only way to profit from the buy-and-hold straddle is through an unexpected and sustained trend in the price of the underlying security. This is particularly ironic, given the lack of a directional insight implicit in the long straddle position.

Unlike the buy-and-hold approach, the Gamma Scalping trade management described in this chapter is consistent with the Greeks of the properly-weighted ATM straddle: Delta-neutral, positive Gamma, positive Vega, and negative Theta. The Gamma Scalping trade management strategy is also designed to generate profits when realized volatility over the holding period exceeds implied volatility, and when implied volatility increases (if the long staddle is exited before expiration) - *regardless of the terminal price of the underlying security.*

Gamma Scalping Objective

Gamma Scalping is a form of *dynamic hedging*, where periodic trades are executed to "rebalance" the aggregate position to a Delta-neutral or market-neutral state. There are many different forms of Gamma Scalping, but I will present a very specific methodology in this chapter. This Gamma Scalping trade management system will allow us to *"extract"* the *realized* value of any option or option strategy (including the long Delta-neutral straddle). Note:

this is the *realized* value of the option (derived from *realized* volatility over the holding period), which will be different from the *implied* value of the option (derived from *implied* volatility at trade inception). If held until expiration, Gamma Scalping will extract the *realized* value of the option, but we would pay the *implied* value of the option. This suggests that the Gamma Scalping trade management strategy would generate profits whenever realized volatility exceeds implied volatility – exactly consistent with our objective.

I will explain the Gamma Scalping implications for *partial holding periods* later in this chapter. For now, let's focus on evaluating the Gamma Scalping trade management strategy when implemented until option expiration. I have claimed that Gamma Scalping will allow us to extract the realized value of an option or option strategy when managed until expiration. If realized volatility equals implied volatility, then the present value of the cash flows generated by the Gamma Scalping strategy should equal the value of the option. We can use this hypothesis to test or validate the Gamma Scalping strategy. Before doing so, I will explain the Gamma Scalping methodology and will review several detailed Gamma Scalping examples using ATM options that expire in 21 trade days.

Gamma Scalping Example: Options Expiring in 21 Trade Days

I will begin with a more academic example and analysis, using paths derived from a binomial lattice, coupled with standard BOM / BSM assumptions (regarding borrowing and lending, transaction costs, no margin requirement, etc.). Later in the chapter, I will present and evaluate Gamma Scalping results derived from actual SPX return data. I will use insights from this analysis to explain the implications for employing a Gamma Scalping strategy in practice.

So, how do we implement the Gamma Scalping trade management strategy to extract the realized value of an option or option strategy? The following methodology applies to individual call and put options, as well as option strategies.

Gamma Scalping Methodology
1) Purchase option or options at trade inception
   At Every Rebalancing Period (Including Inception):
   2) Calculate option or option strategy Delta at prevailing stock price
   3) Buy or sell required number of shares of underlying security to achieve Delta-neutral position
   4) Borrow or lend cash as needed to buy or sell required number of shares

Gamma Scalping (GS) Validation Methodology:
1) Calculate GS cash outflows or inflows resulting from share purchases or sales at each   rebalancing period (-1 x number of shares x share price)
2) Calculate GS cash flow from cash-settlement or option exercise at expiration
3) Calculate present value discount factor for each rebalancing date (using risk-free rate)
4) Calculate the realized GS value: sum of the present values of all discounted GS cash flows above
5) Compare the GS to the initial option or option strategy value

Note: The initial cost of the option or option strategy is *not* included in the calculation of the realized GS Value.

Figure 10.1 below is an example of applying the GS trade management system to an ATM call option, expiring in 21 trade days (TD). Figures 10.2 and 10.3 apply the same GS trade management system to a 21-TD ATM put option, and a 21-TD ATM straddle. These three examples are overly simplistic by design and are not intended to reflect the practical implementation of the Gamma Scalping strategy. After demonstrating the GS trade management system in the following three examples, I will use the standard BSM assumptions to demonstrate that the PV of the cash flows from the GS strategy exactly equal the BSM option value. I will then use the same GS trading strategy on approximately 20 years of actual data to generate and evaluate the GS results and develop practical insights into how the GS strategy should be implemented.

Let's continue with our earlier scenario and assume the initial stock price equals 1000, the strike prices both equal 1000, the annualized implied volatility equals 20%, and the continuously compounded risk-free interest rate equals 4% (the Flat Base Case Scenario). Furthermore, we will assume daily, end-of-day rebalancing, including at trade inception. This equates to

21 intervals. As you will recall from the JAF validation Chapters and the Supplement, we routinely used 8,192 N & N+1 intervals. Finally, in these examples, we will only be evaluating the results for a *single path* through the binomial lattice, or a single set of 22 prices for the underlying security – one for each node.

The purpose of the following three examples is to demonstrate how the GS trade management strategy is implemented, not to validate the results (which will be presented in the next section). It is much easier to understand the framework when using a single path of prices, over only 21 intervals.

Each row of the table in Figure 10.1 represents the end of a trade day; zero represents the inception date. The present stock price at each node is derived from the binomial lattice, using a random number probability generator, in conjunction with the risk-neutral binomial probabilities of the Up and Down states. The resulting stock price from the binomial lattice is used with the standard BSM Delta formula to calculate the Delta of the option.

At time zero, the Delta of the call option equals 0.5345 on a per share basis. This requires a transaction of negative 0.5345 shares of stock, or a sale of 0.5345 shares of stock. I recognize that we could not sell 0.5345 shares of stock, and we could simply multiply all of these values by 100,000 shares if you would prefer, but it is much more intuitive to work with Greeks and hypothetical transactions on a per share basis.

The resulting GS cash flow is positive 534.5063 at time zero (sale of 0.5345 shares x stock price of 1000). Since the cash flow occurred at time zero, the present value factor was 1.0, resulting in a present value (PV) of +534.5063 for the first cash flow.

At the end of the first trade day, the stock price increased to 1,012.6785 (randomly selected from the binomial lattice). The resulting Delta of our long call option increased to 0.6210, requiring the sale of an additional 0.0865 shares of stock to return to a Delta-neutral position. The resulting cash flow was positive 87.5957 (0.0865 x 1,012.6785). Finally, the present value of the same cash flow was positive 87.5818 (87.5957 x 0.9998413).

The last cash flow includes two components: 1) the liquidation of all outstanding GS shares at the prevailing stock price (Buy: -1 x 1.00 x 1,065.0205), plus 2) the exercise value of the option (max(1065.0205-1000),0) = negative 999.9689 (rounded). The present value of the final cash flow at the end of TD 21 equals negative 996.6412 (- 999.9689 x 0.9966722).

The sum of the present values of all GS cash flows for the call option equals 24.886, which is remarkably close to the BSM call option value of 24.694. Remember, we are only looking at one single path of stock prices over a very limited number of intervals (21). While we will use many more paths to validate the GS results, the results for a single path are impressive.

Conceptually, the GS trade management system is simple: use the underlying security to Delta-hedge the option or option strategy at the end of each rebalancing period. The validation methodology is equally simple: calculate the sum of the present values of all GS cash flows over the life of the option and compare that to the value of the option or option strategy at inception.

					# Shares:			Sum: PV of
	Present			Required #	Buy(+) or		PV of GS	GS Cash
Trade Day	Value Factor	Stock Price	Call Delta	Stock Shares	Sell(-)	GS Cash Flow	Cash Flow	Flows
0	1.0000000	1,000.0000	0.5345	-0.5345	-0.5345	534.5063	534.5063	
1	0.9998413	1,012.6785	0.6210	-0.6210	-0.0865	87.5957	87.5818	
2	0.9996826	1,025.5178	0.7058	-0.7058	-0.0848	86.9764	86.9488	
3	0.9995239	1,038.5198	0.7844	-0.7844	-0.0786	81.6536	81.6148	
4	0.9993653	1,051.6867	0.8527	-0.8527	-0.0683	71.7802	71.7346	
5	0.9992067	1,065.0205	0.9075	-0.9075	-0.0548	58.3820	58.3357	
6	0.9990481	1,078.5234	0.9476	-0.9476	-0.0401	43.2778	43.2366	
7	0.9988895	1,065.0205	0.9203	-0.9203	0.0274	-29.1292	-29.0968	
8	0.9987310	1,051.6867	0.8805	-0.8805	0.0398	-41.8351	-41.7820	
9	0.9985724	1,038.5198	0.8242	-0.8242	0.0563	-58.4787	-58.3952	
10	0.9984140	1,051.6867	0.8977	-0.8977	-0.0735	77.3306	77.2079	
11	0.9982555	1,038.5198	0.8434	-0.8434	0.0544	-56.4443	-56.3458	
12	0.9980971	1,051.6867	0.9177	-0.9177	-0.0744	78.2038	78.0549	
13	0.9979386	1,065.0205	0.9657	-0.9657	-0.0480	51.0927	50.9874	
14	0.9977802	1,078.5234	0.9898	-0.9898	-0.0241	25.9453	25.8877	
15	0.9976219	1,092.1975	0.9982	-0.9982	-0.0084	9.1619	9.1401	
16	0.9974635	1,078.5234	0.9968	-0.9968	0.0014	-1.4753	-1.4715	
17	0.9973052	1,065.0205	0.9944	-0.9944	0.0024	-2.5218	-2.5150	
18	0.9971469	1,051.6867	0.9904	-0.9904	0.0040	-4.2165	-4.2045	
19	0.9969887	1,038.5198	0.9841	-0.9841	0.0063	-6.5096	-6.4900	
20	0.9968304	1,051.6867	1.0000	-1.0000	-0.0158	16.6438	16.5910	
21	0.9966722	1,065.0205	0.0000	0.0000	1.0000	-999.9689	-996.6412	24.886

Figure 10.1: 21-TD Call Option Gamma Scalping (GS) Value - Flat Base Case (BSM = 24.694)

Figure 10.2 below is an example of applying the GS trade management system to an ATM put option, expiring in 21 trade days (TD). The methodology is exactly the same, so I will not review the calculations in the same level of detail. However, there are a few important observations. First, note that the initial Delta of the put option is obviously negative. This requires a *purchase* of 0.4655 shares of stock, which results in an initial *cash outflow*. This is the opposite of the call option example in Figure 10.1.

It is also interesting to note that the required transactions for all interim periods are exactly the same for the call option and the put option. This is because of put-call parity and the fact that the Gamma of a call option will equal the Gamma of a put option (with the same strike price and expiration date). As a result, the interim Gamma Scalping transactions will all be the same.

The final cash flow for the put option is different, but has the same components as the call option: 1) the liquidation of all outstanding GS shares at the prevailing stock price (Sell: -1 x 0.00 x 1,065.0205), plus 2) the exercise value of the option ((max(1000.00 - 1065.0205),0) = 0.000). The present value of the final cash flow at the end of TD 21 equals positive 0.0310 (+ 0.0311 x 0.9966722). Note: the intermediate calculations are all rounded to four decimal places, but the final values use the full precision of the intermediate values.

The sum of the present values of all GS cash flows for the put option equals 21.558, which is remarkably close to the BSM put option value of 21.366. In fact, the difference between GS and BSM values of the put option was 0.192, exactly the same as the difference between the GS and BSM values of the call option above. This is not an accident. It is the result of put-call parity and the equivalence of the Gamma of the call and put option.

In addition, I intentionally avoided calling the difference an "error" in the GS value. The GS value is the realized value of the GS transactions in the specific scenario (given the assumptions). The difference between the GS and BSM values are the result of using a single path over a limited number of intervals as a proxy for the continuous BSM model.

| | | | | | # Shares: | | | Sum: PV of |
Trade Day	Present Value Factor	Stock Price	Put Delta	Required # Stock Shares	Buy(+) or Sell(-)	GS Cash Flow	PV of GS Cash Flow	GS Cash Flows
0	1.0000000	1,000.0000	-0.4655	0.4655	0.4655	-465.4937	-465.4937	
1	0.9998413	1,012.6785	-0.3790	0.3790	-0.0865	87.5957	87.5818	
2	0.9996826	1,025.5178	-0.2942	0.2942	-0.0848	86.9764	86.9488	
3	0.9995239	1,038.5198	-0.2156	0.2156	-0.0786	81.6536	81.6148	
4	0.9993653	1,051.6867	-0.1473	0.1473	-0.0683	71.7802	71.7346	
5	0.9992067	1,065.0205	-0.0925	0.0925	-0.0548	58.3820	58.3357	
6	0.9990481	1,078.5234	-0.0524	0.0524	-0.0401	43.2778	43.2366	
7	0.9988895	1,065.0205	-0.0797	0.0797	0.0274	-29.1292	-29.0968	
8	0.9987310	1,051.6867	-0.1195	0.1195	0.0398	-41.8351	-41.7820	
9	0.9985724	1,038.5198	-0.1758	0.1758	0.0563	-58.4787	-58.3952	
10	0.9984140	1,051.6867	-0.1023	0.1023	-0.0735	77.3306	77.2079	
11	0.9982555	1,038.5198	-0.1566	0.1566	0.0544	-56.4443	-56.3458	
12	0.9980971	1,051.6867	-0.0823	0.0823	-0.0744	78.2038	78.0549	
13	0.9979386	1,065.0205	-0.0343	0.0343	-0.0480	51.0927	50.9874	
14	0.9977802	1,078.5234	-0.0102	0.0102	-0.0241	25.9453	25.8877	
15	0.9976219	1,092.1975	-0.0018	0.0018	-0.0084	9.1619	9.1401	
16	0.9974635	1,078.5234	-0.0032	0.0032	0.0014	-1.4753	-1.4715	
17	0.9973052	1,065.0205	-0.0056	0.0056	0.0024	-2.5218	-2.5150	
18	0.9971469	1,051.6867	-0.0096	0.0096	0.0040	-4.2165	-4.2045	
19	0.9969887	1,038.5198	-0.0159	0.0159	0.0063	-6.5096	-6.4900	
20	0.9968304	1,051.6867	0.0000	0.0000	-0.0158	16.6438	16.5910	
21	0.9966722	1,065.0205	0.0000	0.0000	0.0000	0.0311	0.0310	21.558

Figure 10.2: 21-TD Put Option Gamma Scalping (GS) Value - Flat Base Case (BSM = 21.366)

Figure 10.3 below is an example of applying the GS trade management system to an ATM straddle, expiring in 21 trade days (TD). The methodology is exactly the same, so I will not review the calculations in the same level of detail. However, there are a few important observations. First, note that ALL straddle values represent the sum of the call and put values from Figures 10.1 and 10.2. The initial Delta of the straddle is positive, but could be either positive of negative – depending on the initial Deltas of the call and put option. When the strike prices equal the stock price, the resulting call and put Deltas will not exactly offset.

While the straddle values in Figure 10.3 always equal the sum of the call and put values, it makes much more sense to treat the straddle as an individual strategy and use the GS Methodology described above to manage the straddle strategy. In other words, calculate the Delta of the straddle and solve for all of the resulting cash flows, present values, and overall GS value.

The required transactions for all interim periods are exactly equal to the sum of the transactions for the call and put options. However, as explained above, it is more intuitive to apply the GS methodology to the straddle strategy, rather than breaking it up into its component parts. The resulting interim cash flows and present values of the interim cash flows also represent the sum of the call and put values from Figures 10.1 and 10.2, by definition.

The sum of the present values of all GS cash flows for the straddle option equals 46.444, which is remarkably close to the BSM straddle value of 46.059. The difference between GS and BSM values of the put option was 0.385 (rounded), which equals the sum of the differences between the GS and BSM values for the call and put options above, as expected.

The GS straddle value (PV of the GS straddle transactions) would have been 46.444 in the specific binomial lattice path described in Figures 10.1 – 10.3 (given the assumptions). While it is encouraging that the resulting GS values are close the corresponding BSM values, our objective is to generate profits. Before validating the GS methodology, let's use a similar 21-TD straddle example to demonstrate how the GS trade management strategy could be used to generate profits.

Trade Day	Present Value Factor	Stock Price	Straddle Delta	Required # Stock Shares	# Shares: Buy(+) or Sell(-)	GS Cash Flow	PV of GS Cash Flow	Sum: PV of GS Cash Flows
								Figure 10.3: 21-TD Straddle Gamma Scalping (GS) Value - Flat Base Case (BSM = 46.059)
0	1.0000000	1,000.0000	0.0690	-0.0690	-0.0690	69.0126	69.0126	
1	0.9998413	1,012.6785	0.2420	-0.2420	-0.1730	175.1915	175.1637	
2	0.9996826	1,025.5178	0.4116	-0.4116	-0.1696	173.9528	173.8976	
3	0.9995239	1,038.5198	0.5689	-0.5689	-0.1573	163.3073	163.2295	
4	0.9993653	1,051.6867	0.7054	-0.7054	-0.1365	143.5603	143.4692	
5	0.9992067	1,065.0205	0.8150	-0.8150	-0.1096	116.7641	116.6714	
6	0.9990481	1,078.5234	0.8953	-0.8953	-0.0803	86.5556	86.4732	
7	0.9988895	1,065.0205	0.8406	-0.8406	0.0547	-58.2584	-58.1937	
8	0.9987310	1,051.6867	0.7610	-0.7610	0.0796	-83.6702	-83.5640	
9	0.9985724	1,038.5198	0.6484	-0.6484	0.1126	-116.9574	-116.7904	
10	0.9984140	1,051.6867	0.7955	-0.7955	-0.1471	154.6612	154.4159	
11	0.9982555	1,038.5198	0.6868	-0.6868	0.1087	-112.8885	-112.6916	
12	0.9980971	1,051.6867	0.8355	-0.8355	-0.1487	156.4075	156.1099	
13	0.9979386	1,065.0205	0.9314	-0.9314	-0.0959	102.1853	101.9747	
14	0.9977802	1,078.5234	0.9795	-0.9795	-0.0481	51.8906	51.7754	
15	0.9976219	1,092.1975	0.9963	-0.9963	-0.0168	18.3238	18.2802	
16	0.9974635	1,078.5234	0.9936	-0.9936	0.0027	-2.9505	-2.9430	
17	0.9973052	1,065.0205	0.9888	-0.9888	0.0047	-5.0435	-5.0300	
18	0.9971469	1,051.6867	0.9808	-0.9808	0.0080	-8.4330	-8.4090	
19	0.9969887	1,038.5198	0.9683	-0.9683	0.0125	-13.0191	-12.9799	
20	0.9968304	1,051.6867	0.9999	-0.9999	-0.0317	33.2876	33.1821	
21	0.9966722	1,065.0205	0.0000	0.0000	0.9999	-999.9377	-996.6102	46.444

Gamma Scalping Profits: 21-TD Straddle

The Gamma Scalping trade management strategy is designed to generate profits when realized volatility over the holding period exceeds implied volatility, and when implied volatility increases (if the long staddle is exited before expiration) - *regardless of the terminal price of the underlying security*. For now, we are not contemplating exiting the straddle before expiration, but let's assume that we expect annualized *realized* volatility to equal 25% over the next 21 trade days, but implied volatility remains at 20% in the base case scenario.

Subject to discrete characteristics of the specific path over the limited number of only 21 intervals, the Gamma Scalping methodology should be able to extract the approximate *realized* value of the straddle given a 25% realized volatility, but we would only be required to pay the *implied* value of the option at a 20% implied volatility.

Figure 10.3B provides all of the GS calculations for the ATM straddle expiring in 21 trade days, but all stock prices were derived from the binomial lattice generated with a 25% annualized volatility. All of the GS transactions, cash flows, and present values reflect the higher-than-expected level of realized volatility (25%), relative to implied volatility (20%). In general, the number of shares traded and the cash flow amounts will be slightly larger, given the higher level of realized volatility scenario.

If our forecast was accurate and the resulting realized volatility was 25% over the life of the option, the GS trade management strategy would be able to *extract a realized* GS straddle present value of 58.052, but we would only be required to *pay the implied* BSM straddle value of 46.059. The difference between the realized GS straddle value (58.052) and the implied BSM straddle value (46.059) represents a profit of 11.993, on a per share basis.

The per share profit from the GS strategy is not random. Given that the GS value approximates the BSM value for a given level of volatility, we should be able to estimate the profit generated if the volatility is 5% higher. Ignoring any biases in the discrete path selected, the expected profit should approximately equal the Vega of the straddle (at 20%) multiplied by the difference between the expected realized volatility (25%) and the implied volatility (20%).

In this case, the Vega of the ATM straddle with 21 trade days until expiration equaled 2.295. If we multiply the initial Vega of the ATM straddle (2.295) by the 5% expected excess realized volatility (times 100), we calculate an *approximate expected* profit of 11.475 points, which equates to an expected profit of almost 25% in one month.

Why is the expected profit 11.475 not exactly equal to the actual excess profit of 11.993? Because we are only using a linear approximation of the effect of Vega, and the GS from the actual single discrete path (with only 21 intervals) will not exactly replicate the BSM value of the straddle.

The key observation is that we can use this GS approach to exploit volatility pricing anomalies directly when realized volatility is expected to exceed implied volatility – without implicit directional exposure and regardless of the terminal price of the underlying security in any specific realized path. This is why I designed the AI Volatility Edge platform specifically to forecast realized volatility across the entire term structure of volatilities (see Resources Chapter for additional information).

Figure 10.3B: 21-TD Straddle Gamma Scalping (GS) Value @ 25% Realized Volatility (BSM20% = 46.059, BSM25% = 57.535)								
Trade Day	Present Value Factor	Stock Price	Straddle Delta	Required # Stock Shares	# Shares: Buy(+) or Sell(-)	GS Cash Flow	PV of GS Cash Flow	Sum: PV of GS Cash Flows
0	1.0000000	1,000.0000	0.0656	-0.0656	-0.0656	65.5699	65.5699	
1	0.9998413	1,015.8732	0.2388	-0.2388	-0.1732	175.9729	175.9450	
2	0.9996826	1,031.9983	0.4088	-0.4088	-0.1700	175.4398	175.3841	
3	0.9995239	1,048.3794	0.5665	-0.5665	-0.1577	165.3733	165.2945	
4	0.9993653	1,065.0205	0.7036	-0.7036	-0.1371	145.9678	145.8751	
5	0.9992067	1,081.9258	0.8138	-0.8138	-0.1102	119.2047	119.1102	
6	0.9990481	1,099.0994	0.8945	-0.8945	-0.0807	88.7239	88.6394	
7	0.9988895	1,081.9258	0.8395	-0.8395	0.0550	-59.4704	-59.4044	
8	0.9987310	1,065.0205	0.7597	-0.7597	0.0799	-85.0619	-84.9540	
9	0.9985724	1,048.3794	0.6467	-0.6467	0.1130	-118.4172	-118.2481	
10	0.9984140	1,065.0205	0.7943	-0.7943	-0.1476	157.2341	156.9847	
11	0.9982555	1,048.3794	0.6853	-0.6853	0.1090	-114.2912	-114.0918	
12	0.9980971	1,065.0205	0.8346	-0.8346	-0.1493	159.0014	158.6988	
13	0.9979386	1,081.9258	0.9310	-0.9310	-0.0964	104.3000	104.0850	
14	0.9977802	1,099.0994	0.9794	-0.9794	-0.0484	53.1782	53.0601	
15	0.9976219	1,116.5456	0.9963	-0.9963	-0.0169	18.8540	18.8091	
16	0.9974635	1,099.0994	0.9935	-0.9935	0.0027	-3.0221	-3.0144	
17	0.9973052	1,081.9258	0.9888	-0.9888	0.0048	-5.1443	-5.1305	
18	0.9971469	1,065.0205	0.9807	-0.9807	0.0080	-8.5653	-8.5409	
19	0.9969887	1,048.3794	0.9682	-0.9682	0.0126	-13.1658	-13.1262	
20	0.9968304	1,065.0205	0.9999	-0.9999	-0.0318	33.8225	33.7153	
21	0.9966722	1,081.9258	0.0000	0.0000	0.9999	-999.9364	-996.6089	58.052

Gamma Scalping Validation: 5000 Lattice Paths, 5000 Binomial Intervals

Figure 10.4 below summarizes the Gamma Scalping validation results for a hypothetical call option with 252 trade days until expiration, in the base case scenario (20% implied and realized volatility and 4% risk-free rate). Note, I intentionally limited the GS validation analysis to the base case scenario. I have devoted several chapters, plus the 70+ page Supplement to validating the JAF and the JVAF.

The Gamma Scalping trade management strategy described in this chapter can be integrated with the JAF and JVAF and applied to any term structure of volatilities and any term structure of interest rates. However, given the significance of the GS strategy and the importance of realized volatility, I did not want to shift the focus of this chapter to the JAF. As a result, I did not include the GS validation results for the Normal and Inverted cases. For readers who are interested in this exercise, use the binomial framework described earlier to calculate the unique UP and DOWN state values and probabilities *for each forward interval* and use a random probability generator to determine the path of underlying stock prices. The validation process is the same.

Unlike the simple single path, 21-interval example above, the validation analysis summarized in Figure 10.4 is much more comprehensive, averaging the GS results over 5000 random paths through a binomial lattice with 5000 intervals. The objective is to demonstrate that the realized option value extracted by the Gamma Scalping trade management strategy is equal to the BSM option value on average – for a large number of paths and intervals. This is not intended as a practical rebalancing plan (5000 in 252 trading days). It is a validation analysis to verify the GS valuation results approach the BSM valuation results at the limit. I will present a practical GS strategy later in this chapter.

Figure 10.4 compares the GS and BSM values and implied volatilities over 5000 random paths, through a binomial lattice with 5000 intervals, for one-year, in-the-money (ITM), at-the-money (ATM), and out-of-the-money (OTM) call options. As you will recall, the JAF validation analysis regularly used 8,192 N & N+1 intervals.

Even with only 5000 paths and intervals, the GS values for all three call options were accurate to within 0.004, and the implied volatilities were accurate to the nearest 0.001%. Both of these differences could be made arbitrarily small by continuing to increase the number of paths and intervals – approaching a comprehensive selection, drawn from a continuous distribution.

Figure 10.4: Call Option Gamma Scalping, BSM Assumptions, 5000 Intervals							
GS Paths	Initial Stock Price	Strike Price	Average GS Call Value	Average BSM Call Value	Average GS IV	Average BSM IV	Average GS IV Error
5000	1100	1000	169.687	169.687	20.000%	20.000%	0.000%
5000	1000	1000	99.245	99.251	19.999%	20.000%	-0.001%
5000	900	1000	47.627	47.624	20.001%	20.000%	0.001%

Figure 10.5 compares the GS and BSM values and implied volatilities over 5000 random paths, through a binomial lattice with 5000 intervals, for one year, ITM, ATM, and OTM put options. Even with only 5000 paths and intervals, the GS values for all three put options were accurate to within 0.004, and the implied volatilities were accurate to the nearest 0.001%.

Figure 10.5: Put Option Gamma Scalping, BSM Assumptions, 5000 Intervals							
GS Paths	Initial Stock Price	Strike Price	Average GS Put Value	Average BSM Put Value	Average GS IV	Average BSM IV	Average GS IV Error
5000	1100	1000	30.476	30.476	20.000%	20.000%	0.000%
5000	1000	1000	60.034	60.040	19.999%	20.000%	-0.001%
5000	900	1000	108.416	108.414	20.001%	20.000%	0.001%

Gamma Scalping Analysis: 5000 Lattice Paths, 252 Binomial Intervals

Now that we have verified that the option values extracted by the GS trade management strategy approach the BSM option value at the limit, let's begin to make the analysis more realistic by reducing the number of intervals to a more reasonable number. It would not be practical or advisable to rebalance the GS strategy 5000 times in a single year. However, it would certainly be possible to do the required GS Delta-hedging transactions at the end of every trade day.

Figure 10.6 compares the GS and BSM values and implied volatilities over 5000 random paths, through a binomial lattice with only 252 intervals, for one-year, ITM, ATM, and OTM call options. It is still desirable to use a large number of paths, because we need a representative sample to evaluate the accuracy of the GS trade management strategy over a practical number of intervals.

Even with 5000 paths and only 252 intervals, the GS values for all three call options were accurate to within 0.071, and the implied volatilities were accurate to the nearest 0.019%. To put these differences in context, we would only attempt to exploit volatility anomalies between expected realized volatility and implied volatility if they were significant, perhaps 5% as in the earlier hypothetical example. Of course, this threshold will vary across the term structure of volatilities, as will the accuracy of any forecasting model. Using a standardized z-score is an excellent way to evaluate prospective anomalies.

GS Paths	Initial Stock Price	Strike Price	Average GS Call Value	Average BSM Call Value	Average GS IV	Average BSM IV	Average GS IV Error
			Figure 10.6: Call Option Gamma Scalping, BSM Assumptions, 252 Intervals				
5000	1100	1000	169.710	169.687	20.007%	20.000%	0.007%
5000	1000	1000	99.180	99.251	19.981%	20.000%	-0.019%
5000	900	1000	47.627	47.624	20.001%	20.000%	0.001%

Figure 10.7 compares the GS and BSM values and implied volatilities over 5000 random paths, through a binomial lattice with only 252 intervals, for one-year, ITM, ATM, and OTM put options. Even with 5000 paths and only 252 intervals, the GS values for all three put options were accurate to within 0.071, and the implied volatilities were accurate to the nearest 0.019%. As we would expect, the differences between the average GS realized values and

the BSM derived values were comparable for calls and puts – due to put-call parity and identical Gammas at the end of every rebalancing interval.

			Average	Average			
	Initial	Strike	GS Put	BSM Put	Average	Average	Average
GS Paths	Stock Price	Price	Value	Value	GS IV	BSM IV	GS IV Error
5000	1100	1000	30.499	30.476	20.007%	20.000%	0.007%
5000	1000	1000	59.969	60.040	19.981%	20.000%	-0.019%
5000	900	1000	108.417	108.414	20.001%	20.000%	0.001%

Figure 10.7: Put Option Gamma Scalping, BSM Assumptions, 252 Intervals

Gamma Scalping Validation: Actual SPX Daily Returns 1/2000 – 1/2020

To be practical, the Gamma Scalping trade management strategy must be applicable to real-world data. As a result, I used actual SPX data from 1/2000 to 1/2020 to compare the value extracted by the GS strategy to BSM option values. For each day of the 20-year historical period, I created a hypothetical ATM option with 252 trade days remaining until expiration. I calculated the realized volatility from the actual SPX daily returns for the subsequent 252 trade days. I then calculated the value extracted by the GS trade management strategy over the life of each option (252 trade days) and compared the result to the BSM option value using the same realized volatility.

To help standardize the analysis, I assumed the beginning index value was 1000 and the strike price was 1000. Actual risk-free interest rates were derived from U.S. T-bills at the beginning of each trading day. The resulting analysis included over 4800 overlapping GS analysis periods, each spanning 252 trade days. Given that the realized volatility is different for every 252 trade-day period, the average GS value and BSM price is not meaningful. As a result, I elected to focus exclusively on implied volatilities derived from the extracted GS values and the BSM option values.

Figure 10.8 shows the average GS implied volatility and average BSM implied volatility over all 4800 overlapping GS analysis periods. The average GS implied volatility (derived from the extracted GS value) was 16.837%, which was 0.269% lower than the average BSM implied volatility of 17.106%. The good news is that the average difference of negative 0.269% is much smaller than any reasonable threshold for exploiting prospective volatility pricing anomalies.

Figure 10.8: GS, SPX ROR 1/2000 - 1/2020, 252 Intervals				
Initial Stock Price	Strike Price	Average GS IV	Average BSM IV	Average GS IV Error
1000	1000	16.837%	17.106%	-0.269%

However, the lower average GS implied volatility (- 0.269%) indicates that the GS strategy systematically extracted slightly less value than the BSM option value, at the same level of realized volatility. Before attempting to implement a GS strategy in practice, this warrants further investigation.

To understand why the extracted GS value in each period deviated from the BSM option value in the same period, I created a hypothesis about the potential sources of these deviations and used a regression analysis in MS Excel to test my hypothesis. The dependent variable was the difference between the GS implied volatility and the BSM implied volatility. In other words, the regression would attempt to explain why the GS extracted value deviated from the BSM value and deliver an explanatory model that would quantify the causes of these differences. The purpose is to develop insights that will help us design a practical, tradable GS strategy.

I came up with two primary, potential sources for the deviation. First, the rebalancing periods were discrete (daily), rather than continuous. Second, for a given level of realized volatility, there are an infinite number of return paths. The specific pattern of return paths would be important. Specifically, if the largest daily returns occurred when Gamma was the highest (near the money and/or late in the 252 trade-day period), this would *increase* the value extracted by the GS strategy. Conversely, if the largest daily returns occurred when Gamma was the lowest (away from the strike price and/or early in the 252 trade-day period), this would *decrease* the value extracted by the GS strategy.

Based on this reasoning, for each 252-day period, I calculated the correlation between the Gamma at the end of each daily interval and the squared daily return. In the regression, the explanatory or independent variable was the difference between this correlation and the average correlation over all 4800 paths. The value of the regression coefficient for this variable (titled Corr: Gamma vs ROR2) should be positive and significant.

The impact of using discrete rebalancing periods is less obvious. Fortunately, I have traded the GS strategy extensively, using many different instruments. We will explore the practical aspects of this strategy later, but I frequently had the opportunity to rebalance multiple times on days when realized volatility was higher than usual. Toward that end, I had already calculated the realized volatility for each 252-trade-day period, so I created a new explanatory variable for each of the 4800 periods that equaled the deviation from the average realized volatility. For example, if the realized volatility in a specific period was 20.000% and the average over all periods was 17.106%, the volatility deviation (explanatory variable) for that specific period would be 2.894% (20.000% - 17.106%). The value of the regression coefficient for this variable (titled RV Deviation from Average) should be negative and significant.

Figure 10.9 is a table of the regression results for the 4800 return paths from 1/2000 to 1/2020. The regression includes an intercept term, plus the two explanatory variables described above. The R Square of the regression was 66.843%, which indicates that the two independent variables explained 66.843% of the variation in the GS results.

The intercept term equaled -0.269%, which is the same average deviation reported in Figure 10.8 above. The intercept was highly significant with a t-statistic of -14.97. The coefficient for the Gamma/ROR2 correlation variable was positive 10.669%, and was even more significant, with a t-statistic of 81.67. Finally, the coefficient for the realized volatility variable was negative 9.777%, and was also highly significant, with a t-statistic of -43.12.

All of the hypotheses above were confirmed. Higher realized volatility did lower the value extracted by the GS strategy, presumably due to more missed intra-day rebalancing opportunities. Similarly, the analysis assumes EOD daily rebalancing and does not include *any* intra-day rebalancing. It is likely that this also explains the fact that the average value realized by the GS strategy is slightly lower (-0.269%) than the BSM value.

The regression analysis also confirmed that higher correlations between Gamma and squared daily returns increased the value extracted by the GS strategy. We will be able to use all of these insights when designing an actual GS strategy.

Figure 10.9: 1/2000 - 1/2020 SPX Gamma Scalping (GS) Error Analysis								
Regression Statistics								
Multiple R	0.817576473							
R Square	66.843%							
Adjusted R Square	0.668293107							
Standard Error	1.246%							
Observations	4802							
ANOVA								
	df	SS	MS	F	Significance F			
Regression	2	1.502861284	0.751430642	4837.310716	0			
Residual	4799	0.745479433	0.000155341					
Total	4801	2.248340717						
	Coefficients	Standard Error	t Stat	P-value	Lower 95%	Upper 95%	Lower 95.0%	Upper 95.0%
Intercept	-0.269%	0.000179859	-14.97	1.48934E-49	-0.003045114	-0.002339903	-0.003045114	-0.002339903
Corr: Gamma vs ROR2	10.669%	0.00130645	81.67	0	0.104131493	0.109253974	0.104131493	0.109253974
RV Dev from Avg	-9.777%	0.0022675	-43.12	0	-0.102219558	-0.093328879	-0.102219558	-0.093328879

Gamma Scalping in Practice

The Gamma Scalping trade management strategy is designed to generate profits when realized volatility over the holding period exceeds implied volatility, and when implied volatility increases (if the long staddle is exited before expiration). The strategy should only be employed when there is a material and exploitable positive spread between the expected level of realized volatility and implied volatility. While I have applied the GS strategy to call options, put options, and straddles for validation purposes, ATM straddles would be used in practice. We are interested in a Delta-neutral strategy and ATM straddles are close to Delta-neutral at inception. In addition, we are attempting to exploit volatility pricing anomalies using Gamma scalping, so we would like Gamma to be as large as possible – hence the ATM straddle.

If held to expiration, I have demonstrated that the GS profits would be approximately equal to the Vega of the option or option strategy, multiplied by the percentage difference between the volatility realized over the life of the option and the implied volatility of the option. Since we have expressed Vega as a sensitivity to a 1% change in volatility, the resulting value must also be multiplied by 100. As we confirmed with the regression analysis, there are a few other causal factors that will also affect the profit extracted by the GS trade management strategy.

So, the expected profits are approximately equal to the product of Vega and the spread between expected realized volatility and implied volatility (multiplied by 100). But that is only the case if the GS trade strategy is maintained until option expiration. What happens if we exit the strategy earlier in the holding period (before expiration)? This is a particularly important question, because if the volatility pricing anomaly corrects (removing our edge), we should exit the strategy, reduce our exposure, and free up our capital.

If we exited the GS strategy before expiration, we would still be able to extract the GS value over the shorter holding period, and we would use the exact same methodology for determining the required rebalancing transactions. When we exited the GS strategy, we would liquidate the holdings in the underlying security used to Delta-hedge the straddle. However, instead of waiting for the payoff from the long straddle position at expiration, we would also need to sell the long straddle position when we exited the GS strategy. If the realized volatility over the holding period exceeded the initial implied volatility (as planned), the value extracted during the holding period from the GS rebalancing transactions would more than offset the long straddle's loss from Theta. This would be the first component of the GS profit.

When exiting the GS strategy before expiration, there would also be a second profit component: the change in the value of implied volatility on the straddle. Remember the rationale for the trade was the expectation for realized volatility to exceed implied volatility *AND* for implied volatility to increase if exited before expiration. Fortunately, these criteria are aligned. If the realized volatility exceeds the market's expected level of volatility (which is the implied volatility), it is likely that the implied volatility will increase as market participants adjust their volatility expectations. If the implied volatility converged to the realized volatility over the shorter holding period, the total profit of the GS strategy would again be approximately equal to the product of Vega (*at inception*) and the spread between expected realized volatility and implied volatility (multiplied by 100).

If the implied volatility changed, but did not converge to the realized volatility, the second component of the GS profit could be approximated by the product of the change in implied volatility multiplied, and the Vega of the strategy *on the exit date* (multiplied by 100). As a result, the product of the initial Vega and the spread between the estimated realized volatility and the implied volatility can be used to generate an estimated profit for the GS straddle strategy.

Designing and Trading a GS Strategy

Now that we have explored the possibility of exiting the GS straddle before expiration, let's consider other practical aspects of the strategy. First, the GS strategy can be applied to many different underlying instruments, but futures (with futures options) have many advantages. I trade the GS straddle strategy on futures and futures options exclusively, but not just equity index futures. I use have traded this strategy on many different types of futures contracts: equities, bonds, currencies, metals, softs, etc.

The primary advantage of using futures and futures options in the GS strategy is margin efficiency. Since futures trade in discrete contracts, I trade a minimum size of 10 contacts for the initial ATM straddle (preferably with multiples of 10 contracts for larger size). With a 10-contract ATM straddle (10 long ATM calls, plus 10 long ATM puts), we would potentially be required to be long or short as many as 10 futures contracts during the GS holding period. Unlike stocks, the required GS hedging transactions in futures do not require borrowing funds or punitive margin requirements. The futures margin requirements are quite minimal, especially given that all short or long futures positions are "covered" by the long call and put futures options.

Unlike typical short-Gamma option income strategies (OIS), large discrete price changes in the underlying futures contract are highly beneficial to the GS strategy. There are only two factors that generate losses in the GS strategy. The first is the negative Theta of the straddle. Fortunately, the negative Theta is partially or fully offset by the interim GS rebalancing transactions. Even if the volatility realized during the holding period was less than expected (and less than implied), the GS strategy would not suffer the full effects of negative Theta.

The other factor that could generate losses in the GS strategy is a decline in implied volatility. Any decline on implied volatility would act on the BSM Vega of the straddle. While a decline in implied volatility is always a possibility, the Gamma Strategy should only be entered when the realized volatility is expected to exceed the implied volatility AND the implied volatility is expected to increase. As a result, if we have a demonstrated edge in identifying volatility anomalies, any temporary decline in Vega should be minimal.

It is typically easier and more reliable to identify near-term volatility pricing anomalies than longer-term anomalies. However, there are occasionally longer-term volatility anomalies that can be exploited. This tends to favor near-term GS strategies. In addition, the liquidity of near-term futures options is much better than longer-term options. This also favors near-term GS strategies. However, if implied volatility was significantly understated, we would like enough Vega to generate a significant profit. As a result, using futures options expiring in the next few months would be desirable, often coinciding with the most liquid near-term futures contract for that specific instrument.

Using our 10-contract ATM straddle example, we would only need to rebalance if the required number of futures contacts changed by an integer number of contracts. We would rebalance to the nearest number of contracts at the end of the normal trading session for each futures market.

Using our insights from the regression analysis, we would also rebalance during the normal and evening sessions if the Delta of the GS position increased or decreased by a specified number of contracts (for example: 1 or 2 contracts for a 10-contact straddle). While I used simple BSM Delta calculations for the GS validation analysis, it would certainly be beneficial to use True Delta metrics if they were available. I typically use OptionVue for my GS True Delta metrics, backed up by my own analysis.

With access to an options analytics platform, it is possible and advisable to model the expected GS adjustment levels in advance. This allows you to enter Good-Till-Cancelled (GTC) limit orders in advance to buy more contracts if the price of the futures contract declines and sell more futures contracts as the futures price rises. I also use text alerts at each of these levels to notify me immediately if the rebalancing trigger levels are hit during a trading session. After confirming the limit order was filled, a new limit order would need to be entered in the opposite direction. For example, if a new purchase was made at a lower price, a new GTC sell limit order would need to be entered at a higher price. Several GTC limit orders could be maintained in each direction.

Rebalancing intra-session in response to realized volatility is designed to extract the additional GS value not included in the EOD validation calculations. On volatile days, it is not unusual to have several intra-session rebalancing transactions, sometimes in opposite directions. These situations are highly profitable for the GS straddle strategy. This trade plan modification addresses the negative intercept and negative relative volatility coefficient from the regression analysis.

So, what about the last regression coefficient: the correlation between relative Gamma and the squared daily returns of the underlying instrument? You will recall that the coefficient was positive and highly significant, indicating that the GS strategy extracted more value from the option when larger price moves occurred when Gamma was relatively high (near the money) and smaller price moves occurred when Gamma was relatively low. On the surface, it does not seem that we would have much control over the timing of price moves. While that is true, there is another adjustment we can make to the GS trade management strategy to address this issue.

Adjusting the GS Strategy in Practice

The Gamma Scalping strategy was designed to use the underlying futures contract (instead of futures options) to rebalance the position. The reason is that futures are much more liquid and have significantly lower transaction costs than futures options. However, to prevent the situation where the larger price moves occur when Gamma is relatively low, we could close the initial straddle and re-open a new ATM straddle if the Gamma of the original straddle declined significantly. This would occur if the price of the underlying security departed significantly from the initial strike price, which would also cause the Delta of the call option to move materially away from 0.5, and the Delta of the put option to move materially away from negative 0.5. In this scenario, the Gammas of the call and put option would both decline significantly, reducing the future payoffs from the GS straddle strategy. Gamma is symmetric, so this problem would exist for material increases or decreases in the price of the underlying security.

However, we still need to consider transaction costs. We would need to weigh the additional transaction costs against the potential for extracting more value from the straddle. Figure 10.10 is a scatter plot of the percentage of maximum straddle Gamma versus the Delta of a 21-TD call option in the base case scenario. As you can see from the graph, as the Delta of the call option moves away from 0.5, the Gamma of the straddle declines at a decreasing rate.

Given the benefit of maintaining a sufficient Gamma level in the position, it would be logical to set a minimum threshold for the Gamma of the call option. I included three possible thresholds in the Figure 10.10 graph. For a Delta of 0.25 or 0.75, the hypothetical 21-TD straddle would retain 82.7% of its maximum Gamma. For a Delta of 0.20 or 0.80, the hypothetical 21-TD straddle would retain 73.7% of its maximum Gamma. For a Delta of 0.15 or 0.85, the hypothetical 21-TD straddle would only retain 61.7% of its maximum Gamma. Smaller threshold Delta deviations (from 0.5) would generate higher transaction costs, and higher potential value extracted from the straddle. Larger threshold Delta deviations (from 0.5) would lower transaction costs, and lower potential value extracted from the straddle.

Before deciding to close and re-open any GS straddle, it would be particularly important to verify the rationale for the long GS straddle still exists: the expected level of realized volatility over the remaining holding period should materially exceed implied volatility of the prospective ATM straddle, and the implied volatility should still be expected to increase. In addition, there should still be sufficient time remaining until expiration to warrant paying the incremental transaction costs associated with closing and reopening the straddle. Remember, the expected GS straddle profit is a direct function of the Vega of the straddle, and the spread between the expected realized volatility and implied volatility. If there was limited time remaining until option expiration, the relatively small Vega would limit potential profits. In this scenario, it would make sense to close the current straddle and reopen a new ATM straddle using longer-term options (provided the volatility edge still existed).

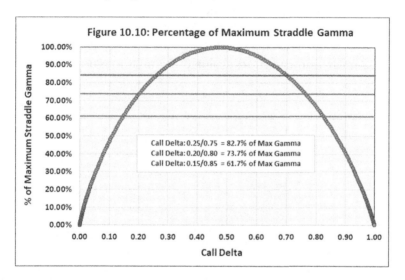

Figure 10.10: Percentage of Maximum Straddle Gamma

Call Delta: 0.25/0.75 = 82.7% of Max Gamma
Call Delta: 0.20/0.80 = 73.7% of Max Gamma
Call Delta: 0.15/0.85 = 61.7% of Max Gamma

There is one final benefit to using futures and futures options in the GS straddle strategy. While volatility tends to be positively correlated across many different markets, futures prices are not highly correlated in general. As a result, it is possible to employ several GS straddles in different futures markets simultaneously, without taking an inordinate amount of risk.

Summary

Gamma Scalping is a very unique strategy that can extract the value of an option or option strategy from the volatility of the underlying security realized over the life of the option. It is designed to exploit volatility pricing anomalies when realized volatility is expected to exceed implied volatility, and implied volatility is expected to increase – without implicit directional exposure and regardless of the terminal price of the underlying security in any specific realized path. This is a far superior and more consistent approach than conventional methods of managing straddles.

We reviewed GS examples in detail, including an analysis of all required EOD rebalancing transactions. I provided several GS validation analyses, which demonstrated that the extracted GS value converges to the BSM value as the number of paths and intervals increases (under standard BSM assumptions).

We examined the results of applying the GS strategy to 20 years of SPX daily return data and we applied the insights from the regression analysis to design a practical GS strategy that could be applied to many different markets. Finally, we reviewed how the GS strategy can be applied in practice, particularly using futures options and the underlying futures contracts, with intra-day and EOD rebalancing, plus adjustments. In the next chapter, we will use a similar framework to evaluate the infamous Portfolio Insurance strategy.

11) PORTFOLIO INSURANCE & OPTION VALUATION

Portfolio Insurance (PI) is a notorious example of a deeply flawed *dynamic option replication* strategy. When coupled with an equity portfolio, it can also be considered a form of dynamic hedging. It is widely considered to be a key contributor to the 1987 crash, when the S&P 500 index lost 20.47% in a single day. The annualized volatility for that one-day loss: 364%!

Portfolio Insurance requires the sale of an increasing number of futures contracts as equity prices decline. By its very nature, it is destabilizing. In fact, it requires the exact *opposite* rebalancing transactions as the Gamma Scalping trade management strategy outlined in the last chapter. As a result, we can use the cash flows from the resulting PI transactions to calculate the realized cost of the replicated option. I still find it remarkable that we can use trade management strategies, such as Gamma Scalping and Portfolio Insurance, to calculate the value of an option or option strategy -provided we use a sufficient number of intervals and return paths.

Gamma Scalping is very powerful and is arguably the optimal way to extract the realized value of an option or option strategy. If Portfolio Insurance is deeply flawed, why should we evaluate the strategy further? Because it is closely related to all negative Gamma Option Income Strategies (OIS). The insights we glean from examining PI can help us manage our OIS trades.

Portfolio Insurance – Trade Management

Unlike Gamma Scalping, there is no corresponding option purchase with Portfolio Insurance. Instead, the objective of Portfolio Insurance is to replicate the profit of an option or option strategy by dynamically buying and selling the underlying security. In an insurance context, PI typically attempts to replicate the profit of a long put option, with the goal of hedging a long equity portfolio. As a result, I will primarily use put option examples, but I will include one example of a PI call option strategy (which could be used to hedge a short equity position). This chapter will use the same layout as the GS chapter, but the insights and conclusions will be very different.

Portfolio Insurance Example: Options Expiring in 21 Trade Days

I will begin with a more academic example and analysis, using paths derived from a binomial lattice, coupled with standard BOM / BSM assumptions (regarding borrowing and lending, transaction costs, no margin requirement, etc.). How do we implement the Portfolio Management trade management strategy to replicate the profit of an option or option strategy? The following methodology applies to individual call and put options, as well as option strategies, but our focus will be primarily on put options.

Portfolio Insurance Methodology
At Every Rebalancing Period (Including Inception)
   1) Calculate option or option strategy Delta at prevailing stock price
   2) Buy or sell required number of shares of underlying security to match the Delta of the option
   3) Borrow or lend cash as needed to buy or sell required number of shares

Portfolio Insurance (PI) Validation Methodology:
1) Calculate PI cash outflows or inflows resulting from share purchases or sales at each rebalancing period (-1 x number of shares x share price)
2) Calculate present value discount factor for each rebalancing date (using risk-free rate)
3) Calculate the realized PI value: sum of the present values of all discounted PI cash flows above The resulting PI value in this step is comparable to the present value (PV) of the profit from the option or option strategy being replicated
4) Calculate the implied cost of the PI strategy, by subtracting the PV of the option payoff from the PI value in step 3
5) Compare the implied PI cost to the initial cost of the option or option strategy

Figure 11.1 below is an example of applying the PI trade management system to an ATM put option, expiring in 21 trade days (TD). Figure 11.2 applies the same PI trade management system to a 21-TD ATM call option. These cases are identical to the simplistic examples used to introduce the GS strategy. After demonstrating the PI trade management system in the introductory examples, I will use the standard BSM assumptions to demonstrate that the PV of the cash flows from the PI strategy exactly equal the present value of the profit of the option, derived using the BSM option value. I will then evaluate the PI trading strategy using the same 20 years of actual SPX return data that we used to evaluate the GS strategy in the last chapter.

Figures 11.1 and 11.2 assume the initial stock price equals 1000, the strike prices both equal 1000, the annualized implied volatility equals 20%, and the continuously compounded risk-free interest rate equals 4% (the Flat Base Case Scenario). Furthermore, we will assume daily, end-of-day rebalancing, including at trade inception. This equates to 21 intervals. As you will recall from the JAF validation Chapters and the Supplement, we routinely used 8,192 N & N+1 intervals. Finally, in these examples, we will only be evaluating the results for a *single path* through the binomial lattice, or a single set of 22 prices for the underlying security – one for each node.

The purpose of the following introductory examples is to demonstrate how the PI trade management strategy is implemented, not to validate the results (which will be presented in the next section). It is much easier to understand the framework when using a single path of prices, over only 21 intervals.

Each row of the table in Figure 11.1 represents the end of a trade day; zero represents the inception date. The stock price at each node is derived from the binomial lattice, using a random number probability generator, in conjunction with the risk-neutral binomial probabilities of the UP and DOWN states. Note: the random paths in these examples are identical to those used to introduce the GS strategy in the last chapter. The resulting stock price from the binomial lattice is used with the standard BSM Delta formula to calculate the Delta of the option.

At time zero, the Delta of the put option equals negative 0.4655 on a per share basis. This requires a transaction of negative 0.4655 shares of stock, or a sale of 0.4655 shares of stock. The resulting PI cash flow is positive 465.4937 at time zero (sale of 0.4655 shares x stock price of 1000). Since the cash flow occurred at time zero, the present value factor was 1.0, resulting in a present value (PV) of +465.4937 for the first cash flow.

At the end of the first trade day, the stock price increased to 1,012.6785 (randomly selected from the binomial lattice). The resulting Delta of the long put option we are attempting to replicate would have increased to negative 0.3790 (become less negative), requiring the purchase of an additional 0.0865 shares of stock to replicate the Delta or market exposure of the long put option. The resulting cash flow from the first rebalancing transaction was negative 87.5957 (-1 x 0.0865 x 1,012.6785). Finally, the present value of the same cash flow was negative 87.5818 (- 87.5957 x 0.9998413). Note: the initial and interim PI rebalancing transactions and the resulting cash flows are exactly the opposite (the negative) of the GS transactions and cash flows.

Unlike the GS strategy, the PI strategy does not own the corresponding option, so there is only a single component of the final PI cash flow: the liquidation of all outstanding PI shares at the prevailing stock price (Buy: -1 x 0.00 x 1,065.0205. The present value of the final cash flow at the end of TD 21 equals negative 0.0310 (- 0.0311 x 0.9966722). Note: the intermediate calculations are all rounded to four decimal places, but the final values use the full precision of the intermediate values.

The sum of the present values of all PI cash flows from replicating the put option equals negative 21.558, which is remarkably close to the present value of the BSM profit of the 21-TD put option (- 21.366). In this case, the replicated BSM put option would have expired worthless, so the PV of the BSM "profit" would equal the negative of the initial option BSM put option value (-21.366).

The difference between the PI profit and the BSM profit was *negative* 0.192 over the single return path. The difference between the GS and BSM values for the same 21-TD put option over the same return path was *positive* 0.192, exactly equal to negative one multiplied by the difference from the PI strategy. This is because the PI and GS strategies require *opposite* transactions, so all PI and GS deviations from the BSM values should be exactly offsetting.

Conceptually, the PI trade management system is simple: replicate the Delta of the option or option strategy at the end of each rebalancing period. The validation methodology is equally simple: calculate the sum of the present values of all PI cash flows over the life of the option and compare that to the present value of the BSM profit of the associated option or option strategy.

					# Shares:			Sum: PV of PI	PI Implied
Trade Day	Present Value Factor	Stock Price	Put Delta	Required # Stock Shares	Buy(+) or Sell(-)	PI Cash Flow	PV of PI Cash Flow	Cash Flows (Profit)	Cost of Option
0	1.0000000	1,000.0000	-0.4655	-0.4655	-0.4655	465.4937	465.4937		
1	0.9998413	1,012.6785	-0.3790	-0.3790	0.0865	-87.5957	-87.5818		
2	0.9996826	1,025.5178	-0.2942	-0.2942	0.0848	-86.9764	-86.9488		
3	0.9995239	1,038.5198	-0.2156	-0.2156	0.0786	-81.6536	-81.6148		
4	0.9993653	1,051.6867	-0.1473	-0.1473	0.0683	-71.7802	-71.7346		
5	0.9992067	1,065.0205	-0.0925	-0.0925	0.0548	-58.3820	-58.3357		
6	0.9990481	1,078.5234	-0.0524	-0.0524	0.0401	-43.2778	-43.2366		
7	0.9988895	1,065.0205	-0.0797	-0.0797	-0.0274	29.1292	29.0968		
8	0.9987310	1,051.6867	-0.1195	-0.1195	-0.0398	41.8351	41.7820		
9	0.9985724	1,038.5198	-0.1758	-0.1758	-0.0563	58.4787	58.3952		
10	0.9984140	1,051.6867	-0.1023	-0.1023	0.0735	-77.3306	-77.2079		
11	0.9982555	1,038.5198	-0.1566	-0.1566	-0.0544	56.4443	56.3458		
12	0.9980971	1,051.6867	-0.0823	-0.0823	0.0744	-78.2038	-78.0549		
13	0.9979386	1,065.0205	-0.0343	-0.0343	0.0480	-51.0927	-50.9874		
14	0.9977802	1,078.5234	-0.0102	-0.0102	0.0241	-25.9453	-25.8877		
15	0.9976219	1,092.1975	-0.0018	-0.0018	0.0084	-9.1619	-9.1401		
16	0.9974635	1,078.5234	-0.0032	-0.0032	-0.0014	1.4753	1.4715		
17	0.9973052	1,065.0205	-0.0056	-0.0056	-0.0024	2.5218	2.5150		
18	0.9971469	1,051.6867	-0.0096	-0.0096	-0.0040	4.2165	4.2045		
19	0.9969887	1,038.5198	-0.0159	-0.0159	-0.0063	6.5096	6.4900		
20	0.9968304	1,051.6867	0.0000	0.0000	0.0158	-16.6438	-16.5911		
21	0.9966722	1,065.0205	0.0000	0.0000	0.0000	-0.0311	-0.0310	-21.558	-21.558

Figure 11.1: 21-TD Put Option Portfolio Insurance (PI) - Flat Base Case (BSM Profit = -21.366, BSM Cost = -21.366, PV Payoff = 0.000)

Figure 11.2 below is an example of applying the PI trade management system to an ATM call option, expiring in 21 trade days (TD). The methodology is exactly the same as the PI strategy replicating the put option, so I will not review the calculations in the same level of detail. However, there are a few important observations. First, note that the initial Delta of the call option is obviously positive. This requires a *purchase* of 0.5345 shares of stock, which results in an initial *cash inflow*. This is the opposite of the put option example in Figure 11.1.

It is also interesting to note that the required transactions for all interim periods are exactly the same for the call option and the put option. This is because of put-call parity and the fact that the Gamma of a call option will equal the Gamma of a put option (with the same strike price and expiration date). As a result, the interim PI transactions will all be the same. We observed this same phenomenon in the Gamma Scalping examples.

As was the case for the PI put option strategy, there will only be a single element to the final PI cash flow: the liquidation of all outstanding PI shares at the prevailing stock price (Sell: -1 x -1.00 x 1,065.0205 = 1064.9894). The present value of the final PI call option cash flow equals 1061.4453 (1064.9894 x 0.9966722).

The sum of the present values of all PI cash flows for the call option equals 39.918, which is remarkably close to the present value of the BSM call option profit of 40.111. The present value of the BSM profit equals the initial BSM cost of the call option (-24.694), plus the present value of the BSM call option payoff at expiration (Max(1065.0205 – 1000, 0) x 0.9966722). The resulting PV of the BSM profit was positive 40.111 (-24.694 + 64.804), rounded to three decimal places.

The difference between PI and BSM values for the call option was negative 0.192, exactly the same as the difference between the PI and BSM values for the put option above. This is not an accident. It is the result of put-call parity and the equivalence of the Gamma of the call and put option. As we observed for the put option above, the difference between the PI and BSM values are exactly the opposite (the negative) of the difference between the GS and BSM values for the call option.

Figure 11.2: 21-TD Call Option Portfolio Insurance (PI) - Flat Base Case (BSM Profit = 40.111, BSM Cost = -24.694, PV Payoff = 64.804)									
Trade Day	Present Value Factor	Stock Price	Call Delta	Required # Stock Shares	# Shares: Buy(+) or Sell(-)	PI Cash Flow	PV of PI Cash Flow	Sum: PV of PI Cash Flows (Profit)	PI Implied Cost of Option
0	1.0000000	1,000.0000	0.5345	0.5345	0.5345	-534.5063	-534.5063		
1	0.9998413	1,012.6785	0.6210	0.6210	0.0865	-87.5957	-87.5818		
2	0.9996826	1,025.5178	0.7058	0.7058	0.0848	-86.9764	-86.9488		
3	0.9995239	1,038.5198	0.7844	0.7844	0.0786	-81.6536	-81.6148		
4	0.9993653	1,051.6867	0.8527	0.8527	0.0683	-71.7802	-71.7346		
5	0.9992067	1,065.0205	0.9075	0.9075	0.0548	-58.3820	-58.3357		
6	0.9990481	1,078.5234	0.9476	0.9476	0.0401	-43.2778	-43.2366		
7	0.9988895	1,065.0205	0.9203	0.9203	-0.0274	29.1292	29.0968		
8	0.9987310	1,051.6867	0.8805	0.8805	-0.0398	41.8351	41.7820		
9	0.9985724	1,038.5198	0.8242	0.8242	-0.0563	58.4787	58.3952		
10	0.9984140	1,051.6867	0.8977	0.8977	0.0735	-77.3306	-77.2079		
11	0.9982555	1,038.5198	0.8434	0.8434	-0.0544	56.4443	56.3458		
12	0.9980971	1,051.6867	0.9177	0.9177	0.0744	-78.2038	-78.0549		
13	0.9979386	1,065.0205	0.9657	0.9657	0.0480	-51.0927	-50.9874		
14	0.9977802	1,078.5234	0.9898	0.9898	0.0241	-25.9453	-25.8877		
15	0.9976219	1,092.1975	0.9982	0.9982	0.0084	-9.1619	-9.1401		
16	0.9974635	1,078.5234	0.9968	0.9968	-0.0014	1.4753	1.4715		
17	0.9973052	1,065.0205	0.9944	0.9944	-0.0024	2.5218	2.5150		
18	0.9971469	1,051.6867	0.9904	0.9904	-0.0040	4.2165	4.2045		
19	0.9969887	1,038.5198	0.9841	0.9841	-0.0063	6.5096	6.4900		
20	0.9968304	1,051.6867	1.0000	1.0000	0.0158	-16.6438	-16.5910		
21	0.9966722	1,065.0205	0.0000	0.0000	-1.0000	1064.9894	1061.4453	39.918	-24.886

Portfolio Insurance Flaws: 21-TD Put Option

The Portfolio Insurance trade management strategy is designed to replicate the present value of the profit of an option or option strategy over its life. Given the insurance context, I will return to the 21-TD put option example. The objective of buying insurance or implementing a PI put option replication strategy is to protect against losses in extreme environments. Unfortunately, even if we required all BSM assumptions to be true in practice (which is not the case), the PI trading strategy would still have a fatal flaw: the PI trading strategy replicates the profit from the put option based on the *realized* volatility actually experienced over the life of the option – not based on the implied volatility at the implementation of the strategy.

This is the same distinction we made when evaluating the GS strategy. However, in the GS strategy, we used anomalies between the expected realized volatility and implied volatility to extract profits from the GS strategy. In other words, these anomalies presented value-added opportunities, not additional risk. In the case of Portfolio Insurance, it is not possible to know the cost of insurance in advance.

Instead, the cost of Portfolio Insurance is determined by the actual market environment experienced over the life of the option. This is a little like buying hurricane insurance and letting the insurance company retroactively set the insurance premium after the devastation of a Cat 5 hurricane! Not only is this a colorful analogy, it is particularly relevant to the 1987 crash with a negative 20.47% daily return and an annualized realized volatility of 364%.

In the actual 1987 crash, sell orders forced the NYSE to halt trading in many stocks, which made it impossible to calculate an accurate value of stock indices and the corresponding futures contracts. This resulted in index futures contracts trading at deep discounts to fair value, which doomed the PI strategies that were required to sell an ever-increasing number of contracts. The resulting PI futures transactions eventually accounted for as much as 30% of all sales volume. Conversely, Gamma Scalping would have been a stabilizing force and would have directly benefited from purchasing deeply undervalued futures contracts, while extracting the realized value from an extreme event with an annualized realized volatility of 364%.

Let's return to the GS example from the last chapter and evaluate the effects of experiencing *realized* volatility of 25% over the next 21 trade days, instead of the implied volatility of 20% of the inception of the PI put option replicating strategy.

Subject to discrete characteristics of the specific path over the limited number of only 21 intervals, the realized profit of the PI put replication strategy should be materially less on average, due to the *realized* cost of the put option at a 25% realized volatility, relative to the BSM cost of the put option at a 20% implied volatility.

Figure 11.3 provides all of the PI calculations for the ATM put expiring in 21 trade days, but all stock prices were derived from the binomial lattice generated with a 25% annualized volatility. All of the PI transactions, cash flows, and present values reflect the higher-than-expected level of realized volatility (25%), instead of the implied volatility (20%). In general, the number of shares traded and the cash flow amounts will be slightly larger, given the higher level of realized volatility scenario.

The resulting realized profit of the PI put replication strategy in the 25% realized volatility environment would have been negative 27.362, compared to negative 21.558 in a 20% realized volatility environment. In other words, the realized profit of the put option strategy would have declined by 5.804 and the implied cost of the put option would have increased by 5.804.

The change in the per share profit from the PI strategy is not random. Given that the PI value approximates the BSM profit for a given level of volatility, we should be able to estimate the profit generated if the volatility is 5% higher. Ignoring any biases in the discrete path selected, the expected profit should approximately equal the Vega of the put option (at 20%) multiplied by the difference between the expected realized volatility (25%) and the implied volatility (20%).

In this case, the Vega of the ATM put with 21 trade days until expiration equaled 1.1475. If we multiply the initial Vega of the ATM put option (1.1475) by the 5% expected excess realized volatility (times negative 100), we calculate an *approximate expected* change in profit of negative 5.737 points, which equates to an implied increase in the cost of the PI put replicating strategy of approximately 25%.

Why is the expected profit not exactly equal to the actual excess profit? Because we are only using a linear approximation of the effect of Vega, and the PI from the actual single discrete path (with only 21 intervals) will not exactly replicate the BSM profit value of the put option. The key observation is that we cannot use the PI trade strategy to reliably hedge long or short positions at a known cost. The opposing relationship between GS and PI strategies will also yield additional insights into managing OIS trades. Before we apply these insights, we will review the validation results for the Portfolio Insurance trade management strategy, using the same scenarios used to validate the GS strategy in the last chapter.

					# Shares:			Sum: PV of PI	PI Implied
	Present			Required #	Buy(+) or		PV of PI Cash	Cash Flows	Cost of
Trade Day	Value Factor	Stock Price	Put Delta	Stock Shares	Sell(-)	PI Cash Flow	Flow	(Profit)	Option
0	1.0000000	1,000.0000	-0.4672	-0.4672	-0.4672	467.2150	467.2150		
1	0.9998413	1,015.8732	-0.3806	-0.3806	0.0866	-87.9865	-87.9725		
2	0.9996826	1,031.9983	-0.2956	-0.2956	0.0850	-87.7199	-87.6920		
3	0.9995239	1,048.3794	-0.2167	-0.2167	0.0789	-82.6866	-82.6473		
4	0.9993653	1,065.0205	-0.1482	-0.1482	0.0685	-72.9839	-72.9376		
5	0.9992067	1,081.9258	-0.0931	-0.0931	0.0551	-59.6024	-59.5551		
6	0.9990481	1,099.0994	-0.0528	-0.0528	0.0404	-44.3619	-44.3197		
7	0.9988895	1,081.9258	-0.0802	-0.0802	-0.0275	29.7352	29.7022		
8	0.9987310	1,065.0205	-0.1202	-0.1202	-0.0399	42.5310	42.4770		
9	0.9985724	1,048.3794	-0.1766	-0.1766	-0.0565	59.2086	59.1241		
10	0.9984140	1,065.0205	-0.1028	-0.1028	0.0738	-78.6170	-78.4923		
11	0.9982555	1,048.3794	-0.1573	-0.1573	-0.0545	57.1456	57.0459		
12	0.9980971	1,065.0205	-0.0827	-0.0827	0.0746	-79.5007	-79.3494		
13	0.9979386	1,081.9258	-0.0345	-0.0345	0.0482	-52.1500	-52.0425		
14	0.9977802	1,099.0994	-0.0103	-0.0103	0.0242	-26.5891	-26.5301		
15	0.9976219	1,116.5456	-0.0019	-0.0019	0.0084	-9.4270	-9.4046		
16	0.9974635	1,099.0994	-0.0032	-0.0032	-0.0014	1.5110	1.5072		
17	0.9973052	1,081.9258	-0.0056	-0.0056	-0.0024	2.5722	2.5652		
18	0.9971469	1,065.0205	-0.0096	-0.0096	-0.0040	4.2827	4.2705		
19	0.9969887	1,048.3794	-0.0159	-0.0159	-0.0063	6.5829	6.5631		
20	0.9968304	1,065.0205	0.0000	0.0000	0.0159	-16.9113	-16.8577		
21	0.9966722	1,081.9258	0.0000	0.0000	0.0000	-0.0318	-0.0317	-27.362	-27.362

Figure 11.3: 21-TD Put Option Portfolio Insurance (PI) 25% RV (Base Case: BSM Profit = -21.366, BSM Cost = -21.366, PV Payoff = 0.000)

Portfolio Insurance Validation: 5000 Lattice Paths, 5000 Binomial Intervals

Figure 11.4 below summarizes the Portfolio Insurance validation results for a hypothetical put option with 252 trade days until expiration, in the base case scenario (20% implied and realized volatility and 4% risk-free rate). Note, I intentionally limited the PI validation analysis to the base case scenario. I have devoted several chapters, plus the 70+ page Supplement to validating the JAF and the JVAF. I did not want to shift the focus of this chapter to the JAF. As a result, I did not include the PI validation results for the Normal and Inverted cases.

For readers who are interested in this exercise, use the binomial framework described earlier to calculate the unique UP and DOWN state values and probabilities *for each forward interval* and use a random probability generator to determine the path of underlying stock prices. The validation process is the same.

Unlike the simple single path, 21-interval example above, the validation analysis summarized in Figure 11.4 is much more comprehensive, averaging the PI results over 5000 random paths through a binomial lattice with 5000 intervals. The objective is to demonstrate that the realized option value extracted by the Portfolio Insurance trade management strategy is equal to the present value of the BSM option profit on average – for a large number of paths and intervals. This is not intended as a practical rebalancing plan (5000 in 252 trading days). It is a validation analysis to verify the PI profits approach the BSM profits at the limit.

Figure 11.4 compares the implied PI and BSM put option costs, and implied volatilities over 5000 random paths, through a binomial lattice with 5000 intervals, for one-year, in-the-money (ITM), at-the-money (ATM), and out-of-the-money (OTM) put options. As you will recall, the JAF validation analysis regularly used 8,192 N & N+1 intervals.

Even with only 5000 paths and intervals, the implied PI values for all three put options were accurate to within 0.004, and the implied volatilities were accurate to the nearest 0.001%. Both of these differences could be made arbitrarily small by continuing to increase the number of paths and intervals – approaching a comprehensive selection, drawn from a continuous distribution. The average implied PI costs for the put options are exactly equal to negative one multiplied by the GS values for the same 5000 paths in the last chapter.

Figure 11.4: Put Option Portfolio Insurance, BSM Assumptions, 5000 Intervals							
GS Paths	Initial Stock Price	Strike Price	Average Implied PI Put Cost	Average BSM Put Cost	Average PI IV	Average BSM IV	Average PI IV Error
5000	1100	1000	-30.476	-30.476	20.000%	20.000%	0.000%
5000	1000	1000	-60.034	-60.040	19.999%	20.000%	-0.001%
5000	900	1000	-108.416	-108.414	20.001%	20.000%	0.001%

Portfolio Insurance Analysis: 5000 Lattice Paths, 252 Binomial Intervals

Now that we have verified that the option profits derived from the PI trade management strategy approach the BSM option profits at the limit, let's begin to make the analysis more realistic by reducing the number of intervals to a more reasonable number. It would not be practical or advisable to rebalance the PI strategy 5000 times in a single year. However, it would certainly be possible to do the required PI Delta-replicating transactions at the end of every trade day.

Figure 11.5 compares the implied PI and BSM costs and implied volatilities over 5000 random paths, through a binomial lattice with only 252 intervals, for one-year ITM, ATM, and OTM put options. It is still desirable to use a large number of paths, because we need a representative sample to evaluate the accuracy of the PI trade management strategy over a practical number of intervals.

Even with 5000 paths and only 252 intervals, the implied PI costs for all three put options were accurate to within 0.071, and the implied volatilities were accurate to the nearest 0.019%.

Figure 11.5: Put Option Portfolio Insurance, BSM Assumptions, 252 Intervals							
GS Paths	Initial Stock Price	Strike Price	Average Implied PI Put Cost	Average BSM Put Cost	Average PI IV	Average BSM IV	Average PI IV Error
5000	1100	1000	-30.499	-30.476	20.007%	20.000%	0.007%
5000	1000	1000	-59.969	-60.040	19.981%	20.000%	-0.019%
5000	900	1000	-108.417	-108.414	20.001%	20.000%	0.001%

Portfolio Insurance Validation: Actual SPX Daily Returns 1/2000 – 1/2020

To yield practical insights, the Gamma Scalping trade management strategy must be applicable to real-world data. As a result, I used actual SPX data from 1/2000 to 1/2020 to compare the implied volatilities derived from the implied costs of the PI and BSM. For each day of the 20-year historical period, I created a hypothetical ATM put option with 252 trade days remaining until expiration. I calculated the realized volatility from the actual SPX daily returns for the subsequent 252 trade days. I then calculated the implied costs of the put options from the PI trade management strategy over the life of each option (252 trade days) and compared the result to the BSM option cost using the same realized volatility.

To help standardize the analysis, I assumed the beginning index value was 1000 and the strike price was 1000. Actual risk-free interest rates were derived from U.S. T-bills at the beginning of each trading day. The resulting analysis included over 4800 overlapping PI analysis periods, each spanning 252 trade days. Given that the realized volatility is different for every 252 trade-day period, the average implied PI and BSM costs are not meaningful. As a result, I elected to focus exclusively on implied volatilities derived from the implied PI and BSM costs.

Figure 11.6 shows the average PI implied volatility and average BSM implied volatility over all 4800 overlapping PI analysis periods. The average PI implied volatility (derived from the implied PI values) was 16.837%, which was 0.269% lower than the average BSM implied volatility of 17.106%. The average difference of negative 0.269% is exactly the same as the average difference between the GS and BSM IVs in the last chapter – as we would expect.

Figure 11.6: PI, SPX ROR 1/2000 - 1/2020, 252 Intervals				
Initial Stock Price	Strike Price	Average PI IV	Average BSM IV	Average PI IV Error
1000	1000	16.837%	17.106%	-0.269%

The PI and GS strategies must generate identical implied volatilities when using the same data. As a result, the PI regression analysis in Figure 11.7 is identical to the GS regression analysis in Figure 10.9. The R Square of the regression was 66.843%, which indicates that the two independent variables explained 66.843% of the variation in the PI results.

The intercept term equaled -0.269%, which is the same average deviation reported in Figure 11.6 above. The intercept was highly significant with a t-statistic of -14.97. The coefficient for the Gamma/ROR2 correlation variable was positive 10.669%, and was even more significant, with a t-statistic of 81.67. Finally, the coefficient for the realized volatility variable was negative 9.777%, and was also highly significant, with a t-statistic of -43.12. Again, all of these statistics are identical to the GS regression.

Figure 11.7: 1/2000 - 1/2020 SPX Delta Hedging (DH) Error Analysis							
Regression Statistics							
Multiple R	0.81757647						
R Square	66.843%						
Adjusted R Square	0.66829311						
Standard Error	1.246%						
Observations	4802						
ANOVA							
	df	SS	MS	F	Significance F		
Regression	2	1.502861284	0.75143064	4837.31072	0		
Residual	4799	0.745479433	0.00015534				
Total	4801	2.248340717					
	Coefficients	Standard Error	t Stat	P-value	Lower 95%	Upper 95%	Lower 95.0%	Upper 95.0%
Intercept	-0.269%	0.000179859	-14.97	1.4893E-49	-0.003045114	-0.0023399	-0.00304511	-0.0023399
Corr: Gamma vs ROR2	10.669%	0.00130645	81.67	0	0.104131493	0.10925397	0.104131493	0.109253974
RV Dev from Avg	-9.777%	0.0022675	-43.12	0	-0.102219558	-0.0933289	-0.10221956	-0.09332888

OIS Trading Insights

Dynamic option replication strategies like Portfolio Insurance, require destabilizing trades in the direction of market trends. These types of trades are prone to slippage and excessive transaction costs. The fact that it is not possible to know the cost of the Portfolio Insurance strategy in advance, and that the actual cost of Portfolio Insurance is determined after the fact, by the realized market environment experienced over the life of the option, are fatal flaws for any insurance-type product. As a result, we will not focus our attention on designing a practical Portfolio Insurance strategy.

However, the Portfolio Insurance trading strategy shares many common traits with Option Income Strategies, all of which have negative Gamma. Specifically, all of these strategies require comparable adjustment trades in the same direction as the market trend – selling as prices decline and buying as prices increase. The purpose of OIS adjustment trades is to limit and manage the magnitude of losses, arising from negative Gamma.

The key observation is that GS adjustments lock in profits (but limit further market-directional gains) from positive Gamma, while PI and OIS adjustment trades lock in losses (but limit further market-directional losses). When Gamma Scalping long straddles, we discovered that EOD rebalancing, coupled with intra-day rebalancing is often optimal during periods of high volatility. We also determined that trading discrete futures contracts automatically limits transaction costs, and that we could use Delta and Gamma to help us identify when to close the initial straddle and if and when to re-establish the position.

Conversely, typical negative Gamma (and negative Vega) OIS trades should be employed when the expected level of realized volatility over the holding period *is less than* implied volatility, and when implied volatility is *expected to decline*. Given that OIS adjustments and PI adjustments effectively lock in losses, it is critical to identify the appropriate time to execute adjustments. Daily OIS adjustments are not practical, necessary, or advisable. The reason is that prices are mean-reverting over the typical holding period of most OIS trades. Given that PI and OIS adjustments lock in losses, it is more profitable to avoid rebalancing, unless it is absolutely required to mitigate excessive market risk.

Without rebalancing trades, mean reversion in the price of the underlying security benefits PI and OIS trades and harms GS straddle trades. That is why regularly rebalancing GS straddle trades is desirable, while judicious rebalancing of OIS trades is preferable. In my first book, *Option Strategy Risk Return Ratios*, I examined the mean-reversion probabilities of call and put options. Below is an excerpt from *Option Strategy Risk Return Ratios* that demonstrates and quantifies the benefits of eschewing OIS adjustments for small to moderate price changes.

"I calculated the realized probabilities of the price of the underlying security "touching" the strike price of the OTM option sold any time during the holding period. I then compared the realized touch probabilities to the theoretical probabilities of touching the short strike to determine the historical probability advantage or disadvantage. The

mechanical details of calculating the theoretical touch probabilities are beyond the scope of this book, but the calculations used 5000-path Monte Carlo simulations from an arbitrage-free binomial lattice.

The following probabilities were calculated on the S&P 500 (SPX), Russell 2000 (RUT), and NASDAQ 100 (NDX) indices from 2000 through late 2013, using rolling holding periods ranging from one day to 60 days. Rolling holding periods means that a new holding period began every day, which means the holding periods overlapped. This provided more observations (over 9000), although the overlapping observations were not independent.

I chose the year 2000 as the starting point to ensure that two bull and two bear cycles were represented in the data. There was still an upward price bias in the equity indices from 2000 through 2013, but that is consistent with the performance of equity indices over most long-term periods.

For each holding period, I calculated the probability advantage of selling OTM options from 0.25 standard deviations (SD) out of the money to 2.0 SD out of the money, in 0.25 SD increments. The probability advantage equals the theoretical (Monte Carlo) probability of touching the strike price of the option sold, minus the realized probability of touching the same strike price.

Remember, when selling options, we would prefer that the theoretical probability of touching the short strike price be greater than the realized probability of touching the short strike. When this probability difference (theoretical – actual) was positive, that indicated a historical trading advantage. When this probability difference was negative, this signified a trading disadvantage."

The negative numbers in the table below indicates that rebalancing OIS trades in response to price changes of less than one standard deviation were costly for call options, over the majority of option expiration dates. The sweet spot was approximately 1.25 standard deviations, which also tends to generate a reasonable risk/return tradeoff for most OIS trades.

OTM Short Call Probability Advantage										
#σ/#Days	1	2	3	4	5	6	10	15	20	40	60
0.25	8.19%	4.63%	2.32%	1.37%	0.97%	0.06%	-1.66%	-2.19%	-2.75%	-4.36%	-4.86%
0.50	6.21%	3.55%	1.34%	-0.16%	-0.58%	-1.30%	-3.10%	-4.77%	-5.61%	-6.47%	-6.70%
0.75	7.44%	4.17%	2.73%	1.65%	1.44%	0.83%	-0.90%	-2.19%	-3.07%	-3.13%	-3.47%
1.00	7.66%	5.58%	4.61%	4.59%	3.53%	3.21%	2.80%	2.49%	1.91%	1.78%	1.18%
1.25	6.62%	6.04%	5.99%	5.56%	5.26%	4.99%	5.49%	5.53%	5.65%	4.34%	4.04%
1.50	5.59%	5.87%	6.00%	6.19%	5.91%	6.05%	5.83%	5.98%	6.32%	5.91%	5.52%
1.75	4.50%	4.75%	5.25%	5.32%	5.28%	5.35%	5.29%	5.51%	5.48%	5.46%	5.59%
2.00	2.87%	3.30%	3.65%	3.57%	3.72%	3.70%	3.67%	3.96%	4.14%	4.25%	4.21%

Summary

Portfolio Insurance (PI) is a notorious example of a deeply flawed *dynamic option replication* strategy. When coupled with an equity portfolio, it can also be considered a form of dynamic hedging. Dynamic option replication strategies like Portfolio Insurance, require destabilizing trades in the direction of market trends. These types of trades are prone to slippage and excessive transaction costs. The fact that it is not possible to know the cost of the Portfolio Insurance strategy in advance, and that the actual cost of Portfolio Insurance is determined after the fact, by the realized market environment experienced over the life of the option, are fatal flaws for any insurance-type product.

However, we were able to validate the accuracy of the PI trade strategy and demonstrate that the implied theoretical cost of the PI trade strategy converges to the BSM cost as the as the number of paths and intervals increases (under standard BSM assumptions). I still find it remarkable that we can use simple, objective GS and PI trade rules to accurately determine the theoretical value, profit, and cost of any option or option strategy.

Finally, we examined the results of applying the PI trade strategy to 20 years of SPX daily return data and we extrapolated the lessons learned from the PI and GS analyses to provide insights into the optimal OIS trade adjustment process.

I coined the term Realized Volatility (RV) many years ago. I have written about RV extensively and taught the concept to my graduate and undergraduate derivatives classes for many years. Realized volatility is one of the most important factors in determining the realized values of all option strategies. Unfortunately, it is rarely discussed in the literature and its importance is not widely understood by most option traders.

The last two chapters on Gamma Scalping and Portfolio Insurance demonstrated and validated the direct link between realized volatility and the value, cost, and profit of all options and option strategies. Furthermore, these two chapters also illustrated that pricing anomalies between expected realized volatility and implied volatility can be systematically exploited through Gamma Scalping and through traditional Option Income Strategies.

12) APPLIED VOLATILITY FORECASTING

Before we can attempt to exploit volatility pricing anomalies, we need to identify the ideal market environments for long and short volatility strategies. If we expected future *implied volatility* to increase more than the market's expected change in implied volatility (the forward projection of the term structure of volatilities) we would benefit from positive *Vega* strategies – and vice versa. If we expected *realized volatility* to be greater than the market's anticipated level of volatility (the implied volatility of ATM options), we would prefer positive *Gamma* strategies – and vice versa. Both of these types of volatility pricing anomalies often occur together, and typically in the same direction. As a result, it is often productive to exploit volatility pricing anomalies using both Vega and Gamma exposures. Finally, larger pricing disparities have higher probabilities of success, lower risk, and greater profit potential.

Identifying Volatility Pricing Anomalies

In order to identify volatility pricing anomalies, it is necessary to have a means of forecasting volatility. There are many different types of qualitative and quantitative methods used to forecast volatility in practice, from pure discretionary judgment to various models including: mean-reversion, GARCH, AI, fundamental, structural, and hybrid. A comprehensive exploration of these methods is beyond the scope of this book, but we do need some context to evaluate the volatility trades in this chapter.

I developed two tools to help identify volatility pricing anomalies in my proprietary trading. The AI Volatility Edge (AIVE) platform and the Option Income Strategy Universal Filter (OISUF) algorithm. These tools are tangential to the book, but are representative of the types of tools that could be used in volatility trading. Brief descriptions of the AIVE platform and the OISUF algorithm are included below. I will refer to AIVE forecasts and OISUF values when applicable in the trade discussions below. However, I will not typically provide screenshots, charts, or comprehensive tables from these tools in this chapter. Please see the Resources Chapter at the end of this book, or the TraderEdge.Net website if you would like more information about these tools.

AI Volatility Edge (AIVE) Platform Overview

The Johnson Aggregation Framework (JAF) was specifically designed to apply the complete term structure of volatilities and the complete term structure of interest rates to quantify theoretically correct and internally consistent current and projected option values and risk metrics, in risk-neutral and risk-averse environments. My JAF research and programming highlighted the profound importance of forward volatility estimates, which is why I simultaneously developed the AI Volatility Edge platform.

The purpose of the AI Volatility Edge (AIVE) platform is *to utilize the latest in AI technology to forecast, identify, and quantify anomalies between the AI expected future volatilities and the entire term structure of volatilities expected by the market (priced into index options and volatility index futures).*

The AIVE platform aggregates the results from 360 separate AI / Machine-learning models to forecast: four different volatility measures, for three different equity indices (SPX, NDX, and RUT), for 13 future time periods (5, 10, 15, 21, 31, 42, 63, 84, 105, 126, 189, 252, and 504 trade days).

The algorithm also interpolates or extrapolates as required to calculate volatility forecasts for any specific option expiration date in the future. The AI Volatility Edge platform can calculate volatility estimates based on end-of-day (EOD) historical data, current EOD data, or even based on the latest real-time (intra-day) price and volatility data.

The AIVE platform forecasts four different volatility measures that are essential for the option trader: *future realized volatility, future realized terminal volatility, future realized extreme volatility, and the modeled value of the volatility index itself* (VIX, VXN, or RVX). *Future realized volatility* represents the expected annualized root mean square of the log of the future daily equity index returns. That sounds complicated, but the important point is that the resulting forecasts are directly comparable to both ATM implied volatility for the equity index options and the corresponding volatility index.

The *future realized terminal volatility* is not annualized and represents the expected continuously compounded percentage price change (plus or minus) of the equity index from the forecast date *until the end of the forecast period*. In other words, it is the *magnitude of expected price change*. The *future realized extreme volatility* is similar and is also not annualized. It represents the *maximum interim* expected continuously compounded percentage price change (plus or minus) experienced by the equity index *at any time* between the forecast date and the end of the forecast period. Said differently, it is the *maximum expected price change*. Both of these values are extremely useful when evaluating alternative strike prices and determining prospective adjustment points for all option strategies.

The final volatility estimate is of the volatility index itself. We obviously know the value of the volatility index, but that value may be unusually high or low relative to the AI model's algorithmic evaluation of the recent price and volatility history.

The advantage of using quantitative models is the ability to quantify the standard error of the models on out-of-sample data. The AIVE platform uses the standard error from each model to calculate standardized z-scores for each forecast. Larger z-scores (positive or negative) indicate trades with higher probabilities of success, lower risk, and greater profit potential. A pattern of positive or negative z-scores indicate a systematic mispricing of volatility across all instruments.

Option Income Strategy Universal Filter (OISUF) Overview

I have been trading and studying Option Income Strategies (OIS) for many years and I have spent much of that time developing, analyzing, and testing many different types of trade filters. The Option Income Strategy Universal Filter (OISUF) algorithm represented the culmination of my research efforts through 2016. The OISUF is a standardized metric calculated by an algorithm that exclusively uses historical and current prices and implied volatilities. It captures the fundamental relationships between price, implied volatility, and OIS performance. It was not derived from a specific dataset and the *parameters were not optimized*. As a result, the *parameters in the algorithm will never change and will never be re-estimated*. The limited number of non-optimized parameters greatly enhances the robustness of the OISUF.

The parameter values were structural and were chosen before strategy testing. Structural means the OISUF parameter values were a byproduct of the market-edge hypothesis itself. They were the only parameter values tested. Despite the use of structural, pre-determined parameter values, the OISUF algorithm is very responsive to changing market conditions. It can be used to systematically quantify the attractiveness of OIS trade entry environments in real time.

The OIS Universal Filter algorithm produces a standardized OIS score. In this context, the word "standardized" means the resulting OIS scores are directly comparable across all underlying securities. OIS scores are not bounded, but typically fall between negative 200 and positive 100. Scores below zero indicate unfavorable OIS environments and scores above zero signify favorable OIS environments. Furthermore, higher OIS scores imply more advantageous OIS environments across the entire spectrum of prospective OIS values.

In the context of identifying volatility pricing anomalies, *high OIS scores* indicate *overpriced volatility* environments - when realized volatility is expected to be *lower* than implied volatility (IV), and implied volatility is expected to *decline.* Conversely, *large negative OIS scores* (coupled with implied volatility at or below the long-term median IV) indicate *underpriced volatility* environments - when realized volatility is expected to be *higher* than implied volatility (IV), and implied volatility is expected to *increase.*

Overpriced Volatility Example

The easiest way to understand volatility trading is through specific examples. Before we begin to evaluate prospective trades, the first question we always have to ask is whether there is anything unique about the current environment or any known material events that will be occurring in the future that could compromise the model forecasts derived exclusively from current and historical price and IV data.

The first example uses closing prices from October 1, 2019. In this case, I specifically chose a date that was not influenced by known material events, such as upcoming Presidential elections, etc. When those types of near-term, discrete events are present, an additional layer of qualitative analysis and judgment is required.

In an overpriced volatility environment, implied volatility is higher than warranted – given the past, current, and anticipated future market conditions. In a genuine overpriced volatility environment, the resulting realized volatility would be less than implied volatility (positive Theta & negative Gamma), implied volatility would be expected to decline (negative Vega), or both. This is the ideal environment for conventional Option Income Strategy (OIS) trades.

On 10/1/2019, the annualized implied volatility of the ATM S&P 500 option expiring on 12/20/2019 was 16.70% and the AIVE annualized Realized Volatility (RV) forecast was only 12.45%. The resulting option was overpriced by 4.25%. Given a standard error of 5.47%, this error equated to a z-score of + 0.78. In other words, the actual implied volatility exceeded the forecast Realized Volatility by 0.78 standard errors. The z-score of 0.78 translated to a one-tailed probability (assuming a normal distribution) of 21.9%. This represents the significance of the observation, specifically the probability of a +0.78 z-score occurring by chance.

In addition, the actual implied volatilities exceeded the AIVE Realized Volatility forecasts for every ATM option. The entire term structure of ATM implied volatilities was overpriced on 10/1/2019 with z-scores ranging from + 0.20 to + 0.78. The 12/20/2019 expiration was the most overvalued with a z-score of + 0.78, making it an ideal candidate to target in our strategy.

This example uses the S&P 500 index, so we also have reliable data for the futures contracts on the corresponding 30-day volatility index – the VIX. The 10/1/2019 AI Volatility Index (VX) price forecast for the VIX futures contract expiring on 11/20/2019 (36 trading days in the future) was only 15.90%. The corresponding VIX futures price was 19.18%, which means the 11/20/2019 VIX futures contract was overpriced by 3.28%. Given a standard error of 5.14%, this error equated to a z-score of + 0.64. In other words, the actual November 2019 VIX futures price exceeded the 2019 VIX forecast by 0.64 standard errors. A z-score of + 0.64 translates to a one-tailed probability (assuming a normal distribution) of 26.1%. This represents the significance of the observation, specifically the probability of a +0.64 z-score occurring by chance. Calculating z-scores for every VIX ATM SPX option and every VIX futures contract allows us to compare the relative value across instruments. In the case of the VIX, the VIX index itself, and every VIX futures contract (except for the 2/19/2020 contract) was overvalued, with z-scores for the overvalued instruments ranging from + 0.14 to + 0.89. As was the case for the SPX options, the VIX index and futures contracts were systematically overpriced on 10/1/2019.

It is interesting to note that the most overvalued ATM option and most overvalued futures contract are related. The VIX futures contract expiring on 11/20/2019 corresponds to S&P 500 Index options expiring in December - 30 days after the 11/20/2019 expiration date. As you will recall, the 12/20/2019 ATM S&P 500 options were the most overvalued as well. This is particularly encouraging, *especially since the models for different volatilities and different dates are entirely unique. They are completely separate models – and they are all generating consistent results.* Ideally, distinct volatility forecasts for different dates and for different equity indices should always be compared and contrasted to look for inconsistencies, discrepancies, and outliers before attempting to exploit volatility pricing anomalies in practice.

Overpriced Volatility Trade Entry

The above analysis strongly suggests that the level of volatility priced into ATM equity options and volatility index (VIX) futures on 10/01/2019 was too high – relative to historical relationships between price, implied volatility, and future volatility. This suggests we should attempt to construct trades that have negative Gamma (and therefore positive Theta), which would benefit from a lower-than-expected level of Realized Volatility, and negative Vega, which would benefit from a prospective decline in implied volatility.

This is the desired environment for employing Option Income Strategies. As you will recall from my OISUF introduction, OIS scores below zero indicate less favorable OIS environments and scores above zero signify favorable OIS environments. Furthermore, higher OISUF scores imply more advantageous OIS environments across the entire spectrum of prospective OIS values and vice versa. On 10/01/2019, the OISUF score was + 54.06. I intentionally selected a date when the AI Volatility Edge forecast was consistent with an attractive OISUF score. Filtering trades based on multiple models is highly effective.

We have identified S&P 500 options expiring on 12/20/2019 and the VIX futures contract expiring on 11/20/2019 as particularly overvalued, so our proposed strategies will focus on these expiration dates in our example strategies.

Let's begin with an options trade, a simple broken-wing butterfly (BWF), constructed with a put spread and a call spread. The OptionVue Greeks and graphical analysis as of 10/01/2019 are shown in Figures 12.1 and 12.2 below, respectively.

I have been a subscriber to OptionVue for many years, and OptionVue offers a discount for annual OptionVue subscriptions on the TraderEdge.Net site. Please use the link on the RHS of the TraderEdge.Net site to take advantage of the OptionVue annual discount; see the Resources Chapter for additional information.

Summary **Figure 12.1**

	Net Reqmts	Gross Reqmts				
			Cash Flow	+$20,614	Delta	10.40
Init	$19,386	$40,000	Cur. Value	-$20,626	Gamma	-0.13
Maint	$19,386	$40,000	Gain/Loss	-$11	Vega	-464.6
Cash/Init	1.06	0.52	Commis	$5.60	Theta	25.67

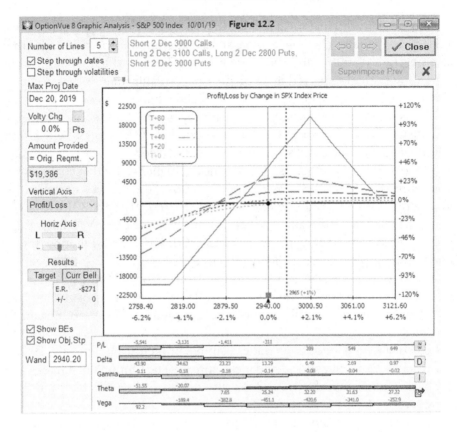

Figure 12.2

The BWF trade required $19,386 of capital (Reg-T margin) and had the desired negative Gamma (-0.13), negative Vega (-464.6) and positive Theta (+25.67), which was consistent with the volatility pricing anomalies implied by the overpriced volatility environment. You will also note the Delta was also slightly positive (+10.4). That was intentional. Volatility and equity prices are strongly negatively correlated. Given that we are forecasting a decline in volatility, that *implies* the bias will be toward higher equity prices. This is why I constructed a slightly bullish broken-wing butterfly trade, to be consistent with our volatility forecast. However, keep in mind that the volatility models are not directional; they forecast volatility, not price direction. It is up to the individual trader to determine how or when to leverage the historical relationship between price and volatility.

I used the AIVE forecasts of Realized Terminal and Extreme Volatility to estimate the potential magnitude of the price changes when selecting the strikes and designing the BWF strategy. The BWF is one of many flavors of Option Income Strategies, which are typically exited well before expiration – to avoid increasing risk due to increases in negative Gamma as the expiration date approaches. As a result, when reviewing the terminal and extreme volatility forecasts, we should focus on the near-term potential holding period, not the expiration date of the options in the strategy.

Overpriced Volatility Trade Exit

It is not practical to provide a daily analysis of the BWF trade during the holding period, but I will provide additional information on the prospective exit date: 11/01/2019. I reran the AIVE Realized Volatility analysis for all ATM options on 11/01/2019. The AIVE Realized Volatility z-score for the 12/20/2019 option expiration (used to construct the BWF trade) dropped to near zero, which removed most of the edge from our trade. Similarly, the degree of overvaluation had also declined to near zero for the corresponding 11/20/2019 VIX futures contract, which further reinforced the justification for exiting the trade. The term structure of volatilities was still overpriced in general, but not materially for the option expiration dates of interest for our strategy.

You will recall that we used the attractive OISUF score of +54.06 as additional support for entering the BWF trade on 10/1/2019. As of the proposed exit date of 11/1/2019, the OISUF score had dropped to *negative* 5.24, which would be considered an *unattractive* OIS environment. The 11/1/2019 AI Volatility Edge forecasts and the OISUF score no longer supported an edge for the BWF trade.

If we look at OptionVue's graphical analysis (Figure 12.3) and Greeks (Figure 12.4) for the BWF trade on 11/01/2019, we also see that we were at the top-end of the sweet-spot of the payoff distribution (which is undesirable) and Delta had turned negative (-14.61), which was inconsistent with the persistent overpriced volatility environment.

Option trading is inherently a zero-sum game. We should only risk our capital when we have a demonstrated edge. There are definitely anomalies that can be exploited, but when our edge is gone, we should exit the trade. In this case, the trade would have generated a $3,189 profit over the one-month holding period, representing a return on required capital of 16.45%.

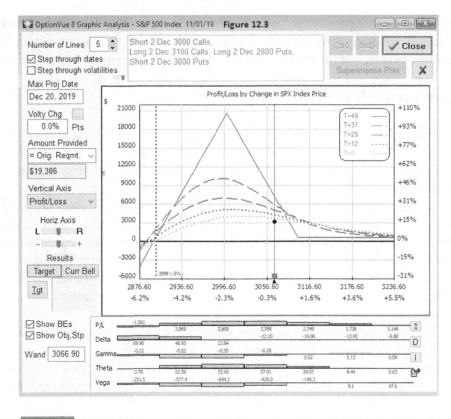

Figure 12.3

Summary Figure 12.4

	Net Reqmts	Gross Reqmts				
			Cash Flow	+$20,614	Delta	-14.61
Init	$19,386	$40,000	Cur. Value	-$17,426	Gamma	-0.21
Maint	$19,386	$40,000	Gain/Loss	+$3,189	Vega	-377.1
Cash/Init	1.06	0.52	Commis	$5.60	Theta	52.16

Alternative Overpriced Volatility Trades

I will not go into the same level of detail, but I wanted to provide two alternative trades that would have been consistent with the overpriced volatility environment. Note, the interpretation of the Greeks is very different due to the VIX as the underlying index (instead of the S&P 500 index), which I will not explore here. Both alternative trades assume the same entry and exit dates of 10/1/2019 and 11/01/2019, respectively. The first alternative trade was a bear put spread using November 2020 VIX put options (anticipating a decline in the VIX). The OptionVue graphical analysis for the VIX bear put spread on the exit date of 11/1/2019 is shown in Figure 12.5 and the Greeks summary on the exit date is shown in Figure 12.6.

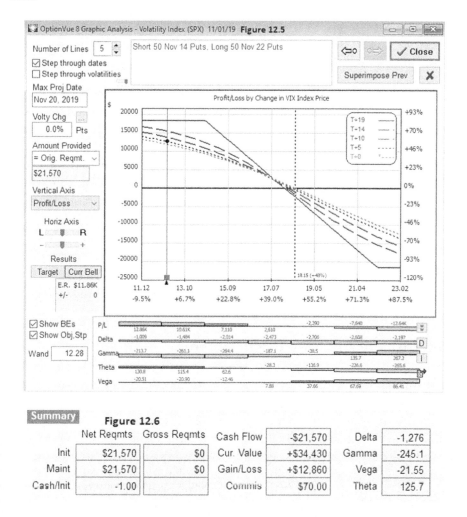

Figure 12.5

Figure 12.6

	Net Reqmts	Gross Reqmts	Cash Flow	-$21,570	Delta	-1,276
Init	$21,570	$0	Cur. Value	+$34,430	Gamma	-245.1
Maint	$21,570	$0	Gain/Loss	+$12,860	Vega	-21.55
Cash/Init	-1.00		Commis	$70.00	Theta	125.7

As you can see from the above exhibits, the VIX bear put spread would have earned a profit of $12,860 on a capital requirement of $21,570, which would have resulted in a return on required capital of 59.62% over the one-month holding period.

The second alternative trade was a long November 2020 VIX 14 put option (anticipating a decline in the VIX). The OptionVue Greeks summary for the long VIX put option on the exit date of 11/1/2019 is shown in Figure 12.7.

Summary						
	Net Reqmts	Gross Reqmts	Cash Flow	-$21,425	Delta	-19.85K
Init	$21,425	$0	Cur. Value	+$54,825	Gamma	1,225
Maint	$21,425	$0	Gain/Loss	+$33,400	Vega	265.6
Cash/Init	-1.00		Commis	$175.00	Theta	-1,456

Figure 12.7

As you can see from the above exhibits, the long VIX put option would have earned a profit of $33,400 on a capital requirement of $21,425, which would have resulted in a return on required capital of 155.89% over the one-month holding period. However, the outright purchase of the VIX put option would have been a much riskier trade, particularly due to the negative Theta of the long VIX put option. Using VIX futures and VIX options is a very efficient way to implement strategies designed to exploit volatility pricing anomalies, but only for the experienced trader.

One critical comment about short volatility trades; they should ALWAYS be covered. In other words, they should have a maximum possible loss and that maximum loss should be consistent with your account size and degree of risk-aversion. If necessary, hedges should be employed to further reduce the maximum loss.

Underpriced Volatility Environment

In an underpriced volatility environment, implied volatility is lower than warranted – given the past, current, and anticipated future market conditions. In a genuine underpriced volatility environment, the resulting realized volatility would be greater than implied volatility (positive Gamma), implied volatility would be expected to increase (positive Vega), or both.

On 11/7/2018, the annualized implied volatility of the ATM S&P 500 option expiring on 01/18/2019 was 14.50% and the AIVE annualized Realized Volatility (RV) forecast was 23.21%. The resulting option was underpriced by 8.71%. Given a standard error of 5.52%, this error equated to a z-score of negative 1.58. In other words, the Realized Volatility forecast exceeded the actual implied volatility by 1.58 standard errors. The corresponding one-tailed probability was only 5.7%.

In addition, for 8 out of 10 of the ATM options in the AIVE analysis, the actual implied volatilities were less than the AIVE Realized Volatility forecasts. In other words, the vast majority of the term structure of ATM implied volatilities was underpriced on 11/07/2018. The 01/18/2019 expiration was the most overvalued with a z-score of negative 1.58, making it an ideal candidate to target in our strategy.

As was the case in the first example, I specifically chose a date that was not influenced by upcoming Presidential elections, etc. When those types of near-term events are present, an additional layer of qualitative analysis and judgment is always required.

I also compared the AI Volatility Index (VX) forecasts to the VIX futures prices for the same trade date: 11/07/2018. The price of the VIX futures contract expiring on 12/19/2018 was 17.27% and the annualized AIVE VIX forecast was 22.13%. The resulting VIX futures contract was underpriced by 4.86%. Given a standard error of 4.90%, this error equates to a z-score of negative 0.99. In other words, the December 2018 VIX forecast exceeded the actual December 2018 VIX futures price by 0.99 standard errors. A z-score of negative 0.99 translates to a one-tailed probability (assuming a normal distribution) of 16.1%.

Unlike the ATM IV analysis on 11/07/2018, the undervaluation of the December 2018 futures contract appeared to be more of an anomaly, although the VIX index itself was also undervalued. It is interesting to note that the most undervalued ATM option and most undervalued VIX futures contract were related. The VIX futures contract expiring on 12/19/2018 corresponds to S&P 500 Index options expiring in January of 2019 - 30 days after the 12/19/2018 expiration date. As you will recall, the 01/18/2019 ATM S&P 500 options were the most undervalued as well. This same phenomenon occurred in the undervalued option example. This is encouraging because *the models for different volatilities and different dates are entirely independent. They are completely separate models – and they are generating consistent results.*

Underpriced Volatility Trade Entry

The above analysis strongly suggests that the level of volatility priced into near-term ATM equity options and December volatility index (VIX) futures on 11/7/2018 was too low – relative to historical relationships between price, implied volatility, and future volatility. This suggests we should attempt to construct trades that have positive Gamma, which would benefit from a higher-than-expected level of Realized Volatility, and positive Vega, which would benefit from a prospective increase in implied volatility.

Positive Gamma (negative Theta) and positive Vega strategies are the opposite of Option Income Strategies. You will recall that OISUF scores below zero indicate less favorable OIS environments and scores above zero signify favorable OIS environments. It would seem the opposite should be true for positive Gamma and positive Vega strategies, and that is true – with one important caveat. *Low (negative) OISUF scores are desirable for positive Gamma and positive Vega strategies, but implied volatilities must be lower than average as well.* On 11/07/2018, the OISUF score was negative 97.32. *And* implied volatilities were below the long term mean and median. I intentionally selected a date when the AI Volatility Edge forecast was consistent with an appropriate OIS score and IV environment. Filtering trades based on multiple models is highly effective.

We have identified S&P 500 options expiring on 01/18/2019 and the VIX futures contract expiring on 12/20/2018 as particularly undervalued, so our proposed strategies will focus on these expiration dates in our example strategies. Let's begin with an options trade, a put ratio backspread (PRBS). The OptionVue Greeks and graphical analysis as of 11/7/2018 are shown in Figures 12.8 and 12.9 below, respectively.

Summary	**Figure 12.8**						
	Net Reqmts	Gross Reqmts	Cash Flow	-$11,136	Delta	-81.13
Init	$23,636	$12,500	Cur. Value	+$11,140	Gamma	0.57
Maint	$23,636	$12,500	Gain/Loss	+$4	Vega	1,548
Cash/Init	-0.47	-0.89	Commis	$10.50	Theta	-205.4

The PRBS trade required $26,636 of capital (Reg-T margin) and had the desired positive Gamma (+0.57), positive Vega (+1,548), which was consistent with the volatility pricing anomalies implied by our analysis. You will note the Delta was also negative (-81.13). That was intentional, although adding directional exposure to volatility trades does add an additional layer of risk and requires additional conviction. Volatility and equity prices are strongly negatively correlated. Given that we are forecasting an increase in volatility, that implies the bias will be toward lower equity prices. This is why I constructed a bearish put ratio backspread example, to be consistent with our volatility forecast. However, non-directional volatility trades could definitely be used instead, one of which I will include in the alternative trade section.

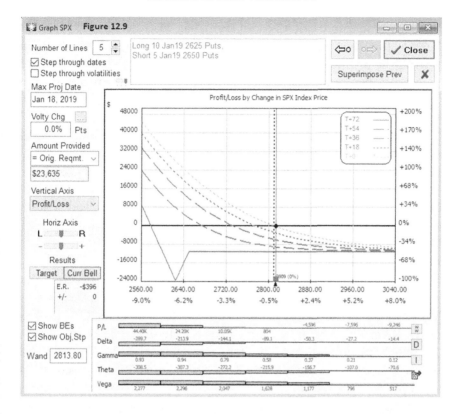

I used the AIVE Realized Terminal and Extreme Volatility forecasts to estimate the potential magnitude of the price changes when selecting the strikes and designing the PRBS strategy. The AI Volatility Edge model was forecasting a 10% move in prices by December 21, far more than suggested by implied volatility at the time. The PRBS was well-positioned to profit from a large downside move in price and increase in volatility.

Underpriced Volatility Trade Exit

As was the case with the BWF trade, it is not practical to provide a daily analysis of the PRBS trade throughout the holding period, but I will provide a brief analysis on the prospective exit date for the trade: 11/23/2018. The ATM IV of the SPX option expiring on 01/18/2019 increased materially over the holding period, from 14.5% to 18.6%. While it was still slightly undervalued relative to the volatility forecasts on the proposed exit date of 11/23/2019, the z-score had increased sharply (become less negative), from negative 1.58 to negative 0.42, which removed the majority of the edge from our trade.

Similarly, the degree of overvaluation had also declined to near zero (+0.01%) for the 12/19/2018 VIX futures contract, which further reinforced the justification for exiting the trade. The term structure of ATM implied volatilities and VIX futures prices were both overpriced in general on the exit date, although a few of the securities were still slightly underpriced.

You will recall that we used the OISUF score of negative 97.32 (*and* implied volatilities were below the long term mean and median) as additional support for entering the PRBS (long volatility) trade on 11/01/2018. As of 11/23/2018, the OISUF score had returned to near zero (-5.61), which would be considered a neutral volatility environment, *and* implied volatilities had reverted closer to the long-term mean and median values. The 11/23/2018 AI Volatility Edge forecasts and the OISUF score no longer supported an edge for the PRBS trade.

If we look at OptionVue's graphical analysis (Figure 12.10) and Greeks (Figure 12.11) for the PRBS trade on 11/23/2018, we see that we were still well-positioned for further gains, but the magnitude of all the Greeks (Delta, Gamma, Vega, and Theta) had increased sharply since the inception of the trade, which magnified the risk. Unfortunately, the AI Volatility Edge forecasts indicated a materially smaller edge. The result: increased risk and reduced prospective return.

When our edge is gone – or no longer justifies the level of risk, we should exit the trade. In this case, the trade would have generated a $20,504 profit over the two-week holding period, representing a return on required capital of 86.75%.

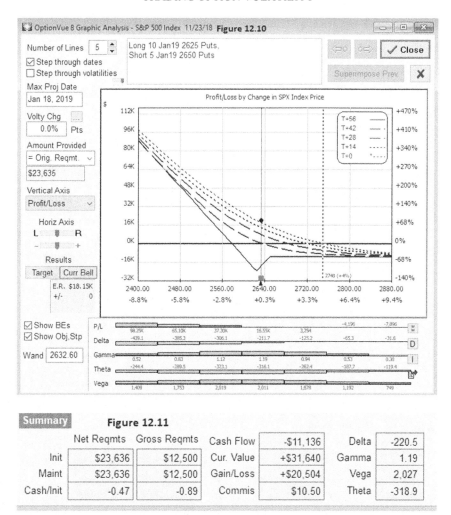

Figure 12.11

	Net Reqmts	Gross Reqmts	Cash Flow	-$11,136	Delta	-220.5
Init	$23,636	$12,500	Cur. Value	+$31,640	Gamma	1.19
Maint	$23,636	$12,500	Gain/Loss	+$20,504	Vega	2,027
Cash/Init	-0.47	-0.89	Commis	$10.50	Theta	-318.9

Alternative Underpriced Volatility Trades

I will not go into the same level of detail, but I wanted to provide four alternative trades that would have been consistent with the underpriced volatility environment on 11/7/2018. The first alternative trade was a long ATM straddle using January 2019 call and put options on the SPX (anticipating a higher level of realized volatility and an increase in implied volatility). The OptionVue graphical analysis for the SPX straddle on the exit date of 11/23/2018 is shown in Figure 12.13 and the Greeks summary on the exit date is shown in Figure 12.14.

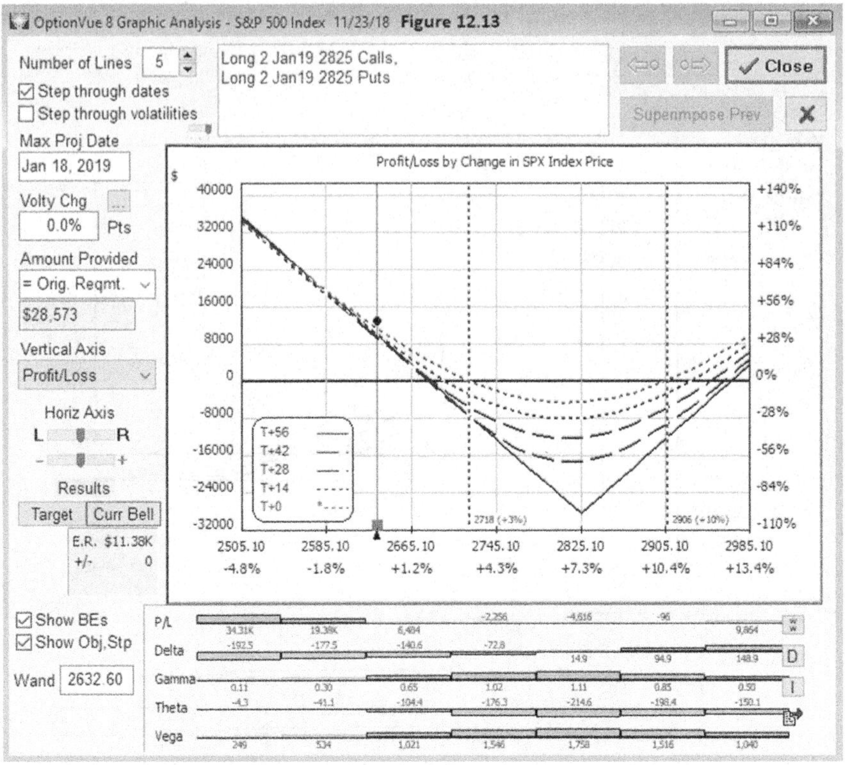

Summary **Figure 12.14**

	Net Reqmts	Gross Reqmts				
			Cash Flow	-$28,573	Delta	-159.1
Init	$28,573	$0	Cur. Value	+$41,597	Gamma	0.49
Maint	$28,573	$0	Gain/Loss	+$13,024	Vega	802.6
Cash/Init	-1.00		Commis	$2.80	Theta	-75.81

As you can see from the above exhibits, the SPX long straddle would have earned a profit of $13,024 on a capital requirement of $28,573, which would have resulted in a return on required capital of 45.58% over the two-week holding period. The long straddle would have benefited from positive Gamma and positive Vega, but was Delta-neutral at inception (unlike the PRBS trade). This explains why the PRBS trade outperformed the long straddle: the directional negative Delta at inception coupled with a large decline in the price of the SPX. It would also have been possible to use the Gamma Scalping methodology to manage the long straddle.

The final three alternative trades use VIX futures and VIX options, instead of SPX options to exploit the underpriced volatility environment on 11/07/2018. Note, the interpretation of the Greeks is very different for all three of these trades due to the VIX as the underlying index (instead of the S&P 500 index), which I will not explore further.

All three remaining alternative trades assume an entry on 11/07/2018 and an exit on 11/23/2018. The next alternative trade was extremely simple: the purchase of five Dec 2018 futures contracts. This is a pure long volatility strategy and has no option or SPX component. Note: unlike short volatility strategies, it is not always necessary (or even desirable) to use covered strategies when being long volatility. The OptionVue graphical analysis for the long VIX futures contract on the exit date of 11/23/2018 is shown in Figure 12.15 and the Greeks summary on the exit date is shown in Figure 12.16.

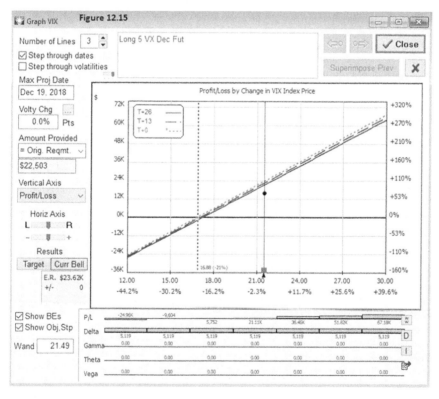

Figure 12.15

Figure 12.16

	Net Reqmts	Gross Reqmts	Cash Flow		Delta	5,119
Init	$22,503	$22,498	Cur. Value	$0	Gamma	0.00
Maint	$16,670	$16,665	Gain/Loss	+$15,995	Vega	0.00
Cash/Init	0.00	0.00	Commis	$5.00	Theta	0.00

As you can see from the above exhibits, the long VIX futures strategy would have earned a profit of $15,995 on a capital requirement of $22,503 (and an initial notional value of $86,350), which would have resulted in a return on required capital of 71.08% (and a return on notional value of 18.52%) over the two-week holding period. Notional value represents the value of the underlying asset or instrument in a derivatives trade. In this case, the notional value ($86,350) equals the initial price of the VIX contract ($17.27), multiplied by the size of each contract (1000), multiplied by the number of contracts traded (5).

The next alternative trade was a long Dec 2019 VIX 16 call option. The OptionVue graphical analysis for the long VIX call option on the exit date of 11/23/2018 is shown in Figure 12.17 and the Greeks summary on the exit date is shown in Figure 12.18.

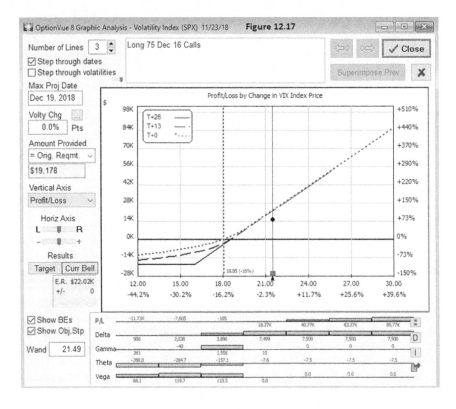

Summary **Figure 12.18**

	Net Reqmts	Gross Reqmts					
Init	$19,178	$0	Cash Flow	-$19,178	Delta	7,500
Maint	$19,178	$0	Cur. Value	+$34,448	Gamma	0.00
Cash/Init	-1.00		Gain/Loss	+$15,270	Vega	0.00
			Commis	$52.50	Theta	-7.54

As you can see from the above exhibits, the long VIX call option would have earned a profit of $15,270 on a capital requirement of $19,178, which would have resulted in a return on required capital of 79.62% over the two-week holding period.

The final alternative trade was a bull call spread using Dec 2019 VIX call options. The OptionVue graphical analysis for the VIX bull call spread on the exit date of 11/23/2018 is shown in Figure 12.19 and the Greeks summary on the exit date is shown in Figure 12.20.

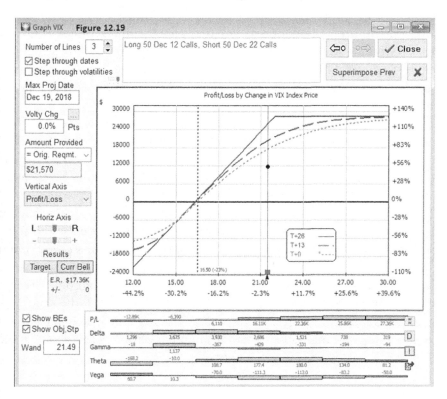

Figure 12.19

Summary **Figure 12.20**

	Net Reqmts	Gross Reqmts	Cash Flow	-$21,570	Delta	2,477
Init	$21,570	$0	Cur. Value	+$33,430	Gamma	-422.5
Maint	$21,570	$0	Gain/Loss	+$11,860	Vega	-114.4
Cash/Init	-1.00		Commis	$70.00	Theta	182.7

As is evident in the above exhibits, the VIX bull call spread would have earned a profit of $11,860 on a capital requirement of $21,570, which would have resulted in a return on required capital of 54.98% over the two-week holding period.

Conclusion

My goal in writing this book was to introduce a practical new analytical framework that generates theoretically correct and internally consistent, current and future option prices, volatility index futures prices, and risk metrics (Greeks) - for all term structures of volatilities and all term structures of interest rates. All of the required documentation, formulas, and examples are included to allow the dedicated reader to implement the JAF and JVAF in practice

I also felt it was important to include pragmatic new tools and volatility-related insights that would be new to many traders, including a practical Excel workbook that solves for the JAF forward volatilities and uses those forward volatilities to calculate structurally-consistent JAF True Vega values for ATM options, VIX futures, and corresponding calendar spreads.

I still find it fascinating that the simple, objective trade management strategies of Gamma-Scalping and Portfolio Insurance can be used to solve for the theoretical values and profits of any option or option strategy. Even more important, the Gamma-Scalping strategy can extract the realized value from an option over time, completely offsetting the loss from time decay – in the appropriate realized volatility environment. Evaluating the notorious Portfolio Insurance strategy even provided insights into managing Option Income Strategies. Finally, we reviewed a number of practical volatility trade examples in actual market environments.

* * *

Please see the Resources Chapter at the end of this book for a description of reader discounts available on the products and services I personally use in my proprietary trading and research. In addition, the Resources Chapter also has information on how to download the TOV spreadsheet and JAF Validation Supplement that accompany this book.

ABOUT THE AUTHOR

Brian Johnson designed, programmed, and implemented the first return sensitivity based parametric framework actively used to control risk in fixed income portfolios. He further extended the capabilities of this approach by designing and programming an integrated series of option valuation, prepayment, and portfolio optimization models.

Based on this technology, Mr. Johnson founded Lincoln Capital Management's fixed income index business, where he ultimately managed over $13 billion in assets for some of the largest and most sophisticated institutional clients in the U.S. and around the globe.

He later served as the President of a financial consulting and software development firm, designing artificial intelligence-based forecasting and risk management systems for institutional investment managers.

Mr. Johnson is now a full-time proprietary trader in options, futures, stocks, and ETFs primarily using algorithmic trading strategies. In addition to his professional investment experience, he also designed and taught courses in financial derivatives for MBA, Masters of Accounting, and undergraduate business programs - most recently as a Professor of Practice at the University of North Carolina's Kenan-Flagler Business School.

He is the author of three groundbreaking books on options: 1) *Option Strategy Risk / Return Ratios: A Revolutionary New Approach to Optimizing, Adjusting, and Trading Any Option Income Strategy*, 2) *Exploiting Earnings Volatility: An Innovative New Approach to Evaluating, Optimizing, and Trading Option Strategies to Profit from Earnings Announcements*, and 3) *Trading Option Volatility: A Breakthrough in Option Valuation, Yielding Practical Insights into Strategy Design, Simulation, Optimization, Risk Management, and Profits*.

He recently authored two in-depth (100+ page) articles on option strategy. The first, *Option Income Strategy Trade Filters*, represents the culmination of years of research into developing a systematic framework for optimizing the timing of Option Income Strategy (OIS) trades. The second, *Option Strategy Hedging and Risk Management*, presents a comprehensive analytical framework and accompanying spreadsheet tools for managing and hedging option strategy risk in real-world market environments.

He has also written articles for the *Financial Analysts Journal, Active Trader,* and *Seeking Alpha* and he regularly shares his trading insights and research ideas as the editor of https://www.traderedge.net/.

Mr. Johnson holds a B.S. degree in Finance with high honors from the University of Illinois at Urbana-Champaign and an MBA degree with a specialization in Finance from the University of Chicago Booth School of Business.

Email: BJohnson@TraderEdge.Net

RESOURCES

Brian Johnson writes a wide range of free, informative articles on https://www.traderedge.net/. The goal of Trader Edge is to provide information and ideas that will help you enhance your investment process and improve your trading results. The articles cover many different topics: economic indicators, technical analysis, market commentary, options, futures, stocks, exchange traded funds (ETFs), strategy development, trade analysis, and risk management. You will find educational articles that appeal to the beginner, as well as advanced tools and strategies to support more experienced traders. I have also created several instructional spreadsheet videos, which are associated with my books and articles: https://traderedge.net/category/video/

Brian Johnson's Books & Articles

Option Strategy Risk / Return Ratios: A Revolutionary New Approach to Optimizing, Adjusting, and Trading Any Option Income Strategy

For the first time, the pivotal concepts of risk and return have been integrated into a consistent approach for managing option income strategies. The risk/return ratios introduced in this book will allow you to evaluate, compare, adjust, and even optimize any option income strategy, on any underlying security, in any market environment. The accompanying Excel spreadsheet will allow every trader to integrate these new tools into their investment process.

Exploiting Earnings Volatility: An Innovative New Approach to Evaluating, Optimizing, and Trading Option Strategies to Profit from Earnings Announcements

The analytical framework introduced in this book will allow you to evaluate, compare, and even optimize option earning strategies on any underlying security, in any market environment. The accompanying Excel spreadsheets will help every trader integrate these new tools into their investment process. The spreadsheets include a comprehensive volatility model and a strategy optimizer. The toolset even calculates "True Greeks," including a new Greek risk metric designed specifically for earnings strategies.

Option Income Strategy Trade Filters: An In-Depth Article Demonstrating the Use of Trade Filters to Enhance Returns and Reduce Risk.

Option Income Strategy Trade Filters, represents the culmination of years of research into developing a systematic framework for optimizing the timing of Option Income Strategy (OIS) trades. The research was based on the analysis of 15,434 OIS trades, each with a comprehensive set of objective, tradable entry and exit rules. The OIS strategy back-test results for ten different types of filters are evaluated in this article, including unique filter combinations that delivered exceptional results. The results of over 100 different back-tests are provided.

Option Strategy Hedging & Risk Management: An In-Depth Article Introducing an Interactive Analytical Framework for Hedging Option Strategy Risk.

Option Strategy Hedging and Risk Management presents a comprehensive analytical framework and accompanying spreadsheet tools for managing and hedging option strategy risk. Brian Johnson developed these practical techniques to hedge the unique and often overlooked risks associated with trading option strategies. These revolutionary new tools can be applied to any option strategy, in any market environment and can be used to help identify the most cost-effective hedging solutions for actual option strategies in real-world market environments.

Option Income Strategy Universal Filter (OISUF) Subscription

Trading Insights, LLC offers a monthly subscription to the proprietary Option Income Strategy Universal Filter (OISUF) algorithm, which I introduced in my recent article *Option Income Strategy Trade Filters: An In-Depth Article Demonstrating the Use of Trade Filters to Enhance Returns and Reduce Risk*. The OISUF algorithm calculates a real-time, standardized option income strategy (OIS) score that quantitatively differentiates among the entire spectrum of favorable and unfavorable OIS environments. The OISUF algorithm is run via macros on an Excel spreadsheet, which requires a one-time download.

The spreadsheet is simple to use and has built-in macros to import free (as of this writing) Yahoo (price) and CBOE (IV) data. Data from alternative sources can also be copied and pasted as desired. The OISUF may be applied to options on any underlying security that has a corresponding volatility index. An explanation of the OISUF follows, but a more detailed description of the OISUF is available via this link: https://traderedge.net/order/ois-universal-filter/. The link is also available in the RHS side-bar of the TraderEdge.Net site. Please see the *Option Income Strategy Trade Filters* article for the most comprehensive discussion of the OISUF.

The published performance results were based on the analysis of 15,434 iron condor trades, each with a comprehensive set of objective, tradable entry and exit rules. The results for each of the 15,000 plus trades were scaled to a constant dollar amount at risk, to ensure all trades were equally-weighted when calculating the performance metrics. I ran the back-tests using end-of-day data on options with monthly expiration dates from May 2004 to May 2016. The back-test results were all based on actual option prices.

The OIS Universal Filter (OISUF) is a standardized metric calculated by an algorithm that exclusively uses historical and current prices and implied volatilities. The volatility index is used as a proxy for implied volatility, which limits the application of the OISUF to underlying securities that have corresponding volatility indices.

The OISUF algorithm has very few parameters. It captures the fundamental relationships between price, implied volatility, and OIS performance. It was not derived from a specific dataset and the *parameters were not optimized*. As a result, the *parameters in the algorithm will never change and will never be re-estimated*. The limited number of non-optimized parameters greatly enhances the robustness of the OISUF.

The parameter values were structural and were chosen before strategy testing. Structural means the OISUF parameter values were a byproduct of the market-edge hypothesis itself. They were the only parameter values tested. Despite the use of structural, pre-determined parameter values, the OISUF algorithm is very responsive to changing market conditions. It can be used to systematically quantify the attractiveness of OIS trade entry environments in real time.

I call it the OIS Universal Filter because it can be applied to enhance the risk-adjusted returns of option income strategies almost universally. It is applicable to any Delta-neutral option income strategy that does not require time (calendar) spread components.

The OIS Universal Filter algorithm produces a standardized OIS score. In this context, the word "standardized" means the resulting OIS scores are directly comparable across all underlying securities. OIS scores are not bounded, but typically fall between negative 200 and positive 100.

Scores below zero indicate unfavorable OIS environments and scores above zero signify favorable OIS environments. Furthermore, higher OIS scores imply more advantageous OIS environments across the entire spectrum of prospective OIS values.

Below is a brief overview of the OISUF performance metrics in Figure R.1. A much more comprehensive explanation is available in the article *Option Income Strategy Trade Filters*. The first two columns on the left-side of Figure R.1 describe the OISUF condition. The next three columns show the performance metrics (profit factor, percentage of winning trades, and average return on margin) for each filter condition. The final column documents the percentage of the 15,434 managed iron condor trades that met the OISUF conditions.

All three performance metrics were an increasing function of the OIS scores across the entire spectrum of OIS score thresholds. In fact, there was only a single case when the performance metrics did not increase for a corresponding increase in OIS score. Despite this minor inconsistency, the OIS score threshold and the performance metrics were almost perfectly positively correlated.

The OISUF algorithm was able to objectively differentiate among favorable and unfavorable OIS trading environments across the entire spectrum of OIS scores. More information about the OISUF subscription is available via the following link: https://traderedge.net/order/ois-universal-filter/.

Figure R.1: 1TPS - OIS Filter (RUT, SPX, NDX)

OIS Condition	OIS Score Threshold	Profit Factor	% Winning Trades	Avg. Return on Margin	% of Total Trades
N/A (ALL)	N/A (ALL)	2.10	85.10%	3.22%	100.00%
OIS Score <=	-200	0.63	61.72%	-3.67%	0.83%
OIS Score <=	-180	0.70	64.25%	-2.87%	1.25%
OIS Score <=	-160	0.77	66.53%	-1.99%	1.53%
OIS Score <=	-140	0.84	68.66%	-1.34%	1.84%
OIS Score <=	-120	0.89	70.18%	-0.83%	2.22%
OIS Score <=	-100	1.16	75.32%	0.99%	3.07%
OIS Score <=	-80	1.25	77.01%	1.40%	4.20%
OIS Score <=	-60	1.47	80.30%	2.19%	6.97%
OIS Score <=	-40	1.65	82.58%	2.57%	13.54%
OIS Score <=	-20	1.98	84.89%	3.16%	27.18%
OIS Score >=	0	2.29	85.86%	3.46%	49.59%
OIS Score >=	20	2.80	87.78%	4.10%	25.14%
OIS Score >=	40	5.15	92.89%	5.53%	11.12%
OIS Score >=	60	7.52	95.32%	6.34%	4.15%
OIS Score >=	80	6.01	94.27%	6.45%	1.24%
OIS Score >=	100	20.69	98.36%	8.13%	0.40%
OIS Score Correlation		N/A	0.996	0.994	N/A

AI Volatility Edge (AIVE) Subscription

Trading Insights, LLC offers a monthly subscription to the proprietary AI Volatility Edge platform, which I mentioned several times in this book. The AI Volatility Edge (AIVE) platform aggregates the results from 360 separate AI / Machine-learning models to forecast: four different volatility measures, for three different equity indices (SPX, NDX, and RUT), for 13 future time periods (5, 10, 15, 21, 31, 42, 63, 84, 105, 126, 189, 252, and 504 trade days).

The algorithm also interpolates or extrapolates as required to calculate volatility forecasts for any specific option expiration date in the future. The AI Volatility Edge platform can calculate volatility estimates based on end-of-day (EOD) historical data, current EOD data, or even based on the latest real-time (intra-day) price and volatility data.

The AI Volatility Edge platform forecasts four different volatility measures that are essential for the option trader: *future realized volatility, future realized terminal volatility, future realized extreme volatility, and the modeled value of volatility index itself* (VIX, VXN, or RVX). *Future realized volatility* represents the expected annualized root mean square of the log of the future daily equity index returns. That sounds complicated, but the important point is that the resulting forecasts are directly comparable to both ATM implied volatility for the equity index options and the corresponding volatility index.

The *future realized terminal volatility* is not annualized and represents the expected continuously compounded percentage price change (plus or minus) of the equity index from the forecast date *until the end of the forecast period.* In other words, it is the *magnitude of expected price change.* The *future realized extreme volatility* is similar and is also not annualized. It represents the *maximum interim* expected continuously compounded percentage price change (plus or minus) experienced by the equity index *at any time* between the forecast date and the end of the forecast period. Said differently, it is the *maximum expected price change.* Both of these values are extremely useful when evaluating alternative strike prices and determining prospective adjustment points for all option strategies.

The final volatility estimate is of the volatility index itself. We obviously know the value of the volatility index, but that value may be unusually high or low relative to the AI model's algorithmic evaluation of the recent price and volatility history.

This is the purpose of the platform: *to utilize the latest in AI technology to forecast, identify, and quantify anomalies between the AI expected future volatilities and the entire term structure of volatilities expected by the market (priced into index options and volatility index futures).*

The AI Volatility Edge platform is delivered via three separate Excel spreadsheets, one for each equity index (SPX, NDX, and RUT). The volatility forecasts are run via macros on Excel spreadsheets, which requires a one-time download.

The platform is simple to use and has built-in push-button macros to import free (as of this writing) Yahoo (price) and CBOE (IV) data. In addition, the platform also provides alternative push-button macros to import data from daily files provided by the third-party vendor Commodity Systems Inc. (CSI). Please see the CSI section later in this Resources Chapter for more information.

Data from alternative sources can also be copied and pasted as desired. A more detailed description of the AI Volatility Edge Platform and monthly subscription is available via this link: https://traderedge.net/order/ai-volatility-edge/. The link is also accessible in the RHS side-bar of the TraderEdge.Net site.

OptionVue

Through our referral agreement, OptionVue is offering an exclusive 15% discount on the initial purchase of any *annual* subscription of any OptionVue product and on all Discover Options educational products. However, the discount is not available to current OptionVue clients with an active OptionVue subscription. Please use the coupon code "traderedge" (*lower case with no spaces or quotation marks*) to receive your 15% discount when ordering applicable products from OptionVue online or over the phone.

I encourage you to visit http://www.optionvue.com/traderedge.html and take advantage of the exclusive 15% Trader Edge referral discount. If you would prefer to evaluate the OptionVue software before placing an order, the above link will also allow you to enroll in a free 30-day trial of OptionVue's option analytical platform. This link is also available in the RHS sidebar of the TraderEdge.Net site.

Trading options without a comprehensive option analytical platform is not advisable and the OptionVue software is one of the most powerful tools available. Unlike most broker platforms, OptionVue evaluates both the horizontal and vertical volatility skews, resulting in much more realistic calculations and more accurate risk and valuation metrics. In addition, I worked with OptionVue to help them apply the aggregate implied volatility formula to quantify the effects of earnings volatility before and after earnings events in the OptionVue software.

The OptionVue software also includes a very powerful "Trade Finder" module, which is similar to the strategy optimization tool in the *Exploiting Earnings Volatility* Integrated spreadsheet. Trade Finder allows the user to specify an objective, strategy candidates, filters, and forecast adjustments and uses those inputs to search for the best possible strategy. Most important, *Trade Finder uses the aggregate implied volatility formula to accurately incorporate the effects of earnings volatility in its analysis.*

OptionVue also offers a subscription service specifically designed for "Earnings Plays." OptionVue's description of the five Earnings Play's strategies follows:

- Prime Movers: Stocks that make big moves - options tend to be undervalued.
- Prime Non-Movers: Stocks that make smaller-than-expected moves, options tend to be overvalued.
- Earnings Pairs: Two stocks in the same industry, only one of which is announcing earnings.
- Echoes - Two stocks in the same industry, with one announcing 1-18

days after the other.

- Runners - Stocks that tend to run in price after the earnings announcement.

This system is based on the hypothetical results actual trades would have experienced in the past and shows you a quality ranking for each trade along with its past success rate.

OptionVue offers real-time and historical option prices, which can be used to back-test option strategies, even with adjustments. OptionVue also offers subscriptions to proprietary strategies, including their VXX Trading System.

Finally, Discover Options, the educational arm of OptionVue, offers one-on-one personal option mentoring from professional option traders with decades of experience.

OptionSlam.com

During the course of my research for my second book (*Exploiting Earnings Volatility*), I collaborated with the owners of OptionSlam.com on several enhancements for their site that will help all traders who use option strategies to trade earnings announcements.

Given the strong synergies between OptionSlam.com and the tools in my second book, OptionSlam.com has agreed to offer an exclusive 15% discount on annual INSIDER Memberships to my readers.

The following benefits are provided to all INSIDER OptionSlam.com Members:
- View Earnings History of Individual Stocks
- View Volatility History of Individual Stocks
- View Straddle Tracking History of Individual Stocks
- View and Customize the Upcoming Earnings Filter
- View and Customize the Earnings Calendar
- View Weekly Implied Volatility Report
- View and Customize the Best Trending Stocks Report
- View and Customize the Current Monthly and Weekly Straddles Report
- View and Customize the Historical Straddles Report
- View Trades from All Members
- Customize and Schedule Email Alerts of Personalized Reports
- Export Earnings Statistics to Excel

OptionSlam.com's historical earnings data provides all of the return and volatility data necessary to evaluate past earnings performance. The "Upcoming Earnings Filter" is a powerful and flexible tool that will help you efficiently identify both directional and non-directional trading candidates.

I encourage you to visit https://www.optionslam.com/partner_info/traderedge and take advantage of the exclusive 15% Trader Edge referral discount. Note underscore ("_") between "partner" and "info" in above link. The Option Slam link is also available in the RHS side-bar of the TraderEdge.Net site. You may also contact OptionVue via phone (847-816-6610) and ask for the Trader Edge discount.

CSI

Reliable prices are essential for developing and implementing systematic trading strategies. Commodity Systems Inc. (CSI) is one of the leading providers of market data and trading software for institutional and retail customers. Please use the CSI link in the RHS sidebar of the TraderEdge.Net site to learn more about CSI's pricing subscriptions.

Affiliate Relationships

I am a customer of OptionSlam, OptionVue and CSI. Trading Insights, LLC, also has an affiliate referral relationship with OptionSlam.com, OptionVue, and CSI.

TOV Spreadsheet & JAF Validation Supplement Files

Purchasing this book entitles you to an individual user license to download and use the associated Excel spreadsheet and JAF Validation Supplement PDF for your own research. However, you may not transfer, distribute, copy, or share the copyrighted spreadsheet, supplement, passwords, or download links.

There is an Excel spreadsheet and a PDF file that accompany this book. The name of the spreadsheet is "TOV Estimate TSV 32.xlsb, and the name of the PDF file is "TOV JAF Validation Supplement.pdf." The spreadsheet and PDF supplement were both referenced throughout this book.

The spreadsheet is available for download as a stand-alone .xlsb file. Many cells in the spreadsheet are protected, hidden, and/or validated to maintain the integrity of the spreadsheet. In addition, the VBA project environment is also password protected, as are each of the worksheet tabs. However, you may still use the worksheets interactively, by entering data into the cells with blue background or blue text or by clicking on the buttons that run macros.

To download the .xlsb file and the PDF file, go to the following page on TraderEdge.net: https://traderedge.net/tov-files/ and follow the download instructions.

You may need the *case-specific password* to *download* both files. If required, the password to *download* the both files is: TOV7537.

Once downloaded, you will also need the *case-specific password* to *open* the files. The password required to *open* both files is: TOV9519.

If the Trader Edge website is not accessible, please send an email *with an explanation of the specific error* received to BJohnson@TraderEdge.Net. *Include your copy of the electronic receipt* for the purchase of this book and I will send you a copy of the .xlsb and PDF files as email attachments – subject to file size limitations.

The TOV spreadsheet was tested using Excel 2013 32-bit, Excel 2019 32-bit, and Excel 365 64-bit – all in a MS Windows 10 environment. Given the use of macros in the TOV spreadsheet, it is highly likely that there will be compatibility problems with third-party spreadsheet software and with Mac versions of Excel.

It is possible that a few spreadsheet coding or formula errors survived the debugging process. If so, it is likely that these would be discovered after publication. Please send me an email with a detailed description of any coding or formula errors that meet *both of the following criteria*:

1. IS reproducible in the *above versions of Microsoft Excel*.

2. IS NOT a function of a specific set of user data or input values.

As explained earlier, the Terms tab includes a partial disclaimer and a link to the full terms and conditions on the TraderEdge.Net site that govern the use of the spreadsheet.

I do not offer user spreadsheet support or investment advice. However, if I can replicate and correct a structural (non-data-specific) TOV spreadsheet error, I will upload a corrected copy of the spreadsheet to the Trader Edge download page and I will update the file origination date on the same page. Please check the download page periodically for the latest versions of the spreadsheets.

I hope you enjoy these tools and find them useful in your option trading and research.

Made in the USA
Coppell, TX
10 August 2024

35827710R00164